AUDEN

Richard Davenport-Hines was born in 1953 and lives in London. His first book was awarded the Wolfson Prize for History and Biography in 1985. His more recent books include *Sex, Death and Punishment* (1990), *The Macmillans* (1992) and a literary anthology, *Vice* (1993). He is a regular reviewer for the *Times Literary Supplement*, and has contributed to numerous periodicals and newspapers including the *Independent on Sunday*, the *Observer*, and the *Sunday Times*. He is currently working on a book on Gothic art and literature.

Also by Richard Davenport-Hines

DUDLEY DOCKER
SEX, DEATH AND PUNISHMENT
THE MACMILLANS
GLAXO
VICE

Richard Davenport-Hines

AUDEN

Minerva

A Minerva Paperback
AUDEN

First published in Great Britain 1995
by William Heinemann Limited
This Minerva edition published 1996
by Mandarin Paperbacks
an imprint of Reed International Books Limited
Michelin House, 81 Fulham Road, London SW3 6RB
and Auckland, Melbourne, Singapore and Toronto

Copyright © 1995 by Richard Davenport-Hines
The author has asserted his moral rights

A CIP catalogue record for this title
is available from the British Library
ISBN 0 7493 9648 2

Printed and bound in Great Britain
by BPC Paperbacks Ltd a member of the British
Printing Company Ltd

For

Christopher Phipps

Contents

Contents

List of Illustrations

PROLOGUE

'What goal but the black stone?'

'Life, as I experience it,' Auden said, 'is primarily a continuous succession of choices between alternatives.' He depicted himself as a voyager. 'The journey of life,' he wrote in 1944, 'is infinitely long and its possible destinations infinitely distant from one another, but the time spent in actual travel is infinitesimally small. The hours the traveller measures are those in which he is at rest between the three or four decisive instants of transportation which are all he needs and all he gets to carry him the whole of his way.' The decisive instants in his life after he began writing poetry in 1922 were his visions of love and of violence in 1933 and 1936, his decision in 1938 to emigrate to the United States, the conception of his lifelong passion for Chester Kallman in 1939 and his return to Christian beliefs shortly afterwards. There was an element of arbitrary choice in each of these decisions. Later there were lesser moments of transportation, as when he settled in New York in 1946, or bought his house in Austria in 1957, or returned to live in Oxford in 1972.

Always the destination of his journey was exceptional. 'From this nightmare of public solitude,' he asked in his great prose poem on the limitations of the artist, Caliban's speech in 'The Sea and the Mirror', 'what relief have you but in an ever giddier collective gallop ... toward the gray horizon of the bleaker vision ... what goal but the black stone on which the bones are cracked, for only there in its cry of agony can your existence find at last an unequivocal meaning and your refusal to be yourself become a serious despair?' This biography of Auden is an account of a traveller who thought his goal was the black stone. Its subject drove himself as hard and ruthlessly as a tycoon.

It is also a book about gratitude and even a tract against twentieth-century self-pity. Auden was suspicious of creeds of personal development and distrusted the introspective tendencies in himself and other people. He thought their result was too often to make people sorry for themselves and to diminish their powers of free choice. Neuroses, he decided in 1929, should be welcomed as a potential source of strength and originality; they could vitalise people rather than weaken them. Suffering (so he believed after his return to Christianity) was integral to God's love and the forgiveness of sins. But both neuroses and suffering were useless if they were not received with gratitude rather than self-pity. In his elegy to Yeats of 1939, Auden wrote:

> Follow poet, follow right
> To the bottom of the night,
> With your unconstraining voice
> Still persuade us to rejoice.
>
> With the farming of a verse
> Make a vineyard of the curse,
> Sing of human unsuccess
> In a rapture of distress
>
> In the deserts of the heart
> Let the healing fountain start,
> In the prison of his days
> Teach the free man how to praise.

These lines, so his friend Hannah Arendt commented, are 'praise that pitches itself against all that is most unsatisfactory in man's condition on this earth and sucks its strength out of the wound – somehow convinced, as the bards of ancient Greece were, that the gods spin unhappiness and evil things to mortals so that they may be able to tell the tales and sing the songs'. Auden expected himself to be brave enough to bear intensities of pain. One sign of courage is the suffering persistence of the lover whose feelings are unreciprocated, or impossible to match and satisfy: this was a role that Auden repeatedly chose for himself. Arendt thought Auden's sacrifices were not only exceptional but ultimately excessive. 'God knows,' she burst out to Mary McCarthy on the day that Auden's death was announced in 1973, 'the price is too high, and no one in his right mind could be willing to pay it knowingly.'

Auden distrusted biographies of poets because they were so often studies in personality. 'Poetry is not a turning loose of emotion, but an escape from emotion; it is not an expression of personality, but an escape from personality,' T. S. Eliot famously wrote. 'Of course, only those who have personality and emotions know what it means to escape from these things.' Auden wanted to escape from the detestable celebrity that had surrounded Shelley, Swinburne and the *fin de siècle* poets. He instead dedicated himself to producing work which at its strongest was impersonal, never confessional. In 1942 he quoted a phrase of Kierkegaard – 'Genius has only an immanent teleology, it develops itself, and while developing itself this self-development projects itself as work' – and then added his own explanation: 'Self-development is a process of self-surrender, for it is the Self that demands the exclusive attention of all experiences, but offers none in return.' Auden put passionate energy into his self-development, but detested the cult of personality with its vulgar rites of credit and fame. His efforts were not a connivance to become a permanent character in the *dramatis personae* of the twentieth century, though that was certainly a result. All his journeying – his emotional and sexual choices, the necessity of religious faith, his changes of domicile – involved self-transformation. He did not transform himself in an escapist spirit, to hide himself from others, strike poses, attract newspaper profiles, but in order to improve his poetry. 'If biographies of writers are justifiable,' he wrote in 1942, 'it is because, in their case, the ways in which they accept and revolt against their immediate situation are peculiarly easy to watch, and the acceptance of and revolt against the immediate is the central human problem of free will.'

There is a character in Alan Bennett's play *Kafka's Dick* who has not read a word of Auden but knows that the poet never wore underpants. Auden rightly mistrusted this outlook that reduces aesthetics to gossip. He loathed the trivialisation of literary biography into something less than a study of free will. He was particularly shrewd to mistrust sexual tale-telling. Though in private he enjoyed erotic speculation ('I don't think Browning was very good in bed,' he told a friend in 1948: 'Mozart, I suspect, was a oncer. Beethoven was certainly trade'), he did not tell dirty stories to drag people down. In a memoir published after Auden's death Cyril Connolly described an incident during the Spanish Civil War in 1937 when he and Auden, having had 'a good lunch', went walking in some public gardens: 'Auden retired to pee behind a bush and was immediately seized by two militia men.' Connolly's anecdote has since been conscripted and redeployed. A right-wing publicist, ostensibly

offering *A History of the Modern World from 1917 to the 1980s*, has only one
use for Auden: castigating the involvement of foreign intellectuals and
communist leaders like Harry Pollitt in the Spanish war, he declares, 'The
poet W. H. Auden was saved by his "Pollitt letter" from a prison sentence
when he was arrested for indecency in a Barcelona park.' The implications
are that writers are reprehensible, that Auden was lascivious while men
were dying on nearby battlefields, that he was surprised in a sexual act, and
that only political influence saved him from justice. This canard has been
repeated elsewhere and more carelessly falsified. In this biography I have
never tried to vilify or diminish my subject; indeed I think that to do so is
decadent and envious, like the stuntedness of the London crowds
described by Wordsworth in lines admired by Auden:

> The slaves unrespited of low pursuits,
> Living amid the same perpetual flow
> Of trivial objects, melted and reduced
> To one identity, by differences
> That have no law, no meaning, and no end.

The private life of a poet (so often trivialised and reduced) is in any case the
lesser part of his existence.

Auden was attentive to a short story by Henry James called 'The Private
Life'. Several English travellers, including a great author called Clare
Vawdrey, are congregated in an inn by a Swiss glacier. The narrator is
puzzled by the dullness of Vawdrey's conversation in contrast to the
brilliance of his books until he goes to spy on his manuscripts. He knows
Vawdrey is downstairs, but finds his double in the bedroom writing
intently in a dim light and oblivious of the intruder. He concludes that
there are two Vawdreys: 'One goes out, the other stays at home. One is the
genius, the other is the bourgeois, and it's only the bourgeois whom we
personally know. He talks, he circulates, he's awfully popular ... for
personal relations this admirable genius thought his second-best enough.
The world was vulgar and stupid, and the real man would have been a fool
to come out for it.' Auden thought the insight of James into creative acts
was unparalleled, and took up the image of Clare Vawdrey in the title
poem of his volume *Nones*. 'Our dreaming wills may seem to escape,' he
wrote,

Through gates that will not relatch
   And doors marked Private, pursued by Moors
   And watched by latent robbers,
To hostile villages at the heads of fjords
   To dark châteaux where wind sobs
In the pine-rooms and telephones ring
   Inviting trouble, to a room
Lit by one weak bulb where our double sits
   Writing and does not look up.

That while we are thus away our wronged flesh
   May work undisturbed, restoring
The order we destroy, the rhythm
   We spoil out of spite.

Auden, like Vawdrey, was a double man, and his poetry worked to restore the order and rhythm that the ordinary world marred from malice.

That is another great feature of Auden's thought and work: he was always striving for integration, struggling to unify experience and objects, synthesising the ideas of traditional religion and twentieth-century psychoanalysis. It was as if he hoped to heal the schisms of human knowledge and feeling. He wanted, in the end, an all-arching reconciliation. His chief means of attaining this harmony were literary, for he was a man who always felt compelled to write. 'Unless I write something, anything, good, indifferent, or trashy, every day, I feel ill,' Auden told his friend James Stern. 'To me the only good reason for writing is to try to organise my scattered thoughts of living into a whole, to relate everything to everything else.'

'To mature means to become conscious of necessity, to know what one wants and to be prepared to pay the price for it,' Auden noted in 1939. 'Failures either do not know what they want, or jib at the price.' Auden did not falter in his journey nor hesitate at the sacrifices which he thought Christians and artists were required to make. He wanted from boyhood to be a great poet; knew always that his goal was the black stone.

CHAPTER 1

'A typical little highbrow and difficult child'

My father's forbears were all Midland yeomen
Till royalties from coal mines did them good

Auden wrote, but his immediate roots were in the Church of England: the 'gun-shy myopic grandchild of Anglican clergymen' was his self-description. Originally the Audens were settled at Rowley Regis in Staffordshire. Three brothers, who were born into this family in the 1830s, were educated on the proceeds of the coal royalties and were ordained into the Church of England. This trio married three sisters called Hopkins from nearby Dunstall. The eldest of the brothers, John Auden, the poet's grandfather, became Vicar of Horninglow in Staffordshire and was a typically fecund Victorian cleric who fathered a daughter and seven sons, the eldest of whom was sixteen and the youngest two when he died of heart failure at the age of forty-five in 1876. The second-youngest son of these children, George Augustus, who was four when his father died, was the poet's father.

Many of those who have written about Wystan Auden have stressed the importance of his mother to the course of his life; but the influence of his father has been underrated. John Betjeman in the 1920s was one of the few to notice that Auden 'much reverenced his father' at a time when it was fashionable among his set to dismiss 'their parents as brutal philistines'. Born in 1872, George Augustus Auden was educated at Repton School and Christ's College, Cambridge. After taking a first-class degree in natural sciences in 1893, he trained in medicine at St Bartholomew's Hospital in London, where he won several scholarships and medals. He was interested in children's medicine, publishing articles by the age of thirty on such subjects as diphtheria in the newly born or tuberculosis in children. It was at Bart's that he met Constance Rosalie Bicknell, a nurse three years his senior. She had been orphaned when young, and had been brought up by an unmarried uncle, with whom she was staying in Italy when he died suddenly. She was then eighteen, on her first foreign journey, and had to shoulder alone the arrangements for his burial. Evidently she was a redoubtable young woman. At a time when few women went to university, she studied French at Royal Holloway College at Egham, graduating with a gold medal in 1891. Unlike Wystan Auden she was a Francophile, and between the wars held soirées for those Birmingham University undergraduates studying French language and literature. She was a devout Christian, with High Church tastes, and qualified as a nurse with the intention of becoming a medical missionary.

Wystan Auden's maternal grandfather, Richard Henry Bicknell, was a Norfolk rector, and like John Auden a Cambridge graduate: he fathered six daughters and two sons in such 'rapid succession' that his wife (the daughter of a Suffolk clergyman, Henry William Rous Birch) 'retired to the sofa ... which gave some degree of immunity from importunate demands'. He died suddenly of a heart attack in early middle age, and was 'evidently a sadist', Auden wrote, 'for his sons danced round the table for joy when they heard he was dead'. The Bicknells had finer associations than the Audens. Charles Bicknell had been Solicitor to the Royal Navy and to the Prince Regent, afterwards King George IV, and was rewarded with sinecures: the Prince Regent put him on a committee to administer the royal parks and forests, he was a commissioner of bankruptcy and a deputy bailiff of the City of Westminster as well as treasurer of the Society for the Propagation of the Gospel in Foreign Parts. His daughter married the landscape artist John Constable in 1816, after a long and troubled courtship which had initially seemed detestable to the family because Constable's father was a miller at East Bergholt and therefore in trade. Intermarriage with the Birches was more attractive to the Bicknells, for the Reverend Henry Birch's mother was the daughter of Sir John Rous, fifth baronet and sometime MP for Suffolk, who had once been put on trial for the murder of his brother-in-law and 'lived under a cloud of suspicion which was only dispersed by a deathbed confession of a valet'. Henry Birch, whose uncle the sixth baronet was created Earl of Stradbroke on the occasion of King George IV's coronation in 1821, married Lydia, daughter of Daniel Mildred, of the prosperous Anglo–Spanish import–export firm of Mildred Goyeneche & Company. Their sons were high achievers. The eldest, Henry Mildred Birch, was captain of the school at Eton and a fellow of King's College, Cambridge before his selection in 1849 by Queen Victoria as principal tutor to her eldest son, afterwards King Edward VII. Henry's palace connections helped his brother Augustus Frederick, a housemaster at Eton who was consequently so favoured by the nobility that his house 'was called the House of Lords because of the great number of noblemen who boarded there'. The remaining Birch brothers were also successful. Ernest joined the Bengal civil service and ended his career as a judge of the High Court in Calcutta. Arthur entered the Colonial Office and was eventually appointed Lieutenant Governor of Ceylon with a knighthood. John went into the family firm of Mildred Goyeneche and was Governor of the Bank of England in 1880. He disliked procrastination as much as his great-nephew Wystan Auden. On the mantelpiece of his office there was a large, prominent card reading: 'Business. Call on a business man in business hours only on business; transact your business, and go about your business, in order to give him time to finish his business.'

The Bicknells and Birches, then, enjoyed more worldly distinctions than the Audens, as Wystan Auden's mother reminded her family and friends: her obituary in a Birmingham newspaper devoted most of its space to listing the titles and offices enjoyed by her uncles. Wystan Auden knew of the Constable connection, and doubtless had much about his mother's family drummed into him by her. When she became engaged to Dr Auden in 1898, one of her sisters, a clergyman's wife, warned in the same exclusive spirit that had recoiled from a Bicknell marrying trade like John Constable, 'If you marry this man, you know nobody will call on you.' Medicine had a precarious social status which Constance Auden felt keenly. A physician took his standing from the class of his patients. Five years before Wystan Auden's birth Francis Laking and Frederick Treves, the two physicians most closely involved in operating on King Edward VII for appendicitis, had both been rewarded with baronetcies. If they were less lucky, physicians ended as sawbones on a level with the slum-dwellers whom they treated. But apart from the insecure social standing of medical families, Constance Auden deplored her husband's family as less polished than hers, despite the fact that his many Auden cousins were studious, precise and devout, shrinking from flamboyant behaviour or mercenary cunning. She was hardened in this view because, like the men of many medical familes, Dr Auden and his sons 'had a very earthy, low sense of humour which annoyed her', according to her granddaughter Jane Hanly.

The turns in Dr Auden's career were indications of his constructive and virtuous outlook. He held several medical appointments in London before settling at York, where he was appointed physician to the County Hospital and seemed set on a career of prosperous conventionality. But in 1908 he abandoned this steady, easy course for a more arduous and unremunerative job as school medical officer for Birmingham. He was the first such appointment by the municipal authorities there: this was a job of high responsibility, suited to a practical reformer, who wanted to lay the groundwork of improved public health in Birmingham, then the greatest industrial city of the kingdom. It required talents as innovator, organiser and delegator, up-to-date ability in medicine and administration, as well as tenacity, patience and tact. He became a pivot in the administrative machinery that in the Midlands disposed of misery and dirt. As a colleague testified, 'Dr Auden was extremely popular with his staff, always thoughtful and kindly, unassuming in his manner, with a strong sense of humour.' He remained school medical officer until his retirement in 1937, and was also for many years Professor of Public Health at Birmingham University.

Despite their common background, the families of George Auden and Constance Bicknell were temperamentally dissimilar. 'On the whole the members of my father's family were phlegmatic, earnest, rather slow, inclined to be miserly, and endowed with excellent health, my mother's were quick, short-tempered, generous, and liable to physical ill health, hysteria and neuroticism,' Wystan Auden wrote in 1965. 'I don't know if it is a universal habit of children, but everybody whom I have asked about the matter tells me that he classified his parents as I did: one parent stood for stability, common sense, reality, the other for surprise, eccentricity and fantasy.' His parents, who married in 1899, did not adjust their differences. There was an atmosphere of suppressed contention about their household, especially after their move from York to the sanitary Birmingham suburb of Solihull. Constance Auden was often ill, perhaps as a sign of her dissatisfaction: 'the true index of a man's character is the health of his wife', as Cyril Connolly believed. Wystan Auden liked to dogmatise about other people's marriages, just as he speculated about the causes of psychosomatic illness, and his parents were not exempt from his analysis. 'Ma should have married a robust Italian who was very sexy, and cheated on her,' he said in 1971. 'She would have hated it, but it would have kept her on her toes. Pa should have married someone weaker than he and utterly devoted to him. But of course, if they had, I shouldn't be here.' There was irony in this comment, for he had long known that, when he was aged about ten, his father had become involved with a nurse while on war service in Egypt; though Dr Auden remained close to his wife, his feelings for the nurse persisted in the 1920s.

'He was the gentlest and most unselfish man I have ever met – too gentle, I used sometimes to think, for as a husband he was often henpecked,' Wystan Auden wrote of his father. On a visit home in 1929 he noted a trivial incident involving his father. 'My father goes to buy stamps. They give him halfpenny ones, and he takes them as he doesnt want to trouble the girl to change them.' This very English diffidence typified Dr Auden's non-professional dealings with the outside world. He disliked fuss or trouble, yet had married someone who seemed to excite them. Their home was a place of outcries and repressed disturbances. Wystan Auden also recorded a brief dialogue which revealed the tension at home, and Dr Auden's weariness with histrionics: his brother caught in an accident, his mother starting to make a scene, and his father's exasperated repression of the incipient drama:

John (on the stairs) – I've knocked a hole in the wall.
Mother (going out) – O John
Father – For God's sake, dont say anything.

This implies that Constance Auden said too much. Certainly she was excitable and domineering. 'Taller than her husband, and a powerful personality, she had a refined and remote dignity,' in the words of Wystan Auden's schoolfriend Robert Medley, who first met her in 1922. To Christopher Isherwood she was 'this solemn, intense woman with her austere nose'. She was not malleable or aloof where her sons were concerned; she watched over them, and enquired vigorously. Nor was she a woman to evade difficulties or slur over duties. Years later, in conversation with the poet John Heath-Stubbs, Wystan Auden 'spoke of

Edwardian virtues and how his mother would punish him if he ever lolled about in an easy chair'. On another occasion he recalled:

> as a small boy ... my elder brother repeated at a tea-party, where a certain lady was present, a remark of my aunt's to the effect that the lady smelt. For the next few days, to all his toys, to his sponge and tooth-brush and all his belongings, he found a paper pinned on which were written the words, 'Never Repeat'. As my aunt was an inveterate gossip, whose stories were often only remotely connected with the truth, we both thought this unfair at the time, but now I think the punishment was just.

His identification with maternal discipline became increasingly eccentric after his mother's death in 1941. He turned the admonishing internal voice of guilt into a maternal voice. He would say, almost as her deputy, of some act, 'Mother would never have allowed that'; as his brother John wrote, 'he developed a fetish about punctuality which he attributed to an imaginary ... image of gongs and peremptory summons to the table by mother'. John thought this behaviour was exaggerated, especially as their mother had not scolded about late arrivals at table. In fact it was Dr Auden who was ritualistic about time: as one of his neighbours wrote, 'his was a strictly disciplined life, and his day was methodically apportioned, beginning at 6 a.m. with breakfast'.

George and Constance Auden had three sons. The eldest, Bernard, was born in 1900. He and the youngest, Wystan, were not close as children, though Bernard remembered reading stories to him when he had bronchitis at the age of eight. (This childhood illness quickened Wystan's interest in industrial landscapes: the fumes of gas-works were then used as a remedy for bronchitis, and it was on such a cure that Auden added to the names on his 'numinous map' that of 'Solihull gas-works, gazed at in awe by a bronchial boy'). The Audens' academic ambitions for Bernard were foiled by the fact that he was not bookish. Perhaps partly as a result of their evident disappointment in this, Bernard was so lacking in self-confidence that he was not commissioned as an officer after being conscripted into the army in 1918 despite having served in his school's Officer Training Corps. Bernard loved animals, and wished to be a veterinary surgeon, but his parents considered this an unsuitable profession, and sent him on an economics course at Birmingham University which he flunked after a year. He then went to Canada, where he received a land grant and began farming. After he became engaged to a schoolmistress, Elizabeth Jeeves, his mother travelled to Canada to forbid the marriage on the ground that his fiancée 'wasn't out of the top drawer'. Bernard submitted to this interdiction for a time, and then rebelled. His mother's attitude thereafter was bossy and snobbish. As Bernard's elder daughter Jane Hanly recalls, Constance Auden 'told my mother that her clothes were inappropriate to her daughter-in-law, and they were all scooped up and given away to charity and substitutes in the style that my grandmother approved of were bought'. Bernard was afterwards persuaded to sell up in Canada, and briefly managed the estate of a Bicknell cousin in Monmouthshire. When this arrangement failed, 'his family, particularly Aunt Mildred Bicknell, became exasperated and unsympathetic, and despaired of finding a course of action for him, so he ended up for the rest of his life as a farmworker'. There was, then, some unkind family discomfiture about Bernard. Perversely this may have given Wystan Auden a bond with some of his early friends like Christopher Isherwood, Edward Upward and others who also had brothers who were in greater degrees considered family oddities. Bernard was a gentle, hard-working, unresentful man who endured his reverses with passive dignity. Though there was no quarrel, Wystan Auden latterly tended to avoid Bernard, who died in 1978.

The middle son, John Auden (1903–91), was closer to the poet and resembled him in some ways. John, like Wystan, had a scrupulousness about his motives and actions that amounted almost to masochism. As a young man he hoped to write poetry, and suffered from bouts of depression. Cecil Day Lewis described him as 'an extreme neurotic' in the early 1930s, but he resolved many of his difficulties and was successful in a career which was as constructive as his father's, and required much of the solitary intellectual concentration which characterised Wystan. He was an intelligent and generous man, with quiet wit and shrewdness, strong and admirable without being smug. Landscape, which gave such delight to Dr Auden and fascinated his youngest son, was John Auden's life work. He read geology at Cambridge and then joined the Indian geological survey, working for ten years in the Himalayas. His explorations of the glaciers of K2 (Mount Godwin-Austen), the highest mountain in the world after Everest, which he first mentioned to Wystan Auden in 1929, inspired the title of *The Ascent of F6*, Auden and Isherwood's mountaineering play with its theme of lethal maternal love. The play was dedicated to John, who commented that when he was on an expedition near K2 in 1937, 'our anxieties were not then connected with Oedipus but with remaining alive between food dumps and the crossing of torrents swollen every afternoon with glacier-melt water'. After learning to fly in 1939, he made reconnaissance flights over unmapped areas, and in the late 1940s undertook a survey of all major dam sites, hydro-electric projects, irrigation works and water-supply schemes in India – a vast and challenging task of far-reaching practical benefit. His first wife, Margaret Marshall, apparently made a decisive intervention in the life of Wystan Auden in the late 1920s (as described in chapter three). In 1940 he re-married Sheila Bonnerjee, granddaughter of the first President of the Indian National Congress, and daughter of a barrister who had been educated in England and knew Latin and Greek better than his native Bengali. John Auden converted to Roman Catholicism in 1951, rather as Wystan had returned to Anglicanism twelve years earlier. Later, during the 1960s, he worked for the United Nations, before retiring to Kensington, where he lived within walking distance of the Geological Museum. 'His fierce devotion to accuracy, his love for the precision of minutiae, were part of a larger respect for truth,' wrote an obituarist. There was a continued sympathy between John and Wystan, though they met seldom and spent most of their lives in different continents. In the early 1950s, at Ischia, Auden said to his niece Jane, 'I am very fond of my family, at a distance' (a remark which he often repeated); she afterwards reflected, 'but one doesn't avoid people one is very fond of'.

Wystan Hugh Auden (named after St Wystan, a Mercian prince associated with Repton, where Dr Auden was educated) was born at York on 21 February 1907. He was always pleased to have been the youngest child and youngest grandchild in his family. He told his sister-in-law Sheila 'that, as in the fairy stories, being the youngest he was the most loved and was destined to find great treasure'.

> I, after all, am the Fortunate One,
> The Happy-Go-Lucky, the spoilt Third Son,

he wrote in 1937. He believed in his luck, and when as an adult others had better luck in card games, he was, he admitted, 'a very bad loser'. He was a clever child who was usually the youngest in his class, which experience implanted in him 'the lifelong conviction that in any company I am the youngest person present'. Precocious as a child, until the 1940s he kept the manner of preternatural youth: 'in our few meetings in after years, he seemed an adult boy', wrote John Pudney, who knew him at school.

Though his personality as a child was memorable, his appearance also was distinctive. He was 'a sturdy, podgy little boy, whose normal expression was the misleadingly ferocious frown common to people with very short sight', Christopher Isherwood remembered him as a young boarding boy. There was a large brown mole on his right cheek. Another early schoolfriend gave a similar description: 'A rather chubby, smooth-cheeked little boy, with very fair hair, who stared you in the eye and whose nickname, "Dodo", didn't suit him, being merely inherited from an elder brother, whom it did.'

His upbringing was bourgeois. 'I grew up in a middle-class professional family', he recalled in 1939.

> My father was a doctor, my mother had a university degree. The study was full of books on medicine, archaeology, the classics. There was a rain-gauge on the lawn and a family dog. There were family prayers before breakfast, bicycle-rides to collect fossils or rub church brasses, reading aloud in the evenings. We kept pretty much to ourselves. Mother was often ill.
>
> In one way we were eccentric: we were Anglo-Catholics. On Sundays there were services with music, candles, and incense, and at Christmas, a crèche was rigged up in the dining-room, lit by an electric torch battery, round which we sang hymns.
>
> There I learnt certain attitudes, call them prejudices if you like, which I shall never lose: that knowledge is something to seek for its own sake; an interest in medicine and disease, and theology; a conviction (though I am unaware of ever having held any supernatural beliefs) that life is ruled by mysterious forces; a dislike of strangers and cheery gangs; and a contempt for businessmen and all who work for profits rather than a salary.

He cherished these values. 'Most of the best people are from the middle classes because it is a class without: an orphan class, with no fixed residence, capable of snobbery in both directions,' he wrote in 1929.

'From class insecurity it has developed the family unit as a defence. Like the private bands in the tribal migrations. It is afraid of its fortunate position.' After his move to the United States in 1939, he redevised his English childhood as something as idyllic as a Thomas Hardy pastoral: 'unsophisticated and provincial', he wrote with pride in 1940, 'a world still largely Victorian, in which one ... did not know divorced persons or artists' and 'relied for amusements on family resources, reading aloud, gardening, walks, piano duets, and dumb crambo; above all a world which had nothing to do with London, the stage, or French literature'. This attitude hardened with age and its almost complacent expression exasperated his earliest admirers: near the end of his life he wrote a 'Profile' of himself which began,

> He thanks God daily
> that he was born and bred
> a British Pharisee.

He had few illusions about his character, except perhaps to think himself worse than he was. Writing of his schooldays for Graham Greene in 1934, he described himself as 'mentally precocious, physically backward, short-sighted, a rabbit at all games, very untidy and grubby, a nail-biter, a physical coward, dishonest, sentimental, with no community sense whatever, in fact a typical little highbrow and difficult child'. He was a keen eater – 'Your god is your belly,' an aunt rebuked him as a child – and 'always a thirsty man', according to a paternal aunt. In most of these respects he changed little.

There were many advantages in his early life: not least that George Auden was such a discreet but accomplished mentor to the young. 'His learning, his clarity of thought, his energy, and the simplicity – even austerity – of his life were known far and wide,' wrote a younger colleague after his death. Dr Auden was a man of versatile interests. Unlike his clumsy youngest son, he was a successful wood-worker. His son recognised this peaceable and unneurotic hobby as the mark of a good man:

> But little crime we see in Quakers
> And least of all is found to be
> 'Mongst those engaged in carpentry.

Dr Auden was punctilious and attentive, but never demonstrative, a lively and faithful correspondent, sending charming and knowledgeable letters to a wide circle of acquaintances in old age. His letters are both formal and affectionate, suggesting a proud, self-sufficient, kind and intelligent man, responsive to the beauty of high and remote places.

Dr Auden liked to relate his recreational reading to his work, so that for example in 1910 he published in *Nature* a reading of Sophocles' *Philoctetes* which was endorsed by the great physician Sir William Osler for its account of malaria in ancient Greece. His conjunction of medical and literary interests made him proud of 'the long line of physician–poets, which includes Akenside, Crabbe, Goldsmith, Wendell Holmes, Keats' and Bridges (who had also trained at Bart's), and he ended his most ambitious essay on a psychological subject (published in 1926) with a quotation from Spenser which his youngest son might have endorsed:

> For of the soul the body form doth take,
> For the soul is form and doth the body make.

He was an amateur archaeologist who in 1910 excavated earth mounds near his old school at Repton in Derbyshire. These were believed to be a Roman camp or Saxon remains, but he in typically downright manner concluded they were a medieval refuge for cattle in time of floods. He translated into English the guide to the prehistoric collections of the National Museum at Copenhagen as well as a treatise on the preservation of antiquities: he was a devoted student of Norse antiquities, and persuaded himself that the surname of Auden indicated that the family had Icelandic origins. This theory tantalised Auden, who visited Iceland twice and developed a set of warrior myths about his ancestors. 'I'm nordic myself,' he wrote in 1952. Strangers also saw a Nordic look about him. During the Second World War some American neighbours denounced Wystan Auden to the Federal Bureau of Investigation as a spy ('They obviously thought I'd come off a submarine'): the agent who came to interview him asked, 'You're a Scandinavian, aren't you?'

His father's love of Nordic history had an early and lasting influence on young Wystan's imaginative development. He identified himself with northernness, and constructed a world of private associations around latitudes and longitudes: his artistic, moral and sensual criteria were all related to his personalised reordering of the planet. As he wrote in 1947,

My feelings have been oriented by the compass as far back as I can remember. Though I was brought up on both, Norse mythology has always appealed to me infinitely more than Greek; Hans Andersen's *The Snow Queen* and George Macdonald's *The Princess and the Goblin* were my favorite fairy stories, and years before I ever went there, the North of England was the Never-Never Land of my dreams. Nor did those feelings disappear when I finally did; to this day Crewe railway Junction marks the wildly exciting frontier where the alien South ends and the North, my world, begins.

North and South are the foci of two sharply contrasted clusters of images and emotions.... North – cold, wind, precipices, glaciers, caves, heroic conquest of dangerous obstacles, whales, hot meat and vegetables, concentration and production, privacy. South – heat, light, drought, calm, agricultural plains, trees, rotarian crowds, the life of ignoble ease, spiders, fruits and desserts, the waste of time, publicity. West and East are relatively neutral. West is more favorable, i.e., more northern, but conjures up the unheroic image of retired couples holding hands in the sunset; East is definitely southern and means dried figs and scorpions.

Auden's images for these compass points derived from his voracious childhood reading and vivid imagination.

'Were it possible to escape from our duties to God and our neighbor into our private islands of schizophrenic bliss', Auden wrote in 1947, most people would retreat with 'those books which, read in childhood, formed our personal vision of the public world.' His mother began reading to him when he was a small child in the nursery, and the influence of her choices was never effaced from his imagination. He listed the titles that had formed his early vision: *Icelandic Legends*, *Machinery for Metalliferous Mines*, Dean Farrar's *Eric, or Little by Little*, Stanley Smith's *Lead and Zinc Ores of Northumberland and Alston Moor*, Hoffman's *Struwwelpeter*, Mrs Beeton's *Book of Household Management* in the 1869 edition, *The Edinburgh School of Surgery*, *Hymns Ancient and Modern* (with tunes) and *Dangers to Health*, 'a Victorian treatise on plumbing with colored plates'. He had no interest in poetry as a child, 'but a passion for words, and appalled my aunts by talking like a professor of geology' – especially, perhaps, the aunt whom he scorned for mispronouncing the geological term 'pyrites'. He had a taste for the macabre: 'It's a great pleasure to think,' he wrote in 1936, 'that all the best nursery poetry shocks the Neo-

Hygienic-child lover.' When young his favourite tale was Hans Christian Andersen's *Ice Maiden*, a story of a lonely boy who climbs alone in high places and is eventually claimed by the glacier of the book's title: 'He beheld the walls of ice shining like blue-green glass; endless crevasses yawned around him, and the waters dripped with a sound like the chime of bells…. The Ice-maiden kissed him; it chilled him through his whole body. He uttered a cry of horror, broke resolutely away from her, stumbled and fell; all became dark to his eyes, but he opened them again. The evil powers had played their game.' Such imagery stayed with him through his life.

Perhaps the most important writer in his childhood was George MacDonald, whose story *The Princess and the Goblin* (mentioned previously) he considered was 'the only English children's book in the same class as the Alice books'. It is a richly written and exciting tale set, for the most part, in the huge caverns, great deep pits and subterranean passages that transect the interior of a mountain whose possession is contested by miners and evil-minded troglodyte goblins. MacDonald's tale sparked the young Auden's fascination with limestone geology, and developed his poetic imagination perhaps partly because of his mother's connection with the author. Her uncle Clarence Bicknell had persuaded MacDonald to buy a villa at Bordighera on the Italian riviera, where the novelist became a leader of the English community. Constance Auden visited Bordighera at least once in the 1880s: another uncle, Charles Bicknell, a Cambridge mathematician in holy orders, had set up the Studia Liguria at Bordighera as a study centre of flora, fauna and minerals. MacDonald was a friend of these Bicknells, and Constance herself probably met him. For a small child to be told that his mother knew the author of a book which she is reading aloud would imbue it with the semblance of vivid reality. The goblins in MacDonald's story wage a fearsome campaign of mischief against the human beings above ground. ('These hills may be hollow, I've a horror of dwarfs,' says Rosetta in *The Age of Anxiety*.) There is however one way in which their attacks can be warded off: 'the chief defence against them was verse, for they hated verse of every kind, and some kinds they could not endure at all'. Curdie Peterson, a twelve-year-old miner's boy who is the novel's hero, is celebrated in his community as an ingenious extemporiser of rhymes, 'for although there were certain old rhymes which were very effectual, yet it was well known that a new rhyme, if of the right sort, was even more distasteful to them, and therefore more effectual in putting them to flight'.

As a small boy Wystan Auden identified with Curdie Peterson: as an older boy he became his own version of him. From the age of six to twelve, around the period of his infatuation with Curdie Peterson, he was 'the sole autocratic inhabitant of a dream country of lead mines, narrow-gauge tramways, and overshot wheels'. He elaborated what he called in 1965 'a private sacred world, the basic elements of which were a landscape, northern and limestone, and an industry, lead mining'. Under his self-imposed rules, the young Auden could incorporate real objects like turbines but not wizardly devices or imaginary inventions of his own. Though this 'sacred world contained no human beings' and 'was constructed for and inhabited by myself alone', Auden needed help in its construction. His father procured textbooks, maps, catalogues, guide-books and photographs for him, and took him down mines. 'It sounds more than a little mad now, but I enjoyed myself enormously and never felt lonely or bored.' Inanimate objects peopled this world:

> Perhaps I always knew what they were saying:
> Even the early messengers who walked
> Into my life from books where they were staying,
> Those beautiful machines that never talked
> But let the small boy worship them and learn
> All their long names whose hardness made him proud;
> Love was the word they never said aloud.

It is not surprising that Constance Auden was anxious, or felt always she needed to screen, manage and protect her odd son.

In a speech in Austria in 1970 Auden said of his childhood, 'it is no doubt psychologically significant that my sacred world was autistic – that is to say, I had no wish to share it with others nor could I have done so'. Around the same time, in the coded autobiography of his commonplace book *A Certain World*, Auden quoted an autistic child as saying, 'Machines are better than people. People go further than they should.' As a child he felt similarly. At the age of four, travelling by train with his grandmother:

> the line
> Passed through a coalfield. From the corridor
> I watched it pass with envy, thought 'How fine!

Oh how I wish that situation mine.'
Tramlines and slagheaps, pieces of machinery,
That was, and still is, my ideal scenery.

He envied machines and did not relish people: as a young adult in 1929
'strict beauty of locomotive' still meant as much to him as human gestures
or looks, and as late as 1951 he still preferred battleships to sailors, for
'without a human will / To tell them whom to kill / Their structures are
humane'. Auden resembled those children whom he later described who
disbelieve in the existence of others, 'think of questions / To prove the
stranger real', and perhaps those adults whose 'faith in the existence of
other selves, normally rather wobbly, is greatly strengthened' by alcohol.
Even as a young man he doubted the existence of other humans: he noted,
for example, that his jealousy was 'of two kinds, the fear that I dont exist,
and the fear that he or she doesnt exist', though he was seldom jealous,
'because I am so conceited I dont believe my rivals exist'. He had a lifelong
craving for physical confirmation of the existence of other people. 'What
man, alone in a strange city, does not feel tempted to visit a brothel?' he
asked during a later stay in Berlin in 1964. There was 'even in the crudest
lust, desire for personal contact'. Again in *A Certain World* Auden quoted
Samuel Butler: 'Eating is touch carried to the bitter end.' The ferocity and
greediness of Auden's eating as a child were the despair and disgust of his
mother: perhaps just another way to escape isolation or keep in touch.

It is important to add that 'autism' has a different meaning now from
that current in Auden's boyhood. The word had been coined in 1911 by
the psychiatrist Eugen Bleuler to describe an extreme narrowing of
relationships either with external reality or with other people. It was not a
phenomenon of disturbance or insanity: Bleuler emphasised that 'we find
amongst all normal people many and important instances where thought is
divorced both from logic and reality'. The word in its earliest meaning was
an extreme version of Freud's concept of introversion. Its more precise
meaning to describe a childhood development disorder dates from the
1940s. Dr Auden had a professional interest in idiots savants who were
sometimes considered as autistic phenomena – he contributed some notes
on 'Arithmetical Prodigies' to the *Lancet* in 1922 – and the looser early
conceptualisation of 'autism' seems to have interested his youngest son.
His quotation from an autistic child has already been noted; elsewhere in
the same 'sort of autobiography' Wystan Auden wrote, 'the world an

autistic child creates is based upon total doubt', before quoting this passage from Bruno Bettelheim:

> All autistic children demand that time must stop still. Time is the destroyer of sameness. If sameness is to be preserved, time must stop in its tracks.... In the autistic child's world the chain of events is not conditioned by the causality we know. But since one event does follow another, it must be because of some timeless cosmic law that ordains it. An eternal law. Things happen because they must, not because they are caused.

Auden in his poetic maturity did not want time to stop still, but otherwise the conquering of doubt, the assertion of belief, the identification of eternal law developed into his great poetic concerns. It would be reckless to claim that Auden was an autistic child: it is enough to report that as an adult he considered his imaginary childhood world to have been essentially autistic and that in the oblique self-portrait of *A Certain World* he referred on several occasions to autism.

Books were the first good objects in his life, but they led him to imbue machinery with goodness and through books he developed his fascination with a special type of landscape, limestone moors. With his father, and often accompanied by his brothers, he explored this terrain on trips that brought feelings of 'intense joy and reverence' to the participants. 'You know, I feel sadly separated from you,' Dr Auden wrote affectionately to Wystan in New York in 1940. 'Years ago, we were such companions on so many expeditions.' The terrain of limestone landscape and derelict lead-mines became, as Auden wrote of the old mine at Rookhope which he visited in 1922, 'my symbol of us all'. There he:

> was first aware
> Of Self and Not-self, Death and Dread:
> Adits were entrances which led
> Down to the Outlawed, to the Others,
> The Terrible, the Merciful, the Mothers.

His love for such terrain was symbolic of his need to offer a love that was so strong as to be unreciprocable. The ungiving limestone was a preparation for imperfect love: an early model of the great test which he set himself in his love for Chester Kallman. It also became a way in which he could

imagine the love of God, and the redemption in which he came to believe
as a Christian.

> How, but with some real focus
> of desolation
> could I, by analogy,
> imagine a love
> that, however often smeared,
> shrugged at, abandoned
> by a frivolous worldling,
> does not abandon?

'Father by son', Auden wrote in 1929, 'lives on and on.' Certainly in later
life Auden harked back to his father's medical background and tried to
perpetuate its associations. He pursued friendships with New York
physicians like David Protetch and Oliver Sacks, and used to ruminate on
medical themes to visitors. Depending on the quality of his ideas, the
response was sometimes appreciative. On one occasion in the 1960s he was
visited in New York by the British neurologist Peter Nathan and Martin
Starkie, an actor and Chaucerian scholar. Auden regaled them with a
stream of old medical jokes at which Nathan laughed politely, although
they were hoary and not particularly funny. For Auden however medical
anecdotes had become precious relics, like shards of ancient urns. He was
comforted by talking about medicine with Nathan, but was dogmatic in
his opinions and seemed to fancy that he understood neurology. Nathan
was not offended by this hectoring, though Starkie thought that Auden
would have resented a non-poet talking to him about poetry in that tone.
To the end of his life, Auden thought of himself as the son of a physician,
and stressed the fact.

A special interest shared by father and son was psychology. Before the
First World War Dr Auden began collecting data to help classify all sorts
of mental types. He was elected to the Royal Medico-Psychological
Association in 1910, and contributed to the *Journal of Mental Science*. He
became honorary psychologist to the children's hospital in Birmingham
and medical adviser to an institution for the mentally handicapped. Many
of his publications related to the more practical side of child psychology:
for the *Journal of Children's Diseases* he considered 'Mirror-writing'
(1910); for the *Journal of Criminal Law and Criminology* he discussed
'Feeblemindedness and Juvenile Crime' (1911); for *Psyche* in 1923 he

examined 'The Biological Factors in Mental Deficiency'. His approach was essentially practical, with a special interest in medical reasons for juvenile delinquency. As early as 1912 he investigated the condition in children now recognised as dyslexia, discovering that all of a sample of fifty-three children from a special school had difficulties in sequencing sounds which had led them to be marginalised in their education, or treated as a social problem. Having himself contracted encephalitis in the epidemic after the First World War, he afterwards wrote an account of its behavioural sequel in children as part of an attempt to modify perceptions of delinquency. In 1926 he published a study of insanity as represented in ancient Greek literature. The depiction by Sophocles of the madness of Ajax he regarded as consummate in its clinical accuracy: so much so that he claimed Sophocles as a member of the medical profession.

This interest in psychology was part of Dr Auden's fierce but systematic curiosity: it was no dilettante or speculative indulgence, but part of his lifelong dedication to doing good. For his youngest son, though, psychology served other purposes. His 'pre-pubescent' feeling had been that 'people seemed rather profane' compared with 'a cliff of savage fells' or 'the relics of old mines'; but when, with adolescence, his interest in people quickened, psychology provided a way in which he could approach them with what looked like clinical detachment but was in fact a way of keeping their dangers at a distance. For him psychological categorisation was a way of asserting control. There was a moment in his life when every child is fearful: arrival at a new school. Revealingly, as Auden repeated himself,

> My first remark at school did all it could
> To shake a matron's monumental poise
> 'I like to see the various types of boys.'

Psychology was a way of knowingness, of superiority; but it was also fun. Auden's contemporary Graham Greene also became interested in psychology when young. His parents were old-fashioned and artless people who at breakfast would recount any bizarre dream of the previous night. The young Greene, who had discovered Freud, 'would leave the bacon cooling on his plate as he listened with the fascination of a secret detective'. He would lure them into imparting more details, to which he could usually attach some scandalous significance. Young Auden too was thrilled by this role of secret detective (like Freud, who called his ideas 'a secret science'). Auden's access to his father's books was a privilege which brought greater privileges. As an adolescent he studied Freud and Jung, and their more influential critics like Rivers; then, with a certitude that dazzled his friends, he analysed motives and reinterpreted other people's words in a way which threw up startling new meanings. For people barely familiar with Freudian theories of motivation, Auden's tricks and accusations could seem unimaginably provocative, exciting fun or offensive nonsense. It was partly a game for him: it helped him to dominate: and it was also an intensely serious effort to explain the apparently inexplicable, or impose a theory of order on random acts and thoughts. He had a mind powerfully attracted to synthesis; psychology was for him a way of assimilation. It is not known which of Freud's books Auden read in the early 1920s, but it is certain that he acquired a knowledge of human motives and passions – or at least of doctrines that seemed to explain them – that was rare at that time. It must have made him feel very powerful, and very clever.

Auden wanted to understand and believe. The world of 'total doubt' which he attributed to autistic children held no attraction. As an adolescent he hankered after a belief in magic. Several poems in his juvenilia are about fairies. There is for example a poem of 1922 or 1923, 'Faith' (its variant title is 'Belief'):

> We do not know
> If there be faeries now or no
>   But why in pain yourself involve
>   With question's that you cannot solve
>   O let's pretend it's so
>   And then perhaps if we are good
>   Someday we'll meet them in the wood.

In another verse of 1923, inspired by de la Mare's 'Mocking Faery', Auden is lying awake in bed at night when he is wooed by a fairy who wants him to go out to play.

> But Reason said within me
> There are no fairies now
> You are a fool; best stay in bed.

He is too rational, and fears the scorn of others, and sends the fairy away, but is 'ashamed' of his doubt. These fairy poems have been persuasively analysed by Katherine Bucknell as expressing young Auden's uncertainty about his poetic vision. But they also yield another reading: that of his rational, self-conscious, inhibited self clashing with his yearning for magical revelation and the conflict shaming him. Even the act of thinking, when it involved myths, or symbols, or analogies, seemed to have supernatural ingredients. 'Thought' he once likened to 'fairyland'. Freud, Jung, Groddeck and the other new psychologists were the fairies he allowed himself. Psychoanalytical interpretations were the magic that he did not forbid: especially as he came to believe that 'the use of magic is to disenchant people'. In a poem of 1934 which Eliot apparently dissuaded him from publishing he charted the ruin of old superstition and the rise of new beliefs for an 'unfairied' world.

> Charitable men, kind fathers, pillars of the churches,
> Meaning to do no more than use their eyes,
> Each from his private angle, then sapped belief.
>
> At dusk across our windows fell no longer
> The shadow of the giant's enormous calves,
> The kobbold's knocking in the mountains petered out;
>
> The dateless succession of midsummer dances broken,
> The moulds of green turf were unfairied; in marsh after marsh
> The sterile dragons died a natural death.
>
> All the specific projections of our human fears
> Whose lives and features were our artists' stock in trade,
> For whose propitiation we had long devised
>
> Excellent machinery, created a profession
> In which the retinue at the magician's house,
> Down to the pages, felt a pride of membership,
>
> Have vanished into air. Each to his neighbour blind
> He totters giddy on the slipping fringe of madness,
> And, powerless as children to locate his terror, whimpers.

Yet even in the incredulous, fearful modern world there were still a few men with a 'vision … of one great meaning', intellectuals to be honoured for 'creating a new myth of the Austere Observer' who offered ways to unprecedented comprehension and belief: chief among them 'Freud, who made a new Vienna famous', but also Marx, Einstein, Planck, Rutherford, J. J. Thomson and others. Freudian interpretations could seem as clinically scientific as the physics of Rutherford and Thomson, but chiefly they 'showed us what evil is', Auden wrote in 1939: 'our lack of faith'.

In many unostentatious and attractive ways, George Auden influenced his son's intellectual and imaginative development, yet Wystan Auden would have emphasised the intensity of his mother's involvement – perhaps because he was influenced too soon, and too profoundly, by Freudian theories. In this context of neurosis and childhood trauma it is essential to remember Auden's warning in 1941 when writing of Kafka, 'the artist who comes nearest to bearing the same kind of relation to our age that Dante, Shakespeare and Goethe bore to theirs'. Auden noted that 'the psychoanalysts go to town over his relationship with his father', but added this caution:

> Kafka understood this better than they when he wrote: 'All these so-called diseases, pitiful as they look, are beliefs, the attempts of a human being in distress to cast his anchor in some mother soil.' Psychotherapy will not get much further until it recognizes that the true significance of a neurosis is teleological, that the so-called traumatic experience is not an accident, but the opportunity for which the child has been patiently waiting – had it not occurred, it would have found another, equally trivial – in order to find a necessity and direction for its existence, in order that its life may become a serious matter. Of course it would be better if it could do without it, but unconsciously it knows that it is not, by itself, strong enough to learn to stand alone: a neurosis is a guardian angel; to become ill is to take vows. The questions with which Kafka dealt, the nature of his genius, have very little to do with his father; what the latter could do for him was to compel him to accept his vocation, to help him to resist the temptation to deny his vision by accepting a cosy conventional belief.

Auden was always full of Oedipal preoccupations. This was perhaps intensified by the fact that St Wystan, after whom he was named, was sanctified because 'he objected to the uncanonical marriage of his widowed mother to his godfather, whereupon they bumped him off', as Auden recorded. (St Wystan's godfather was king of Mercia, which made it 'a rather Hamlet-like story'.) 'In England sex is a secret between mother and son,' he told Alan Ansen in 1949. 'Your mother is always drawing you aside and telling you your duties toward your father, your father your duties toward your mother, the maid duties toward your parents.' There is no doubt, though, that Auden's beliefs on this point were strongly held, and were reflected in his writing. In his early country-house charade, *Paid on Both Sides* (1928), it is the mothers who perpetuate feuds and incite murders. Later in *The Dog Beneath the Skin* (1935) he and his collaborator Christopher Isherwood devised a deluded woman whose mad, vengeful love for her sons supposedly killed by German snipers is one of the ugliest features of the play. Her name Mildred Luce they derived from Mrs Auden's ancestress who had married the Revd Henry Birch and from the maiden name of Isherwood's paternal grandmother. It is Mildred who, in the final scene as revised by Auden, kills the hero Sir Francis Crewe when he challenges her delusions. In their next play, *The Ascent of F*6, its hero Michael Ransom climbs a mountain with four companions because his mother insists on it. All perish, Ransom last of all. Given this attack on maternal destructiveness, it is not surprising that at the first performance of *The Ascent of F*6 in 1937, 'poor Mrs Auden sat there restless and agitated', to quote Kathleen Isherwood, who was nearby. In the final Auden–Isherwood play, *On the Frontier*, it is the villain who is killed when he teases the young soldier Grimm for being a mother's pet, 'the son who was to achieve wonders'.

'What is the use of pretending one can treat the members of one's own family as ordinary human beings?' Auden asked in 1963. This was a crucial question in understanding his emotional evolution. Equipped from youth with his layman's understanding of psychoanalysis, he was always quick to represent parents as mythical symbols, planetary constellations, metonymic omnipotents or fractured deities. As he said, 'in poetry all dogmas become myths'. In his poem 'Father and Mother, twin-lights of heaven' (1929), which took its imagery from a metaphor in an article of his father's on human character, he depicted the Sun as:

> patriarch, whose male authority
> Takes without weakness from reluctant Nothing
> Her imagined perfection....
> Brought to maturity by you I see
> The intimate fusion of soul and body

The interdependence of good and evil.

The Moon though is mother,

> whose irrational will
> From unapproachable distance without sign
> Controls the movements of the enormous sea

> ...

> Keeper of the sexual mystery,
> The wave-like motions of love and hate,
> Conspicuous patron of lovers and maniacs.

He fell early and irredeemably into the routine of thinking in this form.
Initially, as a new and inventive way of thought, it gave him freedom and a
sort of mental vivacity. But for an adult to persist in thinking of his parents
as extraordinary human beings, or to continue to invest them with mythic
significance or symbolic power, is likely to be a retarding and impoverish-
ing experience. It is not adult, it hinders adult decisions, it limits the
possibilities of change. Auden's imagination was taken over in this way
because it was necessary to his development as an artist: 'In poetry as in
life, to lead one's own life means to relive the lives of one's parents and,
through them, of all one's ancestors; the duty of the present is neither to
copy nor to deny the past but to resurrect it,' he wrote in 1947. The
emotional debit of this was that in some of the most crucial areas of his
non-working life he became increasingly remote from the concrete.

It was his mother supremely whom he would not treat as an ordinary
human being. It was her mythic influence that became almost an
obsession. He identified 'landscape' with the maternal body, and
elaborated great symbolic roles for all mothers; yet Constance Auden's
concrete influences were great enough. Pre-eminently these were musical
and religious. When he was eight, she taught Wystan the words and music
of the love-potion scene in Wagner's *Tristan and Isolde*, which mother and
son would sing together, 'Wystan taking the part of Isolde', as his brother
John called, 'with implications of which she was evidently totally
unaware'. This must have been a scene of lovely tenderness at the time,
although those who think too much about the 'causes' of male
homosexuality fasten a more narrow and dismal meaning on it. Wagnerian
love duets were an intense and demanding exaction by a mother on a small

boy, but they were the early making of a great librettist: the sort of experience that raises a sensitive child out of the pleasant, facile creativity of a cultivated amateur into the disciplined power that creates enduring compositions. One meaning of these moments was shown after Mrs Auden's death in 1941, when her son chose to write a Christmas oratorio in her memory: *For the Time Being* is one of his neglected masterpieces, and his most direct treatment of sacred subjects. Its dedication to her is a fit tribute to the positive effects on him of her musical and religious intensity. In another way his early exposure to Wagner gave him a lasting insight and set a life-long pattern. 'The Tristan–Isolde myth is more dangerous to us than the myth of Don Giovanni,' he wrote in 1966 to a friend. 'We have – at least I know I have – to beware in our relations with others of becoming emotional leeches – and in this sphere the one who appears to be giving the blood may well be the greatest leech of the two.' In adult affairs, Auden liked to feel that he was the lover with the strongest feelings, the one who appeared to be giving most blood but was in fact the greedier leech. It is as if he saw emotional relations as an equivalent of 'the second law of thermodynamics' which he gave prominence in a self-analytical passage in *The Orators* in 1931: a law stating that when heat is exchanged between two objects, the hotter loses energy to the colder. This habit of feeling perhaps began in his relations with his mother.

The music in the Audens' lives was inseparable from religion and equally important. 'Religion was something you didnt talk about in public,' Wystan Auden wrote in 1934 of the English middle classes of his generation. 'It belonged to mother's bedroom; in some cases it was what father did.' The Audens were 'unusually devout, though not in the least repressive or gloomy', he added twenty years later. 'My parents were Anglo-Catholics, so that my first religious memories are of exciting magical rites (at six I was a boat-boy) rather than of listening to sermons.' As a boat-boy he would be bedecked in a red cassock and white linen cotta, and carry the boat of incense-grains to the altar. His participation in these rituals implanted in him (as he gratefully acknowledged in 1956) 'what I believe to be the correct notion of worship, namely, that it is first and foremost a community in action, a thing done together, and only secondarily a matter of individual feeling'. Auden developed an early taste for liturgical dispute. 'By the time I could walk, I had learned to look down with distaste upon "Prots" – they were said never to kneel properly but only to squat – to detest the modernism of our bishop and mildly deplore the spikiness of Aunt Mill, who attended a church where they had the Silent Canon and Benediction,' he wrote. For a later agnostic age it can be difficult to realise how central were religious beliefs to the lives of the Audens and Bicknells, or how literally religious stories were lived. In 1947 he recalled the 'dear chilblained mittened hand' of his 'favourite aunt', Daisy Bicknell.

> She was said to be what is called 'mentally retarded' and was looked after in a convent (from which she occasionally ran away), and used to come to us for the Christmas holidays, when her brilliant skill at Happy Families belied her reputation for not being 'quite all there'. She had an obsession; being totally deaf in one ear, she would implore us to promise that, when she died, we would not bury her too deep, for then she might never hear the last trumpet. Sure enough, at her funeral, when the coffin was being lowered into the grave, it stuck halfway down and refused to budge.

Auden believed that his churchgoing as a child contributed to his poetic development. 'As a choirboy, I had to learn, not only to sight-read music, but also to enunciate words clearly – there is a famous tongue-twister in the Jubilitate "For why, it is He that hath made us and not we ourselves" – and to notice the difference between their metrical values when spoken and when sung, so that, long before I took a conscious interest in poetry, I had acquired a certain sensitivity to language which I could not have acquired in any other way.' Recitation aloud was basic to understanding him as a poet. The first adult poetry which he could remember enjoying was Tennyson's 'In Memoriam', which his father read aloud, and Poe's 'The Raven' and 'The Bell'. Aged twelve he recited at a school entertainment at which he also provided impetuous musical accompaniment to a country dance; socially he used to recite Christina Rossetti and R. H. Barham to fellow pupils; once he began to write his own poetry, he would recite his latest productions to friends, sometimes through closed doors, as they tried to sleep.

Constance Auden had prudish tendencies which her youngest son resisted and mocked when he was young, but perpetuated in middle age himself. In 1929 he wrote,

> The mother had wanted
> To be a missionary in Africa
> So the son's novel
> Must be published in Paris.

Intense maternal religiosity, he teasingly implied, was bound to produce the sort of imagination in a son which would not be tolerated under Britain's obscenity laws and could only be expressed in French stewpots. Yet in later life he affected to become as prudish as any missionary, for example in the 1960s walking out from the New York opening of an adaptation of Chaucer's *Canterbury Tales* by Nevill Coghill and Martin Starkie in protest at the farting on stage. But he had almost predicted this in 1936:

> We imitate our loves: well, neighbours say
> I grow more like my mother every day.

One incident may have distorted his relations with his mother, or (to paraphrase his comments on Kafka) have provided the opportunity for which he had patiently waiting to suffer a neurotic reaction. At the age of seven, in 1914, about the time that he went to boarding school and his father went away to war, he was circumcised. Circumcision was then a common practice among the English middle classes, though usually undertaken at birth: a Hertfordshire doctor had written in the *Hospital Reports* of Dr Auden's training hospital, Bart's, in 1899 that 'of late years most parents' of his private practice asked him to circumcise new-born boys. This fashion for male circumcision among the English middle classes arose partly because it was considered hygienic for men who worked in Britain's tropical colonies; it was also a response to parental or medical anxiety about 'precocious' sexual feelings in boys, the foreskin drawing attention to the genitals at an age when interest in them was assumed to be latent. Neither parents nor physicians foresaw the effect on some middle-class Englishmen of Auden's generation, whose frantic hunting for rough trade was related to their pleasure in foreskins, and their identification of them with real men rather than the effete and circumcised of their own class: the 'comparison of circumcised with uncircumcised and vice versa', as Auden wrote in 1929. Certainly to be circumcised at the age of seven might aggravate a boy's sense of being impaired, damaged or incomplete; Freudian doctrine presented circumcision as symbolic castration, and Groddeck (a psychologist whom Auden read in 1929) observed that to boys, 'the fact first became clear comparatively late, that a castrated man, a eunuch, is something distinct from a circumcised man'.

Auden's operation remained an unpleasant memory. It possibly influenced his sexual behaviour as an adult. Certainly, from adolescence onwards, he was dissatisfied with the size of his own penis, and preoccupied with the size of other men's.

> To hear the tenor in the opera call
> You'd never dream the penis is so small

he wrote in 1929. Nearly forty years later he was still dwelling on the subject. 'Offered a choice between becoming the most powerful man in the world and having the biggest cock in the world, most men would choose the latter,' he noted in 1964. 'It is men, not women, who suffer most from penis-envy. They can also suffer, of course, as women cannot, from penis-variety ... Cocks have a personal characters [sic] every bit as much as their owners, and very often the two are quite different.'

Possibly there is further significance in Auden's late circumcision. Small boys of Auden's generation were often threatened by their mothers for masturbating, and he conceivably came to see women as potential castrators. This may be indicated in his analysis in *A Certain World* of one of the most important poems of his childhood, 'The Story of Little Suck-a-Thumb' in Heinrich Hoffmann's *Struwwelpeter*. In this poem Mamma forbids her little boy Conrad to suck his thumb while she is away, and threatens that, if he disobeys, 'the great, long, red-legged scissors man' will cut his 'thumbs clean off'. She goes away, he sucks, the scissor-man amputates. Walter Allen, who met Auden in the 1930s, suspected that *Struwwelpeter*'s 'influence was never far away from him throughout his life', and recalled an incident in the 1930s when Auden visited a Birmingham University don who was married to a scold. 'He'll cut her hands off,' he said excitedly to Allen afterwards. 'One day, he'll cut her hands off.' Just as Conrad was mutilated after he was separated from Mamma, so Auden was circumcised at the time when he was separated from his mother and sent to boarding school. As an adult Auden thought this poem was 'not about thumb-sucking ... but about masturbation, which is punished by castration'. Though he did not mention his mother in his comments on the scissor-man, he ends this section of *A Certain*

World with a remark which shows that for him it is actual women, not notional scissor-men, who are castrators. 'Very different is the fear aroused in me by spiders, crabs, and octopi, which are, I suspect, symbols for me of the castrating Vagina Dentata.' He used these ideas poetically. In 'The Witnesses' (1932) he ended a list of ominous forces with the phrase 'the women in dark glasses, the humped-back surgeons and the scissors man'. A decade later, in 'The Sea and the Mirror', he alluded to the idea of *vagina dentata*:

> In their Royal Zoos the
> Shark and the octopus are tactfully
> Omitted.

We cannot know the exact association in Auden's mind between late circumcision and castrating women, but we can suspect that he made such an association, and that it was integral to a disagreeable circle of fear, resentment and guilt.

Childhood for Auden was the usual mixture of security, benevolence and destructiveness. The difference between the outward reality of Auden's life and the neurosis of the artist is one that must be treated gingerly by a biographer. 'Let each child have,' he urged in 1936, 'as much neurosis as the child can bear.' He was a fortunate boy with fewer horrid monsters in his childhood than many people suffered; but as a younger man, at least, he believed in pushing neuroses to their limits: he relished the way that neurotic fears could be aroused from dark, forgotten places to disturb the placidity of ordinary life. As he wrote in 1935,

So, under the local images your blood has conjured,
We show you man caught in the trap of his terror, destroying himself.
From his favourite pool between the yew hedges and the roses, it is no fairy-
   tale his line catches
But grey-white and horrid, the monster of his childhood raises its huge
   domed forehead
And death moves in to take its inner luck.

If neuroses rooted in childhood appeared later, it was partly because he sought them out to test his inner luck.

CHAPTER 2

'I knew that very moment what I wished to do'

Educational influences as well as parental were important to Auden. He was a precocious child whose school years marked a stage in his literary development. He started serious writing at the age of fifteen; he made discoveries and decisions at school which changed the direction of his life; and the surface, at least, of his character was altered by his experiences in those years. He knew this himself, though he sometimes expressed it negatively. 'It is impossible to understand modern English literature unless one realizes that most English writers are rebels against the way they were educated, and it is impossible to understand the strength of the English ruling class until one realizes where it comes from,' Auden wrote in 1939 while reviewing Cyril Connolly for Americans. 'For the English are right; character and personal charm are politically more important than Intellect.'

In his case rebellion started after he was sent away, in the autumn of 1915, to board at St Edmund's School at Hindhead in Surrey, a preparatory school with some fifty pupils, including his brother John. He arrived at the school with an advanced, home-bred sensibility which was a delight for the more imaginative of his schoolfellows but less amenable to the school authorities. As he recalled after settling in the United States in 1939, 'My political education began at the age of seven when I was sent to a boarding school. Every English boy of the middle class spends five years as a member of a primitive tribe ruled by benevolent or malignant demons, and then another five years as a citizen of a totalitarian state.' These first adult contacts 'outside the family circle' were 'hairy monsters with terrifying voices and eccentric habits, completely irrational in their bouts of rage and good-humour, and, it seemed, with absolute power of life and death. Those who deep in the country at a safe distance from parents spend their lives teaching little boys, behave in a way which would get them locked up in ordinary society. When I read in a history book of King John gnawing the rush-mat in his rage, it did not surprise me in the least: that was just how masters behaved.' Auden's feelings were not unique: nor were parents indifferent to the childish suffering. One of Auden's earliest friends at St Edmund's was Christopher Isherwood, whose mother's diary is an endless source of illumination on the two boys over the next quarter-century. 'The last day,' wrote Kathleen Isherwood at the end of the Christmas school holidays of 1915–16, '& each hour grudged by poor C., the going back is really hateful.' The separation must have been painful for such a coddling mother as Constance Auden; but it may have benefited her son to move into less dependent relationships.

Dr Auden enlisted in the Royal Army Medical Corps after the outbreak of war in 1914 around the time that the lease of their house at Solihull expired. Constance Auden did not renew it, but during each school holiday took furnished rooms for herself and her sons in a different part of England. A holiday spent at Bradwell in Derbyshire stimulated Wystan's passion for limestone landscape, although his brother John felt 'he probably came to love Alston Moor in Cumberland more than any other place'. (An ordnance-survey map of Alston Moor hung on the wall of Auden's shack on Fire Island in 1947.) During such holidays, his contribution to war work was to knit mufflers in the evening while his mother read aloud. Otherwise he does not seem to have been caught by world events. Admittedly St Edmund's impressed Kathleen Isherwood as 'very military now', after a visit in June 1917, but she was perhaps duped by the military pretensions of 'the new master', Captain Reginald Gartside-Bagnell – 'a very keen soldier', she wrote, 'somehow now unfit for service' – who was a laughing-stock among boys like Auden. Generally the school's militarism did not seem serious. 'We drilled with wooden rifles and had "field days" when we took cover behind bushes and twirled noisemakers to represent machine-gun fire,' Auden recalled. Dr Auden was in Gallipoli, Egypt and France for four years, but mostly behind the firing line, and the danger to him 'had no reality' for his youngest son (rather as he denied that the castrating scissor-man had not been frightening because 'not a real person'). 'At school one morning, Christopher Isherwood appeared wearing a black armband; I knew this meant his father was dead, but the words "killed in action" brought no image to my mind.'

Humour was the best defence against the oppressive apprehensions of the time: and jokes were the basis of Auden's friendship with Isherwood. He remembered walking together one Sunday near Hindhead, and Isherwood (who was two years older) saying, 'God must have been tired when he made this country,' which was the first time 'I heard a remark which I thought witty.' Together they developed that arcane and inpenetrable intimacy of private language and private jokes that is the most valuable coinage of boarding-school life. Auden valued friendship as a 'fellow conspiracy' hard for outsiders to breach – an alliance against the rest of the world like 'Seven against Thebes'. In the conspiratorial cells of schoolboy life, Auden was a leader by virtue of his seeming omniscience. As Isherwood described him at St Edmund's,

> He was precociously clever, untidy, lazy and, with the masters, inclined to be insolent. His ambition was to become a mining engineer; and his playbox was full of thick scientific books on geology and metals and machines, borrowed from his father's library. His father was a doctor.... To several of us, including myself, he confided the first naughty stupendous breath-taking hints about the facts of sex.... With his hinted forbidden knowledge and stock of mispronounced scientific words, portentously uttered, he enjoyed among us, his semi-savage credulous schoolfellows, the status of a kind of witch-doctor. I see him drawing an indecent picture on the upper fourth form blackboard, his stumpy fingers, with their blunt bitten nails, covered in ink; I see him boxing, with his ferocious frown, against a boy twice his size; I see him frowning as he sings opposite me in the choir, surpliced, in an enormous Eton collar, above which his great red flaps of ears stand out, on either side of his narrow scowling pudden-white face.

Auden was a scuzzy boy: as an adult he still disliked 'antiseptic objects' and remained unprepossessing in some of his manners. 'Wystan hasn't changed in the least,' Isherwood noted in 1936. 'His clothes are still out at the elbows, his stubby nail-bitten fingers still dirty and sticky with nicotine; he still drinks a dozen cups of tea a day ... he still eats ravenously – though not as much as he once did – and nearly sheds tears if the food isn't to his taste.' At meals he still shovelled food into his mouth while reading.

Despite his interest in science, Auden at the age of thirteen, in 1920, became the first president of a literary society started by boys and teachers at St Edmund's. In its early months it concentrated on Shakespeare readings, initially *The Merchant of Venice* and *Midsummer Night's Dream* (with Auden as Antonio and Portia, and Hermia and Bottom). There were however other diversions, like toffee and cake, and on 27 March 1920, so the society's minute book recorded, the 'defenestration of the president'.

In the autumn of 1920 Auden went to his public school, Gresham's School at Holt in north Norfolk. It had been founded in 1554 by Sir John Gresham, Lord Mayor of London and Prime Warden of the Fishmongers' Company, a City livery company which still supported the school and dominated its governing body in the twentieth century. Despite its endowments by the Fishmongers, the school had only a local reputation until the appointment of George Howson as headmaster in 1900. The school showed no signs of vitality, and consisted only of the relics of the ancient grammar school; but Howson raised Gresham's into the ranks of recognised public schools, while burnishing it with an exceptional liberal brightness. The original Tudor buildings in the centre of Holt were handed over to the preparatory school, and new buildings were erected outside the town. Set in spacious grounds, with a grassy amphitheatre for Shakespearean productions, the architectural style of the new red-brick buildings was 'a rather clumsy Queen Anne with a Flemish flavour'. Howson had the hardihood to take Greek off the curriculum and gave an almost unprecedented emphasis to science. He exerted himself in cultivating a special kind of school spirit. Gresham's had virtually no fagging or beating, no privileges for older boys, few bounds set on boys roaming outside the school grounds, no caps or colours for good gamesmen, and no inter-school matches. 'The result was apparent in the high tone that prevailed throughout the school, and in the courteous attitude of the boys towards visitors and strangers, to whom they gave a friendly welcome, which was as noticeable as it is rare,' wrote one observer in 1919. Howson's ideas attracted middle-class parents of cultivated or progressive tastes. The number of pupils rose from 44 in 1900 to about 250 in 1920.

Auden's headmaster was J. R. Eccles, who had been Howson's science master. A bachelor and teetotaller who was so anxious about masturbation that all Gresham's boys had their trouser pockets sewn up, he was a pompous man who bustled about carrying an armful of books. Many of his mannerisms and accents seemed risible. He once addressed the upper-sixth divinity class on the theme of a pamphlet entitled 'Jesus Christ Cuts No Ice in California': Auden, who was a wicked mimic, exploited this absurdity for weeks. (He imitated Eccles to more serious effect later; his brilliant 'Address for a Prize Day', written in 1931 for *The Orators*, is taken from his recollections of Cyril Morgan-Brown at St Edmund's mixed with later memories from Gresham's.) Eccles believed that in a small school, where he could know each boy individually, he could apply what he called his 'honour system'. He interviewed every pupil soon after his arrival. Each boy was adjured to promise his housemaster to avoid 'indecency, bad language and smoking', and to tell his housemaster should he fail in that promise. 'I like every boy to feel that he is pledged to allow nothing to go on in the School, if he can help it, which reflects upon the good name of the School' – a mealymouthed way of indicating that boys were expected to persuade a fellow pupil to report himself if they saw him breaking a rule, or, failing that, to denounce him themselves to the housemaster. Eccles's technique of moral induction to the school was resented by Auden's friends and seemed tantamount to imposing on Gresham's, so Auden wrote in 1934, the conditions of 'a fascist state'. Auden conceded that the system eliminated smoking, swearing or smut by boys in public, but felt that 'no more potent engine for turning them into neurotic innocents, for perpetuating those very faults of character which it was intended to cure, was ever devised'. Of the two promises extracted by Eccles, 'the second, the obligation to interfere with one's neighbours', meant 'that the whole of our moral life was based on fear, on fear of the community, not to mention the temptation it offered to the natural informer'. These fears only made the pupils 'furtive and dishonest and unadventurous'.

Auden's reaction to this system was inseparable from his 'lost interest' in Christianity. He had been confirmed at the age of thirteen, while a pupil at St Edmund's, during a period of religious enthusiasm. 'Essentially the reason why any person in any age who has been brought up a Christian loses his faith is that he wants to go his own way and enjoy the pleasures of the world and the flesh,' Auden wrote in 1956; but 'to say that ... I lost my faith would be melodramatic or false'. His change of outlook was partly attributable to his realisation that 'unredeemed eroticism' had lain behind his 'pseudo-devout phase' at St Edmund's: he went to confession with the Revd Geoffrey Newman, who had been appointed school chaplain there in 1920, because he had been attracted to him. (Newman, who was born in 1886, headed a list which Auden made in the early 1940s of the fifteen men and boys whom he had loved, culminating with Chester Kallman.) With his increasing interest in psychology, and with the snobbish contempt and arrogance of adolescence, he had also noted 'that, of those who take religion most ardently, a number are unfortunate in one way or another, suffer from physical or mental ill-health, or are unhappily married or too unattractive to get married'. But his disenchantment with Christianity was increased by the cant of worship at Gresham's. Eccles used to preach on moral courage in the school chapel. 'Don't hoard your life,' he sermonised, 'spend it for the good of others.' Hortatory clichés like this delivered from the pulpit would exasperate a boy with an Anglo-Catholic upbringing, accustomed to the spiritual imagination, aesthetic appeal and intellectual astringency of the worship in Mrs Auden's church. There were forms of religious behaviour that were 'a scandal to the imagination', Auden later wrote; one such scandal was surely to preach in secularised commonplaces rather than with the authority that requires spiritual obedience. The Christian Churches, as Auden said, were 'all too ready to make shady deals with any temporal power which would advance what it believed to be its interests': it was despicable to hear religious beliefs being reduced to the mean and dispiriting level that accommodated school discipline.

Nevertheless Auden had many good memories of the school. He felt 'an immense debt' to a few masters: Tyler, the senior classics master, 'who was never tired of showing us the shallowness of those who despised the classics, had the most magnificent bass reading voice I have ever heard, and from listening to him read the Bible and Shakespeare I learnt more about poetry and the humanities than from any course of University lectures'. With the music teacher Walter Greatorex he enjoyed 'my first friendship with a grown up person'; in contrast with the intensity of emotions and expectations that he had endured with his mother, Greatorex 'was in the best sense of the word indifferent'. In his final year at the school he was impressed by a young master called Frank McEachran, an engineer's son from Wolverhampton who had recently returned from

Leipzig, where he had lived during the height of the Weimar inflation, researching a book on Herder, the German philosopher of nationalism. McEachran became a contributor to periodicals like T. S. Eliot's *Criterion* and Cyril Connolly's *Horizon*, as well as to more specialised philosophical publications. Like Tyler he stimulated Auden's commitment to the spoken word as a means of approaching poetry though, like other masters, he could not instil in Auden the rules of punctuation: 'I can only think of them as breathing indications,' Auden admitted in 1936. McEachran built his teaching techniques around his collection of 'Spells': an eclectic and provocative set of extracts from the great literature of several cultures – chiefly but not exclusively poetry – which he would recite, or make his boys recite standing on chairs, as a way of showing the glory of words and of celebrating his own passionate love of poetry. They were a compelling teaching aid, unforgettable to his brighter pupils, and impressive even in the dry form in which they were later published. (The largest sources of McEachran's spells were the Bible, Shakespeare, Eliot and later the adult Auden, followed by Dante, Goethe and Nietzche; with Blake, Sir Thomas Browne, Donne, Hopkins, Keats, Milton, Pascal, Virgil and Wordsworth figuring prominently.) Both of the Auden parents had read poetry aloud to their boys: Wystan as a young chorister had made his own discoveries about enunciation and metre: and the importance of recitation aloud was reinforced by Tyler and McEachran. Otherwise he was not a great respecter of schoolmasters. 'Far, far too many are silted-up old maids, earnest young scoutmasters, or just generally dim.' The reasons for this were clear to him by early adulthood. Those who were attracted to teaching after leaving university were 'only too often those who are afraid of the mature world, either the athletic whose schooldays were the peak of their triumph from which they dread to recede, or else the timid academic whose qualifications or personal charm are insufficient to secure them a fellowship; in either case the would-be children'.

But the great catalyst in Auden's life – sexually and creatively – was Robert Medley. Medley was two years older than Auden, born in 1905; he was a clever, imaginative boy with an agnostic father. In March 1922, when Auden was fifteen, the school's sociological society visited a boot factory at Norwich; on the return journey, Auden contrived to sit next to Medley on the bus. 'He told me he had wanted to speak to me for a long time; he was very determined and it was quickly arranged that we should go for a walk on the following Sunday,' Medley recalled. 'I have no idea what we talked about, for Wystan did most of the talking, except that we soon discovered that we had a good deal in common, including a detached attitude towards the school.' Years later, in 1939, ostensibly writing of Pascal, Auden observed:

> Even the ablest could recall a day
> Of diagnosis when the first stab of his talent
> Ran through the beardless boy and spoilt the sadness
> Of the closed life the stupid never leave.

For Auden the crucial moment of his day of diagnosis was spent with Medley. He still intended to be a mining engineer, and his most recent 'crazes' had been 'for motor-bikes, photography, and whales'. But in the spring of 1922, on a walk together, Medley made some irreligious remarks and was then startled to find Auden flushed with annoyance (despite his professed dislike of Howson's Christianity). To cover their discomfiture Medley changed the subject. As Auden recounted,

> indecision broke off with a clean-cut end
> One afternoon in March at half-past three
> When walking in a ploughed field with a friend;
> Kicking a little stone he turned to me
> And said, 'Tell me, do you write poetry?'
> I never had, and said so, but I knew
> That very moment what I wished to do.

He was already so fascinated with words that the draw of poetry would eventually have proved irresistible; but this moment in the ploughed field was intense and mastering. As he said in a television interview of 1965 about this decision, 'It did come like a revelation.' Appropriately Medley had been talking of Christianity only moments before Auden's life vocation was revealed, for poets and Christians share an analogical sense of the world and rely on a similar inheritance of symbolic language.

At other times Auden related his sudden turn to poetry to his distress at Gresham's life. 'I have yet to meet a poetry-lover under thirty who was not an introvert, or an introvert who was not unhappy in adolescence,' he wrote in an autobiographical fragment of 1940. At boarding school, the poetry-lover 'sees the extrovert successful, happy, and good and himself unpopular or neglected; and what is hardest to bear is not unpopularity, but the consciousness that it is deserved, that he is grubby and inferior and frightened and dull'. His consolations in this suffering are solitary and introspective. 'Unable to imagine a society in which he would feel at home, and warned by some mysterious instinct from running back for consolation to the gracious or terrifying figures of childhood, he turns away from the human to the non-human: homesick he will seek, not his mother, but mountains or autumn woods, friendless he will mutely observe the least shy of the wild animals, and the growing life within him will express itself in a devotion to music and thoughts upon mutability and death. Art for him will be something infinitely precious, pessimistic, and hostile to life.' Auden developed a voracious appetite for poetry, browsing in his school library, taking up a poet like de la Mare, whom he would soon drop for another like W. H. Davies. De la Mare's anthology *Come Hither*, published in 1923, 'more than any book before or since, taught me what poetry is', he later testified. Medley introduced him to Arthur Waley's recent translations of ancient Chinese poems. 'Their straightforward flatness – so unromantic appealed to me then, and this appeal grows stronger in 1964,' he noted forty years after.

But Auden's supreme early influence was Wordsworth. He identified his earliest poem as a Wordsworthian sonnet about a tarn in the Lake District; it has not survived, and his mother in 1926 identified his poem 'California' as his earliest effort (presumably dating from the spring of 1922). Inspired perhaps by a coastal district in Norfolk, it is also imitative of Wordsworth, whose visionary experiences in boyhood provoked a mortified desire in Auden for similar revelation. He longed for equivalent vision, but felt inadequate to it. As an adolescent, and indeed later, Auden 'suspected' that his nature was 'colder' than many other people's, and 'envied those who found it easy to feel deeply'. One proof of deep feeling, or of innate poetic gift, would have been a revelatory vision such as had transformed Wordsworth. But Auden had no such vision, and perhaps felt himself debarred from such experiences by his loss of religious faith. Instead he developed a personal poetic theory of gratitude for both suffering and human imperfection. As he wrote in 1937,

O look, look in the mirror,
O look in your distress;
Life remains a blessing
Although you cannot bless.

> O stand, stand at the window
> As the tears scald and start;
> You shall love your crooked neighbour
> With your crooked heart.

Yet though in substitution for a boyhood vision he set himself tests of emotional endurance to invigorate his creativity, he was also, as he wrote years later, the sort of 'would-be poet who serves his apprenticeship in a library', imposing his own meaning and emotion on the work of whoever he had chosen as his current Master. 'This has its advantages', Auden said ('his Master is deaf and dumb and gives neither instruction nor criticism'), but studying an inanimate master in a book could seem cold and mechanistic when compared to the revelations about Nature which Wordsworth experienced: especially because at this time Auden thought 'Nature's griefs were infinitely more' impressive than 'the petty griefs of man'. 'California' begins with the poet looking up a hill at the night sky. He feels inspired and capable of greatness.

> A man could walk along that track,
> Fetch the moon and bring it back,
> And gather stars up in his hand
> Like strawberries on English land.

But confronted with the wholeness and magnificence of nature, he lapses into an impoverished timidity and shrinks away in self-reproach:

> Then turned with slow steps down the hill.
> But how should I, a poor man, dare
> To meet so close the full moon's stare?
> And so I stopped and stood quite still,
> Then turned with slow steps down the hill.

He dares neither to act nor to let his imagination run riot. He opts for nullity. As Auden understood, art for the introverted adolescent is 'hostile to life'.

In the summer of 1923 he discovered Thomas Hardy. 'For more than a year I read no-one else, and I do not think that I was ever without one volume or another of the beautifully produced Wessex edition in my hands: I smuggled them into class, carried them about on Sunday walks, and took them up to the dormitory to read in the early morning, though they were far too unwieldy to read in bed with comfort,' as he wrote gratefully on the centenary of that poet's birth. In some respects Hardy was familiar and unthreatening. 'To begin with, he looked like my father: that broad, unpampered moustache, bald forehead and deeply lined sympathetic face.' He was a safe father-figure, because not impeccable or impossible to compete with: 'Hardy's faults as a craftsman, his rhythmical clumsiness, his outlandish vocabulary were obvious even to a schoolboy, and the young can learn best from those of whom, because they can criticize them, they are not afraid.' Hardy's provincialism suited young Auden too. 'There were several Londoners at school, alarming elegant creatures – one even who was said to read Racine for pleasure,' he recalled in 1940. 'Looking back, I realize how lucky it was that I felt too gauche and frightened to get to know and imitate them, for their favourite authors could only have encouraged me into pretending a life which had no contact with my own experience: the dangers of too early a sophistication and contact with "modern" writers are so great.' Auden continued hankering for the features of the Hardy country for the rest of his life. He persuaded himself (it was an over-simplification) that the more idyllic side to Hardy had been his own experience. 'The properties of Hardy's world were the properties of my own childhood: it was unsophisticated and provincial, and it was the England of the professional classes' – so he wrote shortly after settling in the United States and beginning the redepiction of his English boyhood. In truth Hardy's Dorset had little in common with Solihull, and was not as cosy as Auden suggested.

What Auden valued most in Hardy was 'his hawk's vision, his way of looking at life from a very great height': a characteristic too of Dr Auden, who kept by his bedroom door a carved wooden screen with a Greek inscription which read in translation, 'Live as on a mountain.' ('The debris of broken systems and exploded dogmas form a great mound, a Monte Testaccio of shards and remnants of old vessels which once held human beliefs,' Dr Auden had told a medical conference in 1921: 'If you take the trouble to climb to the top of it, you will widen your horizon.') It was Hardy's hawk vision, Auden thought, which gave him such magnificent powers of synthesis: 'To see the individual life related not only to the local social life of its time, but to the whole of human history, life on the earth, the stars, gives one both humility and self-confidence.' It was such a synthesis of the ethical, emotional and physical needs of humanity that Auden's greatest poetry later attempted; but as an adolescent he naturally felt self-conscious and inadequate. In a poem of 1925 (influenced by Wordsworth as well as Hardy) he described turning off a track and hurriedly, eagerly scrambling upwards towards a tarn in high terrain, as if to the hawk's eyrie:

> all at once
> Three crags rose up and overshadowed me
> 'What are you doing here, the road's your place'
> – Between their bodies I could see my tarn –
> What could I do but shift my feet awhile
> Mutter and turn back to my road again
> Watched out of sight by three tall angry hills.

He feared the same guilty presumption about approaching the poetic higher-ground. Auden had mentioned a tarn before, in a poem in which he looked down from rocks on two beautiful boys bathing in a tarn's dark water. In this 1924 poem he did not approach the swimmers; like the poet on the hill in 'California', he turns away from experience. The attractiveness of the boys was a special note: his early development as a poet was inseparable from his developing sense of masculinity and masculine relations.

Auden's school friendships with Medley and others had erotic undercurrents, but they were essentially intellectual or literary with a smaller sexual element, rather than the other way around. He 'simply walked across from his house to mine and forcefully initiated a friendship which, though brief, was romantic and grandiose', recorded John Pudney, who afterwards was a poet. Auden overwhelmed Pudney with:

> urgent monologues about D. H. Lawrence, Havelock Ellis, Wilfrid Gibson, psychology, sexual hygiene, homosexuality and Socialism. For a person of my age and environment this was an explosive experience. On long didactic walks Wystan did not talk like a boy. He spoke a language which was mature, worldly, intellectually challenging. I wondered then, and still wonder, if he had ever had any boyhood at all.

Ten years later Auden was rueful that he had been sexually inhibited in his overtures. 'At Holt I was a bloody little funk; Had I not been we should have had much fun,' he told Pudney in 1932.

This failure to consummate his friendships with Medley and Pudney by sexual activity was mainly a matter of diffidence; but it was part of a pattern which became clearer in the future. The sort of adolescent who develops a taste for poetry, Auden wrote in 1940, prefers 'love frustrated, for all success seems to him noisy and vulgar', and thinks that 'the authentic poetic note' is struck by such lines as Housman's:

> Lovers lying two and two
> Ask not whom they sleep beside
> And the bridegroom all night through
> Never turns him to the bride.

The small boy who preferred machines because people went too far, or demanded too much emotionally, still turned in adolescence to machinery in his images and compassion. He had been taken aged eight to the gasworks at Solihull, where the fumes were thought good for his bronchitis, and at seventeen he celebrated the derelict land littered with 'old drain-pipes' surrounding the gas-works:

> this is dear
> To pour his joy into; he always sings
> His loveliest among these broken things.

Like the literary masters to whom he paid tribute in libraries, abandoned machines were deaf and dumb, insensate and unresponsive, giving neither instruction nor criticism. He supplied the emotion for them, as Katherine Bucknell has noted of 'The Traction Engine' (1924):

> Here now it lies; unsheltered, undesired,
> Its engine rusted fast; its boiler mossed, unfired,
> Companioned by a boot heel and an old cart wheel,
>   In thistles attired.
>
> Unfeeling, uncaring; imaginings
> Mar not its future; no past sick memory clings,
> Yet seems it well to deserve the love we reserve
>   For animate things.

Nor did his tastes change. 'In my Eden we have a few beam-engines, saddle-tank locomotives, overshot water wheels and other beautiful pieces of obsolete machinery to play with,' he wrote in 1954.

Auden's love had to exceed everyone else's bounds. His feelings had to be unreciprocated, or at least impossible to match in strength. He did not respond at this time when he was the object of love. His music master, Walter Greatorex, who was homosexually inclined, introduced him as a lover of poetry to Michael Davidson, a young journalist living in Norwich. 'I was bewitched at the first meeting; not by a physical attractiveness, which I didn't find (beyond the general one of adolescence), but by the blinding discovery, as in a revelation, that here was wonderfully joined that divine freak called genius with the magical age of sixteen', Davidson wrote. 'The maturity of even his smallest remarks, a kind of inspired wisdom which, in his company, one couldn't help being aware of, was alarming; and I knew instantly that, though ten years older, I was shamefully his inferior in intellect and learning.' Auden intoxicated him 'like one's second Pernod', and was romanticised as a 'Chatterton, on whom I would lavish all I could muster of literary maternalism'. Davidson replaced Medley (who had left Gresham's for art school) as the most immediate influence on Auden in 1923. He was supremely a literary influence. Letters, poems and books flowed between Norwich and Holt. 'He sent me every new poem he wrote (in his small, adult hand; that looked much more legible than it sometimes was), and I returned long letters of criticism or rather discussion; and through the post we discovered to each other any exciting writers that had come fresh to us – remember particularly Edward Thomas, Robert Frost, Jefferies and de la Mare – or copied out passages of special relevance in our reading,' Davidson recorded. Years later, on Ischia, Auden told him, 'Michael, you don't know what you did for me in those days.' He not only bombarded Davidson with letters and sheaves of poems, but also wrote often and lengthily to Medley. These messages Medley would stuff in his pockets, to read on walks or buses; but, as Medley confessed, they were soon lost or torn, and he became the friend who 'answered some / Of his long marvellous letters but kept none'. (Auden never kept letters either.)

Auden often visited Medley's home in London. 'He fitted well into a family of six, being an avid player of card games,' Medley wrote almost sixty years later. His untidiness and nervous energy, typified by 'his habit of banging out fugues and popular hymn tunes on the piano before breakfast', were 'tolerable, but life could not go on being lived at such a pitch. Although everybody felt a bit flat after Wystan had gone, there was also a sense of relief.' As Auden perhaps required, the nervous intensity of his behaviour and feelings could not be matched. In London Medley and Auden made expeditions of cultural discovery. They visited Harold Monro's poetry bookshop and attended the more innovative theatrical productions of 1923. The first of these was Karel Capek's futuristic play about robots, *RUR*, staged in April by Basil Dean. The plot concerned the Rossom Universal Robot Company, whose managers set out to free humankind from the curse of toil and to transform themselves into a Nietzschean aristocracy nourished by millions of mechanical slaves. These robots turn against their masters, exterminate the human race, only to be doomed to early extinction as they have no means of regeneration or renewal. The robots' survival is ensured, however, when two of their number are transformed into humans by falling in love. Soon afterwards Medley and Auden saw another Capek production, *The Insect Play*. This was a satire on ethnology and the 'Human Ant Heap' which was exciting but unevenly written. To some of its audience in 1923, it was objectionable for its talk of love being 'consummated', but the evening was memorable to Medley half a century later, and aspects of it seem to have imprinted themselves on Auden's imagination: in 1970 he wrote a poem about insects, entitled 'The Aliens', which is reminiscent of Capek's play and ends tellingly, 'they are to us quite simply what we must never become'.

Yet when Medley stayed with Auden in Birmingham, his visit was overtaken by crisis. A year or so earlier, in the Gresham swimming pool where the boys swam naked, Auden had asked Medley for a double dive: a manoeuvre in which Auden clung pick-a-back to Medley, who then jumped from the top diving board. 'I cannot conceive of anything else I would rather be able to do well,' Auden said of diving in 1936. 'It's such a marvellous way of showing off.' But in the Gresham's pool the double dive was a fiasco. 'Wystan predictably came unstuck on the way down and emerged from the water with a badly bleeding nose.' Now in Birmingham there was an emotional sequel. Auden had written a poem about this pool, which he left on the floor of his bedroom where his mother found it. The two youths were summoned to Dr Auden's study. 'Dr Auden explained gently that he himself as a young man had enjoyed a "close friendship" but that such a thing was not desirable, nor had he gone "that far". Had we gone "that far"? We gave him an assurance that our relationship had always been and would remain purely platonic and left the study, numbed by the implications of the discovery but thankful that it had not been worse.' Dr Auden destroyed the poem. Around the same time Auden's contacts with Davidson were prohibited by the Gresham's authorities and Mrs Auden, which interdiction only goaded him into further meetings. His defiance may have owed a little to his sense of sexual difference; but in chief it arose from the impatience of an intelligent boy confronted by the narrow dominion of schoolmasters. When he schemed to stay with Davidson in Norwich, and had other assignations, it was intelligent sympathy that he needed rather than sexual solidarity or pleasure (their friendship remained chaste). 'He knew, of course – better than I, having the entire psychological pentateuch at his finger-tips – the nature of my feelings for him,' Davidson realised. 'He rather enjoyed them – he could study me, so to speak, clinically; he once told me, as if stating an interesting scientific fact, that I was the first adult homosexual he had met.' When Davidson sent him feeble love verses, he never referred to them; 'he abhorred easy emotionalism and sentimentality'.

These incidents with Davidson and Medley could have been far more unpleasant: compared with many boys in his position, Auden's troubles with his parents were thin. He had, overall, a secure, happy and comfortable childhood, with enough anxiety to keep him alert and enough minor grievances to give a sense of justice. At the age of seventeen, he had a rare coherence in his view of who he was, what he believed and what his future required. He knew what he wanted, and he was poised to act. 'I wanted to be left alone, to write poetry, to choose my own friends and lead my own sex-life,' he recalled in 1939. He was making himself ready for that happy relegation that transforms fear and misery, passion and effort, into experience and knowledge.

As an adolescent the poetry of Housman appealed to him. Writing of Housman in 1938, he summarised the choices facing any writer with hopes of greatness:

> Heaven and Hell. Reason and Instinct. Conscious Mind and Unconscious. Is their hostility a temporary and curable neurosis, due to our particular pattern of culture, or intrinsic to the nature of these faculties? Can man only think when he is frustrated from acting and feeling? Is the intelligent person always the product of some childhood neurosis? Does Life only offer two alternatives: 'You shall be happy, healthy, attractive, a good mixer, a good lover and parent, but on condition that you are not overcurious about life.

On the other hand you shall be attentive and sensitive, conscious of what is happening around you, but in that case you must cease to expect to be happy, or successful in love, or at home in any company. There are two worlds and you cannot belong to them both. If you belong to the second of these worlds you will be unhappy because you will always be in love with the first, while at the same time you will despise it. The first world on the other hand will not return your love because it is in its nature to love only itself.'

Auden had the fortitude and endurance to make the harder choice.

CHAPTER 3

'I mean to be a great poet'

Auden went to Oxford in the autumn of 1925 and left in the summer of 1928. It was, he wrote forty years later,

> a time to wear odd clothing,
> behave with panache
> and talk nonsense as I did,
> ambling in Oxford's
> potamic meadows with friends:
> one austere dogma
> capped another, abstract noun
> echoed abstract noun,
> to voice our irreverent
> amoebean song.

He was an authentically rare type. Stephen Spender said Auden's most impressive feature was 'that, at such an early age, he was so confident and conscious a master of his situation'; but that was an impression that he worked hard to make on Spender. Underneath this self-confidence he was riven by his own interior questioning. Years later, in 1963, Auden asked his brother John, 'Why must one do academic study during the very years when the only thing one really wants is to know "Who am I?"' As an Oxford undergraduate he had addressed this question in all its emotional and intellectual aspects. He developed his consciousness, personal and poetic; found new sympathies and antipathies; transgressed, disgusted himself, went back on his ideas; then set himself new tests and challenges as part of his search for a fitting identity. This was little different from the experiences of any undergraduate of intelligence and sensitivity, though Auden's intensity and single-mindedness were more extreme than many people could have managed. But there was more to his situation at Oxford than this. He studied hard, even if he did not impress his examiners, and was continually working as a poet. By the age of twenty he was recognised as a prodigy, co-editor of a collection of *Oxford Poetry*; someone with a small, dedicated readership, not just another adolescent limited in his own private meanings, but a poet whose work had started to transcend his life and was starting to alter other lives. Cecil Day Lewis, for example, was three years his senior yet 'willingly became his disciple where poetry was concerned', felt his 'emulative faculty' was 'roused to its utmost' by Auden.

Auden's college was Christ Church, the domain of aristocrats and Etonians. Their self-assurance impressed him, so much so that in middle age he sometimes wished he had been educated at Eton. Christ Church awarded him a minor scholarship in natural science which partly paid his fees, but early in 1926 he changed to a course in politics, philosophy and economics (known as PPE or Modern Greats), before again transferring after a few months to the English School. 'The exclusiveness of the rich undergraduates and the cynicism of the dons were remarkable' in Oxford in the mid-1920s, as Auden's near-contemporary James Lees-Milne has recorded. The 'most intellectual' of the dons were often 'those who toadied to the *jeunesse dorée* to the neglect of the struggling scholars'. Tuition was minimal because tutors were too busy or too lazy to be bothered. So long as undergraduates attended the prescribed number of lectures they were not penalised. 'To pass three hours a week feverishly trying to take down notes, or memorise a string of platitudes or paradoxes – usually the latter since most lecturers tend to show off – is utterly useless,' Lees-Milne decided. 'A student does far better to read the stuff quietly in his room. It will take him a quarter of the time, and he will thus be able to concentrate without distractions. But he will need personal guidance as well.' Auden knew this, kept to his room; 'Auden then, as always, was busy getting on with the job,' MacNeice recalled of the Oxford years, 'reading very fast and very widely.' After his changes of course in 1926, Auden was lucky to have personal guidance as well.

His first mentor was Roy Harrod, the young don at Christ Church responsible for modern history and economics who also supervised PPE there. The family tradition of the Harrods was that 'literary and artistic ... conversation was by far the greatest, if not the prime object, of life' and he liked to exercise this taste with the more sympathetic undergraduates. The two men found an affinity, and it was through Harrod that Auden met Bill

McElwee, an undergraduate with whom he fell in love. The PPE course though was less appealing, and after a few months Auden abandoned it. As he explained to Harrod, 'To an introvert like myself, the social conditions of the poor in the 19th century as expounded by G.D.H. Cole do not click.' In any case PPE had not fitted with his life-plan. 'My ambitions are all literary ... at all other forms of intellectual activity I am incompetent and only half-interested.' English literature best served his purpose.

His reunion in December 1925 with his old schoolfriend, Christopher Isherwood, was critical to his decision to transfer to the English School. Isherwood, who had left Cambridge that summer after deliberately spoiling his examination results, was working in London as a personal and social secretary. He was living uneasily in Kensington with his widowed mother and trying to write a novel. His meeting with Auden was a chance affair, but he found him little changed.

> His small pale yellow eyes were still screwed painfully together in the same short-sighted scowl and his stumpy immature fingers were still nail-bitten and stained – nicotine was now mixed with the ink. He was expensively but untidily dressed in a chocolate-brown suit which needed pressing, complete with one of the new fashionable double-breasted waistcoats. His coarse woollen socks were tumbled, all anyhow, around his babyishly shapeless naked ankles. One of the laces was broken in his elegant brown shoes. While I and his introducer talked he sat silent, aggressively smoking a large pipe with a severe childish frown. Clumsy and severe, he hooked a blunt dirty finger round the tops of several of the books in my shelves, over-balancing them onto his lap and then, when his casual curiosity was satisfied, dropping them face downwards open on the floor – serenely unconscious of my outraged glances.

But after this inauspicious beginning they revived the old jokes and mimicry from St Edmund's, and developed a new cipher or private dialect for their conversations. Auden – 'deliberately a little over-casual' – revealed that he was writing poetry, and was soon consulting Isherwood about his work. Isherwood's opinions counted for more than anyone else's with Auden at this time, and a pattern of loving friendship developed which remained little altered until the war. Reviewing the poems of their mutual friend William Plomer in 1937, Auden made a comparison based on his view of Isherwood and himself which went deep into his sense of their identities. 'A novelist must be painstaking, cautious, objective, non-committal, or he makes an utter fool of himself. Good lyric poetry depends upon the opposite qualities, on throwing caution to the winds, accepting the subjectives as God-given, wildly taking sides, becoming in fact what Mr Yeats has described as "a foolish passionate man".'

One common point between Auden and Isherwood was their rebellion against the small, smothered morality of their mothers. It seemed to many of their generation that most of the personal and real emotions which this morality had supported had been knocked to oblivion by the war. The preface to *Oxford Poetry* 1927 described 'the chaos of values which is the substance of our environment': Auden hoped the poets would show the way to order. 'Puritanism,' Eliot had written recently, 'became repulsive only when it appeared as the survival of a restraint after the feelings which it restrained had gone.' Isherwood described his youthful self as 'an upper-middle-class Puritan, cautious, a bit stingy, with a stake in the land'. But Auden, who was peremptory in his interference in the lives of his friends, conspired with Isherwood's friend Edward Upward to overturn the assumptions and loyalties of this Puritan from the Cheshire gentry. Auden incited rebellion and resentment. 'During the strike I worked for the T. U. C. and have quarrelled bitterly with certain sections of the family in consequence, which is all to the good,' he wrote to Isherwood in 1926. The Isherwood family became a long-term interest in his life. He indulged in amateur psychologising about their relations, and wrote poems about them. 'The Photograph of a Boy in Costume' (1926) describes Isherwood's younger brother Richard dressed for a recent school play; 'Uncle Henry' (?1931) is an imaginative version of the sex life of his friend's rich uncle.

Isherwood was a youth of limited sexual experience when he re-met Auden in 1925. Auden set out to broaden his outlook with shameless and inflammatory anecdotes of his own escapades: both young men recognised that transgressive sexuality would serve their literary needs. As Auden wrote twenty years later, 'without these prohibitive frontiers we should never know who we were or what we wanted. It is they who donate to neighbourhood all their accuracy and vehemence.' After a few months Auden and Isherwood began to have sex together: not in a spirit of romantic passion, but as two men who understood one another well, giving and sharing pleasure, relieving tension and having fun. 'For years we fucked like rabbits every chance we got,' Isherwood later told Thom Gunn. They continued as lovers in this way, at intervals, until 1939.

The authorities at Christ Church were too 'snooty' to have a don to teach the upstart new course in English literature, and in autumn 1926 sent Auden to study with a fellow at Exeter College, Nevill Coghill, who became a lifelong friend. Coghill often told the story of his first interview with Auden. Wanting to plan their work with relevance to Auden's needs, Coghill asked what he wished to be in later life. 'I'm going to be a poet,' Auden answered. Coghill made some patronising reply ('Ah yes! … It will give you insight into the technical side of your subject') only to be crushed by Auden: 'You don't understand at all. I mean to be a great poet.' Coghill was eight years older than Auden. His father had been an Irish baronet who painted landscapes, and his aunt Edith Somerville was a luminary of Anglo-Irish literature. He was a tall, vivacious, gracefully leonine man valued for his witty, arresting conversation and letters of glittering, discursive eccentricity. He had read history as an Oxford undergraduate, and was a practising Christian, both of which had broadened his sympathies and appreciation of literature. His chief interest was medieval English – notably Chaucer and *Piers Plowman* – and he was acclaimed for spectacular open-air productions of Shakespeare's plays. He published little, and for years 'was better known in Oxford as a personality than as an academic', according to his friend Lord David Cecil. 'He had gifts of sensibility and ardour which enabled him to feel and to make others feel the works of past authors to be as alive and significant as those written by contemporaries.' Though he married in 1927 and fathered a child while Auden was his pupil, his tastes were predominantly homosexual, and the marriage soon disintegrated.

Coghill relished his hourly tutorial with Auden as the 'liveliest' moment in his week. They met in the small, mullioned fifteenth-century dungeon where Coghill lived in Exeter College. 'Before the ritual of his reading his weekly essay aloud to me was reached – always the clou of the occasion – there would be a torrent of other things, some joke or scandal of the week, some ironical anecdote, lightly touched with a grin of Schadenfreude, some political fulmination, some discovery in psychoanalysis, some Communist proposition, some new poetic enthusiasm,' Coghill recalled. 'He would talk of the sayings and doings of his friends, Christopher Isherwood, Cecil Day Lewis, Stephen Spender, and others, then unknown, now famous, and at the centre of strange excitements in new politics, new writing, new morals, new anathemas, new hosannas.' If this was the effect that he had on his teacher, his impact on his contemporaries was overwhelming. His conversation with them was exceptional: there was no invective, he did not offer the usual dreary little exactitudes of a swot, spoke neither with the suggestive lisp of an aesthete nor with the interrogative quaver of an adolescent nervous wreck. As Coghill delighted to remember,

> He had great intellectual prestige in the University at large; he used words ... which nobody else knew. His sayings were widely mis-quoted, and would appear, in their garbled form, in the essays of my other pupils. These being cross-examined, and their nonsense laid bare, still held the trump, which they would play when nothing else would save them: 'Well, anyhow, that's what Wystan says.' It was the armour of God to them.

Thirty years later, after Auden had been elected Professor of Poetry at Oxford, he remembered his undergraduate pontifications to Coghill with distress. 'Really, how do the dons stand it, for I'm sure this scene repeats itself year after year. When I recall the kindness of my tutors, the patience with which they listened, the courtesy with which they hid their boredom, I am overwhelmed by their sheer goodness.'

In his talks with Coghill Auden often mentioned other young poets. Cecil Day Lewis, 'sardonic, restless, intolerant, but basically romantic and naive' as he described himself, first met Auden in the latter's rooms at Christ Church, the windows of which were covered in sackcloth curtains because he preferred to work by artificial light. Auden was not 'the first exceptional intelligence that I had encountered, but he was the first young man I met here who had already dedicated such an intelligence to poetry', Day Lewis judged. 'It was his vitality, though, rather than his intellectual power, which most impressed itself upon me at the start – a vitality so abundant that, overflowing into certain poses and follies and wildly unrealistic notions, it gave these an air of authority, an illusion of rightness, which enticed some of Auden's contemporaries into taking them over-seriously.' For Day Lewis such 'exuberance redeemed ... the dogmatism, the intellectual bossiness, and the tendency to try and run his friends' lives for them, all of which were by-products of this excess of life'.

Day Lewis recognised that Auden could be a bully or a poseur, and studied those mannerisms which were, according to taste, endearing or ludicrous: later he wrote a series of crime novels under the alias of Nicholas Blake, and took the more singular of Auden's social tics for the character of Nigel Strangeways, his detective hero. Auden enjoyed the Blake novels, writing in 1968 that they had 'given more pleasure to more people than, in our age, any verses can ever hope to'. In the summer of 1927 the two apprentice poets often walked together in the Oxford area. 'Wystan's favourite walk was past the gas-works and the municipal rubbish dump – he moving with his phenomenally long, ungainly stride, and talking incessantly, his words tumbling over one another in the hurry to get out, a lock of tow-coloured hair falling over the brow of his rather puffy but wonderfully animated white face,' Day Lewis recollected. 'As likely as not, he was carrying a starting-pistol and wearing an extraordinary black, lay-reader's type of frock coat which came half way down to his knees and had been rescued by him from one of his mother's jumble sales.'

Another of these mutinous children was Stephen Spender. They met at Oxford when Spender was nineteen and Auden two years older: Auden took hold over Spender's mind declaring, 'You are so infinitely capable of being humiliated. Art is born of humiliation.' Yet Spender was shrewd in return. 'Auden, despite his perceptiveness, lacked something in human relationships. He forced issues too much, made everyone too conscious of himself and therefore was in the position of an observer who is a disturbing force in the behaviour he observes.' Twenty years later Spender still doubted if Auden 'completely broke away from the isolation in human relationships which was simply the result of his overwhelming cleverness as a young man'. Their affection was lifelong, and was perhaps even preserved by the vinegary traces in their relations. 'When a friend forms an idea of one when both he and you are very young and retains the same attitude throughout one's life, one feels a bit resentful,' Spender later said. In the 1940s Auden described:

> that anxiety about himself and his future which haunts, like a bad smell, the minds of most young men, though most of them are under the illusion that their lack of confidence is a unique and shameful fear which, if confessed, would make them an object of derision to their normal contemporaries. Accordingly they watch others with a covert passionate curiosity. What makes them tick? What would it feel like

to be a success? Here is somebody who is nobody in particular, there even an obvious failure, yet they do not seem to mind? How is that possible?

Mutually vigilant competitiveness of this sort characterised the friendship of Auden and Spender. It is notable that with MacNeice, whom Auden did not know intimately until the mid-1930s when they were both based in Birmingham, Auden was far less domineering. There was less jealousy, or poetic competitiveness, in MacNeice than in other contemporaries, and the two men's relations were more relaxed (although privately Auden disparaged MacNeice as a reviewer). MacNeice too shared Auden's gleeful eye for the farcical.

Auden's desire to impress, yet characteristically English pretence of indifference, was demonstrated in his attitude to the class-mark of his degree. He professed not to be competitive with 'the common herd' about examination results. 'I can take no interest in what class I get,' he claimed to his brother John in 1927. His course with Coghill 'interests me immensely and I get much benefit therefrom I think, but the benefit is all that concerns me'. This was a temporary pose; by the Easter vacation of 1928 he confessed that the prospect of his final examinations was 'becoming a nightmare'. He wept with mortification during his final examinations in the early summer, according to his fellow undergraduate J. I. M. Stewart, who sat opposite him: 'this was astonishing, even unnerving, but there could be no doubt about it: the tears were coursing down his pale and ample, if as yet unformed, cheeks'. When he received only a third-class degree, Auden was ashamed and found no consolation in Coghill's remark that the examination questions were clumsy. 'I certainly expected to do better,' he told Harrod. 'No one likes making a fool of himself or being set down by others as an intellectual charlatan.' His poor results were held against him by some academics. They enabled A. L. Rowse to conclude, 'Wystan's cleverness was verbal, pyrotechnical – not intellectual, it did not extend into the realm of thinking.' In fact his third-class degree may have reflected the anti-modernist prejudices of those who marked his papers. The external examiner was Ernest de Selincourt, an authority on Wordsworth's texts who held the chair of English literature at Birmingham University and loathed modernism. De Selincourt was certainly proud of his part in humbling Auden. A few years later he discovered that one of his Birmingham pupils admired Auden's poetry.

'"And would it surprise you Mr Allen," the rejoinder was triumphant, "to learn that Mr (*sniff*) Auden (*sniff*) got a third at Oxford, and a bad third at that? I know, because I was the external examiner." '

Auden wrote that after a school regime like Gresham's, with its inhibitions on sexual expression, pupils were likely to 'remain frozen or undeveloped, or else, their infantilised instinct suddenly released, they plunge into foolish and damaging dissipation'. Certainly he celebrated his arrival at Oxford with an eruption of sexual activity. When his schoolfriend Medley saw him early in his undergraduate career, he found Auden 'with new-found independence was enjoying the part of grand seigneur'. On one visit (after talking half the night) they went to bed together: a consummation long desired by Auden, but one which was symbolic rather than passionate. 'Neither of us was an experienced lover and did not know how to make the best of the occasion, and there was something typically clinical and Wystan-like in his remarking as the sheets were pulled back that "everybody's resistance" was "at its lowest by three o'clock in the morning",' Medley recalled.

Auden's sexual self-confidence may have owed something to his friendship with another Christ Church undergraduate, Tom Driberg, who was two years older than himself and afterwards became a distinguished journalist and Labour politician. The two youths had a shared preference for fellatio, though they were too similar in type to be attracted to one another. Their attitude to private domestic histories was similar too. Driberg considered the family to be 'an institution destructive of true affection, a nexus of possessiveness, vindictiveness and jealousy', and judged 'the people of my grandparents' and parents' generations were great haters, and the hatred was concentrated most intensely within the family'. Auden, who loved to study other people's families, might have thought the Dribergs resembled the Bicknells: as he later wrote, 'every family snapshot album is an argument for the doctrine of Original Sin'. Driberg was proud of the fact that he accompanied Auden in his discovery of T. S. Eliot's *The Waste Land*: a moment of excitement which neither man forgot. As Driberg recalled half a century later, they stood side by side in his rooms scanning a copy of Eliot's review, the *Criterion*; 'read it, at first, with incredulous hilarity (the Mrs Porter bit, for instance); read it, again and again, with growing awe'.

As well as the excitement of literary revelation, Driberg and Auden had political and sexual interests in common. In some respects these were inseparable. Public schoolboys like Auden came to university in a state of political naivety. Pupils were not 'given any real sense of the problems of the world, or how to attack them, other than in vague ideals of service', Auden wrote of Gresham's. As a result 'the public school boy's attitude to the working-class and to the not-quite-quite' was that he should be 'fairly kind and polite, provided of course that they return the compliment, but their lives and needs remain as remote to him as those of another species'. Some middle-class left-wingers like Driberg dealt with this shortcoming by sexual contact: Auden's attitude resembled that of his poem 'Rain' which, so he told Isherwood in 1926, did not 'idealize the labourer in any way', least of all 'the damnable half-educated kind'. Such snobbishness proved ineradicable in him. It 'really gratifies my sex snobbery', he recorded when in Berlin in 1929 he discovered that a previous client of his rent-boy Pieps had been 'Lord Revelstoke, the banker who died in Paris, a friend of the king'. In the same period he described himself trying to pick up a youth in an alley, 'brandishing my cigar, picturing myself as the Baron de Charlus', but, though he posed as peremptory in sexual matters, he knew that he was 'a middle-class rabbit' rather than a successful predator. Years later he wrote in New York,

> Too timid to cruise,
> in his feudal day-dream no
> courage is needed.
> The Cardinal halts his coach:
> 'Dear Child, you please me. Hop in!'

This gentle platonic idyll evokes Auden's preferred mode of *droit de seigneur*. He maintained, so he told a New Yorker in 1947, 'the European attitude that the lower classes simply ought to go to bed when asked', adding that Chester Kallman, like other Americans, 'was horribly shocked when I told him I felt that way'. Similarly he thought that the Vision of Eros – the 'infinite sacred importance' invested in a beloved by a lover, as described in Plato's *Symposium* or Shakespeare's sonnets – was demarcated by 'class feelings': no one could have such a vision about an individual belonging 'to a social group which he has been brought up to regard as inferior to his own, so that its members are not, for him, fully persons'. These class boundaries to visionary experience seem peculiarly English in their narrowness; but the significance in Auden's case is as a reminder of his difficulty in appreciating the individuality of other people, or the reality of their existence. Until about 1946 he tended to treat other people as types.

'Caricatures', he told his wife Erika Mann in 1936, 'are really my favourite kind of picture.' A particular favourite was Honoré Daumier (1808–79), who depicted people for what they represented as social subjects rather than as individuals with special needs and feelings: his cartoons of lawyers, for example, represent the truth of Lord Radcliffe's definition of justice, 'a word that the people in power use to give a moral cover to what is really their own material interest'. Auden had similar tendencies to Daumier. He believed that 'the analysis of character' was exclusively 'the province of the novel', so much so that the people in his own dramatic writings were variously described as 'types (no characters)' or 'cartoon-like'. As John Bayley has written, 'though Auden never regards people wantonly or inhumanly he does depersonalise them and transform them into a bizarre extension of object or place. Their significance to the poet as emblems of some general condition may be large, but they are always seen against some appropiate background or linked to their unique and revealing properties of clothing, accent, or facial tic.'

The attitudes of Driberg and Auden were a reaction against school and parents. 'School life taught me that I was an anti-political,' as Auden recalled in 1939.

> The Enemy was and still is the politician, i.e. the person who wants to organise the lives of others and make them toe the line. I can recognise him instantly in any disguise, whether as a civil servant, a bishop, a schoolmaster, or a member of a political party, and I cannot meet him however casually without a feeling of fear and hatred and a longing to see him (or her, for the worst ones are women) publicly humiliated.

In Auden's case there was a special factor. The politician wants power as a way of taking people into relations of dependence. But as an undergraduate Auden propounded to Spender his theory that art was born of humiliation rather than of power. He saw the artist as someone to whom steady emotional durability and financial anxiety were inimical. 'Apart from the homosexual question, marriage for me would be fatal,' he wrote to his brother John. 'It would mean doubling the pressure of an already oppressive environment; the insistent craving for money would mean artistic deterioration.' He wanted the freedom to write and, although at Oxford he was a leader of his set, he never offered that dependability which is the basic conceit of his enemy, the politician.

The chief political event in Britain during Auden's undergraduate years was the General Strike of 1926. Most Oxford undergraduates volunteered as strike-breakers to keep transport and other public services operating: an activity which was interpreted by the Conservative government as a sign of support for the authorities and opposition to trade unions. Auden had a more persuasive explanation: that 'it was the day-dream of almost every middle-class English boy to drive a train or bus, to do something which his social position normally forbade, like loading a ship or directing traffic'. The volunteers were indulging no more than wish-fulfilment. Auden – 'out of sheer contrariness', so he claimed later – drove a car for the Trades Union Congress. It belonged to the historian Sir George Clark, and Auden was supposedly so poor a motorist that it took him two days to drive two miles from Clark's house to central Oxford, where he collided with a lamp-post. In later life he tended to be dismissive of his early political beliefs. 'I don't remember being interested in politics when I was an undergraduate,' he told Coghill in 1972. 'I certainly wouldn't have dreamed of opening a newspaper.'

For Auden politics were subordinate to poetry. Reading *The Waste Land* in the spring of 1926, as Driberg said, had an awesome impact. The result for Auden was first of all a liberation: followed by poetic distraction and confusion: then recovery, and a massive process of intellectual consolidation. In his early excitement Auden read more of Eliot's poetry and literary criticism. 'I have torn up all my poems,' he announced to Coghill, 'because they were no good. Based on Wordsworth. No good nowadays.... I've been reading Eliot. I now see the way I want to write. I've written two new poems this week. Listen!' In time Auden found hidden consonances between Eliot and Wordsworth as well as their obvious dissimilarities: when Eliot died in 1965, Auden suggested that, like Wordsworth, 'his inspiration for nearly all he wrote arose out of a few visionary experiences, which probably occurred quite early in life' (though Auden in 1926 knew nothing of Eliot's visions). Eliot was a contaminating influence on Oxford undergraduate poetry in the 1920s. Auden later recognised that his generation had misread *The Waste Land* as grievously as schoolmasters who used Kipling's 'If' as a moral exhortation to their pupils. 'Had the undergraduate really read his poem,' Auden wrote in 1943, 'he would have to say: "Now I realise I am not the clever young man I thought, but a senile hermaphrodite. Either I must recover or put my head in the gas-stove." Instead, of course, he said, "That's wonderful. If only they would read this, Mother would understand why I can't stay home nights, and Father would understand why I can't hold a job".' Auden's emulation of *The Waste Land* initially resulted in the worst sort of mimic originality. His poetry became increasingly disarrayed and disjunctive, mixing styles and forms, choked with allusions and uninteresting ambiguities, clumsy and meretricious. One example of this messiness is 'Thomas Epilogises' written in May or June of 1926. With an epigraph from Gertrude Stein, it alludes to Rembrandt, Grendel, Ulysses, Nebuchadnezzar, Mozart, Byron, Eliphar, Zophar, Bildad, Handel and a satyr called Silenus, and contains repeated debased echoes of Eliot. Yet the next major poem that he wrote, 'Humpty Dumpty', dating from July or August 1926, while not yet emancipated from Eliot's thrall, is a significant advance. Its opening lines (beginning 'Dawn rose for hunting, trampling on the hills') suggest the ominous mood and images that Auden in the 1930s would work more adeptly. The poem raises many ideas that would be characteristic of the later Auden. There is mistrust of the pretensions of poetry and an expiatory disparagement of the poet 'indulging his plush insincerity,/His gulping courage, and his sexual day-dreams'. There are presentiments too of the subjects that would preoccupy Auden from the 1940s: original sin, pre-eminently, and the mythopoeic symbolism to which he returned in his great poem of 1952, 'The Shield of Achilles'. 'Humpty Dumpty' ends with the poet emerging from dreams of 'Tom o' Bedlam at the edge of Things', waking to the fact that his real subjects are mundane, rather than lying in the emotional extremities, and yet immense in their implications: 'crocuses/And waltzes still have something to recall/Of Adam's brow and the wounded heel'.

Eliot influenced Auden in other ways. His essay 'Tradition and the Individual Talent' (1919) was fundamental to Auden's choices at this time. The poetic apprentice, so Eliot adjured, must 'by great labour' acquire an 'historical sense' which is 'nearly indispensable to anyone who would continue to be a poet beyond his twenty-fifth year; and the historical sense involves a perception, not only of the greatness of the past, but of its presence; the historical sense compels a man to write not merely with his own generation in his bones, but with a feeling that the whole of the literature of Europe from Homer and within it the whole of the literature of his own country has a simultaneous existence and composes a simultaneous order'. Eliot's ideas provided Auden's literary motives and methods after 1926. His exacting tone fitted Auden's self-punitive, self-coercive tendencies. 'The progress of an artist is a continual self-sacrifice, a continual extinction of personality,' Eliot had written. This was Auden's choice. 'No man can be a writer without devoting himself to it,' he told his brother John: 'he must order his whole life and reading to one end.' It was to be Auden, rather than Eliot or any other poet, who in 1948 embarked on compiling a five-volume anthology of English-language verse from 1400 to 1914; but his historical sense was far less exclusive and puritanical than most critics who harped on the existence of tradition. His roots in the progressive, scientific professional life of provincial England differed from Eliot's, and Auden was correspondingly more catholic and playful.

Eliot's journal the *Criterion* was an indispensable guide to Auden's critical development. Despite the mediocrity of many of its contributions, its efforts to integrate European cultural tradition into English literary life impressed Auden, as did contributions by younger critics like Herbert Read and I. A. Richards. Auden was enraptured by Eliot's 'extraordinary gift for surprising quotations' in his critical writings: 'his quotation of six lines of Dryden suddenly made me see that poet in a completely new light'. The young man set out, deliberately, systematically and with concentrated effort to develop his historical sense (already stimulated by Coghill's teaching). Auden in his reading was now always observing, comparing, returning, taking notes, finding the excitement of quick transitions, turning it all over with hard responsible judgment, the whole process continuous and intense, all with the intention of remembrance. 'I don't think it can be stressed too strongly, that a writer must undergo a strenuous discipline, and that he must cohere and continue in a tradition,' he wrote to his brother John in 1927. 'Read Catullus, Chaucer, Dante, Marvell, etc.' he urged in another letter. 'The only thing which can hold you up in expression is just a lack of the tradition.' This was an idea that was to recur throughout his career.

Great masters who have shown mankind

An order it has yet to find,

he apostrophised Catallus, Dryden, Hardy, Rilke and others in his 'New Year Letter' of 1940.

> Now large, magnificent and calm,
> Your changeless presences disarm
> The sullen generations, still
> The fright and fidget of the will,
> And to the growing and the weak
> Your final transformations speak,
> Saying to dreaming 'I am deed.'
> To striving 'Courage. I succeed.'
> To mourning 'I remain. Forgive.'
> And to becoming 'I am. Live.'

Eliot had enjoined on a young poet 'a continual surrender of himself as he is at the moment to something which is more valuable'. Auden's efforts to practise this personal extinction entailed, as he recognised himself, a crisis of identity. 'The person who is worth anything is always I think alone,' he wrote to John in June 1927. 'Real artists are not nice people; all their best feelings go into their work, and life has the residue.' His choices were isolating, and he did not expect any simple or straightforward happiness. He meant to be a great poet and had no prevision of failure. Man, he wrote in 1926,

> whimpers to his Gods 'Don't hurt me!' Yet
> Sometimes more bold, finds in him greater things
> Would strip its body of its swaddling clothes
> Of rounded arms, red lips, and warm white buttocks
> To build therefrom bleak masses bit in granite,
> Gaunt shapes that know not passion or decay,
> The Archetype of an eternal Mind.

He wanted to become such an Archetype – according to Spender, at this time 'Auden's life was devoted to an intellectual effort to analyse, explain and dominate his circumstances' – and thought to do so he must put himself beyond coddling comforts or passions. His self-discipline involved him in a series of decisions that are examined in another poem of 1926, 'Thomas Prologizes'. Like most of his poems which are introspective or confessional (excluded by him from collections published as books), it is bad work; still it prompted a revealing letter to Isherwood, who had complained that it was incomprehensible. It is about 'an adolescent, who feels that all his old ideas are breaking up and have taught little but lyric and lechery', yet 'in the usual way of romantic adolescence thinks that he is capable of doing any great and heroic thing though what he isn't quite sure of', Auden explained. Lechery, so he had come to suspect, would prevent him from great or heroic lyricism, perhaps because (as Katherine Bucknell suggests) he believed that unfulfilled wishes produced keener creative tensions than gratification.

His sexuality was causing anxiety at home, where it was confused with his struggle for emotional independence from his mother. Not surprisingly each sign of his potential for sexual transgression made her more tense and controlling. 'The only relief is Wrenson's boy, whom I have taken to the cinema twice,' Wystan wrote to his brother John from their parents' house during the Christmas vacation of 1926. 'He is a cheerful soul, and gives me an admiration which is gratifying if unmerited. I dont think you need expect to see me in jail on a certain charge.' His parents though were dismayed by the talk this friendship might arouse in the neighbourhood: Wrenson was the local grocer, and the interest of the doctor's son in the grocer's boy was easily construed. 'M is a little suspicious about the cinema as yesterday as I was going out with him, she made Dad go with me, and I had to dash out before to tell the boy I couldnt come with him.' Not surprisingly these suspicions and deceptions led to accusations and scenes. The next day at lunch Mrs Auden 'worked herself up into a storm of tears, I remaining quite bovine', Wystan reported to John. 'She is now sitting in martyred silence.' She was still anxious and assertive at a performance of *Parsifal* that evening. 'In the theatre she sshed at every possible occasion, and quarrelled loudly with me for going to have a drink.' This was not a tolerable home-life: its moieties, to use Dr Auden's word, must have been a quickening cycle of resentment and guilt, emotions which may have contributed to Wystan Auden's choice during 1927 to be celibate.

This was a concrete expression of the impulse to sacrifice himself for his art. He was setting himself a calculated difficulty and a real test of self-mastery: isolating himself in a private domain of exclusion, privation and penance. 'As far as I can see it means a complete negation of all the pleasant material things, and nothing in return but ones own somewhat sceptical self-satisfaction,' he wrote to his brother John in June 1927. 'However I don't really complain; it is my own choice, and I believe the most satisfactory cheating of life, bar perhaps the religious.' There was nothing exceptional in his celibacy, which was the state of the great majority of his fellow undergraduates, and some adolescent attitudinising in his phrases; but his intentions were sincere, and part of a consistent train of thought in his life. In poems during the summer and autumn of 1927 he decried love as divisive of personal purpose – 'that notable forked-one' – or sickly, sexy anaesthetic, like 'Gauze pressed over the mouth, a breathed surrender'. A phrase of his in the preface to *Oxford Poetry 1927* published at the end of the year – 'our youth should be a period of spiritual discipline' – was more public and hortatory.

Auden's celibacy partly reflected his difficulties with his homosexuality. Since his days at Gresham's Auden had been outspoken about sex, and from his undergraduate days onwards admiring stories about his risky exploits circulated among his friends: the encounters to which 'pressure of strange knees at cinemas' was only a preliminary; the picking up of a stranger on a train; even on a dark night dropping coins into the boots of a sentryman outside a royal palace, and fellating him in his sentrybox. Yet behind the bravura there was doubt, guilt and consternation. In 'Thomas Epilogises' there is a havering between schoolboy homosexuality with 'young Desmond, whom I met/Behind the fives courts every Sunday night/And Isobel, who with her leaping breasts/Pursued me through a Summer'.

His readings of Freudian and other psychological theorists had given him the sense that homosexuality was immature and indicative of arrested emotional development. In 'Song', written in the summer of 1926, he explored these feelings using imagery from an article by his father recently published in the *Journal of Mental Science*. Dr Auden had likened a child's maturing process to the planetary system. 'He feels himself the centre of a universe of his own, round which the various planets of his little solar system revolve. But, as he grows, the experience of reality, ere long teaches him that there are other solar systems beside his own, the orbits of whose planets cross and re-cross his own.' In 'Song' Auden describes how originally his 'relation seemed ordained' with the Sun as his guiding star (the Sun in his personal mythology represented, as he indicated in a later poem, patriarchal authority and 'maturity'). 'But passion's waywardness has spoiled/The motions I began.' As the direction of his desires was immature, so he was demoted in the natural hierarchy of the constellations. The star whose natural growth had been disrupted was inferior and hurtling towards destruction or madness:

> When I spin rapidly afar
> Till I am burnt away,
> No planet but a shooting star
> Decline my Bedlam way.

Auden also shrank from reciprocity. 'There still lingers in my mind the idea of something indecent in a mutual homosexual relation,' Auden admitted to a friend in July 1927. In the same month he wrote a poem about a homosexual traveller whose 'love' is 'too curious'; he 'stiffens to a tower', but is set apart from 'the natural ending of a day': the fulfilment of his desires is 'deferred'. The mood of this poem suggests hesitancy and non-consummation of desires rather than the repetitive and rampantly cruisy young man whom other writers like to imagine. So, too, does a later poem, written in September 1927, about 'two pathics, who consider themselves living the free, the true life' but are in fact 'shut altogether from salvation' by their homosexuality. Their bravura was a pose. For a time religious guilt and unease keeps them chaste:

> spite of their new heroism, they feared
> That doddering Jehovah whom they mocked;
> Enough for him to show them to their rooms –
> They slept apart though doors were never locked.

Finally they consummate their desire: 'Down they fell; sorrow they had after that.' Sorrow, he thought in 1927, was his fate. 'As a bugger, there are only three courses open to one,' he explained to his brother John. There was the path to 'Middle-aged sentimentalism' in which a schoolmasterly type idealised 'the education of youth', occasionally allowing himself some timid gesture ('the hand on the shoulder') or trite remark ('You have the glorious gift of youth'). Then there was the fate of 'the London bugger. Sucking off policemen in public lavatories. The doors shut. We're all buggers here.' Finally there was 'the pursed mouth' of 'asceticism' for which he thought, without enthusiasm, he must opt.

'The constant bickerings and quarrellings of the parents or other children, may sometimes produce, especially in neuro-pathic children, a state of conflict which finds solution in a return to the "ideal companion" stage of psychic development, or to a world of fantasy with which the ego-schema can find itself in complete harmony,' Dr Auden had written in 1926 in his most important article on psychology. 'This lack of harmony is also the basis of the so-called inferiority complex, which is still another of the more underlying causes of delinquency.' His ideas on the inferiority complex were drawn from those of the psychologist William McDougall, who posited 'a hierarchy of instincts ... grouped under the leadership of the master-instinct of self-regard' (and who incidentally presented 'the maternal instinct ... as something primitive, blind and almost savage', as Wystan Auden came to do in his plays). It is relevant both to Auden's choice of celibacy and to some of his frustrated misery in 1927 that he had a self-diagnosed inferiority complex, and was attracted to extrovert sportsmen rather than the campy aesthetes of Oxford. 'I personally find the public-school-man-in-the-street infinitely more companionable than the awful ... pathicks who buzz about the arts,' he wrote to his brother John in June 1927. By then he had fallen for Bill McElwee, with whom he went to Austria in December 1926. 'William being heterosexual makes sexual behaviour of course impossible,' he explained to John. 'What saves the thing as far as I am concerned is that he is so fond of me as to make me convinced that if he were homosexual, the thing would be mutual.' From this acceptance of the necessity of platonic love for McElwee he moved on to his other consolations. 'Life is inevitably disgusting ... The only satisfaction is in the acquisition of disinterested knowledge such as science or art, just because it has no point or purpose.' Yet even at the height of his feelings for McElwee he realised the transience of his emotions. 'How long it will last I can't say. One always imagines that this one will be the permanent only to be ashamed the next day.' Reliably enough in the autumn of 1927 he developed a new infatuation, for Gabriel Carritt, who welcomed his affection but rebuffed his sexual advances.

Wystan Auden was preoccupied at this time with 'the so-called inferiority complex' about which his father had written. The two of them travelled together in Croatia in this summer of 1927: Wystan was so miserable in his father's company that he 'wished I was dead'. Immediately after their return, he wrote two poems about hereditary ills, those beginning, 'Truly our fathers had the gout' and 'We, knowing the family history'. One possible reading of the second poem, which had a working title of 'Family Likeness' and is a story of medical pathology about 'the lethal factors that were in the stock', would acknowledge that Dr Auden's youngest brother Harry had been in trouble for homosexual acts while a young student in Germany and that Dr Auden believed that 'heredity' had a considerable influence over primary instincts. It was after this miserable holiday with his father that Wystan Auden arranged to undergo psychoanalysis with the 'wish to improve my inferiority complex and to develop heterosexual traits'. He underwent a form of analysis, conceivably at the end of 1927, or in 1928: the identity of his analyst is not certainly agreed, although there is some circumstantial evidence. It is known that he had heard of someone later called Margaret Marshall, whom he had described as 'one of those pleasant pornographic women'. He reported that she had achieved 'the most astonishingly good results' in psychoanalysing a friend of his, probably Cecil Day Lewis. It cannot be proved that Auden himself received treatment from her, but the possibility exists, and it is clear that by the late 1920s she was well known to him.

About seven years older than Auden, Margaret Marshall was said by Day Lewis to have 'trained as a psychiatrist', although it is not clear whether this involved more than reading Freud, Jung and Adler. He did not think her technique counted as analysis, but treasured the memory of her 'sensual mouth, the air of practicality, of clinically earnest attention, lightened from time to time by a lewd giggle'. She exemplified a trend which Chesterton had noted in 1922: 'Psychology was becoming the leading parlour game of the day.' According to John Auden she may have studied the ideas of Emile Coué, the author of such books as *Self-mastery Through Conscious Auto-suggestion* (1922) who is best remembered for coining the phrase, 'Every day, in every way, I grow better and better,' which he recommended his adherents to recite twenty times each morning and evening. Coué was a pharmacist who had once dispensed medicine to a customer with incorrect directions for its use, and was set thinking when it nevertheless had the desired therapeutic effect. He decided that the power of expectation could command the human body, and developed a homespun theory of will and self-motivation. He also experimented with hypnotism and mesmerism. In the 1920s Coué was a world force in demotic psychology denounced variously as the 'incarnation of silliness' and 'a foe to Christianity'. After he visited England in 1922, an editorial in the journal *Psyche*, to which Dr Auden was a contributor and probably a subscriber, concluded 'only a great psychologist could have grasped the simple laws of mental life and have applied them as M. Coué has done'. Coué was so popular that, when he died of overwork in 1926, *The Times* commemorated him with an editorial as well as an obituary. 'Equipped with nothing but the faith of a child and a smattering of psychological medicine,' reported *The Times*,

> he triumphed where men incomparably better equipped mentally have failed again and again. He became a 'rage', almost a religion. Vast numbers of men and women – especially women – in the Old World and the New, put their faith in him without reserve. His clinic at Nancy became a place of pilgrimage, and the pilgrims ... were content to wait long hours until the small, frock-coated figure, so human, so French, should be able to attend to them ... Nothing surprised him; nothing seemed, even, to interest him very much. He had for all the same smile ... the same benediction. All were but human beings to be won to his earnest, immutable dogma ... 'Look into my eyes and believe; repeat my formula: you will be healed.'

If Margaret Marshall did bring Auden under Coué's influence, it has several implications. Coué's crankish religiosity was the muddle of science and faith likely to tempt the young Auden, who was as suggestible at this time to charismatic untrained psychologists as he was to Eliot, Yeats or Graves. More surely Coué's little iron formula of self-mastery was likely to appeal to the sort of young man already given to masterful decisions. His boyhood choice that Sunday afternoon in March 1922 to write poetry – his adolescent determination to Coghill that he was going to be 'a great poet' – were just the acts of will that Coué proposed. He had been encouraged in this at home by his father – 'The man of strong will is one who habitually imagines success,' according to Dr Auden's intellectual hero, W. H. R. Rivers – and showed his will in both extraordinary and quotidian ways. His Oxford friend Gabriel Carritt recalls him at this time discovering that he had dropped three pound-notes on a long country walk. 'We will pick them up on the way back,' he declared; four hours later, in the dusk, they saw the notes fluttering along the grass: without comment Auden picked them up and pocketed them. Such acts of will were Auden's reaction to his mother's scolding (never more incessant than when he was an undergraduate) that he lacked 'self-sacrifice, self-discipline, self-control'. When he got only a third-class degree in his examinations that year, almost his only consolation was that his will had not failed: 'I can acquit myself I think of failure of resolution over this.'

In the mid-1920s Margaret Marshall had left her physician husband for a tubercular invalid named Douglas Marshall. 'Agnostic, unconventional, a bit raffish, deliciously disrespectful,' as Day Lewis describes her at this time, 'she had no tabus; her language could be, on occasion, as foul as mine; her somewhat intense and dominating personality was relieved by that touch of a clown which I have always found so endearing in a woman.' She married Marshall in the late 1920s, but after his early death 'the penchant for disaster which she wryly confessed to – a kind of accident-proneness on a heroic scale – came for a while into the ascendant'; some acquaintances suggested 'that she secretly relished the disasters in which she was involved'. Wystan Auden had written in 1927 to his brother John in India mentioning Margaret Marshall and recommending psychoanalysis in a phrase that hints at Coué: 'I think you might make yourself happier.' In due course John consulted her about his depression, found her 'brilliant and domineering', and was given the Coué treatment. 'She almost succeeded in persuading me to tell myself to leave India,' John recalled in 1982. But instead they married soon after Marshall's death and together returned to India. Day Lewis thought 'she can hardly be blamed for the tragedy that followed, unless it is criminal to marry an extreme neurotic in the mistaken belief that you can cure him'. She became involved with a servant and outraged 'the Auden meanness' with her spending; after what John Auden described as 'bitterness and despair in Calcutta', they separated in January 1932 and were divorced in October 1933. 'I shall always like Margaret and admire her in many ways, but no one who had seen her with Douglas could fail to see, I think, that she never wanted an adult love,' Wystan consoled his brother after the separation 'She wanted such absolute admiration and dependance [sic], and only an invalid could possibly give it to her.'

Wystan Auden's experiences with Margaret Marshall are hard to assess. He indicated that in the summer of 1928 he consulted an unnamed practitioner living at Spa in Belgium: this was possibly Margaret Marshall, who had connections with the town, where she settled after leaving John Auden in 1932. Years later, in 1971, perhaps realising the inadequacy of his treatment, Auden denied having been analysed at all.

But in 1928 he made a jotting on the experience to Isherwood. 'Had a most pleasant week with my analyst,' he wrote facetiously. 'Libido, it is proved, is towards women.' This suggestion might have been hard for him to resist if his analyst was a passionate, dominant young woman given to lewd giggles with the young men who consulted her; harder still if (as Day Lewis said) she thrived 'best in relationships in which she was a nurse'. Auden's mother had been a nurse, his father's girlfriend was a nurse, his fiancée was to be a nurse. It is not surprising that Auden and his analyst agreed the hypothesis, which Auden offered to Isherwood as fact, that 'the trouble is incest'. As Auden himself realised, psychologists and sexologists can be glib on this subject. 'Its quite alright to talk about an incest complex in people, as long as you don't believe they want real incest, in a bed,' he wrote in 1929. He never forgot (as inferior or amateur psychologists might) that fantasies are not real, and knew that he was capable of confusion. On a few occasions Auden referred to his own incest fantasies, but one cannot know if these were any more than ideas suggested by his reading and conversations. It is possible that his emotions and experiences were cut and trimmed to fit the theories of his age. Auden's analysis perhaps focused on his Oedipal complex since he became persuaded that his desire for women was blocked by his fear of incest with his mother. He would already have known from his reading that according to Freudian doctrines his strong identification with his mother had created in him a narcissistic tendency which led him to choose men like himself as sexual objects. But the incestuous desire may have been for his father. In 1922, aged fifteen, Auden had shared a bed with his father when they were on a walking-tour: 'I suddenly had a violent longing to be fucked by him,' he recalled in 1942. 'I have to confess he didn't.' This is all very tentative. All that is certainly known is that his analysis was brief and did not provide any revelations. During his psychological consultations at Spa in August 1928, he wrote only one poem. 'To throw away the key and walk away', it begins, 'makes us well / Without confession of the ill.' With enough deliberate self-mastery, as recommended by Coué, 'the old life', Auden promised himself, could be 'done'. Neurosis could be willed away. A few weeks later he made an abrupt and unexpected decision.

In the autumn of 1928, shortly after his return from Spa, where he had been told his libido was towards women, he became engaged to marry a nurse called Sheilah Richardson. Auden was in limbo – he had left

university a few months earlier, he was planning to go abroad and was
jobless – and it was as if he set about inventing a new version of his
masculinity: mimicking 'the heroic sexual pose / Playing at fathers to
impress the little ladies'. Years later, at a party in New York, he said,
perhaps facetiously, that he had gone out for the evening with Sheilah
Richardson and failing to think of anything else to say, had asked her to
marry him. But at the time he was more serious about graduating into
manhood and trying to make himself the man his father was. ('All
buggers,' he noted in 1929, 'suffer with the reproach, real or imaginary, of
"Call yourself a man".') He seems to have made a resolution worthy of a
disciple of Coué; he told Spender in justification of his proposed marriage,
'It's a matter of will. It's just a question of choosing your object.' Dr Auden
had married a nurse in the 1890s, and for several years had strong and
disruptive feelings for another nurse whom he had met in Egypt around
1916. It seems almost imitative that Sheilah Richardson was also a nurse.

> Now tell me what your children are?
> Pocket editions of their papa

– so Auden wrote in a verse of 1931 about those bourgeois values that he
both mocked and venerated. Years later, in 1947, Auden said that he
doubted it was 'a good idea' to discuss homosexuality with a 'sympathetic
and understanding' woman, 'because, you see, women, even the most
intelligent of them, can never quite grasp the idea that there are such
things as queers. They always feel that the right woman for you just hasn't
come along. But they don't doubt that she will.' It is a remark that implies
criticism of Margaret Marshall's analysis rather than of Sheilah Richardson.

Auden's emotional choices and sexual quandaries of 1926–8 were only
part of his situation in Oxford; one thinks at twenty a great deal of sex, but,
even then, not constantly. This was also the phase of Auden's life when his
poetic personality was maturing, and he became a conduit of ideas and
stylistic influences, imitating or trying to enlarge upon the work of older or
dead poets at the same time that he was influencing a new generation of
tyro poets. He tested the possibilities in himself, and showed his friends
the possibilities in themselves.

Eliot was a colossal but not exclusive influence after 1926; once Auden
had ceased his more slavish imitations in 1927, he was free to use in his

own way Eliot's ideas about tradition. He became sure in his touch and more distinctive in his achievements. He experimented in the style of Housman, and was influenced by Sassoon's *Satirical Poems*, which were published in 1926. Some images can be traced to Edith Sitwell's *Bucolic Comedies* of 1923. But Yeats and Graves he studied more thoroughly and absorbed more deeply than all of these. As a schoolboy, during the most intense phase of his friendship with Michael Davidson, Auden had used Hardy and Thomas to alleviate Wordsworth's influence on his poetry. In the summer of 1927 he similarly resorted to Yeats in an effort to emancipate himself from 'Eliotian Intellectual Bombast', as Auden and Isherwood described it to one another. Next, for a short period, he used the work of Robert Graves. The result was that between August 1927 and January 1928 his poems became his own: Auden became 'Audenesque', and a new idiom was created.

Of all the poetical father-figures adopted by Auden, Yeats is the one whom he repudiated most vehemently. The elegy and magazine article with which Auden marked Yeats's death in 1939 have been described by Stan Smith as 'Oedipal dialogues': simultaneously acts of honour and usurpation. Auden's belief that he was a poetic successor to Yeats was explicitly shown when he came to write of the Irishman again in 1947. He recognised their kinship in 'fascination' with 'what's difficult'. He celebrated the way Yeats had released regular stanzaic poetry from iambic monotony, 'the dead hand of Campion and Tom Moore', but knew that many readers regarded his own work with metre and rhyme as more ambitious. He praised Yeats for such poems as 'In Memory of Major Robert Gregory' (a private elegy of 1918 which acquired symbolic public significance): such work had transformed, he wrote, 'the occasional poem from being either an official performance of impersonal virtuosity or a trivial *vers de société* into a serious reflective poem of at once personal and public interest'. Yet even this compliment is the preliminary to an act of filial usurpation: after Yeats's death Auden was the acknowledged master of such 'occasional poems', perhaps the most notable being 'In Memory of W. B. Yeats' (1939) while others like 'September 1, 1939' vie with Yeats's 'Easter 1916' in both theme and structure. Yeats's cosmology and occultism – his dependence for ideas on his wife's planchette – were risible to Auden by 1947. 'How could Yeats, with his great aesthetic appreciation of aristocracy, ancestral houses, ceremonious tradition, take up something so essentially lower-middle class – or should I say Southern Californian – so ineluctably associated with suburban villas and clearly unattractive faces?' he demanded. 'A. E. Housman's pessimistic stoicism seems to me nonsense too, but at least it is a kind of nonsense that can be believed in by a gentleman – but mediums, spells, the Mysterious Orient – how embarrassing.' But there was a serious ethical objection to Yeats. Poets, Yeats advised Laura Riding in 1935, 'should be good liars': an opinion which became steadily more repellent to Auden. As he wrote of Yeats to Spender in 1964, 'he has become for me a symbol of my own devil of inauthenticity, of everything which I must try to eliminate from my own poetry, false emotions, inflated rhetoric, empty sonorities'.

Auden's relations were equally vexed with Robert Graves, to whom he turned his concentration in 1927. He studied the poetry of Graves, and feasted on his critical ideas. Graves's book *Poetic Unreason*, which had been published in 1922, was an attempt to apply the ideas of analytic psychology to the emotions aroused by reading poetry. It was steeped in views taken from W. H. R. Rivers's treatise *Instinct and the Unconscious* (1920). Rivers's books were in Dr Auden's library, and were cited in his medical articles. According to Isherwood, Rivers was one of the authorities whom Auden would invoke in his Oxford years; as Rivers's influence will be detailed in the next chapter, it is enough to acknowledge here that Auden came to Graves's ideas on 'poetic unreason' already primed by his reading of Rivers or perhaps by family discussions about his neurological investigations and theories on the biological origins of psychoneuroses. Despite these consonances Auden and Graves did not meet at this time, and the attitude of Graves made friendship impossible later. As a boy Graves had forced the resignation of a schoolmaster whom he mistakenly alleged had kissed his best friend, and he remained wary of homosexuality. Consistent with this he deplored Auden personally as a 'homosexual and parlour communist' as well as rejecting his poetic homage. 'Auden is a fraud: that is to say, a synthetic poet, plagiarizing in a curiously wholesale way,' he told Sir Basil Liddell Hart in 1935. 'He gets hold of some good piece of work by someone which is not too well known, and vulgarises it.' Later in his Clark lectures of 1954 he accused Auden of cowardice during the wars of Franco and Hitler. In return, although Auden in 1961 hailed Graves as 'a poet of Honor' in public – 'To read his poems is both a joy and a privilege; they are passionate, truthful and well-bred' – in private he bitched to Coghill about the inaugural lecture given by Graves after he succeeded Auden in the Oxford Professorship of Poetry: 'Between you and me – SSSHHH! – the Old Boy didn't work very hard.'

Graves was jealous of Auden, but his accusations of plagiarism were chiefly stoked up by the vindictive resentments of his lover Laura Riding. Auden reputedly had a phenomenal recall of what he had read, though MacNeice noticed that, when he quoted from memory, 'he nearly always gets it wrong', distorting other people's work to his own sense of things. His susceptibility was not only to written words. To the awe of Spender and others, 'he had at his command at every moment an incredible store of impressions vividly recorded as ideas'. With these Auden sought nothing less than to formulate a coherent and organically unified vision. He described his collection of *Oxford Poetry 1927*, which he edited with Day Lewis, as 'an infinitesimal progression towards a new synthesis, one more of those efforts as yet so conspicuous in their paucity'. It was synthesis that he sought. He was faced, as he wrote of Yeats in 1947,

> with the modern problem, i.e. of living in a society in which men are no longer supported by tradition without being aware of it, and in which, therefore, every individual who wishes to bring order and coherence into the stream of sensations, emotions, and ideas entering his consciousness, from without and within, is forced to do so deliberately for himself what in previous ages had been done for him by family, custom, church and state, namely the choice of the principles and presuppositions in terms of which he can make sense of his experience.

Whereas Eliot attempted a synthesis that was purely artistic, only Auden (with the crankish exception of Pound) 'had the courage to face unpleasant facts and attempt a social synthesis', so Francis Scarfe wrote in 1942.

Auden was more like Graves than Eliot in the use to which he put poetic tradition, and in the traditions which he used. Eliot drew from a small body of writings which he identified as classics: they were the pillars of high culture, or as it might be 'the army of unalterable law'. But for Graves 'in an absolute sense all poetry is of equal value': the poet must 'learn from his enemy the scientist who finds a generic beauty everywhere'. Similarly Auden's criteria were 'rarely purely aesthetic', as he wrote himself; he would 'often prefer an inferior poem from which he can learn something at the moment to a better poem from which he can learn nothing'. When Auden took ideas or phrases from other writers – whether novelists, dramatists, journalists, military strategists, scientists, ethnologists, critics, philosophers, nursery rhymers, folk ceremonialists, travellers or psycho-analysts – he was as keen, acquisitive and ruthless in what he used, with the same mixture of intuition and calculation, as a tycoon planning mergers, annexing and consolidating whatever could be taken into his schemes. Twenty years later he acknowledged his similarities to a bargain-hunting merger-monger in the poem that is his most deliberate self-portrait, 'A Household'. Auden would take anything which served his imagination; but whereas Eliot borrowed from other poets to hint at the timeless immanence of his themes, Auden disguised his borrowings so as to make his themes more his own. 'A quotation', he told his brother John, 'should be used to illustrate some context completely foreign to it.' For this reason 'quotations from contemporary writers are a little dangerous'.

During the 1920s literary criticism in Britain enormously extended its reach. For centuries there had been textual scholars, philologists, gentlemen bookmen and studious parsons; but the affable, discursive approach of Edwardians like Quiller-Couch, Saintsbury and Whibley had little in common with the implacable intensity of concentration and purpose found in Eliot and Pound. It is important that despite Auden's moments of self-revulsion ('had one of those dreadful literary conversa-tions when I always talk such pompous nonsense', he noted in 1929), he began to write poetry in the decade when younger critics took on this new acuity; he scrutinised books and articles as they appeared, pondered their meanings and incorporated their ideas into his own creative plans.

I. A. Richards was a major intellectual influence on Auden. The chapter from his book *Principles of Literary Criticism* (1925) entitled 'The Analysis of a Poem' had originally been published under the title 'Psychology and the Reading of Poetry' in the same volume of the journal *Psyche* to which both Dr Auden and Rivers had also contributed. Richards distilled his *Principles* into a little book *Science and Poetry*, which Auden read shortly after its publication in 1926, adding its doctrines to the medley of opinions that he had been collecting in his Oxford reading. One appeal of Richards was that he offered 'the possibility of emotional experience instigated, if not wholly controlled, through ordered words': an idea irresistible to a young poet who believed that self-control of the emotions was the key. Then again Richards believed that 'the central dominant change' affecting modern poetry was 'the Neutralization of Nature, the transference of the Magical View of the world to the scientific': a question which had preoccupied Auden since boyhood. Richards all but severed the dependence of poetic effect upon any standard of objective belief. 'It is not the poet's business to make scientific statements' of verifiable accuracy, but to make a 'pseudo-statement', the acceptance of which 'is entirely governed by its effects upon our feelings and attitudes', a phrase in other words which is '"true" if it suits and serves some attitude or links together attitudes which on other grounds are desirable'. Richards declared, 'It is never what a poem says which matters, but what it is': a belief that was modish, for in the same year that opportunistic imitator of modernist fashions Archibald MacLeish wrote his much quoted 'Ars Poetica', which concluded, 'A poem should not mean / But be'; a year later in *Oxford Poetry* Driberg (perhaps following a hectoring from Auden) was declaring, 'Brain is deposed, all judgment lies at fault / ... truth's but of lip.'

By 1927 Auden had set these doctrines among his own. 'Works of Art, no matter what the medium, exist for the production of emotion in the observer, and their magnitude is in direct proportion to the quality and quantity of emotion involved,' he wrote to his brother John after reading Richards.

> Musical notes as you say have no meaning or significance taken individually but when arranged in a definite scheme of relations, they present to the hearer an emotional sequence. So with words. The two functions of words must not be confused, the emotive use, and their use for making logical judgments ... In poetry it is immaterial whether the word series is logical or not; what is important is that the emotional sequence should be unbroken (cf. a wet dream, where the dream-events are often highly illogical, but the emotional sequence is perfect).

Ideas, according to Auden's summary of Richards,

> represent the final stage of the reaction to a work of art when emotion has spent itself, and have no emotive significance in themselves. It is

for this reason that it is immaterial if the ideas induced by a poem seem true or false; All ideas in poetry are Richards' pseudo-statements. If the ideas can be reached, the poem is successful. Begin with the stimulus that gave you the ideas, and the ideas will follow in the reader. To secure an orgasm, start with the first sight of your beloved, not of your spermatozoa. The latter only cause disgust and detumescence.

In taking Richards's position Auden was shifting from his schoolboy commitment to the necessity of accurate belief or the virtues of strong faith (exemplified in his poems about fairies of 1923); in turn, his undergraduate commitment to the doctrines of Richards weakened after 1930. Nevertheless MacNeice was still right in 1940 when he wrote of Auden, 'Ideas strike him – as they did Donne – emotionally and so are hardly detachable from their context, from the mood of any particular poem.'

'The language which is more important to us,' Eliot had written in 1920, 'is that which is struggling to digest and express new objects, new groups of objects, new feelings, new aspects.' As an Oxford undergraduate Auden began his pursuit of language. He had no time for the modish or mediocre. 'Written ravishing lines, but has the mind of a ninny,' he said with typical dismissiveness of one for whom Spender had youthful admiration. The meaning in his early poetry was often distorted or unrecognisable. Many passages were baffling, if not unintelligible, but he created a new idiom that combined the jerky, the angular, the sinister and the glamorous. Auden suggests rather than specifies; his reader is forced to inductions and suppositions which leave the widest margins of meaning. There are luminous phrases and darkly obscure passages: it is as if Auden is forcing bewildered readers to patch together the fragments of understanding, and to construct from these a viable account of their own making. There is a prodigious private commentary underscoring Auden's lines of which no one else can ever know the exact intent. Sometimes he forgot his intent himself. The serried erasures of his drafts show that even his mistakes were interesting; but, as James Fenton has hinted of attempts to gloss lines like 'Lands on the beaches of his love, like Coghlan's coffin', the fact that Auden forgot the exact meaning of his allusion suggests his meaning may not have mattered much for long. When in 'Taller To-day' (1928) he wrote of 'the Adversary' who 'put too easy question / On lonely roads', he seems to indicate whichever 'adversary' a reader cares to imagine: the questions are supplied by the reader too, the lonely roads are those of other people's personal landscapes as much as Auden's. The work is divided between writer and reader.

The hypotheses underlying his approach are set out in an essay on 'Writing' which Auden wrote for Naomi Mitchison in 1932. It has been described by Edward Mendelson as 'a manifesto of his private ideology', and it offers special insights into his intentions as a young man. Commissioned for a collection of essays entitled *An Outline for Boys and Girls and Their Parents*, the seriousness of Auden's attention to it shows how highly he valued influencing the young. 'We are shut inside ourselves and apart from each other,' he wrote. 'There is no whole but the self': as Proust indicated, *chaque être est bien seul*. In this state of isolation the possibilities of language are imprecise, contradictory and subjective. 'Most of the power of words comes from their not being like what they stand for,' he wrote in this essay. 'If the word "ruin" for instance was only like a particular ruin, it could only serve to describe that one solitary building; as it is the word conjures up all the kinds of ruin which we know and our various feelings about them, ruined churches, ruined houses, ruined gasworks, loss of money.' Yet associations were vague, and most contemporary civilized speech 'is like a tunnel under which the currents of feeling can pass unseen'. In a passage that seems derived from McDougall's *The Group Mind* (a book esteemed by his father) he explained that 'when communities are small and their interests common to all their members, mere acquaintance with each other is enough to make people use their language well, but as communities increase and interests become specialised, the past history of the language gets bigger and heavier, education in the use of language becomes more and more necessary'. As a result, Auden thought, in the twentieth century there was more clarity in speech. 'Generally speaking, the feeling meaning is transmitted with extraordinary accuracy, as the gestures and the tone of voice which go with the words are remembered also. With a statement in writing it is often impossible after a time to decide exactly what the author meant.' Writing of Auden's early poems, John Matthias has found 'that they communicate with extraordinary energy their rhythms, images, tones of voice, and fields of force – the unique, jagged, and mysterious linguistic universe that Auden's early style creates. They communicate their Sound as they engage the silence around them.'

It is crucial to understanding the early Auden to recognise his commitment to sound. 'In general,' he advised his brother John in 1927, 'the thought should be sensuously apprehendable in poetry.' The importance of recitation aloud was a topic to which he often returned. In what amounts to a sequel to his essay of 1932 on 'Writing', Auden in 1935 wrote an introduction to an anthology of poetry for use in schools entitled *The Poet's Tongue*. Again addressing schoolchildren, he declared that 'memorable speech' was the simplest and best definition of poetry:

> That is to say, it must move our emotions, or excite our intellect, for only that which is moving or exciting is memorable, and the stimulus is the audible spoken word and cadence, to which in all its power of suggestion and incantation we must surrender, as we do when talking to an intimate friend. We must, in fact, make exactly the opposite kind of mental effort to that which we make in grasping other verbal uses, for in the case of the latter the aura of suggestion round every word through which ... it becomes ultimately a sign for the sum of all possible meanings, must be rigorously suppressed and its meaning confined to a single dictionary one. For this reason the exposition of a scientific theory is easier to read than to hear. No poetry, on the other hand, which when mastered is not better heard than read is good poetry.

The arguments of these essays for children of 1932 and 1935 anticipate by a generation some of the theories of French structuralism. These beliefs remained with him. 'I cannot know exactly what I mean,' he wrote in 1959, 'words cannot verify themselves.'

John Bayley has noted of early Auden that 'the gaps his poems make between subject and response' are 'virtually an aesthetic weapon'. The 'cognitive disruption' in Auden's writings of this period seems to enforce the view that without a visionary revelation like that of Wordsworth (or, as Auden later imagined, Eliot) no individual can know very much with certainty. They have to resort instead to conjecture or deduction: to use their own imagination as much as the poet's. It is why Auden's shrewdest critics see such different strengths in his work: the honey of intellect and the imperatives of ethical commitment; romanticism; tense passion; and constant, implacable political concern. These readings are not antagonistic: the meaning is most where the interpretations lie thickest. Auden knew this, and demonstrated it in his criticism and poetry. For example, he arranged parts of *The Dyer's Hand* in the 1960s in notebook form recognising that what a reader brings to its text in the way of imagination, connections and comparisons may be as rich as any detail that he imposed on his text. He preferred *The Dyer's Hand* to be read in the sequence in which his notes were printed, but he claimed no rights as its author. Earlier, in the 1930s, he noted that poets had a separate existence and meaning in the lives of their readers: 'Children swarmed to him like settlers,' he wrote of Edward Lear, 'he became a land'; while Yeats in the act of dying 'became his admirers'.

'If the apprentice is destined to become a poet, sooner or later – in my case when I was twenty – a day arrives when he can truthfully say for the first time: All the words are right and all the words are genuinely mine': so Auden later said. Although 'Humpty Dumpty', written around August 1926, was a crucial poem in the evolution of his authenticity, the poem which marks the end of his apprenticeship, when all the words become Audenesque, is 'The Watershed', written in August 1927. It describes a narrow, elevated tract of ground set in a region of dismantled mines and poor soil – a sterile terrain representing the poet's choice of a life of deflected urges however 'frustrate and vexed'. Such places consoled his misanthropy; as he wrote two years later, 'Country on a fine day always makes one feel, Why do I bother with people? They are insignificant.' The land of the watershed is 'cut off, will not communicate'; even inhuman contact will fail: 'Beams from your car may cross a bedroom wall, / They wake no sleeper.' Once when the mines had been worked the watershed had been busy; but its future is ominous, seems to belong only to solitary figures and wild animals like the hare with which the poem ends: 'taller than grass, / Ears poise before decision, scenting danger'. This chill ending to a poem about a depopulated region recalls a question in Lawrence's *Women in Love*: 'You yourself, don't you find it a beautiful clean thought, a world empty of people, just uninterrupted grass, and a hare sitting up?' Lawrence's novel (published in 1920) seems a strong influence on 'The Watershed', primarily because many of its images resembled the imagery that had been entrenched in Auden's imagination by his childhood reading. The final crisis in Lawrence's novel recalls the conclusion to Andersen's ice-bound stories of Auden's childhood, and anticipates the final scene of the Auden–Isherwood play, *The Ascent of F6*.

Gerald Crich, the central male figure of *Women in Love*, lives among Nottinghamshire colliers who are described as if they were the goblins whom Curdie Peterson had fought or the sacred objects of Auden's autistic imagination in boyhood: 'powerful, underworld men who spent most of their time in darkness', miners with 'mindless, inhuman' voices. 'They sounded also like strange machines, heavy, oiled. The voluptuousness was like that of machinery, cold and iron.'

'The Watershed' was what readers soon meant by 'Audenesque'. The idiom was even more distinctive by January 1928, the month when 'The Secret Agent' was written.

> Control of the passes was, he saw, the key
> To this new district, but who would get it?
> He, the trained spy, had walked into the trap
> For a bogus guide, seduced by the old tricks.
>
> At Greenhearth was a fine site for a dam
> And easy power, had they pushed the rail
> Some stations nearer. They ignored his wires:
> The bridges were unbuilt and trouble coming.
>
> The street music seemed gracious now to one
> For weeks up in the desert. Woken by water
> Running away in the dark, he often had
> Reproached the night for a companion
> Dreamed of already. They would shoot, of course,
> Parting easily two that were never joined.

(Like all of Auden's poems, this is best understood if spoken aloud, as he would have done at the time. He recited 'poems with an intonation which made them seem obscure, and yet significant and memorable', Spender said. 'He had the power to make everything sound Audenesque, so that if he said in his icy voice, separating each word from the next as though on pincers, lines of Shakespeare or of Housman, each sounded simply like Auden ... The poetry which he loved most had this monosyllabic, clipped, clear-cut, icy quality.')

Auden at this time was apparently interested in Coué's auto-suggestive formula, so it is arresting that the opening phrase of 'The Secret Agent' – 'Control of the passes' – seems to echo the title of a Coué-influenced book, Robert Thouless's *The Control of the Mind: A Handbook of Applied*

Psychology for the Ordinary Man, which had been published in June 1927, and was listed in the *Times Literary Supplement* of 8 December 1927 (a few weeks before the writing of 'The Secret Agent') jointly with William McDougall's *Character and the Conduct of Life*. The annual issues of *Oxford Poetry* were usually reviewed by the *TLS* during the first fortnight of December, and Auden, who was the book's co-editor in 1927, would have been looking out for the review (which this time appeared in the second issue of the month). The two books by McDougall and Thouless were guides to practical success rather than works of morbid psychology, showing ways to prepare the human mind to respond successfully to emergencies. McDougall's book was hailed in the *Times Literary Supplement* as 'pure gold' for synthesising philosophy with psychology. Thouless took a more practical approach to 'the management of the emotions' offering particular advice on 'discipline of thought' intended 'to get rid of the inferiority complex'. There are many influences at work in Auden's poem – John Fuller shows that the final line for example invokes the last line of the old English poem 'Wulf and Eadwacer' – but a reading based on the influences of Coué and Thouless is supportable. The passes are those of the mind, whose control Coué and Thouless teach; the 'new district' is fulfilled adulthood. The secret agent is a frustrated adolescent moving against the 'old tricks' of adults, the 'bogus' guides. He is audacious, but he has not imagined success well enough, so that his efforts of will have been inadequate to beat the grown-ups. His emotions have been like water running away in the desert at night: the antithesis of Greenhearth dam, which would harness the immense, wasted power of water. The secret agent's laxity in getting control of the passes – his procrastination in achieving emotional self-mastery – has been fatal: 'the bridges were unbuilt and trouble coming'. It is going to end badly for the secret agent who foresees, 'they would shoot, of course, parting easily who were never joined'. It was mind and body that had never been properly joined: mind that would betray the secret agent if he could not get 'the key'. The whole of this wonderful poem fulfils what Wystan had promised John after reading Richards: an emotional sequence of words that is unbroken and ultimately perfect. He was twenty when he wrote it.

At Oxford Auden occupied an exceptional position. He awed the dons who knew him, and dominated the imaginative development of the best literary talents of his day. He was exceedingly ambitious, intellectually inexhaustible and superbly receptive. His reading was ravenous; he hungered for the sustenance of tradition. Sympathetic to the styles of others, but already rich in ideas and techniques of his own making, his language and images became startlingly innovative. He was an undergraduate prodigy whose dogmatism and erudition daunted and dominated his set. He pervaded, coloured and embellished the ideas of all of them: Day Lewis, Spender, Warner and many lesser poets would have been lost for a vocabulary without him. He seemed to come before them accomplished, infallible and armed at all points. His loud and copious talk was more than an amusement: it provided their topics and social support and was the source of perpetual suspense. Those who had scarcely met him were still changed by his opinions. In the years of their first successes in the 1930s, he was included with them in the same miscellaneous publicity about 'the pylon poets', and was grouped together with them under the soubriquet of MacSpaunday. Later, when this stage of his life had closed in 1939, he summarised his own influence in his poem on Voltaire:

> Cajoling, scolding, scheming, cleverest of them all,
> He'd led the other children in a holy war
> Against the infamous grown-ups; and, like a child, been sly
> And when there was occasion for
> The two-faced answer or the plain protective lie,
> But patient like a peasant waited for their fall.

By 1928 he was ready to leave the emotionally retarding atmosphere of Oxford: that community of excitable, self-pitying undergraduates with 'their syllabus of limitless anxiety and labour, / ... Blaming the times, their parents, all the other people', and the deeply rutted dons, who poked and shuffled in books, or judged the quality of people by their degrees. He had already beaten them in his achievements and at the age of twenty was defining the attitude of a generation. As Randall Jarrell said a quarter-century later of Auden's work in 1928, 'He wrote then some of the strongest, strangest and most original poetry that anyone has written in this century; when old men, dying in their beds, mumble something unintelligible to the nurse, it is some of these lines that they will be repeating.'

CHAPTER 4

'I'm king of Berlin'

Auden, when his father offered to pay for him to live abroad for a year after Oxford, disliked 'the conventional anglosaxon images of Paris as the city of the Naughty Spree – La Vie Parisienne, Les Folies Bergères, Mademoiselle Fifi, bedroom mirrors and bidets, lingerie and adultery, the sniggers of schoolboys and grubby old men'. He thought an aspirant author should endure austerity, and for this reason, as he recalled in 1952, 'I and some of my friends' – Isherwood and later Spender – 'deserted Paris for the much grimmer and disturbing uncartesian world of Berlin.' He went to Germany in October 1928 and lived there until July 1929. For most of that time he was in Berlin. These ten months were eventful. It was in Berlin, he wrote, that he 'ceased to see the world in terms of verse', and embraced experience, accepting, inviting and surmounting all it offered. There were many possibilities. He resolved to sound them as coldbloodedly as when he went to bed with Medley and clinically analysed the best timing for seduction. At one level he was like any young man abroad with a small allowance from his parents and eager for life. 'I am incredibly happy nowadays spending my substance on strumpets, and taking part in the White Slave traffic,' he wrote to Spender from Berlin in 1928. But there was nothing perfunctory about his use of the Weimar vices; they created opportunities for him that were not all instantaneous and carnal. What happened to him in Berlin is recorded in a journal which he kept for a few months from April 1929. With the exception of another journal which he kept briefly in 1964 during a return visit to Berlin, it is the only one of his journals that has been preserved (at least one other existed, dating from about 1939–40). It was found on the floor of his Oxford home by David Luke a few days after his death.

The first forty or so pages contain intimate autobiographical notes on the right of the notebook; on the left are rhymes, jottings and other miscellanea which sometimes seem a commentary on the contents of the facing page. Later pages contain Auden's notes from authors like Freud, Proust and Riding together with his own reflections. The overall impression is of hard living, hard reading and hard thinking. For all its moments of gloom, panic and disgust, it is the record of an intellectual with a glorious zest for life. Auden's poems written in Berlin reflected themes which are explored in the journal; but the great creative sequel to these months is *The Orators*, which he did not begin until the spring of 1931. This ambitiously constructed book, which should be a keystone of his literary reputation, provoked strong reactions in the 1930s. Edith Sitwell prided herself that she had 'never attempted to write a dubious scientific text-book in something which was neither prose nor verse, and label it a poem', but John Hayward in 1932 concluded, 'it is a book which must be read patiently and with care ... more than once, for ... it is the most valuable contribution to English poetry since *The Waste Land*'. Assessing it in 1966, Auden thought it written by 'someone ... near the border of sanity'. He guessed that his 'unconscious motive in writing' *The Orators* had been 'therapeutic, to exorcise certain tendencies in myself by allowing them to run riot in phantasy'. It was his way to end the storm-and-stress period of his sexual adolescence. This was a process of poetic enlargement rather than of some notional personal liberation. Writing *The Orators* was not for Auden any more than psychoanalysis 'a device for getting a brand-new personality'; it did not change him much as a man, for as late as 1954 Arthur Koestler thought him 'more sex-obsessed than anybody I know'. But Auden subscribed to an axiom of Freud's: 'A man should not strive to eliminate his complexes but to get into accord with them: they are legitimately what directs his conduct with the world.' For Auden the artist was someone 'who is all of the time what everyone is some of the time, a man who is active rather than passive to his experience'. *The Orators* is a sign of such activity.

'The real "life-wish" is the desire for separation, from family, from one's literary predecessors,' Auden wrote in his journal. But his wish to be free from 'the immense bat-shadow of home' and concomitant forces – 'from all opinions and personal ties; from pity and shame' – was not a yearning for the void. He was not abstaining or deferring action by going abroad. He was putting himself apart from the timid routine of 'a middle-class rabbit', performing acts far more provocative than the doctor's son taking the grocer's boy to the cinema in Harborne; but it was all with the intention of advancing his self-knowledge and testing his emotional endurance in ways that might improve him as a poet. 'I do enjoy life immensely more than most I think, but just because one lives to understand,' he noted in the journal. 'To me writing is the enjoyment of the living.' Yet this journal, with its assertions of separation from family, was made possible by Dr Auden paying for his son to live abroad for a year after leaving Oxford: it ends with Auden returning to the family home, where he accepted the futility of unfocused rebellion against parents. A few months afterwards he wrote,

> Yours you say were parents to avoid, avoid them if you please
> Do the reverse on all occasions till you catch the same disease.

Moreover the journal has family conversations as its antecedent. In 1927 Dr Auden had published a medical case-note about a masochistic young fishmonger who had been accidentally killed 'by the symbolism of subjection'. The death instrument was 'a woman's high-heeled suede outdoor shoe, which was laced on to a bootmaker's iron boot-last' swathed in women's stockings; this was pinioned across his throat by 'a stout piece of wood' on which was balanced 'the bottom end of a heavy double bedstead, in such a way that the whole weight of the bed was transmitted to the shoe, and so to the throat'. Given his interest in his father's work, it was natural that Wystan Auden in Berlin chose to visit the museum of Magnus Hirschfeld, an authority on transvestism and campaigner for the removal of penal laws against homosexual acts. Hirschfeld in 1919 had opened the world's first institute of sexology, which provided a pioneering service as marriage counsellors, medical and legal advisers and sex educators; there was also an exhibition of his research interests, summarised in the title of his best-known book, *Sexual Anomalies and Perversions*. At one level, as Auden recognised, his Berlin journal is about just that: sexual anomalies and perversions. That is what he indicates at the start:

> It begins with the Hirschfield [sic] museum. We waited in an eighteenth century drawing room with elderly ladies and adhesive trouser boys. Why was this so obscene. H's boy was very earnest and bourgeois yet I felt he was nice. Don't let's have nothing of this pornography for science. A eunuch's pleasure.

Isherwood was more embarrassed than Auden by the museum's display of deviant paraphernalia. In memoirs published in 1977 during the high exuberance of the Californian gay liberation movement, Isherwood hailed his discovery of the Hirschfeld museum as the wonderful moment when 'he was forced to admit kinship with these freakish fellow tribesmen' and recognise that they all stood together 'on the same side'. For Isherwood, then, Hirschfeld's institute was where he began to celebrate special differences; Auden's response was more ambivalent.

Soon after arriving in Berlin Auden met John Layard, an Englishman who was sixteen years older than him. Layard together with Isherwood were the two Englishmen most prominent in Auden's Berlin milieu, and his influence was profound. He had been on an anthropological trip with W. H. R. Rivers in the south Pacific at the time of the outbreak of the war in 1914, and had been stricken with a mental breakdown and physical paralysis on his return to England. Rivers, who was revered by Dr Auden, had far-reaching importance to Layard too. Wystan Auden shared this interest, and, as John Fuller has shown, the trial scene of his charade *Paid on Both Sides*, written in 1928, is based on a passage in Rivers's book *Conflict and Dream*. But if Layard admired Rivers, he idolised the psychologist Homer Lane, who had cured his paralysis. 'Our lives are more formed,' Auden wrote in 1955, 'by the individuals upon whom we try to model ourselves than by any other factor, even if we belong to the minority with an interest in ideas.' He was always experimenting with personal models – in Berlin among others Lawrence, Proust's Baron de Charlus, Lane and Rivers – who pitched him into physical and mental action with experience.

Rivers was the first great connection between Auden and Layard. Trained as a physician at Bart's, where he won prizes which a few years later were carried off by George Auden, Rivers was a neurologist who became interested in anthropology and conducted some of the earliest experiments in cross-cultural psychology in the 1890s. During the First World War he was psychologist at the Craiglockhart hospital for shell-shocked soldiers. Rivers until then had been an isolated, stammering, loveless man, but in the crisis after 1914 he came to love his patients and exuded gregarious contentment. It was 'because he had to heal himself that he could heal others', according to a medical colleague. 'His whole personality expanded as he grew to realize what was his true mission in

Constance Auden teaching her youngest son, aged four, about books – 'those books which, read in childhood, formed our personal vision of the public world'.

bottom left Wystan playing with a donkey in the same year, 1911.

bottom right Five-year-old Wystan Auden dressed as a beetle.

Wystan (standing) and John Auden
photographed by their Aunt Mim at
Monmouth in 1911. Mildred Bicknell was an
intrepid traveller and photographer in the
Balkans, and very close to her sister
Constance. She was a powerful, sometimes
uncomfortable influence in the lives of her
nephews.

The three Auden brothers on a gate at Builth Road in Radnorshire in August 1913. 'We were such companions on so many expeditions,' his father later wrote.

The three Auden brothers at a Welsh slate quarry in 1914. Around them 'those beautiful machines that . . . let the small boy worship them and learn all their long names whose hardness made him proud'.

Wystan Auden (front row, third from right, with mouth agape) at St. Edmund's School in 1917.
An inky, sturdy, precocious and insolent schoolboy, aged ten.

Constance Auden in her garden.
'We imitate our loves: well, neighbours say
`I grow more like my mother every day.'

George Auden in his study.
'Father by son lives on and on.'

George and Constance Auden. 'Ma should have
married a robust Italian who was very sexy, and
cheated on her. Pa should have married someone
weaker than he and utterly devoted to him.'

George Auden aged sixty with his pets, Tinny
and Biddy.

Wystan, John and Bernard Auden as young men. 'I, after all, am the Fortunate One, The Happy-Go-Lucky, the spoilt Third Son.'

Auden as an undergraduate. 'Why must one do academic study during the very years when the only thing one really wants is to know "Who am I?".'

Auden at his parents' house in the Lake District around the time of his graduation in 1928. 'That anxiety about himself and his future which haunts, like a bad smell, the minds of most young men. Accordingly, they watch others with a covert passionate curiosity. What makes them tick? What would it feel like to be a success?'

Auden marked this picture 'Utopian youth grown Old Italian.'
When young he liked to pose as decadent.

life.' This example was a lesson to his admirers. He was one of the earliest English readers of Freud, and did much to introduce Freudian ideas to the medical profession, though his major treatise, *Instinct and the Unconscious*, presented Freudianism as too deterministic and set out a biological theory of the psycho-neuroses. One of the patients at Craiglockhart was Wilfred Owen, whose life was turned to the better. No man had greater intellectual influence on Robert Graves than Rivers. He was 'the chief father-figure' in Siegfried Sassoon's life, a man who 'awakened in me a passionate consciousness of the significance of life'. When he cruised on Arnold Bennett's yacht the two men talked every morning:

> Those talks ... constituted the most truly educational experience I have ever had. Rivers seemed to know something about everything and a lot about nearly everything ... But it was less his universal knowledge that impressed me than his lovely gift of co-ordinating apparently unrelated facts. And it was less his gift of co-ordination that impressed me than the beauty, comeliness and justness of his general attitude towards life ... He read enormously throughout the cruise, assimilating big book after big book.

Rivers, like Auden, tried to see each problem whole. Layard recognised their similarities: 'You know, Wystan, next to Lane and Rivers, I think you are the most intelligent man I have ever met.'

Auden made other impressions on him too. 'His face was absolutely smooth and angelic – the kind of face that turns out to be really "wicked",' Layard recalled years later of their first meeting. 'We talked and talked (a lot about Homer Lane – this was the beginning of Wystan's interest in him) late into the night.' They shared a bed, and Layard made sexual overtures which Auden declined, saying, 'No, I've got a boy.' Though Layard had been living in Berlin for some time, this was the first he had heard of 'street-boys', which shows how self-absorbed and prim he must then have been. In Auden's company he finally found the nerve to commit little crimes and to test his ideal of pleasure without guilt. They became habitués of the Cosy Corner, 'a very small café, rather scruffy, in which there were always half a dozen boys hanging around drinking beer', as Layard recalled. 'All these boys, as far as I know, were heterosexual, but they didn't mind playing around, and they liked a bit of money.' During their first few meetings, so Auden wrote, 'I felt his experience and his exposition of Lane has made a great difference to me.' Auden was prone to that rueful scorn about some of his sexual partners which is usually associated with Victorian males: the equivalent of what Edith Wharton called 'an undisturbed belief in the abysmal distinction between the woman once loved and respected and those once enjoyed – and pitied'. It was like this with Layard. 'Going to bed with him at first though was a great mistake which lasts. I feel guilty about it. It was so dreary and compulsionistic and I didn't get any sleep.'

Auden was once in the Cosy Corner café with Isherwood, John Layard and German friends when it was raided by police searching for three absconding borstal boys. The Englishmen gave their coats to the youths, who, assuming the appearance of rich foreigners, escaped undetected. Afterwards Auden, Layard and some others went to Layard's room with the boys. 'I found myself being kissed by one and having my breast sucked by the other,' Layard recorded. 'That's the only sort of orgy I've ever experienced. It was ecstatic and satisfying because it involved no responsibility and no personal relation whatever; it was just great fun.' In *The Enemies of a Bishop*, the play that Auden wrote in Germany in 1929 with Isherwood, two borstal absconders dress in disguise and cause sexual havoc while police officers from the Flying Squad raid the Nineveh Hotel where they have congregated. For Auden it was almost as Havelock Ellis wrote of Casanova: 'We have lost the orgy, but in its place we have art.'

After the visit to Hirschfeld's institute, Auden's journal cuts to a scene with Layard and Isherwood at the Cosy Corner café. He accuses himself of hypocrisy: 'For half an hour I felt in power. Became intimate with John ... "You've just got to get well. You're much too good a person to be like this." I was vilely insincere, because I don't care a hoot.' At about this time Auden 'inflamed' Layard with stories of the 'power' of his current lover, Gerhart Meyer ('The cord from his balls to his spine was like a 1000 volt cable,' according to Auden). Provoked by this, Layard took Meyer to bed, with humiliating results. 'I had stolen Wystan's boy, I had gone against every rule, and then been impotent.' Auden's journal takes up the story on 3 April:

John meditating suicide. Kisses me. No more than a plate of cold soup. 'It's not one of the things one forgets.' Temper. I start to leave. 'Must go.' 'I don't think this is very profitable.' 'To whom?' 'To you or to me.' Burst into tears. 'I'm so sorry. You're so decent.['] Tried to persuade him to kill himself.

Auden went home, and shortly afterwards Layard shot himself in the mouth, the bullet being deflected from his brain towards his forehead. 'I thought: "My God, I haven't killed myself. But it's all right. I've only got to get Wystan and give him the pistol and he'll finish me off".' Layard took a taxi to Auden's address.

I then had to walk up four flights of stairs with the bullet inside my skull, to Wystan's room. As I went up one or two boys were coming down; Wystan had been having a party. I arrived and said, 'Wystan, I've done it ... But it hasn't killed me. Please finish me off – here's a pistol and ammunition.' I'd had no doubt he'd do it, out of friendship. But he said: 'I'm terribly sorry, I know you want this, but I can't do it, because I might be hanged if I did. And I don't want to be. Lie down on the divan.' So I lay down; then I passed out.

Auden's version was this: 'He wanted me to finish him off. I wished I could. Retched when he vomited blood. Perhaps this is sympathy. Had to kiss him and disliked it. Appropriate snow storm on the way to the hospital. Depressed.' He tried to make himself feel better by the sort of verbal repetitions that had been recommended by Coué and Margaret Marshall: 'I keep saying to myself, "I'm happy you can appreciate his unhappiness".' But Coué's methods were useless, the sentences repeated by Auden at this crisis just seemed 'Lies. His misery is merely a nice background enhancing what I feel.'

Layard survived this incident, which proved to be the catharsis that unblocked his life. He went on to publish a major work of anthropology as well as a study of dream symbolism. His contacts with Auden continued until the war. When Kathleen Isherwood attended a lecture of 1938 on the Sino-Japanese war given by Auden and her son, she noted, 'John Layard and his quite nice looking rather cow like wife sat just in front of us – his whole expression & personality seems softened & normal the cow is evidently a success.' Layard may have been unprepossessing ('helpless and ugly as the embryo chicken', Auden judged), but their discussions in 1928–9 'raised me largely from the dead', so he felt by 1930; 'Nothing but love ... He says is needed for analysis.' Nevertheless when Layard 'talked about Lane and love', Auden 'was ashamed in front of Christopher' and feared that he would be teased: he reflected, 'what we think we believe varies with our company'.

One focus of discussion was D. H. Lawrence's *Fantasia of the Unconscious*, a book published in 1923 which enjoyed a powerful vogue. Lawrence's influence on Auden is identifiable as early as 'The Watershed' in 1927, but it reached its apotheosis after Auden went to Germany a year later. Auden's novel-reading was voracious, almost promiscuous; at times novels were more valued by him than poetry, and mattered as much to his work. 'Novel writing is,' he wrote in 1936, 'a higher art than poetry altogether.' So Lawrence at this time was someone whom he 'quoted in restaurants', although by 1933 he felt 'guilty' about his attraction to Lawrence's fascistic kinks:

> We were to trust our instincts; and they come
> Like corrupt clergymen filthy from their holes
> Deformed and imbecile, randy to shed
> Real blood at last.

Yet this was only an interim reaction. Looking back from the perspective of 1947, Auden felt grateful to Lawrence for giving a mandate to his ambitions: the terms in which he conveyed his gratitude reveal part of his situation as it stood when he went to Berlin.

> The would-be young writer of my generation in Europe grew up under the aesthetic shadow of nineteenth-century France. The serious writer was a solitary *esprit*, writing was an extremely difficult and exhausting sacred task; between the artist's working life and his personal life there could never be anything but antagonism. To encounter a writer who wrote as naturally as he breathed or slept was for us therefore a great liberation. For what the young writer needs is the child's shamelessness and frivolity which is not afraid of making a fool of itself nor asks if its play is important so long as it is having a good time, and we were aesthetically too prudish for our age, so afraid of writing badly or trivially that we were in danger of losing the self-confidence to write at all.

Another influence on Auden was Georg Groddeck, a psychologist with a water-therapy institute at Baden-Baden where Layard had stayed as a patient. Like Lawrence, Groddeck was sarcastic about 'our highly prized intelligence', offering instead a new source of identity (derived from Nietzsche) which he called the It, 'a capricious, unaccountable, entertaining jester' which 'plays marvellous tricks'. Auden believed that his It had a cycle of 'repenting its sins ... every six months' which resulted in periodic illnesses. One definition of a sin is an action which will bring misfortune in the future, and for Auden and Layard one weakness that brought them to sin was discord with their mothers. The misogynistic fantasies which occur in *The Orators* find confirmation in Groddeck's and Lawrence's assertions. Lawrence condemned parents who 'loved' their children 'to perdition', insisting that such love was 'poison to the giver, and still more poison to the receiver'. Groddeck agreed that mothers' love for their children had a counterpart of aversion: 'Man lives under the law: Where love is, there is also hate; where respect, there is also contempt; where admiration, there is also envy.' He also suspected that childbirth was an act of hatred. 'As to ... questions like these,' Auden had written in 1927, 'The story was never more reticent, / Always afraid to say more than it meant'; but Groddeck and Lawrence were strident and emphatic, insisting on the primacy of feelings and never realising that understatement is the language of reality.

Many of their precepts seem now like charlatanism; a charge actually made in legal proceedings against Layard and Auden's third seer, the American Homer Lane: 'a dangerous charlatan and an adventurer, who, for the safety of the public, ought to be out of the country', as prosecuting counsel said at his deportation proceedings in 1925. Lane's doctrines, as revealed by Layard, made a huge impact on Auden's living and working. He believed in releasing unconscious guilt, and turning its negative impulses into enriching powers. Delinquency, neurosis and even psychosis were twisted expressions of positive life-force which had to be 'loved' and honoured in order to be cured. He equated sin with neurosis (as did Auden for most of the rest of his life): if a person's vices were stronger than their virtues, then those vices represented the greater life-force and were therefore more valuable. For some years Lane ran a community for delinquents in Dorset called the Little Commonwealth. His work there convinced the educationalist A. S. Neill that Lane was 'the most brilliant intuitional child psychologist I have known'. But, after accusations of financial and sexual irregularities, the Little Commonwealth was shut in

1918. Though Neill judged that 'he ought never to have handled adults', Lane set up as a psychologist in London until he was deported in 1925 (like Ernest Jones and other analysts, he probably had sexual relations with women patients). Lane was a true healer whose success with some patients was undeniable; but he was a mountebank too. As Neill recalled in 1948, 'Lane would say in a study circle around 1918–19, "Football fans have castration complexes," or some such statement, and we all sat round with open mouths and took it in, never questioning where the Master got his proofs.' Lane knew the importance of play. 'Life was a game to him,' recalled Layard, and he was protean with his patients: he played 'a "naughty boy" with naughty boys. He was a youth (with a youth's youthful longings) when treating a youth. He was sick with the sick.'

Auden in Berlin was reading and thinking with his usual intensity. 'To me illumination is a progressive process,' he wrote. His sources were as varied as ever. For example he combined Chekhov with Rivers to conclude, 'evil is degenerate, not primitive' – not basic to individuals, but the result of the deforming influences of the societies in which they were grouped or the destructive effect of social discipline on individual feelings. On another occasion he drew on his reading of Irving Babbitt's essays on the ethical components of art and coupled it with T. E. Hulme's *Speculations*, essays on humanism and the philosophy of art which had been posthumously published in 1924 under the auspices of Herbert Read. Then he noted how ethical systems endangered individual goodness just as the cultural uniformity of Middle America overwhelmed individuality:

> Ethical values are absolute and not derived from subjective desires. Precisely, that is why it is so disastrous to apply them to human desires ... the Fall is repeated in each individual and is not a single irretrievable event in Human History. Regeneration is not secured by discipline and in the Higher Will of Babbitt, rather is the Fall ensured.

This train of thought (tricked out in the journal) led to some of the ideas about bad rhetoric enforcing twisted ethical discipline that feature in *The Orators*. Under the influence of Lane, Auden propounded: 'Be good and you will be happy is a dangerous inversion. Be happy and you will be good is the truth. Men often speak of their right to happiness. It is their only duty.' In Berlin he started to live out these ideas. 'The substitute of a theory of life for living is a source of nemesis,' Auden concluded. He laid down in his journal Lane's principle that he was practising, 'To cure a disease, encourage it, don't repress ... Use love, not fear.' He reiterated this again on 12 June 1929, after reading Galsworthy's *Forsyte Saga*: 'Every desire if developed far enough develops a course of criticism, destroying itself.' Accordingly, if a cure was needed for homosexuality, then that cure was extravagant indulgence in homosexual acts: the opposite of the chastity which Auden had tried in 1927, and far different from the psychotherapeutic talk cure of 1928.

'I am having the sort of friendships I ought to have had at sixteen and didn't,' he wrote on New Year's Eve 1928. His Berlin friendships had little in common with a sixteen-year-old's crushes. 'I ordered champagne,' he noted of an evening costing 36 marks. 'They giggled like girls which is what I wanted. Its time I learnt to control my phantasies of grandeur.' The roughness of his men friends went beyond schoolboy rowdiness. 'Wystan liked being beaten up a bit,' Layard claimed of their time in Berlin. 'It would start with pillow-fights and end with blows; then they would go to bed together.' Though he tried to hide this masochism from Layard, with other English friends he was defiant. 'My boy', he boasted from Berlin, had left him 'a mass of bruises'. Earlier he had told Coghill, 'I do admire a real swine'; and David Luke identifies in the young Auden a strong element of 'romantic emotional masochism'. Auden attributed this to his artistic commitment. 'How one likes to suffer,' he noted in April 1929. 'Anyway writers do; it is their income.' In Berlin he believed that a man's faults were not dismaying but enhancing. There were emotions to dread, and yet be drawn to. Clinically noting the minor delinquencies of a man called Franz with whom he went to Lunar Park, he concluded: 'This insolence pleases. It was so gratuitous. An anti-life gesture.'

Auden may have been encouraged in these ways by his reading of Gide's *Les Faux Monnayeurs* (1926), which depicted anti-life behaviour as a characteristic of energetic youth rather than of ethical defectives. The more pretentious of Gide's middle-class delinquent boys hope to form a literary elect; some ferret out family secrets, play at criminality and are enlisted by a gang of counterfeiters. One youth makes incestuous advances to his uncle and another is tricked into shooting himself in front of his fellow pupils. The reality behind these idealisations of evil was repre-sented by two adolescent lovers Richard Loeb and Nathan Leopold, who had been convicted of a cruel, sordid child-murder in Chicago in 1924. Yet *Les Faux Monnayeurs* impressed Auden ('the end is a masturbator's daydream – so optimistic', Auden judged in middle age), and its link of nephew with uncle has a sequel in *The Orators*.

The shedding of guilt was one of the priorities of Auden and Layard. 'The sailor on shore is symbolically the innocent god from the sea who is not bound by the law of the land and can therefore do anything without guilt,' Auden later wrote, and the most important of his Berlin toughs, Gerhart Meyer, was a sailor (like himself aged twenty-two). Auden was excited by Meyer's sexual allure for men and women, 'the most extraordinary power I have met in anyone', and admired the 'absence of fear' in this 'truly strong man'. He relished Meyer's strength as a counterpart to his own inferiority complex: 'I posture before the glass,' he wrote after a row with Meyer, 'trying to persuade myself but in vain that I am up to his physical level.' The opening of his journal had indicated that it was to be a scrutiny of 'the truly weak men': almost its earliest doggerel described compensatory strength:

> Pick a quarrel, go to war,
> Leave the hero in the bar.
> Hunt the lion, climb the peak,
> No-one guesses you are weak.

The day after Layard shot himself, Auden went to Hamburg with Meyer.

> Few things are better than a hurried meal when one is packing to go off to a lover. I wondered what books one takes on these occasions. I took Donne, the Sonnets, and Lear. In the tube I had an encounter with a whore. I stared at her feeling, 'I'm king of Berlin'. She promptly came and stood beside me until I got out.

When Auden said, 'I should like to take you to the mountains with me,' Meyer replied, 'I don't like mountains. I only like towns where there are shops.' Meyer's instincts were mercenary, and on 16 April, after their return to Berlin, he left in the middle of the night after a row about money. 'At the same time my dressing gown and John's revolver went with him.' Auden's reaction was characteristically self-critical, even masochistic in its conscientiousness; it bore the impression of the theories of perfect love held by Lane. 'It's too easy to say "He's a bad egg. I made a mistake." If a person does one an injury one is always half to blame.'*

Auden's severance from Meyer occasioned reflections which transcend the fact of a sailor levanting with a purloined dressing-gown. 'When someone begins to lose the glamour they had for us on our first meeting them, we tell ourselves that we have been deceived, that our phantasy cast a halo over them which they are unworthy to bear,' Auden noted on 16 April. 'It is always possible however that the reverse is the case; that our disappointment is due to a failure of our own sensibility which lacks the strength to maintain itself at the acuteness with which it began. People may really be what we first thought of them, and what we subsequently think of as the disappointing reality, the person obscured by the staleness of our senses.' Love was either 'a remnant of something degenerating', he wrote, 'of something which has once been immense, or it is a particle of what will in the future develop into something immense; but in the present it is unsatisfying; it gives much less than one expects'. A few months later, in August, he reused these phrases as if to confirm that his view was developing into something immense.

> So, insecure, he loves and love
> Is insecure, gives less than he expects.
> He knows not if it be seedtime to display
> Luxuriantly in a wonderful fructification
> Or whether it can be but a degenerate remnant
> Of something immense in the past but now
> Surviving only as the infectiousness of disease
> Or in the malicious caricature of drunkenness;
> Its end glossed over by the careless but known long
> To finer perceptions of the mad and ill.

David Luke was one of the most perceptive and staunch of Auden's friends in the 1960s and 1970s. He believes that the theory of love propounded by Auden when he broke with Meyer remained for the rest of his life. The lover, so Luke argues that Auden believed, 'perceives the

---

* In 1955, after visiting Berlin, Auden wrote to friends, 'My name having appeared in the papers, I got a letter from a boyfriend of 1929, then a sailor, as beautiful as the dawn, who behaved very badly to me. I went to see him, and nearly fainted – He had not just put on weight, he was grotesque like something in a circus also owns a lamp shade factory and is obviously pretty rich.'

beloved as he or she "really" is; the eyes of love are not blind but visionary, they behold a deeper, "more real" reality, but only while the passion of love is sustained'. When passion dies, so does the vision. Auden's view is the opposite of the claim in reductive psychology that infatuated lovers are duped by sexual emotion into idealisations of their loved ones which misrepresent that person's true self. Whereas Freud indicated that erotic love was an over-valuation of its object, and therefore false, Auden recognised that it could bring both transfiguration and enrichment. Auden famously treated sexual acts as symbolic or filling an omission (usually familial). Thus he wrote of Meyer, 'I want him to be an elder brother,' and identified his own choice in homosexual acts with motherhood ('I am my mother'). But the symbolism of sexual acts is not the same as love. Auden did not pretend that his feelings for the Berliners were visionary: 'His clap is nothing serious/ He never rips me off,' he versified cheerfully to the tune of the Passion Chorale in 1930, 'At kissing and at sucking/ I give him alpha plus.'

Auden's Christian upbringing treated homosexual acts as sinful; he knew that Freud considered the true aim of human sexuality to be heterosexuality. 'Only the differences between man and woman represent the perfect state of sexual evolution', wrote Iwan Bloch, a venereologist and ethnologist known in Berlin as the Linnaeus of erotic flora. 'The "third sex" is a regressive phenomenon.' The 'childish condition' of homosexuality was to Jung 'always a defective adaptation to external reality': in fact 'a faulty development ... of the otherwise very appropriate need for masculine guidance'. These assertions were mumbo-jumbo given authority by the apparent neutrality of their scientific language: Bloch based his belief that heterosexuality represented a higher form of evolution on the fact that the human penis was longer and thicker than those of mammals. Yet, given the proliferation of such comment, and the general assumption of western culture it is not surprising that Auden identified marriage with maturity; saw homosexuality, to adapt a phrase from the psychologist Trigant Burrow's *Social Basis of Consciousness* (1927), which he read at this time, as 'intercepted growth'.

It was thus a matter of magnitude that on 29 July, having returned to England, he broke his engagement to marry Sheilah Richardson, to whom he had proposed in 1928. 'Bravo Me', he wrote that day to Layard. Earlier, in Berlin on 13 April, he had presaged the break: 'the attraction of buggery is partly its difficulty and torments. Heterosexual love seems so tame and easy after it. I feel this with Sheilah. There is something in reciprocity that is despair.' Now in his journal (echoing *Lear*, which he had taken to read in Hamburg with Meyer) he insisted: 'Never – Never – Never again. She is unhappy. She wants to be pushed. And I should do it. And I won't.' He repeated himself in a letter to McElwee: 'I was but am no longer engaged. Never, never again. This is a criticism of me, not of marriage.' It was a death of sorts. In the conclusion to his 1928 charade *Paid on Both Sides*, the bridegroom died as he celebrated his marriage, as if recalling Auden's favourite book as a child, Andersen's *Ice Maiden*, in which the bridegroom drowned in an Alpine lake after a joyous picnic. This image resurfaced in the great poem which begins 'It is time for the destruction of error' (October 1929). It depicts a momentous occasion, 'the dragon's day, the devourer's', when love fails and death has its triumph.

> we know that love
> Needs more than the admiring excitement of union,
> More than the abrupt self-confident farewell,
> The heel on the finishing blade of grass,
> The self-confidence of the falling root,
> Needs death, death of the grain, our death,
> Death of the old gang; would leave them
> In sullen valley where is made no friend,
> The old gang to be forgotten in the spring,
> The hard bitch and the riding-master,
> Stiff underground; deep in clear lake
> The lolling bridegroom, beautiful, there.

Auden's renunciation of marriage with Sheilah Richardson was a loss, it seemed to him, indeed a personal failure. A few years earlier he had sexual relations with an Austrian woman, Hedwig Petzold, with whom he kept in affectionate contact until the end of her life, but the experience had not engaged him. 'I am not disgusted but sincerely puzzled at what the attraction is' in women, he told the novelist Naomi Mitchison; heterosexuality to him was 'like watching a game of cricket for the first time'. In his attempt to understand the choice of sexual acts Auden consulted the books of Proust, whose 'analysis of the bugger' in *Sodome et Gomorrhe* (published in March 1929 in English translation as *Cities of the Plain*) though 'beautiful' was he concluded 'inadequate'. The ideas in Auden's reading of

Proust originated from self-analysis, though they applied to him in varying ways at different times. Proust 'rightly lays stress on two things', Auden wrote: 'The Buggers as the great secret society and "the inverts terrible nerves".* But all his talk about the "man–woman" seems astoundingly superficial and quite meaningless.' Proust's sense of homosexual acts as 'Revolt against Authority' – clandestine by nature, made more attractive by their secrecy and peril than by their pleasures – and his persistent implication that 'the social ban makes buggery exciting', Auden judged 'of secondary importance, as buggery always flourished where there was no such repression'. There were, Auden realised from his own self-knowledge, a range of more important motives and interests that drew men into homosexual acts. Some he categorised as 'Physical' in origin. Most men were 'interested in the Penis', their own primarily, and felt curiosity or rivalry about other men's. Such factors as 'repression of infantile masturbation or exploration by the Parents' or 'comparison of circumcised with uncircumcised and vice versa' were in this category. So too was 'the need for physical contact', which he thought British middle-class inhibitions prevented ('refusal to undress in public' he specified in *The Orators* as one of the 'enemy traits'). Contact was:

> natural when there is any contact of personality and should be encouraged. The comparative freedom of the lower classes from violent perversion is perhaps due to the habit of sleeping together and dislike of sleeping alone. Among the educated classes the child very soon connects … the idea of physical contact and sexual acts. When he does gratify the first, he thinks he wants the second i.e. when he sleeps with his friend he gets an erection.

There had been an episode with Meyer which showed the reality that Auden had in mind. The sailor teased Auden with sexy fantasies: 'We must get a woman up here and jazz her together. Or I jazz her and you watch. You never done that. You'll get a kick out of it. I bet you find yourself jogging off when I jazz her.' Perhaps this is just smut; but Meyer's suggestion may have been meant as a generous offer, an act of male camaraderie which cheerfully acknowledged the physical curiosity which some men feel about other men's bodies. The antithesis of this candid

---

* This word is indecipherable; instead of 'nerves', it may be 'woes' or 'heroes'.

masculinity was depicted in *The Orators* in the passionless bonding, self-conscious inhibitions and masked emotions of the middle-class golfers: 'frowning, conscious of their pipes, cellular underwear … the tall, capless one in the back row deliberately half-hidden'. Meyer's attraction for Auden was mainly physical, yet it involved the 'Inferiority Complex' which so much troubled Auden and which he listed as the most prominent 'Mental' stimuli for homosexual acts. An inferiority complex might arise from 'Physical trouble like late puberty': as an example from *The Orators*, 'an immature boy wrapping himself in a towel, ashamed in the public baths' because he is seen to lack pubic hair. Another source of inferiority complex is 'lack of skill at games, or anything that tends to make him feel "I'm not a he-man" and in compensation makes him fall in love with boxers': this is the opposite of the male prowess celebrated in the ode in *The Orators* to the Sedbergh rugby team of whom Auden was one of the 'touch-line admirers.' The puny and the clumsy chase after 'he-men', Auden thinks, as if sex relations could be 'an act of sympathetic magic like taking Bovril' which will invigorate and strengthen them. This contrast was reiterated in *The Orators*: 'The muscular shall lounge in bars; the puny shall keep diaries in classical Greek.' Prudery – what Auden called 'false sex idealism' – he also classified as a 'mental' stimulus to homosexuality. 'If the child gets the idea that sex is wicked, he will try to get out of sex. Buggery is the attempt to go without the cake and eat it.' Another cause was 'The Segregation of Maleness and Femaleness'. Education instilled 'the idea that men are men and women women, quite different. This leads to feelings of inadequacy in each and no point of contact. Homosexuality then becomes an attempt to complete oneself.' Auden's thinking and work always strove towards wholeness and the reconciliation of disparities.

After returning from Berlin, Auden endured a series of practical uncertainties about jobs and doubts about more personal choices. He stayed with his parents before starting work as a private tutor in London in the autumn of 1929. It was during this temporary job, in November, that he wrote:

> A long time ago I told my mother
> I was leaving home to find another:
> I never answered her letter
> But I never found a better.
>
> . . .

I've come a long way to prove
No land, no water, and no love.
Here I am, here are you:
But what does it mean? What are we going to do?

A small resolution came in April 1930, when Auden began teaching at
Larchfield Academy, a boys' school in south-west Scotland. Further
encouragement reached him after Faber in September 1930 published
1000 copies of *Poems*, his first commercially published book (Spender had
hand-printed a small edition of twenty Auden poems in 1928). It
contained poems which he had written between August 1927 and April
1930, and opened with his charade entitled *Paid on Both Sides* (which he
privately gave the semi-autobiographical subtitle 'A parable of English
Middle Class (professional) family life 1907–29') about a feud perpetuated
by a hate-ridden mother.

The publication of *Poems* signalled to the young poet William Plomer
that 'guerilla warfare had ... broken out'. MacNeice praised Auden's
'remarkable ear which he runs in harnass with his mind' so that his use of
words is narrowed by neither 'meaning' nor 'sound-value'. Instead, 'the
sound adds to the meaning and by adding makes a new meaning'. He
contrasted *Paid on Both Sides* with Eliot: 'It is tragic where *The Waste Land*
is defeatist, and realist where *The Waste Land* is literary.' William Empson
also enthused about the charade: 'It puts psychoanalysis and surrealism
and all that, all the irrationalist tendencies which are so essential a part of
the machinery of present-day thought, into their proper place; they are
part of the normal and rational tragic form, and indeed what constitutes
the tragic situation.' Even F. R. Leavis found passages to admire, though
his mean and querulous spirit ensured that his praise was only grudging.
'I'm sending you W. H. Auden's poems, on the chance that the "Charade"
may interest you,' he wrote to his protégé Ronald Bottrall. 'Not that I
think Auden's in the same class with you – as I've pointed out to admirers
of his, he can't stand the comparison. Details and general aim are
impressive, but his technique isn't nearly as sure as yours.'

In his talks with Layard Auden had elaborated theories about the
psychosomatic origin of disease. Hatred of the flesh was, he thought,
manifest in boils and skin diseases; hatred of the past in diarrhoea or
nausea; Isherwood's sore throat he called 'a liar's quinzy'; Spender was 'so
tall' because 'he's trying to reach Heaven'. When in February 1930 he

underwent an operation for a rectal fissure he interpreted this as a symbol of buggery (his preferred word at that time for homosexuality), though he himself seldom practised anal intercourse, which he disliked. During his recuperation he amused himself 'writing a textbook of Psychology in doggerel verses'. Fear of spiritual and creative love was diagnosed thus:

> He was a housemaster and a bachelor
> But refused to keep dogs
> So he is dying of cancer.

Sexual guilt was equated with ill health:

> Love your cock
> Stand a shock
> Hate your cock
> Soon a crock.

Healthy attitudes brought immunity from infection:

> If a whore shocks you
> Then she will pox you.

This interest (amusing if taken lightly) was developing in 1929–30 into curiosity about the collective neuroses of his epoch. As Spender wrote in 1937, 'at first though this interest was clinical; he was content to state what he beautifully and profoundly saw without implying an attitude or a remedy'. Auden was not an outright Freudian in his analyses because he thought Freud resembled the Oxford don quoted in *The Orators* as saying, 'I don't feel quite happy about pleasure.' Freud never conceded that childhood could be happy; always earnest about sexual facts, he was never lyrical about sexual pleasure. 'The error of Freud and most psychologists is making pleasure a negative thing, progress towards a state of rest,' Auden noted in his Berlin journal. 'This is only one halt of pleasure and the least important half. Creative pleasure is, like pain, an increase in tension.' A year later he wrote in a poem critical of many kill-joys, including Freud, 'If we really want to live, we'd better start at once to try;/ If we don't, it doesn't matter, but we'd better start to die.' Auden's poetry was more teasing or parabolic than his critical articles, which often represented major phases of his thinking. Thus he wrote in 1932, 'The mere fact that A prefers girls and B boys is unimportant. The real cause for alarm lies in the large number of nervous and unhappy people who are incapable of any intimate faithful relationship at all, in whom sensation has remained at or regressed to the infantile level as an end in itself ... and to whom, therefore, the object is really non-existent. It is true that nearly all homosexual relations are of this kind but so are a large proportion of heterosexual ones and there is nothing to choose between them.'

Most of *The Orators* was written during the summer and autumn of 1931 while Auden was a teacher at Larchfield. The book is meant to tax and bewitch and play games with unconscious associations. Auden's intentions were prefigured in his journal: 'The spirit naturally chooses the difficult rather than the easy. It is so much more interesting.... This also accounts for the success of repression. Half the mind enjoys the difficulty of censoring, the other half of circumventing the censor.' *The Orators* is easy to misjudge. Spender wrote in 1932, 'we can only enter if we are prepared to accept it whilst we are reading about it'; as Gide observed on a visit to Berlin in 1930, 'great works do not so much teach us as they plunge us into a sort of almost loving bewilderment'. Taken on these terms, the impact of *The Orators* can be tremendous. 'When I flew through *The Orators* first,' wrote Berryman, 'I recognized Auden at once as a new master.' For Auden's biographer one excitement of the book lies in its parabolic versions of the perplexities besetting its author: his uncertainties about masculinity, his tendency towards Lawrentian fascism, his efforts to synthesise literary and psychological ideas are all resolved or examined in the book. There are many impersonal influences that could be analysed at great length. As Stan Smith has brilliantly shown, *The Orators* closely reflects the time and place at which it was written. It is full of local references – some taken from the *Helensburgh and Gareloch Times* – of an obscurity intended as derision of the 'metropolitan high priests of culture'. Auden's commemoration of the local businessmen and detached villas of Helensburgh are a postmodern practical joke against the exclusive, privileged Tradition associated with Eliot, a man whose 'day is over' (according to an ode in *The Orators* addressed to Rex Warner's baby son), a poet who spends his time in August 1931 'dreaming of nuns', though the Labour government has collapsed in economic crisis to be replaced by a corrupt coalition. This scoffing was tender, for Auden at this time adulated his publisher Eliot.

The most unsettling aspect of *The Orators* is the difficulty of deciding how far the madder passages reflect Auden's state of mind in 1931. The book is cryptic and fragmentary because communication among the disinherited and excluded dispenses with proofs: there is a reciprocal divination whereby men understand each other with half a word. It is, says Proust, a freemasonry which uses the language of signs, or trusts its meanings to inflexions and hints which are the antithesis of public rhetoric. Many of the figures in *The Orators*, like its young men who pride themselves on being 'persons unknown to our parents', are disinherited or isolated. 'Poetry is the last refuge and asylum for the individual of whom oratory is the enemy,' Yeats's father had written in 1914, and this maxim might serve as an epigraph for *The Orators*; Auden himself later warned, 'Bad men are often good orators.' The book is a disenchanted look at pompous, equivocal public figures who pose as good, plain-spoken fellows or the sort of social controllers who pose as neutral analysts with remarks like 'Speaking as a scientist'. Auden for example contrasts public rhetoric as exemplified by deceptive, lethal patriotic clichés about the British Expeditionary Force in 1914 – sentimentalities which are orotund, dehumanised and insincere instruments of social control – with the authenticity of 'the last desperate appeals of the lost for help scribbled on the walls of public latrines' (pertinent because, as an observer of such phenomena claimed in 1930, until 1914 all sexual graffiti 'in public places was heterosexual in nature: it is now almost invariably homosexual').

The Orators concerns the rhetorical subjugation of humanity's sexual, group and survival instincts. Warfare is a supreme example of group activity, and preparations for aeronautical war take a central part of the book (called 'The Airman's Journal'). One example of social control enforced by rhetoric was the busybodying reclassification of old pleasures by sexologists and psychologists. In response to this Auden makes flying a metaphor for homosexual acts and presents the poet with the sensibility to perform such acts as 'a flying trickster'. Flying is 'unholy hunting and ghostly journey': unholy because ignorant people say, 'if the Lord had intended people to fly He'd have given them wings'. Sublimation of desire is manifest in male 'day-dreams' of 'dragging their chums from the blazing fuselage'. Sublimation is important because *The Orators* suggests modes of masculinity rather than analysing sexual acts. Certainly one of its preoccupations is men's desire for other men. This is most explicit in 'The Airman's Alphabet' in which the arse and the prick, for example, are represented in aeronautical terms like Cockpit – 'Soft seat/and support of soldier/and hold for hero' – and Joystick – 'Pivot of power/and responder to pressure/and grip for the glove'. Yet *The Orators* is addressed to a far wider audience than the 'revolving roarer' and has a far broader subject than sexual inversion. It is about male desire: it celebrates sexual covertness: but it is also about masculine initiation into fascistic groups (as signified in the title of part one, 'The Initiates'). His most exciting type of Berlin friend had resembled 'a rugger hearty', and he later realised that at the time he wrote *The Orators* he might as easily have become a fascist as a communist. Fascism is one symptom of an over-valuation of masculinity. It is an attempt to make a man's world; the fascists' repudiation of weakness is a repudiation of their idea of femininity. As Auden's airman says, 'there is something peculiarly horrible about the idea of women pilots'. Fascist men seek to obliterate their pain by externalising it in war against their supposed enemies. The compensatory manoeuvres of the 'truly weak men' formed the inaugural theme of the Berlin journal, followed by sexual anomalies and perversions: such are the foundations of fascism. But though a fascist's fear of not being manly enough leads him to glorify death, his fear can provoke him into courageous behaviour. He is brave enough to deny fear. This is what people often mean by masculinity; and fortitude, as Auden told Spender, was the quality that he most admired.

Auden's writing about homosexuality in the 1930s had to be coded for the same reason that Isherwood had to destroy his diaries of the period: homosexual acts were criminal in Britain until 1967, and persecuted by the police for longer. Its male practitioners were put beyond the frontier of accepted social bonds unless they engaged in tense and subtle (often self-destructive) complicity with authority. Invisibility was required as a precondition of impunity: social and other sanctions are still visited on men who insist on a public rhetoric of homosexuality or refuse a role of social effacement. There were real risks at the time for men like Auden. At Oxford he had to pay £5 (then a largish sum) to buy the silence of a man who found him in bed with John Betjeman. Candid writing brought legal interdictions from the authorities or personal jeopardy. As recently as 1928 Radclyffe Hall's inexplicit sapphic novel *Well of Loneliness* had been prosecuted for obscenity, and Virginia Woolf had revised *Orlando* to make it less vulnerable to such attack. Auden could not print the word 'bugger' in early editions of *The Orators*, where it appeared as *****; men caught by the police in homosexual activity (or denounced for it by busybodies) were imprisoned. Yet *The Orators* suggests that homosexual acts can be the initiation into a privileged group rather than criminal transgressions.

'Perversions are due to a desire not for pleasure but justice.' Auden declared in his journal. In *The Orators* he revived this idea in Lane's terms: 'The glutton shall love with his mouth ... the sick shall say of love "it's only a phase"; the psychologist, "That's easy"; the bugger, "Be fair".' Justice is inseparable from one of the great symbols of masculinity, heroism, because the necessary counterpart of heroism is injustice in the form of victimisation. As Auden wrote in 1936, the old idealisation of a hero had 'passed away at Ypres and Passchendaele', and had been replaced by Walt Disney's trickster, 'The little Mickey with the hidden grudge'. For Auden one of the chief symbols of the twentieth century were the monuments erected after 1918 to commemorate the Unknown Soldier rather than victorious generals and admirals as in the past. 'About the Unknown Soldier nothing is known except that he lost his life. For all we know, he may, personally, have been a coward. In his monument, that is to say, we pay homage to the warrior, not as a hero, but as a martyr.' Similarly Kafka was the author who best represented, Auden thought, the age in which they lived. 'Previously, the hero is the exceptional individual, exceptional either by his in-born gifts or his acquired virtues,' Auden wrote of Kafka. 'His goal is either to manifest or to achieve individuality; the hero who is saved achieves this positively, the tragic hero who is damned achieves it negatively.' But the publication in 1925 of *Der Prozess* (in English *The Trial*) changed everything. 'K, on the other hand, suffers and fails to achieve his goal precisely because he is an individual.... The fact that he is K is really the evidence of his guilt in *The Trial*; if he were innocent, he would have no name.'

The first sign of Kafkaesque persecution in *The Orators* is in 'Address for a Prize-Day' which opens the section entitled 'The Initiates'. The address is orated by a busybody. He wants his listeners to sacrifice themselves to all the stale, inexorable conventions. Everyone needs putting down, or putting in a new place. He inveighs against solitary, self-sufficient people who do not move with the crowd: they are rubbished as 'excessive lovers of self'. His audience is enjoined to interfere in their ways and disrupt their satisfactions. Later Auden was to quote a remark of Schopenhauer – 'he who does not love solitude will not enjoy freedom' –

and the real transgression of this group is to love private freedom. The busybody authorities of public-school life can no more tolerate individuality than dictators or other political power systems. Lawrence had written in *Fantasia*, 'You have got to base your great purposive activity upon the intense sexual fulfilment of all your individuals' for 'that was how Egypt endured'; but the school orator will have none of that, 'you are no longer living in ancient Egypt' he warns the boys. He incites a brutal round-up of perverted lovers who are thrown into a 'Black Hole' under the floor of the hall: the sort of punishment that is imposed by punishers who fear their own perversion or need to extirpate their own kind. The crudest kind of collective emotion is panic, and 'Address for a Prize-Day' ends with a horrid scene of group panic stimulated by fear of the perverted lovers.

Auden inserts a parable about the *führer-prinzip* as outlined in Lawrence's *Fantasia*. It is orated by an infatuated member of the inner group of a leader. They form a secretive, exclusive, excitable little band vying with one another for their leader's attention: the orator himself has possessive fantasies, imagining self-sacrificial and histrionic gestures of love. Overwhelmed by such emotion, the group destroys itself. It is the sort of proto-fascism that Auden needed to avoid in the early 1930s. There may be better forms of male bonding, he suggests. He has told his readers that the 'undercarriage' of airmen is 'easy to injure', and his ensuing 'Letter to a Wound' refers to his recent rectal fissure. The nature of the wound is unspecified and its symbolism is consequently more powerful: like the old judicial phrases for sodomy, 'a certain charge' or 'the crime not to be named among Christians'. He remembers the aftermath of diagnosis: 'Outside I saw nothing, walked, not daring to think. I've lost everything, I've failed.' Like Auden himself, after his visit to Croatia in 1927 when his 'inferiority complex' over his homosexuality was at its worst, 'I wish I was dead.' But then he makes a positive choice to accept lovingly what he cannot shirk; 'here we are together, intimate, mature', he writes. 'Nothing will ever part us.' His love is almost revelatory. He tells the wound, 'Thanks to you I have come to see a profound significance in relations I never dreamt of considering before, an old lady's affection for a small boy, the Waterhouses and their retriever, the curious bond between Offal and Snig, the partners in the hardware shop on the front.' It is a new pattern of understanding, a specialised sensibility.

That sensibility is explored further. The airman alienates himself from his own safe and dreary past, and fantasises about a secret heritage with its own mysterious signs and community. His 'true ancestor' is his maternal uncle carrying 'the lethal factors that were in the stock' mentioned in a 1927 poem, and anticipating a phrase in a 1938 poem, 'hinting at the forbidden like a wicked uncle'. This idea came partly from the boy in Gide's *Les Faux Monnayeurs* who feels an incestual desire for his uncle; partly from his uncle Harry and Isherwood's uncle Henry, who both had homosexual tastes. The airman recalls that as a child he found his uncle perplexing and intimidating: 'I thought I hated him but I was always eager to please him or run errands, and a word of approval from him made me happy for the rest of the day.' One memorable incident happened around the time of puberty. 'I can remember when I was about thirteen a letter coming from him at breakfast. "Of course I know he's very clever," my mother sniffed, and then there was a silence.' But with adolescence there came recognitions that were a revelation. 'It wasn't till I was sixteen and a half that he invited me to his flat. We had champagne for dinner. When I left I knew who and what he was – my real ancestor.' This champagne initiation taught the airman to scrutinise all uncles. 'Uncle Sam, is he one too? He has the same backward-bending thumb that I have.'

The psychologists Groddeck and Stekel whom Auden had studied in Berlin both identified kleptomania or tremulous hands with sexual acts; Gide in *Les Faux Monnayeurs* equated delinquency with the impulse to life; and this is another case in which Auden combined ideas from contemporary novelists and psychologists for his own purposes. 'Every criminal act is a revolt against death,' he declared. 'Stealing is an attempt to perform a miracle.' Homosexual acts like stealing were offences against criminal law, but the airman provides his own law, 'self-care, or minding one's own business'. This though is opposed by acts of definition which are enemy acts, coming from such people as Christians requiring the abnegation of Self and obedience to the leading of God or psychologists who root homosexuality in narcissism and self-gratification. In Berlin Auden had seen the new psychology as a secular substitute for Christianity relying on a similar play of symbols and therapies. 'The part of psychology is to provide the gospel,' he had written. 'Cures are the miracles.' On later occasions too he likened 'psycho-analyst and Christian minister'.

One of the new psychological doctrines which seemed brave and exciting in the 1920s was that everyone was essentially bisexual, and that all those who practised heterosexual acts, and denied the slightest interest in other acts, were repressing the truth about their desires. One morning in Berlin Gerhart Meyer asked, 'Is the Prince of Wales much so?', and Auden replied, 'I don't think so. Everybody likes both I think ' The twentieth-century western theory of universal bisexuality had its power in Auden's epoch, and did not seem stale or jejune in 1931. Some sexual impulses, Auden had decided in his analysis of Proust, were intended to achieve wholeness. He had condemned in his journal the segregation of masculinity and femininity. The airman represents 'awareness' of the united duality, but the new psychology 'attempts to disturb this awareness by theories of partial priority'. Flying tricksters like the airman believe in 'the unity of passion of which nothing can be said but that it is the effort of a thing to realise its own nature', but the enemy with their 'learned reason' and over-intellectualisation cannot grasp this. 'Their extraordinary idea is that man's only glory is to think.' Freud, so Auden had noted in his Berlin journal, 'really believes that pleasure is immoral, i.e. happiness is displeasing to God. If you believe this the death wish of course becomes the most important emotion.' The airman's enemies include those interpreters whose 'sense of humour' rests on 'verbal symbolism'. They use language as a weapon in an unequal power relationship. A psychologist for example can be a corrupt rhetorician who interprets other people's words, but keeps a privileged place in an enclosed system; he will not have his words analysed. 'He means what he says.' Yet Auden did not wholly repudiate the new psychology. It gave him insights into human motives and misconduct – indeed a power to control and change what happened – that resembled those detectives of pulp fiction Bulldog Drummond or Panther Grayle to whom in *The Orators* he prayed for deliverance 'from all nervous excitement and follies of the will; from the postponed guilt and the deferred pain ... from the encroaching glaciers of despair, from the drought that withers the lower centres'.

'What Freud says is always partly true,' Lawrence began in *Fantasia*; but he was intent to argue, 'All is not sex.... A sexual motive is not to be attributed to all human activities.' Auden's position was similar. He came to Freud steeped in the work of his sympathetic critics like Rivers, who insisted (with relevance to *The Orators*) that the survival instinct was stronger than the sexual.'Freud's error is the limitation of the neurosis to the individual,' Auden believed. 'The neurosis involves all society.' One divergence is that, where Freud began by interpreting dreams, dissidents like George Auden or McDougall with their preference for the concrete began by interpreting character. Character-reading had important antecedents in English literature. Early in the seventeenth century poets like Sir Thomas Overbury compiled prose compendia of human types categorising men and women by characteristics or vocations. Sections of *The Orators* are character-writing in twentieth-century accents too. Cumulatively they are some of the most beautiful and evocative passages in the book. They are like a paradigm of the book too: erotic ('One charms by thickness of wrist; one by variety of positions; one has a beautiful skin, one a fascinating smell'); perverted ('One makes leather instruments of torture for titled masochists'); psychologically odd, like the autistics and idiot prodigies whom Dr Auden studied ('clumsy but amazes by his knowledge of time-tables'); or admirable. Auden lists enemy characteristics as well. The following sample show Auden's dislike in 1931 of the life-diminishing tendencies of the English middle classes: their timidity, inauthenticity, philistinism and regression:

> Three enemy catchwords – insure now – keep smiling – safety first.
> Three signs of an enemy country – licensed hours – a national art – nursery schools.
> Three signs of an enemy house – old furniture – a room called the Den – photographs of friends.
> Three results of an enemy victory – impotence – cancer – paralysis.
> Three counter attacks – complete mastery of the air – ancestor worship – practical jokes.

There had been few moments of humour in Auden's earliest published poems. But in *The Orators* there was a flippancy which came to be a familiar Auden technique. His attitude to joking had coalesced in 1929. 'The only good reason for doing anything is for fun,' Auden had decided in Berlin. Implicit in the ideas of Groddeck and Lane was the belief that play is not trivial. Play is an experience of imagination and symbols: it is easy and allusive in a way that implies trust and pleasure rather than coercion and guilt. It is through play that children learn to communicate, and it is a valid route to adult discoveries. It may seem childish, but it is a sure way to keep one's receptivity and zest. Auden's jokes sometimes suggest that he dreaded to be understood; but in 1931 sly pranks were a

tactic of his flying tricksters which made the fascist tendencies of the
airman less offensive and also upset the solemn controls of the
rhetoricians. The first day of the airman's mobilisation against the enemy
was therefore one of relentless teasing. Auden's campaign is a glorious
mixture of Ronald Firbank's camp prancing and the strategic heroics of
Erskine Childers:

> At the pre-arranged zero hour the widow bent into a hoop with
> arthritis gives the signal for attack by unbending on the steps of St
> Philip's. A preliminary bombardment by obscene telephone mes-
> sages for not more than two hours destroys the morale already
> weakened by predictions of defeat made by wireless-controlled
> crows and card-packs. Shock-troops equipped with wire-cutters,
> spanners and stinkbombs, penetrating the houses by infiltration,
> silence all alarm clocks, screw down the bathroom taps, and remove
> plugs and paper from the lavatories.

The Orators closes with six odes in which Auden addresses his friends
and pupils, intimates chosen to remind us that he thinks 'the smaller
group' is 'the right field of force'. It concludes with an ambiguous
'Epilogue' which reads as if it has some imaginative relationship with
Kafka's *Der Prozess* as it was interpreted by Auden. 'Man ... can never
know the whole truth, because as the subject who knows, he has to remain
outside the truth, and the truth is therefore incomplete': so Auden later
wrote. 'From this follows the paradox that K's only guarantee that he is
following the true way is that he fails to get anywhere. If he succeeded in
getting his way, it would be proof that he failed.'

'We are all sex-obsessed today,' Auden complained in 1932, 'because
there isnt any decent group life left.' *The Orators* is like a preparation for
finishing off one's sex-obsessions so that one can turn to love. There was a
chance that the writing of it could free Auden to seek an identity – poetic
certainly, and perhaps personal – that was less limited by his choice of
sexual acts. But as the Epilogue indicates, if he had complete success in
getting his way, it would be proof that he had failed.

CHAPTER 5

'To love; to be loved; to be a teacher; to be a pupil'

Auden never wavered from the knowledge that, unless you love someone, nothing makes any sense. At its worst love can be barbarous, tedious and puerile – 'the concept of life as an arrogant private dream to be shared by two', as Cyril Connolly said – but it is also the emotion that transfigures and redeems. For Auden love was like the 'numinous object' in a Quest which 'has fallen into the hands of the Enemy or is protected from the unworthy by terrifying guardians; none but the predestined hero can find it'. When young he had darted after versions of love, in his poems and emotional affairs; but it was only after concluding *The Orators* in November 1931 that he concentrated his vision, and it was not until June 1933 that his wishes and experience were coincident. Then consummation came: he had a vision of agape, a feeling of unity and serenity that meant everything to him as a man and a poet. Before then he had been casting about in isolation, almost floundering in his doubts about connections between other people. But his sense of love that developed in 1933 (in Mendelson's words) 'makes possible a union of isolated individual perspectives in a coherent work of art, one broader and larger than any single point of view could allow'. His ideas of love in the 1930s were ecumenical. Love was healing: the works of healers were works of love. He rejoiced at the imaginative awe that came in their train. As he later wrote, 'Poetry can do a hundred and one things; delight, sadden, disturb, amuse, instruct – it may express every possible shade of emotion, and describe every conceivable kind of event, but there is only one thing that all poetry must do; it must praise all it can for being and for happening.'

Auden's first cohesive study of love was the book which was published in London in 1936 as *Look, Stranger!* and in New York in 1937 under the

improved title of *On This Island*. Like *The Orators* it begins and ends with
poems headed prologue and epilogue. There are all types of love in the
book: erotic and sublime, the false and true, the redemptive and
destructive; all sorts of lovers too: the mismatched, the sulky, the self-
absorbed couples, the breakers of vows. Though Auden seems to hope
that love can redeem individuals or groups, the structure of the book
implies that the strongest forces in life are destructive or sacrificial. The
prologue written in May 1932 is a woozy invocation of love as a cure for
modern ills; but its 'facile optimism', in Hecht's phrase, is corrected by the
more coherent and persuasive epilogue written in 1936. This lists great
twentieth-century healers, including Nansen, Schweitzer, Freud, Kafka
and Proust, whose works of love are unprotected and foredoomed:

> For the wicked card is dealt, and
> The sinister tall-hatted botanist stoops at the spring
> With his insignificant phial, and looses
> The plague on the ignorant town.

People are gripped by fierce weary old hatreds. Violence, prejudice and
malevolence have mastery:

> Can
> Hate so securely bind? Are They dead here? Yes.
> And the wish to wound has the power. And tomorrow
> Comes. It's a world. It's a way.

But what was Auden's personal situation in this time of love? The five
years to 1936 were the most diffused of his life. His situation was that of a
young intellectual with no private means. His work went forward on
several different lines: the possibilities before him were so segmented that
though he had no 'moneybug' in 1932 he contemplated becoming a
businessman. Like any serious writer, he wanted money because it was his
means to buy the time to write rather than intrinsically valuable to him.
His father had subsidised him at university and during his year abroad, but
after that he had to support himself. 'I am not ambitious about a job, as
long as I have one to live on,' Auden told Roy Harrod in 1928. He needed
opportunities to write and time to maintain those contacts which help to
develop a young author's literary reputation. He envied friends who
enjoyed private incomes, and was exasperated when they neglected their
chances. 'As the one who has to have the job, I am naturally jealous of you

and Christopher who can do as you please,' he told Spender after three years of schoolmastering. 'I dont think you know all the humiliations and exploitation of ones weakness that a job like mine involves, how hard it is to preserve any kind of integrity.'

He was saved from the gnawing sense of starved aptitudes by his success as a poet. He was in his mid-twenties now: his feelings about his childhood were becoming less intense and questions of his own identity were diminishing; in their place he had a developing curiosity about the worlds of other people. 'What I think I should really like is a BBC job connected with education,' he confided in the spring of 1935, but instead he gave up schoolmastering to work for six months making documentary films. He was also finding celebrity as a dramatist trying to reach people on a scale which no slim volume from Faber could challenge. His closest friends were leftist and interested in the new psychological ideas. Faber's dust-jacket of *Look, Stranger!* (written by Eliot) claimed him as 'a leader of a new school of poetry'. It was in this period, too, that he had his earliest experiences as a collaborator, compiling his first anthology and working with other friends on plays and filmscripts. In the early 1930s he was sometimes in love, mainly with adolescent youths; but his private joys were isolated 'While we were kissing,' he noted, 'these years have seen a boom in sorrow.' He was living in a time of economic collapse, political menace and social exhaustion – 'violent faces are exalted, / The feverish prejudiced lives do not care' – yet he believed that it was his duty to praise rather than repine:

> Lucky, this point in time and space
> Is chosen as my working place.

At the end of this period, in 1936, he noted: 'The four necessary human relationships: to love; to be loved; to be a teacher; to be a pupil.' It was this matrix that he had spent the previous years exploring.

His ideas were enriched at this time by a new friendship with Gerald Heard, one of 'the healers and the brilliant talkers' beloved by Auden. Heard's ideas were as marginal and wayward as those of Coué or Lane, which suited Auden, who preferred to put his healers' words to uses of his own devising. Aged forty-two in 1931, Heard was a clergyman's son, 'witty, playful, flattering, talkative as a magpie, well-informed as an encyclopaedia, and, at the same time, life-weary, meditative, deeply concerned', according to Isherwood. For dinner with Joe Ackerley's parents he wore 'a leather jacket with a leopard-skin collar and pointed purple suede shoes, and lectured my astonished father on the problem of the uneconomic banana skin'. He was expansive in his generalisations about philosophy, psychology and history (thus resembling his close friend whom Auden called 'Huxley knowaldous'), but the substance did not impress everyone. 'He looked very like El Greco, and spoke in long, suavely delivered sentences rich in names like Aloysha Karamasov, Epictetus and St Gregory of Nyassa, and in facts about the salinity of blood and seawater, evolution and probably the transmigration of souls,' wrote Guy Davenport, who met him in the USA. 'Only in some high-toned Methodist preachers have I ever heard such beautiful rhetoric wrap itself around absolutely nothing.' Heard, like Auden, spent much time analysing the impulses to buggery and diagnosed in himself an 'inferiority complex'. His *Social Substance of Religion* (1931) attempted to read history in psychological terms rather than through economic forces or the impact of great men. He believed the conflicts between the individual spirit and the state arose from human duality, but did not accept Freud's view that sex was the basis of this conflict: like Auden he cited 'Malinowski, Rivers ... and others' showing 'how human culture/Shapes our separate lives.' Indeed the positivistic rationalism which represented the highest intellectual virtue for Freud seemed vicious to Heard: part of the over-clinical, objective yet inhibited consciousness imposed by the needs of modern capitalism. For Heard the healthier side of human duality was a natural, subjective, unmediated inner knowledge.

Religious symbolism was important to Auden in the early 1930s though he did not count himself a Christian. In October 1932, for example, apparently after looking at Bellini's picture *The Agony in the Garden* depicting the arrest of Jesus and hanging in the National Gallery, he wrote his ominous ballad beginning 'O what is that sound which so thrills the ear'. It is not a Christian poem, and yet it was Christian imagery that excited him to write it. Correspondingly there was a passage in Heard's *Social Substance of Religion* that impressed Auden not by its religious content but by celebrating primitive Christianity's community spirit. 'The Gospel', Heard declared, 'had nothing to do with orthodoxy', but was 'a matter of feeling, or rapturous conviction and direct experience'. He continued,

The Gospel is not salvationist. For this is its secret and power: it abolishes the individual. It is not a cautious, far-sighted calculation of the individual's chances, a contemptible repetition of Noah's saving of himself and leaving the rest to drown. It is the opposite. It is not a private advice of oncoming destruction, and a secret knowledge of how to escape. It is not fear and lonely flight.... It is a communism so profound that economic communism beside it is but a symptom.... Those who were swept by the gospel, were attempting nothing so cold, individual and intellectual, as the saving of their own souls after death. They threw aside personal salvation.... They found real salvation from the lust for self-salvation in complete devotion to the group, to the new, small, intensely beloved community of like believers.

The images in this passage excited Auden. He believed that ideally such a group would number no more than twelve. 'The Middle Class are well aware of the satisfaction of this kind of group from team games,' he wrote in 1934. 'Those who have complained of athletics in schools as a religion were right in their diagnosis.'

Yet Auden's life was often more mundane than these abstractions suggest. After working briefly as a private tutor in London and recuperating from his operation in Birmingham, he began teaching at Larchfield Academy in Dumbartonshire in April 1930. Day Lewis had taught there before him. Auden's subjects were English and French, though he was also involved in games. 'I teach rugger,' he told Spender. 'Every day I rush about in shorts telling people not to funk.' If he chafed under the austere monotony, he could play up school life's absurdities, as he did to Margaret Marshall and his brother John in November 1931:

Materially I am living miserably like a hen, scratching for food. Otherwise I am very very happy here, only anxious lest the school should go bust and compel me to leave. I'm beginning to have the same sort of feelings for Scotland that many Englishmen seem to get for Bulgaria or Greece.

The school is quite wonderful. Upstairs the headmaster, partially blinded by a recent operation, is moping over a gas stove, worried about his wife going gradually mad in a canvas shelter in the garden. The young Reptonian engaged at a moderate salary to take his work is out rock-climbing with a maiden aunt. My other male colleague is bicycling back to his young wife against a head wind. A mistress is having pregnancy phantasies; and I spend most of my time adjusting the flow of water to the boys' urinals with a brass turn-key.

Tonight is Friday night when the chaps come to play Badminton and to talk about big-ends. To-morrow if I'm lucky, Derek my chum will come to sit on my knee. Now I must go and pump up the footballs.

Derek was a local youth for whom he felt a cheerful, transient ardour.

Auden left Larchfield after about fifteen months, and from the autumn of 1932 until the summer of 1935 (and again briefly in 1937) he worked at the Downs School, Colwall, near the boundaries of Herefordshire and Worcestershire in the west Midlands. The Downs was, he told Coghill, 'a posh liberal quaker school financed by chocolate, good kind people dependant [sic] on usury, which muddles them, poor things'. He taught English, arithmetic, French, gymnastics and biology. 'Frightfully busy here telling the boys about the balls of Frogs,' he reported to Rupert Doone. 'Some of them are starting a geological museum in aid of the unemployed. We sing many hymns, and slap our thighs. Those who loiter in the lavatories are not much thought of.' The school impressed even his more fastidious friends. 'Although this is a Quaker school, run by the Cadburys, it is quite "ordinary",' Brian Howard reported during a visit. 'They are all so happy – with their school paper full of jokes and their art school and their sensible clothes.' Auden himself was so proud of 'our school magazine' that he sent a copy to Walter de la Mare after reading *Early One Morning*.

Some pupils were hugely impressed. 'His arrival was like a glorious firework display,' Michael Yates later wrote. 'Completely unconventional, striding about in a large black Flemish hat, waving an umbrella, he entranced us with his eccentricity, tireless energy and sense of fun. We called him Uncle Wiz.' Yates was thirteen when Auden arrived at the Downs School, and in 1933 moved to his public school, Bryanston in Dorset; but Auden maintained contact, travelling abroad with Yates and others in 1934 and 1936. Auden indeed made overtures in 1934 to join the teaching staff at Bryanston, and befriended several of Yates's fellow pupils. In April 1935, 'full of doubts', he accepted a job at Bryanston, only for the offer to be withdrawn, ostensibly because a letter that he had sent to a schoolfriend of Yates, containing a phrase of facetious sacrilege, was intercepted by its headmaster.

Poetry and schoolmastering were not Auden's only work. He experimented as a prose-writer and earned fees as a contributor to various 'highbrow' periodicals. Eliot at the *Criterion* was the first editor with whom he had contact (initially as the publisher, at Faber, of his books). 'This fellow is about the best poet I have discovered in several years,' Eliot declared. He published *Paid on Both Sides* in the *Criterion* of January 1930, and afterwards sent Auden for review George Binney Dibblee's *Instinct and Intuition: A Study in Mental Duality*, which developed the Rivers –Head theories of epicritic and protopathic sensibility. Auden steadily extended his range of contacts. In November 1930 he approached Max Plowman, a disciple of Homer Lane who was associated with Middleton Murry on *Adelphi*. Plowman was a former friend and patient of Rivers, a pacifist who lived in an agragrian community. His writings presented it 'almost as a duty to enjoy oneself', rather as Auden had been convinced by Layard in Berlin that happiness was the primary human duty. Auden wrote seeking an interview to discuss Lane: 'Through a friend of mine who was a patient of his, he has so profoundly influenced my life that I am anxious to meet anyone' who knew him. Following this overture some short Auden poems were published in *Adelphi* in 1931. These were the first poems by him to be published in a nationally known magazine; so it was through Lane's connections that Auden began his literary networking. Sir Richard Rees, who succeeded Murry as editor of *Adelphi*, ranked Auden in 1932 as one of the 'hopeful young men', albeit 'rather pettifogging in their art', who deserved 'judicious encouragement'; but Plowman, who was a poet himself and a devotee of Blake, found Auden 'a misery to read'. It was probably Auden's choice, and a sign of his self-confidence in such matters, that none of his work was published by them after 1931. As Day Lewis told Rees, their circle found *Adelphi*'s 'affectation of proletarianism and heartiness as offensive ... as the bourgeois affectations of "good taste" which you rightly despise in our more slug-like intellectuals'.

A more successful contact was Janet Adam Smith, deputy editor of the British Broadcasting Corporation's magazine the *Listener*. 'Early in 1932 I read the three poems by Auden in *New Signatures* ... and bought his *Poems*, published by Faber in 1930 in their enterprising pre-Penguin

paperback series of poets at half-a-crown,' she recalled. 'The energy of
these poems, their assurance and irreverence, were immensely exhilarating: Auden's was a voice we had to have in the paper – or voices, for what
was most exhilarating of all was the range of forms and styles.' Shortly
afterwards she met him at a dinner party held by Spender and his sister (it
was a high-spirited affair, and Auden was sent out of the room to eat his
pudding), and asked him for a poem to publish in the *Listener*'s literary
supplement. He sent 'O what is that sound', but Adam Smith was away
when it arrived and aghast to find on her return that it had been rejected in
her absence. Despite the doubts of her superiors, in July 1933 she
published 'The Witnesses'. It was so 'puzzling' to the BBC's Director
General, Lord Reith, that Adam Smith had to seek an endorsement of
Auden from Eliot, whose report 'silenced the critics within the BBC' for a
few years. Joe Ackerley, who became the *Listener*'s first literary editor in
1935, continued to use Auden as a poet and reviewer. The poems
(including Auden's 'Look Stranger' and 'Fish in the Ruffled Lakes') that
Ackerley published in his literary pages were condemned in 1936 by
H. A. L. Fisher, a BBC governor and former Minister of Education, as
'much too precious; angular and contorted'; but Ackerley was loyal to
Auden, who felt a lifelong 'debt' to him.

As a prose-writer Auden was initially diffident and uneven. Thus in the
autumn of 1930 he drafted an article on puritanism for the *Criterion*, but
decided to 'chuck it', he told his brother in November. 'I can't say things
that way. Context and contact are everything. Or else joking verse.' He
sometimes failed to hold together his themes, and it was not until the end
of the decade that he found a consistent tone. Janet Adam Smith believed
that his most characteristic and exciting reviews were those published
anonymously in which any weaknesses could be less easily identified with
him personally. An example given by Adam Smith was a provocative piece
of 1934 on poetic drama beginning, 'This book is an exhibition of
perpetual motion models. Here they all are, labelled Phillips, Davidson,
Yeats, some on the largest scale, some on the tiniest, some ingenious in
design, some beautifully made, all suffering from only one defect – they
won't go.' But though he could not easily satisfy himself as an essayist,
from 1932 the flow of his reviews was continuous. Henceforth he
accumulated ideas from both his reviewing and poetry-writing which
elucidated one another. Thus for *Scrutiny* in December 1933 he reviewed

Hector Bolitho's 'trashily written and exceedingly readable biography' of Lord Melchett, the founder of Imperial Chemical Industries, a proto-fascist whose life presented 'a terrible parable of human folly'. Melchett reappears in *The Dog Beneath the Skin* as the financier Grabstein, for whom poets are 'moral degenerates or Bolsheviks, or both', and Imperial Chemicals is bequeathed sewage in a poem of 1936.

Another important example occurred in 1934 when Auden was commissioned to write a few paragraphs on Basil Liddell Hart's biography of Lawrence of Arabia for the magazine *Now and Then*, the house-journal or 'glorified circular' issued by Liddell Hart's publisher, Jonathan Cape. The ideas that Auden gleaned from this book were reworked by him in April into the sonnet 'Who's Who':

A shilling life will give you all the facts:
How Father beat him, how he ran away,
What were the struggles of his youth, what acts
Made him the greatest figure of his day:
Of how he fought fished hunted, worked all night,
Though giddy, climbed new mountains; named a sea:
Some of the last researchers even write
Love made him weep his pints like you and me.

With all his honours on, he sighed for one
Who, say astonished critics, lived at home;
Did little jobs about the house with skill
And nothing else; could whistle; would sit still
Or potter round the garden; answered some
Of his long marvellous letters but kept none.

Lawrence as both intellectual and man of action epitomised this duality; but there is far more to 'Who's Who' than a poetic version of Liddell Hart's biography. The two friends have their counterparts in *Sodome et Gomorrhe*, read by Auden when he was staying in Berlin with Isherwood in 1929. Proust describes a man living in the country who sometimes walks at night to 'cross-roads where, although not a word has been said', he meets a boyhood friend. 'They begin again the pastimes of long ago, on the grass, in the night, neither uttering a word,' Proust says.

During the week, they meet in their respective houses ... without any allusion to what has occurred between them, exactly as though they had done nothing and were not to anything again, save, in their relations, a trace of coldness, of irony, of irritability ... at times of hatred. Then the neighbour sets out on a strenuous expedition on horseback, and, on a mule, climbs mountain peaks, sleeps in the snow; his friend, who identifies his own vice with a weakness of temperament, the cabined and timid life, realises that vice can no longer exist in his friend now emancipated, so many thousands of feet above sea-level. And, sure enough, the other takes a wife.

Yet when the married explorer returns, he resumes his cross-road meetings with the country recluse. Perhaps the two boyhood friends reminded Auden of himself and Isherwood, who throughout the 1930s went to bed together 'whenever an opportunity offered itself' and whose slightly embarrassed mutual pleasuring was 'rooted in schoolboy memories', according to Isherwood. This Proustian episode certainly mattered to Auden, for in 1940 he wrote again of the cross-roads:

> Two friends who met here and embraced are gone,
> Each to his own mistake; one flashes on
> To fame and ruin in a rowdy lie,
> A village torpor holds the other one,
> Some local wrong where it takes time to die:
> The empty junction glitters in the sun.

Heard as well as Proust influenced 'Who's Who'. There is a chart in *Social Substance of Religion* showing the personality types or 'psychological ramifications which have gone on since the rise of history'. This is an extract:

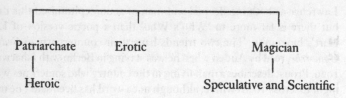

In Auden's poem the explorer is a hero, but also a son of patriarchy: his father's beatings are one of the great facts of his life. His explorations may have romantic power, but they constitute one of those lives (in Heard's phraseology) of 'individual action' or 'heroic caprice' which by the 1930s were no longer enough to 'explain why history has been what it has been'. For all the man of action's seeming invincibility, his life is unsatisfied, for his energy is discharged in action and his discoveries are at an end. He sighs for his friend, the descendant not of patriarchs but of trickster-like magicians whose life has its own inexpugnable speculative richness: sitting still at home he suggests the illumination of Psalm 46 which, after images of swelling mountains and roaring waters, ends with the injunction, 'Be still, and know that I am God.' This sonnet shows a poetic characteristic that was strengthened as Auden fulfilled the repetitive and humdrum duties of a schoolmaster. He celebrated household routine or garden pottering as if they had the mystery and symbolic beauty of rituals. He took pleasure in the most ordinary daily habits, and vested the dependable in parabolic significance – often signifying gratitude.

Auden's attractions for literary journalists were not entirely personal to himself. When the middlebrow *News Chronicle* published extracts from his poetry and dramatic writings a few years later, they boosted him as a representative young author 'presenting the future'. It was a certain sequel to his friendships and contacts with literary editors that he became known as a moving spirit in a new coterie. Auden himself saw this as a perversion of group life. 'The problem is particularly bad in a city like London, which is so large, that the only group you can find, is living with your own kind,' he wrote to John Pudney in 1932. 'This is disastrous. You end up by eating each other. The whole value of a group is its constituents are as diverse as possible, with little consciously in common. Plurality is unity.' Perhaps the most unpalatable form of metropolitan cannibalism was the literary vendetta. Auden was always generous as a reviewer, and regretted the way that critics like Wyndham Lewis 'even when he is attacking fundamental abuses attacks them through certain writers which the majority of people have never read: too often what promises to be really important degenerates into a private squabble between rival literary pushes'.

The poet Michael Roberts's review of *From Feathers to Iron* by Day Lewis – twenty-nine poems published in 1931 concluding with an epilogue entitled 'Letter to W. H. Auden' – was crucial in defining the idea of a young, propagandist school of poetry. Roberts's anthology *New Signatures* (published in February 1932) consolidated this idea. Another anthology by Roberts, *New Country* published in 1933, focused more attention on what Bonamy Dobree called 'the school of which W. H.

Auden is leader, round whom are grouped in particular Stephen Spender and Cecil Day Lewis'. Auden was the leader in *New Country*. This chorus from Rex Warner's 'The Dam' is Audenesque like much else in the anthology:

> Where now is the designer? Has he died?
> When will work start again on the dam, in the mine?
> Will rivers flow backward? Will it be in our time?
> What has happened to Colonel Humphries? Will he come?
> Or has he been waylaid
> somewhere above the falls, below the pool,
> by ghosts, by the financier or by a maid,
> by the clergyman, the professor from the school,
> stuff of our nightmare. Will the Colonel come?

Auden was in the vanguard of a new force, so that when the publisher Rupert Hart-Davis arranged the first English edition of Robert Frost's poetry, 'in the hopes of making it more saleable', he commissioned Auden and Day Lewis as well as Edwin Muir and an American to write introductions. 'I don't know whether Frost ever saw Auden but he certainly didn't like him,' Hart-Davis judged.

Roberts in the introduction to *New Signatures* summarised what unified his chosen authors: they saw life as a set of psychological problems, 'aspects of an emotional discord which can be resolved neither by reasoning nor by action, but only by a new harmonisation such as that which may be brought about by a work of art'. Cyril Connolly had another name for this coterie – the Homintern – and a belittling description of them, 'psychological revolutionaries, people who adopt left-wing political formulas because they hate their fathers or were unhappy at their public schools or insulted at the Customs, or lectured about sex'. (Auden and Isherwood detested 'frontier officials ... in whom private terrors breed a love of insult and interference'). Connolly's remark was malicious, but it is true that the attitudes and techniques of the set were disparate. As Samuel Hynes noted, the only mood common to all the poets in *New Signatures* is apprehensiveness. If apprehension was the keynote, their subordinate emotions were a belief in team-playing and distrust of over-cerebralisation. Politically they were schoolboys. A few months after the publication of *New Signatures* a schoolmaster sent Auden a poem by one of his pupils, John Cornford. 'The only useful criticism is of the personal kind – if I could say "Get into the first XV" or "Shoot your French-master with a water pistol", I might really be of use – but as I can't you must forgive me if anything I say sounds too like a governess,' Auden replied to Cornford in May 1932. 'If it's a choice between reading and doing something else, do something else and remember that everything your housemaster says about the team spirit ... is absolutely right but that it is the tone of his voice which makes it such a lie.'

John Bayley offers a positive interpretation of this: Auden as 'a new type of aesthete, who sees art not as a religion, but as a game, to be played with as skilful and individual a touch as possible'. When Auden visited Edward Upward at Scarborough in 1931, 'he put on a false red beard just before getting out of the carriage', but his clowning was more than a joke. 'The clown', he once wrote, 'doubles his meaning.' Of all the poets consulted by Geoffrey Grigson in 1932 before starting *New Verse* (the ferociously written and critically invaluable magazine of the Auden generation in the years to 1939), Auden's reply was the most casual yet original: 'Why do you want to start a poetry review Is it as important as all that? I'm glad you like poetry but can't we take it a little more lightly. If you do start one and want my stuff, of course you can have it. I hope you'll keep it gay.' This was not flippancy, but Auden saw gaiety as the way to develop curiosity and a sense of marvels. As he wrote with John Garrett in the introduction to an anthology for schools in 1935,

> One of the motives behind poetry is curiosity ... and ... curiosity is the only human passion that can be indulged in for twenty-four hours a day without satiety.... Poetry is not concerned with telling people what to do, but with extending our knowledge of good and evil, perhaps making the necessity for action more urgent and its nature more clear, but only leading us to the point where it is possible for us to make a rational and moral choice.

By contrast Day Lewis was more earnest. 'I am for anything that will help to throw open the park to the public: it makes one despair to think that one is preserved for an aesthetic aristocracy,' he told Grigson. 'They would find plenty in Spender's work and mine and some of Auden's which had meaning for them.... our writing is half propaganda: we can't help it: nobody else seems to be doing anything about "this England of ours where nobody is well". And its so silly to be spilling propaganda only into the mouths of a few incurable neurasthenics.'

Auden considered Geoffrey Hoyland, headmaster of the Downs School, to be 'quite a great man' worth the dedication of one of his finest poems of the early 1930s, 'Out on the lawn I lie in bed'. Yet with his need of emotionally extremist experiences, he wrote as if his headmasters were prototypes for the character of The Leader in his play with Isherwood, *On the Frontier*. 'A private school is an absolute dictatorship where the assistant staff play, as it were, Goering Roehm Goebbels Himmler to a headmaster Hitler. There are the same intrigues for favour, the same gossip campaigns, and from time to time the same purges.' Even fifteen years later a speech in which Stalin's henchman Andrei Zhdanov purged three Russian poets seemed to Auden 'just like one's old housemaster'. Auden was exasperated by complacent definitions of education as the making of useful citizens. 'A state has to train its youth not only to be its good citizens, but ... to destroy its present existence,' he wrote in 1934. 'Educationalists must always be revolutionaries.' The police and politicians, he had written earlier, define 'a useful citizen' as 'a person who won't give you any trouble'. Education for the poor 'is a dope to allay irritation'. The training of a boy under the prevailing system concerned the perpetuation of class privileges:

> If he is poor ... better teach him enough to read the *News of the World* ... If he's rich, your sort, then segregate him with the other young of your sort, let him year by year through his school-days feel all the excitement of a social climber, and make him so afraid of the opinions of your sort, that you may be sure he'll never do anything silly, like forgetting his class. Public school men will always lend each other money.

Auden found it 'topsy-turvy' that although pupils at teaching-training colleges were taught the rudiments of child psychology, 'they ... are given no sort of insight whatever into themselves, which, in a profession where adults are expected ... to profess official opinions on every subject of importance, to lead the private life of a clergyman, where a mask is essential, sets up a strain which only the long holidays ... safeguard from developing into a nervous breakdown'. The febrile atmosphere affected him. 'The tenth week of term, and the enormous hysteria of school life begins to be a little offensive,' he wrote from Larchfield to his brother John. 'Am under a bit of a cloud at the moment as I swore at a boy and a parent overheard.' Auden believed that the only way to survive in a boys' boarding school was by playing the part of a buffoon critic or pedagogic trickster. He found 'occasional exquisite moments of satisfaction' in trying to reach the small minority of boys who were not already sealed up tight in a vacuum of inherited opinions. 'A teacher soon discovers that there are only a few pupils whom he can help, many for whom he can do nothing except teach a few examination tricks, and a few to whom he can do nothing but harm,' he wrote in 1939. 'The children who interested me were either the backward, i.e. those who had not yet discovered their real nature, the bright with similar interests to my own, or those who, like myself at their age, were school-hating anarchists.' To this last precious group he 'tried, while encouraging their rebellion, to teach a technique of camouflage'. His Downs pupil Michael Yates has described his technique. 'His classes were in turn traditional, original or a plain riot of fun,' Yates wrote in the school magazine the *Badger*, which Auden himself initiated. 'The requirements of Common Entrance were replaced by a talk on astronomy and the stars. A surfeit of essays gave way to elaborate impromptu plays. To the sixth form he explained the meaning of sex. And he made us read aloud, endlessly, banishing the monotony of the schoolboy's voice. This was not just play.' Another pupil, Gurney Thomas, recalled Auden's verbal and psychological games:

> He was fascinated by the way small boys' minds work and on one occasion decided that we should imagine ourselves on a sledge being chased by hungry wolves in Russia. The wolves were gaining on us and we took votes to decide which boy should be thrown out to delay their attack on the sledge as a whole. This was repeated until all but one of the class – the most popular boy – had been disposed of. We felt rather sheepish at first, not wanting to be seen to throw out the least popular boy, but Auden was clearly thrilled to see what we thought of each other .. he would have enjoyed a similar vote on the staff even more.

Heard's speculations about group feelings were incorporated (sometimes awkwardly) into Auden's poetic ideas. In a poem of February 1932 (which in its longer, suppressed version was dedicated to Heard) Auden celebrated the group life of a school community as a centre of 'love, satisfaction, force, delight'. It was to explore these possibilities that in March 1932 Auden asked Heard to arrange a visit to Dartington Hall in Devon, where Dorothy and Leonard Elmhirst had in 1925 started a community engaged in agriculture, forestry, woodworking and other crafts together with a progressive school. He liked Mrs Elmhirst, writing to her, 'I shall not easily forget either Dartington or your beautiful hospitality.' Yet he had reservations. 'I've just been down to what seems to me the most remarkable thing in England; An estate in Devonshire run on real community lines,' he reported to John Auden. 'It smells quite genuine; and seems the right English variant on Russia. The snag is the school. Co-ed and all that, a little factory for neuters.' The sillier part of this reaction was misogynistic: he was a man who liked boys and disliked the contamination of girls in his schools. Yet he had also identified an important truth about many of those with the keenest interest in child psychology. 'An excessive interest in child welfare, like an obsession about cruelty to animals, is not a symptom of a healthy society; a preoccupation of those with small independent incomes, it is often a propitiation of the feelings of guilt at not attacking the fundamental abuses of a society, in which an unsatisfactory educational system is one of many results, not a cause.' His father was one of the country's great school medical officers, whose working life was a practical, compassionate and unmannered effort to improve the conditions of childhood. By contrast the emotional and educational nurturing of children in communities in pretty places like Devon or the Cotswolds was one of the signs of what Wystan Auden in a poem of 1933 described as 'the high thin rare continuous worship / of the self-absorbed'.

Censors and busybodies had only to proclaim that their restrictions were intended to protect children, and all opposition to them was disarmed, although the supreme intention was usually to regulate adult lives. Auden despised this child-centred suburbanism in smocks. 'Folk-dancer, remembering a once-sore behind, thinks, "Ah, had the masters loved me, I should have expanded like a flower,"' Auden wrote in 1932 in a review in the second issue of the Leavisite quarterly *Scrutiny*. His acerbity owed something to Leavis himself (for at this stage Auden's prose style often reflected that of his commissioning editors), and he continued his piece on *The Yearbook of Education* and W. N. Marcy's *Reminiscences of a*

Public Schoolboy in terms that were partly attuned to *Scrutiny*'s Lawrentian loathing of Benthamite enlightenment, partly a reflection of his own preference for vigorous sporting youths over febrile hothoused prodigies and perhaps had a trace of his own mild youthful masochism.

> There are some, who, though comfortably off, with no right to fear, have nightmares ... off they go to live with the children, and splendid they are at it too. The children brighten up no end – in their heads. Stupidity which is a natural defence against living beyond one's means collapses under the intense fire of their kindness. Girls of eleven paint like Picasso, boys of sixteen write pastiches of Joyce. Every child responds to the love smarm for a bit. But emotionally it withers. Before a man wants to understand, he wants to command or obey instinctively, to live with others in a relation of power; but all power is anathema to the liberal. He hasn't any. He can only bully the spirit.

Just as Auden deprecated over-protected precocity in children, so he deplored too much fuss over childhood trauma and over-indulgent tenderness about early anxieties.

Auden's sense of history – initially as a young poet studying the traditions of the Great Masters, then as an anthologist and after 1940 as a Christian – was progressive. He thought of the future as (potentially and actually) more significant than the past, and believed that a lone, implacable sequence of private tests and choices was more enriching to human character than cults of personal development. He shuddered at the 'air of injured rightness ... from the cultured smug minority' who thought otherwise. Like his father he diverged from Freudians in his attitude to early experience. He believed psychoanalysts were too susceptible to the quantitative methods of nineteenth-century science. As he wrote later to Ernest Jones, 'I find the influence of this attitude in Freud's tendency – I speak as a fool – to conclude that, if you have a series of related, similar or analogous experiences, the first in time must necessarily be more significant than the second and so on.' The duality that counted for Auden, as he wrote in 1930, was between 'the whole self at different stages of development e.g. a man before and after a religious conversion'. For Auden personally there were several such stages of development in the 1930s: his life underwent the transfiguration of love in 1933; he balanced this in 1936 with the realisation that, as he later wrote, 'we are not, any of us, very nice'; and in 1939 he met Chester Kallman and returned to Christianity.

The transfiguration of love occurred as a spiritual vision at the Downs School:

One fine summer night in June 1933 I was sitting on a lawn after dinner with three colleagues, two women and one man. We liked each other well enough but we were certainly not intimate friends, nor had any one of us a sexual interest in another. Incidentally, we had not drunk any alcohol. We were talking casually about everyday matters when, quite suddenly and unexpectedly, something happened. I felt myself invaded by a power which, though I consented to it, was irresistible and certainly not mine. For the first time in my life I knew exactly because, thanks to the power, I was doing it – what it means to love one's neighbor as oneself. I was also certain, though the conversation continued to be perfectly ordinary, that my three colleagues were having the same experience. (In the case of one of them, I was able later to confirm this.) My personal feelings towards them were unchanged – they were still colleagues, not intimate friends – but I felt their existence as themselves to be of infinite value and rejoiced in it. I recalled with shame the many occasions on which I had been spiteful, snobbish, selfish, but the immediate joy was greater than the shame, for I knew that, so long as I was possessed by this spirit, it would be literally impossible for me deliberately to injure another human being. I also knew that the power would, of course, be withdrawn sooner or later and that, when it did, my greeds and self-regard would return. The experience lasted at its full intensity for about two hours when we said goodnight to each other and went to bed. When I awoke the next morning, it was still present, though weaker, and it did not vanish completely for two days or so. The memory of the experience has not prevented me from making use of others, grossly and often, but it has made it much more difficult for me to deceive myself about what I was up to when I do. And among the various factors which several years later brought me back to the Christian faith in which I had been brought up, the memory of this experience and asking myself what it could mean was one of the most crucial, though, at the time it occurred, I thought I had done with Christianity for good.

This was the moment when Auden had the first glimpse of the numinous object of his quest. As a youth he had felt himself denied a moment of clarity, and had to work as a poet with no personal experience of pure love expanding into eternity. He had resolved to make himself a great poet without the benefit of visionary revelation such as had transformed Wordsworth's life; but he dreaded to be, as he wrote in 1935, one of those 'many writers of excellent sensibility whose work is spoilt by a bogus vision which deprives it of the entertainment value which it would otherwise have had'. His poetic vision was incomplete. As an American reviewer of his early poems noted, 'he knows what is hateful and disgusting more clearly than he knows what he wants to create in their place'. But on the Downs lawn in 1933 he found the substitutes for hate and disgust. He finally experienced those emotions of oceanic unity which he had long believed were the prerequisite of the highest poetic achievement.

His feelings that evening are described in his poem of June 1933 beginning 'Out on the lawn I lie in bed': Despite the usual indifference of things, and all the flattening, pauperising pressures of time, this was one moment in a lifetime when 'the vision seriously intends to stay'. It was a creative transformation which he attributed to others: Pascal, for example, in a poem of 1939 which has some phrases derived from Hardy's great poem about fate and will, 'The Convergence of the Twain':

> at last, one Autumn, all was ready:
> And in the night the Unexpected came.

> The empty was transformed into possession,
> The cold burst into flames; creation was on fire
> And his weak moment blazing like a bush,
> A symptom of the order and the praise:
> And he had place like Abraham and Jacob,
> And was incapable of evil like a star,
> For isolation had been utterly consumed,
> And everything that could exist was holy.

> All that was really willed would be accomplished:
> The crooked custom take its final turning
> Into the truth it always meant to reach.

. . .

Then it was over. By the morning he was cool,
His faculties for sin restored completely,
And eight years to himself.

A few weeks later Auden reviewed for the *Criterion* Violet Clifton's *The Book of Talbot*, a memoir of the Roman Catholic landowner and Arctic explorer Talbot Clifton. 'It is the life of a husband written by a wife who loved him; a man of old family whom fortune enables to realize every phantasy in action, by a woman who, I should imagine, read little but Homer, Dante and Shakespeare.' It was, he wrote in the rapture of his own vision, 'a great book' which had 'that sense of glory which it is the privilege of great art to give'. Violet Clifton's passionate concentration on her man was to Auden resounding evidence 'that the first criterion of success in any human activity, the necessary preliminary, whether to scientific discovery or artistic vision, is intensity of attention or, less pompously, love'. For Auden love had now become the power that gave coherence and completeness to everything.

Love has allowed Lady [sic] Clifton to constellate round Talbot the whole of her experience and to make it significant. One cannot conceive of her needing to write another line; one feels that she has put down everything. One is quite incurious to know whether Talbot was in actual life as magnificent a figure as he is in his book. Whatever his origins he is completely convincing. There is no trace of day-dreaming.

As an Oxford undergraduate, Auden had told Spender 'the subject of a poem is a peg to hang the poetry on', but Auden in the summer of 1933 reversed his opinion that the verbal patterns of poetry mattered more than subject-matter. In Auden's own words, Violet Clifton's passion for her subject provided 'her remarkable technical skill at combining the words of Talbot's diary and her own comments into a consistent texture of narrative'; it was 'possible for her to say things which in isolation look silly' because her love held together in wonderful unity what would otherwise be fragmented and miserable. Mendelson points to the importance of this change in Auden's poetic ideas: the Clifton review 'argues that technical skill results from love of subject: a radically anti-modernist position that Auden would continue to hold, in a less exalted way, throughout the 1930s'. He was now denying 'the formal autonomy of art' and moving towards restoring 'poetry to a didactic relationship with its audience'. It was the beginning of his estrangement from mainstreams of twentieth-century thought.

Auden's discoveries about love were taking place in the context of school life. His interests were juvenile. 'It's such a pity Wystan never grows up,' friends said at this time: Edmund Wilson wrote in 1937 that the poet of *Look, Stranger!*, for all his gifts, 'seems to have been arrested at the mentality of an adolescent schoolboy'. As if trying to recover the opportunities for affairs which he had missed as a schoolboy, Auden's love objects tended to be adolescent. Crucially in 1933 he fell in love with someone more than ten years younger than himself. The poetic result was a series of songs and sonnets which (now he was less screened and secluded from the feelings about which he wrote) were the strongest expressions of love yet written by him. These lyrics, which were sometimes rapturous in their happiness, transcend any occasion or individual: they evoke emotions that readers can recognise from their own experience. Yet they never tell of the simple, unconditional triumph of love.

Auden's 'Song' of February 1936 ('Let the florid music praise') seemed to the adolescent Philip Larkin 'really beautiful – Auden at his greatest and inimitablest. When I read stuff like this I tend to fold up and die.' Yet though it celebrates the lover's beauty as a proud, conquering imperial force, it warns of the revenges of the unloved. Another poem (called 'A Bride in the 30s' to confuse its objects) was composed after a holiday tour of Germany and central Europe which Auden took in August 1934 with Michael Yates and Peter Roger, two former Downs pupils. Love (he says in this poem) brings that heightened sensibility which he had first analysed after that night in 1929 when Gerhart Meyer left him:

> Easy for him to find in your face
> A pool of silence or a tower of grace.
>
>   . . .
>
> Simple to excite in the air from a glance
> Horses, fountains, a side-drum, a trombone,
>   The cosmic dance.

This sensibility increases awareness of political horrors:

> Ten desperate million marching by,

> Five feet, six feet, seven feet high,
> Hitler and Mussolini in their wooing poses.

Sexual relations are celebrated at the start of this poem – 'Lucky his bed' – but the great test is purity of commitment rather than sex. The dangers or sins of consummation had been a theme in Auden's poetry since his own adolescence; more important than sex was the love which taught 'the language of learning and the language of love'. (This was the beginning of his distinction between love and desire which years later in Austria led him to write: 'Oncers do no damage: / only those who could love / can really corrupt.')

As shown by his reaction to Violet Clifton's memoir and by the title of 'A Bride in the 30s', Auden was emotive about marriage. Though his 1936 poem 'As it is, plenty' is ironic about a complacent family man living in empty respectability, he esteemed and even overrated marital status. His own marriage in June 1935 to Erika Mann, though undertaken to provide her with a British passport and an escape from Nazi persecution, was not for him a marriage of convenience empty of meaning. He dedicated to her his next book – the study of love, *Look, Stranger!* – and years later teased his brother John and his nieces Anita and Rita that he was the only one of the Audens not to have got divorced. He was prone to advise other people on their marriages, for example warning Patrick White's cousin Peggy Withycombe that his old Gresham friend Tom Garland 'was perhaps one of those men who was not *meant* to be married': advice which she unfortunately ignored. Erika Mann (who was then running a peregrinatory anti-Nazi cabaret) had first asked Isherwood to marry her. Isherwood however had a 'rooted horror of marriage. To him, it was the sacrament of The Others; the supreme affirmation of their dictatorship.' To Auden, by contrast, marriage (heterosexual or not) remained an ideal. Though he was sniffy when Spender married in 1936 ('rather a dreary affair & no champagne', he told Isherwood's friend Olive Mangeot), he liked arranging marriages of convenience. Erika Mann's cabaret friend Therese Giehse also needed a British passport, and Auden felt one of his friends should marry her. 'What are buggers for?' he asked. His schoolmaster friend John Garrett was offended at the suggestion – 'Wystan wanted me to marry some chorus girl,' he fumed – but John Simpson consented. Simpson worked as a male nurse to a mental defective in Birmingham, and was part of the literary set there centred around Professor and Mrs E. R.

Dodds whom Auden had befriended. (Simpson wrote novels under the pseudonym of John Hampson. His novel *Family Curse* (1936), depicting 'the pomposity, the greed and the narrowness of the Birmingham bourgeoisie', in which, according to Cyril Connolly, one of the most successful characters was 'Johnny, who was queer, and whose queerness was well described', was banned by one Birmingham library, rousing Auden to protest at the 'unjustifiable presumption' of censors acting 'through ignorance or bigotry'.)

Literary collaboration was valued by Auden as a sort of marriage. 'Between two collaborators, whatever their sex, age or appearance, there is always an erotic bonds [sic],' he wrote in 1964. 'Queers to whom normal marriage and parenthood are forbidden, are fools if they do not deliberately look for tasks which require collaboration, and the right person with whom to collaborate – again, the sex does not matter. In my own case, collaboration has brought me greater erotic joy – as distinct from sexual pleasure – than any sexual relations I have had.' His earliest extended collaboration had been with Isherwood in 1929 on the play which became *The Enemies of a Bishop*. They resumed their collaboration to write three plays beginning with *The Dog Beneath the Skin*, which was published in May 1935. He hoped for great things from the collaboration of 'a realist writer like Christopher and a parabolic writer like myself'. Auden in 1934 quoted Gide: 'A friend is someone with whom one does something discreditable.' A decade later he cited Nietzsche: 'Maturity – to recover the seriousness one had as a child at play.' This was the spirit in which Auden and Isherwood collaborated: 'a pair of scamps' according to the landlady of a boarding house where they once stayed. Their high jinks could turn into effrontery. When they accompanied Spender and Plomer to the cinema in 1932, they disrupted the showing with their tittering at the love-making between Greta Garbo playing Mata Hari and the epicene Ramon Novarro as a Russian spy. The woman in front of them turned round to hiss, 'Can't you stop sniggering for five minutes?', which seemed even more hilarious to them.

During 1934 Auden worked with John Garrett on a remarkable poetry anthology for schools which was published as *The Poet's Tongue* in 1935. Garrett was a former Oxford pupil of Coghill's who at the age of thirty-three, in 1935, became headmaster of the new Raynes Park County School in the southern suburbs of London. Garrett was a stylish, flamboyant, discerning man: Rex Warner and the painter Claude Rogers taught at his school, which was also favoured by Day Lewis and Basil Wright. Visitors to the school included Eliot, John Lehmann, Spender, MacNeice, Coghill, Rowse, Sybil Thorndike, Michael Redgrave, David Cecil, Doone and Medley. Auden wrote a 'School Song' for Garrett, and a master produced a less respectful rhyme:

> Have you heard of the wonderful school
> They've built on the Kingston By-pass?
> They say it's no place for a fool,
> But it helps if you've got a nice arse.

The Poet's Tongue was very much a reflection of Raynes Park County School. The reference in its preface to 'the unhappy face' of a commuter 'in the suburban train' points to the connection of the school and the anthology to one of the great twentieth-century misfortunes, the killing of local cultures, whether the extermination of Amazonian communities, the tawdry tourism and bland internationalism that engulfed Mediterranean islands like Ischia or the submergence of the distinct accent, phraseology and oral traditions of early-twentieth-century Hertfordshire or Surrey into the homogeneity of Estuary English. This was exemplified by Garrett and his pupils, the children of socially disconnected, educationally aspirant lower-middle-class people. Garrett himself was a barber's son from Trowbridge in Wiltshire ('over the town hung the smell of brewing hops') who reinvented his speech into a loud, plummy voice, and offered the job of art master to Claude Rogers with the remark, 'You were the only candidate with a halfway decent accent.' He was snobbish in other ways – 'you all live in such horrid little houses,' he told his pupils.

Auden himself, comparing George Orwell's encounters with the English poor in the 1930s 'with those of his great predecessor Henry Mayhew' in the 1850s, was 'struck, and saddened, by the decline in their powers of verbal expression'. He suspected that the inarticulacy of Orwell's paupers, 'compared with the Dickensian exuberance of Mayhew's interviewees', was attributable to 'universal elementary education, which has destroyed their instinctive native speech, but not trained them to do more than read the cheaper newspapers'. In these circumstances the emphasis in *The Poet's Tongue* on the spoken word takes on special meaning. The first half of the anthology is crammed full of folksongs, nursery rhymes, sea shanties, ballads, carols, doggerel from broadsheets, drinking songs, choral verses, narrative poetry, madrigals and so forth; it uses dialect, and plays with accents, and honours the demotic past in a way which led David Jones to call *The Poet's Tongue* 'one of the best anthologies of English stuff I know of'. Like Robert Bridges in *Spirit of Man* and other anthologists, Auden and Garrett printed each poem without its author's name. They also enhanced the catholicity of their selection by printing each item in alphabetical order of their first lines which produced some marvellous juxtapositions. But the real greatness of the anthology (and the key to its extraordinary suggestiveness in the 1930s) is in its unsentimental, hard-headed celebration of the power of the spoken word for semi-literate people and its tribute to the local cultures whose extermination was signalled by the existence of Raynes Park County School, built on a by-pass between a fish- and meat-paste factory and a second-hand car emporium.

Some of this anti-modernist spirit informed Auden's collaborative work in the theatre. His chief interest as a dramatist was in disseminating the pleasure of poetry, but there was a revulsion from the more pretentious, rootless side of modern culture, of which Raynes Park could serve as a symbol. Reviewing a study of *Modern Poetic Drama* for Janet Adam Smith in 1934, Auden was declamatory. Drama was 'so essentially a social art' that all poets should be dissatisfied with the three kinds of modern English poetic drama: 'the romantic sham-Tudor which has occasionally succeeded for a short time on the strength of the spectacle; the cosmic-philosophical which theatrically has always been a complete flop; and the high-brow chamber-music drama, artistically much the best, but a somewhat etiolated blossom'. He wanted popular dramatic forms like 'the variety-show, the pantomime, the musical comedy ... the thriller' to influence new poetic drama. 'All characters who speak verse are as flat as playing-cards,' he wrote. 'Poetic drama should start with the stock musical comedy characters – the rich uncle, the vamp, the mother-in-law, the sheikh and so forth – and make them, as only poetry can, memorable.' For this reason he thought acrobatics were 'poetry's natural allies'. Such a manifesto was not to everyone's taste. 'Auden is a very nice rattled brained boy', Eliot told Virginia Woolf in 1935. 'Some of his plays extremely good, but its superficial: stock figures; sort of Punch figures.'

Drama satisfied several needs in Auden. He had a taste for ritual, for recitation and for the uses of verbal sounds; by his time in Berlin he had also come to see 'play', in all meanings of the word, as a virtuous force which had been neglected under centuries of puritan disapproval. In addition, as Mendelson suggests, theatrical writing became Auden's way of reaching other people. His first effort at theatrical writing, *Paid on Both Sides* (1928), was a charade, that is a private game for people whom he knew (in this case the family and friends of Bill McElwee). It was meant to involve groups and reduce personal remoteness. 'Drama began as an act of the whole community,' he insisted under Heard's influence a few years later. 'Ideally there would be no spectators ... every member of the audience should feel like an understudy.' He wrote a play every summer from 1928 until 1930 (though none was performed) and conceived of *The Orators* in 1931 as 'abstract drama – all the action implied'. He wrote several plays for performance by his pupils. At Larchfield there was *Sherlock Holmes chez Duhamel*, about French reactions to the deductive powers of the Baker Street sleuth, apparently written to improve the boy performers' fluency in French. He was involved in theatricals at Downs School, as Rupert Doone reported in 1934: 'I went down to see Wystan's school play, which I enjoyed very much indeed, and I think I learned things besides, from the children, especially in a short play that Wystan said they made up for themselves.' This was entitled *The Fight for the Cabbage*. 'It bore an uncommon resemblance to a "Folk Play", so one can take it that the "master" guided them,' Doone added. 'It was about a cabbage, and a tree, and a king and his son, and a giant and a doctor and an attendant and a princess and father Xmas and a hare and and and.'

A few years earlier Auden had been asked by Doone to write a play for the Group Theatre. Doone was a dancer (a former lover of Cocteau and pupil of Massine) who had been working in the Ballets Russe at the time of Diaghilev's death, and organised the Group Theatre in 1932 along lines which stressed co-operative training. The Group Theatre was not a club, and did not have a permanent building, but Doone hired rooms for lectures and readings, and arranged productions in theatres leased for the occasion. He drew many talents into his work: Benjamin Britten as a composer; Henry Moore and John Piper as designers; Eliot and Yeats as well as Auden, MacNeice and Spender. Early members of the group included Duncan Grant, William Coldstream and Adrian Stokes among painters; Havelock Ellis, Masefield and Harold Nicolson as representative writers; Anton Dolin, Harley Granville-Barker, Flora Robson and Nevill

Coghill among those involved in performing arts. 'I can't understand half the allusions,' Antonia White noted after attending a rehearsal of *The Dog Beneath the Skin* in 1935: 'The atmosphere is feverishly progressive. Revolution in politics; revolution in art; revolution in one's way of life. Few actual party members but it is taken for granted that one sympathises with communism.' Auden was optimistic about the Group Theatre's potential as an innovatory force and was keen on its ideal of being a community 'who do everything and do it together'.

He did not share Doone's enthusiasm for ballet and found him volatile. The adversities which Doone had endured had been enough to make anyone difficult: he had been an apprentice draughtsman in the Midlands, absconded to London, and survived for a time as a male model; intelligent and a discriminating reader of poetry, he was nevertheless ill-educated and inarticulate, moving in a set where expensive schooling and verbal brilliance were taken for granted; in his milieux of dance and homosexuality, good looks were admired but his odd appearance was likened by Lydia Lopokova Keynes to 'the potato'. It was a measure of Doone's intelligence and charm that, despite his touchiness and vagaries, Auden during the summer of 1933 fulfilled the commission to write *The Dance of Death* (though his hastiness in certain passages is too evident). 'This brash irreverent allegory' about a moribund middle class 'was unlike anything written for the English stage', in Mendelson's description. Auden 'combined German cabaret and English pantomime, presented Marxist analysis in rhymed verse, and offered an active and decisive role to its audience'. The silent dancer (wearing a mask designed by Henry Moore) tried to distract the middle-class chorus from their impending deaths by involving them in various fads and crazes. 'As each of these distractions proves futile, the dancer declines in strength and the audience (through the voices of actors scattered among the ticket-holders) proclaims more loudly its revolutionary impatience.'

The play caused a sensation when it was staged for subscribers in February 1934 and had wider acclaim when produced at the Westminster Theatre in the following year. 'In this episodic play (it might be called a musical comedy if we dared risk misdirecting good, easy people seeking an after-dinner rest cure) Mr Auden assumes an audience ready to jeer at the last struggles of a middle class doomed to extinction,' Charles Morgan reported in *The Times*. 'The members of this class dream of a new life, but secretly desire the old, for there is death inside them, and after enduring vigorous persecution in song, dance and patter, they are "liquidated", and the stage is left to Mr Karl Marx, who, "having gathered all the material facts", pronounces that the instruments of production have been too much for the old order, and hopefully waves the Red Flag over the heads of his armed escort.' Morgan disliked 'the desperate singlemindedness' with which Auden moved towards his 'predetermined end' in which the dancer's death empowered the proletariat. 'It is a pity that the ideas of the present piece should for the most part have the desolating air of schoolboy brilliance.' Yet Morgan thought Auden's language showed 'how poetry, by basing itself upon contemporary speech-rhythms, may regain its old place in the theatre', and applauded the dramatic innovations. 'Those choruses parading in front of a simple backcloth, these performers scattered about the auditorium, the jazz orchestra, the dancer representing Death and the Announcer speaking for Death through a megaphone, all striving to combine realistic incident and fantastic illusion' resulted in 'an expressive and agreeable theatrical form'. Not everyone was impressed. Lord Cromer, who as Lord Chamberlain was in charge of theatrical censorship, wrote of *The Dance of Death*, 'this is a most incomprehensible play, but I suppose some people will say they understand it!' George Street, his reader, commented: 'It is of course impressionist, which means incoherence drifting into sheer nonsense.'

Auden's next theatrical production was the rollicking *The Dog Beneath the Skin*. Its influences were as diverse as Dante and Ira Gershwin, though Brecht was paramount. Its didacticism was weak, as might be expected of a play reminiscent to the *Observer* of Noël Coward. The plot (put together by Auden, with help from Isherwood) was as complicated as that of the Downs school play, *The Fight for the Cabbage*. As Charles Morgan wrote after the play's production in January 1936,

They have invented a little legend which sends a young man and a dog (in the skin of which a lost baronet is concealed) on a journey through the contemporary world. This world, as they see it, is a 'racket' or conspiracy among men to avoid facing the evil truth and taking action to remedy. The evil has its origin in their separation from nature and from the ancient discipline of nature over man. Man by his inventions has become master of nature and is terrified by his own mastery. Being afraid, he submits himself wildly to false gods –

to dictators or to priestly men of science, to rich men or the Press. Or he seeks to escape – in eroticism, medievalism, art, asceticism, faith, even in invalidism. All these are bitterly assailed in little scenes which have generally an ingenuity of rhyming contrivance and a naivety of thought that combine to keep the stage amusingly alive.

Near the end of the play the dog leaves his skin to preach. 'We are to "repent, unite and act" to destroy a social system in which love is governed by money,' Morgan concluded. 'This stage of the proceedings is a trifle embarrassing, but how easily this form of embarrassment might have occupied the whole evening and how long an immunity there is to be thankful for.'

It may seem that Auden and his friends were juvenile in their railing against authority and the dull malevolence of officials. It is too easy to forget the noxious, pompous stupidity that leaked over their epoch like gas-fumes from a defective stove. The reaction of the British theatrical censors to the text of *Dog* is a reminder. It was read for the Lord Chamberlain by George Street, who objected to 'the authors' hatred of society' and obstructed the play's production on political grounds. 'Many people will object to the whole play as Communist propaganda, but it cannot wisely be banned on that score,' Street reported to Lord Cromer, who concurred that it was 'an unnecessary play for public performance'. The official tactic was therefore to insist on a long list of obtuse cuts (the vicar's sermon 'needs modifying', Street advised, because 'there is too much about God'). Street's hope was 'that if the Lord Chamberlain requires all these excisions the authors will withdraw the play. It would not be a great loss. The underlying idea of Vicars and Generals etc oppressing the poor is out of date nonsense.' To test the possibility of banning the play outright, the censors consulted Lord David Cecil, 'a younger intellectual' (who was a colleague of Coghill at Oxford) with irreproachable connections in the Conservative Party. His report was a carefully couched masterpiece designed to ensure that the production would proceed with the minimum bother. He knew the distrust of British officialdom for enthusiasm and, like Eliot reporting for Lord Reith on Auden's contributions to the *Listener*, he knew that he could best mollify the authorities with a lukewarm tone. Cecil advised that 'it would be a very great mistake to ban the whole play'. Auden's reputation stood too high for a summary act of suppression, much though the officials might like it:

Mr Auden is one of the most considered of our younger authors –
and though personally I do not care much for his work, I think it
original, sincere and talented, intended neither to shock or court
notoriety but genuinely to express his literary and other views. Nor
is he an eccentric, not taken seriously; he has a large party of
admirers among reputable and sober critics.

In any case *The Dog Beneath the Skin* ('highly artificial and fantastic ...
modern pantomime with a vaguely communist tinge') was in Cecil's
opinion no more 'demoralising ... than a modernist ballet'.

The third area of Auden's collaborative work was neither as an
anthologist nor as a dramatist. From the autumn of 1935 until February
1936 Auden worked in the GPO Film Unit headed by the documentary
film-maker John Grierson. 'We were experimenting to see whether poetry
could be used in films, and I think we showed it could,' Auden recalled.
His first work in the Unit was the madrigal 'O lurcher-loving collier, as
black as night' for a film about miners entitled *Coal Face*; but most
famously he worked on the documentary *Night Mail* about an express
train taking letters north to Scotland. He was asked to write the
commentary after filming had been completed. 'Then we saw what
enormous stature Auden had,' a colleague recalled. The only place for
Auden to work was in a narrow corridor at the back of the GPO Film Unit
premises. The corridor was also the rendezvous of Post Office messenger
boys, 'fifteen-year-old Cockney kids, wild as hell, and they made their tea
and whistled and played cards'; but Auden sat at an old table nearby, and
wrote poetry with the help of a stop-watch so that each snatch of verse
would fit each filmshot. He liked the busy atmosphere, and on earlier
occasions, according to Medley, had sat writing in a Lyon's Corner House
'because he liked (he said) the "anonymity" '. He once quoted a remark of
T. E. Lawrence – 'Happiness comes in absorption' – and it is good to think
that in this corridor off Soho Square he enjoyed great happiness. There
was no pride about him:

He kept bringing it, and – the cheek of us, in a way we turned down
so much. He'd say, 'Alright. That's quite all right. Just roll it up and
throw it away.' The most magnificent verse was thrown away, and in
that situation, with all that noise going on and being harassed and
used, he turned out the very, very famous lines of *Night Mail*.

This anecdote demonstrates a crucial aspect of Auden's working attitude. He disliked poets being solemn about themselves or precious about their art, and his aesthetic theory against poetic pretensions to change the world, as it had developed by the 1940s, annoyed or disappointed some of his early admirers. It was their perceptions that changed, for his attitude was constant: 'Just roll it up and throw it away.'

Another colleague at the Film Unit was the young composer Benjamin Britten, who had first visited him at Downs School in July 1935. They were introduced by Basil Wright, a film colleague, who afterwards suggested 'that it was Wystan who first awoke Ben's real imaginative and emotional life'. Auden gave great attention to Britten, to whom in March 1936 he addressed the poem 'Underneath the abject willow', which urges him to abandon his 'cold' and 'moping' existence and instead 'warm to action' and love's 'satisfaction'. Auden lodged in London with another of Grierson's associates, William Coldstream, who afterwards painted a portrait of Auden's mother in 1936–37, and with Coldstream's first wife, Nancy, an artist who later married Spender's brother Michael. 'I was on the verge of having an affair with Nancy Coldstream, but just in time I remembered that all women are destructive,' he told his brother John. Though the Coldstreams were good friends, the conjunction of poverty and London was uncongenial. 'Towns take a lot of getting used to, and one must be richer, if one is to live decently in them, than one need be in the country,' he wrote in 1936. He also, as he admitted in the *Listener* in February of that year, found documentary films exasperatingly slow to make and patronising of the poor. When Lawrence Gowing, a pupil who had recently left the Downs School, wrote to Auden at the Film Unit asking his advice, the response was lukewarm. 'You only want to become a film director because you think it is the art of the future,' Auden replied. 'It isn't. Art is the art of the future.' Encouraged, perhaps, by the critical success of *The Dog Beneath the Skin*, which opened on 30 January, Auden resigned from the Film Unit a few weeks later.

CHAPTER 6

'The cold controlled ferocity of the human species'

In the summer of 1936 Auden journeyed to Iceland. During the two months that he spent there, he considered all the great issues which would preoccupy him in the later 1930s: a poet's cultural identity, his relation to political action, the creative enrichment of exile and the dangerous ease of cheating. He had also in Iceland, one day, an experience of searing unpleasantness which would turn his attention towards the subject of violence, and result in further journeys to the war-zones of Spain in 1937 and China in 1938; it involved him briefly with political propagandists, and made him scrutinise the nature of human tyranny and its relation in the 1930s to mechanisation. Apart from two plays with Isherwood, his poetic ideas from this period were published in *Letters from Iceland* in 1937, *Journey to a War* (1939) and *Another Time* (1940). He resembled his own description in 1939 of Voltaire:

> like a sentinel, he could not sleep. The night was full of wrong,
> Earthquakes and executions. Soon he would be dead,
> And still all over Europe stood the horrible nurses
> Itching to boil their children. Only his verses
> Perhaps could stop them: He must go on working.

His work at this time reflects the quandary of a man caught, as he wrote, in 'the clutch of crisis and the bloody hour' and seeking to do his duty by his moment 'in a low, dishonest decade'. There was a sentence of Kafka's that resonated for Auden: 'One must cheat no one, not even the world of its triumph.' He quoted this aphorism in 1941 when he felt that he had cheated or had been implicated in attempts to cheat the world of its triumphs. By then he had reverted to Christian beliefs, abruptly and even arbitrarily as it seemed to some friends, although with hindsight there is an undercurrent of Christian sentiment in many of his phrases in the 1930s.

The preliminaries to Iceland were simple. After resigning from the Film Unit Auden went on 16 March to stay at Sintra in Portugal with Isherwood and his lover Heinz Neddermeyer, who was a refugee from German Nazidom. Together with Isherwood he began writing a play about mountaineering which they entitled *The Ascent of F6*. He returned to England in April, and shortly afterwards visited his schoolboy friends at Bryanston. When Michael Yates then told him that he and three other pupils were accompanying a master to Iceland in August, Auden's response was swift. He negotiated an advance from Faber to write a travel-book about Iceland with MacNeice: then settled to meet Yates there. In July he reached Iceland (the subject of so many boyhood stories told by his father): he was joined after six weeks by MacNeice and later by Yates and the Bryanston party. For Auden this trip (which ended in September) was crucial. 'An effect of travelling in distant places,' he wrote in Iceland, 'is to make one reflect on one's past and one's culture from the outside.' Henceforth he deliberately unsettled himself, and until the final year of his life was always a traveller or voluntary exile, spurred by an intellectual masochist's need of the neurosis of estrangement: 'no one thinks unless a complex makes him', he wrote in Iceland.

A year later in 'Dover' (1937) he described the great port as a place of little material importance: 'Nothing is made in this town.' Instead, he noted, it was a place of emotional ferment. Every day travellers separate or are reconciled. A port builds 'its routine upon ... unusual moments', he wrote:

> The vows, the tears, the slight emotional signals
> Are here eternal and unremarkable gestures
> Like ploughing or soldiers' songs.

In Iceland Auden decided that 'the day of a self-contained national culture is over'; a year later he pictured the people of Dover killing time:

> Above them, expensive and lovely as a rich child's toy,
> The aeroplanes fly in the new European air,
> On the edge of that air that makes England of minor importance

Apart from Iceland in 1936, Auden made several trips to Germany, visited

Belgium in 1934 and 1938, Switzerland in 1934 and 1935, Czechoslovakia
in 1934, Denmark in 1935, Portugal in 1936, Spain and France in 1937, as
well as Egypt, Hongkong, China and the US in 1938; yet his journeys
increased his sense of enclosure. 'I had the feeling,' he wrote in Iceland,
'that for myself it was already too late. We are all too deeply involved with
Europe to be able, or even to wish to escape.' Many of the ideas in *The
Orators* had begun during his isolation in Germany, and were completed
during his seclusion in the cultural oddity of Larchfield, where he was
'paid to teach English to the sons of Scotchmen'. Exile and isolation had
creative uses: as he reassured himself in 1939, Voltaire exiled at Ferney
was 'perfectly happy'.

In Iceland Auden considered the social role of the poet. In his 'Letter to
Lord Byron' written there, he described how 'until the Great Industrial
Revolution', an artist as a dependant of a great patron had the status of 'a
scivvy'. Haydn wore Prince Esterhazy's livery, and Mozart wrote his
music to order. Following industrialisation 'a new class of creative artist
set up', rentiers who 'drew dividends'. Their independence brought new
pretensions and more complex functions. Writers were elevated to the
status of cultural institutions, or like Victoria's Poet Laureate were
smeared with the tawdry gilding of celebrity. Tourists came to gawp at
Tennyson's house, and he became an adjunct of the new consumerism,
with his words appropriated as the motto of a suburban department store,
Bentalls: 'To strive, to seek, to find and not to yield'. His funeral was like
an episode at Warhol's factory in the accents of 1892: burial in
Westminster Abbey, with a duke, two marquesses and two earls as his
pallbearers; tickets for the event sent out by his publishers; the phrases of
the funeral oration telegraphed round the world; the Abbey nave lined by
veterans of Balaclava (the living matter of 'The Charge of the Light
Brigade'); while outside urchins sold broadsheets of 'Crossing the Bar'.
Auden came to loathe such macabre episodes. 'You can't imagine what
I've been through over Eliot's death,' he wrote to Coghill a few days after
the event in 1965. 'Modern publicity is absolutely revolting.' He was
dismayed by the way that journalists pestered him with idiotic questions
or besought glib quotes, and had a disagreeable presentiment of his own
death. It was the Laureate's didacticism, Auden came to think, that was his
undoing. 'Tennyson was a fool to try to write a poetry which would teach
the Ideal,' he wrote in 1944.

Auden was a celebrity of the 1930s, and found in Updike's phrase that celebrity is a mask that eats into one's face. 'Remember you once saw Auden plain,' Janet Adam Smith told her little son Andrew Roberts with mock solemnity after showing him to the poet in 1937. 'Auden made a tremendous impact on me, as on so many of my generation,' Michael Meyer wrote in 1989:

> 'Taller today, we remember similar evenings', 'Sir, no man's enemy, forgiving all', 'Look stranger, at this island now' and
>> Now the leaves are falling fast,
>> Nurses' flowers will not last;
>> Nurses to the graves are gone,
>> But the prams go rolling on.
>
> I had not thought of these lines for decades but, leafing again through the 1930 *Poems*, which I bought in 1937 when I was sixteen, and *Look, Stranger!*, purchased together with *The Ascent of F*6 and *Spain* the following year, I feel again across fifty years the old excitement. Here was someone speaking to us in our own language and on our own level.... He made one feel that poetry was something one might partake in oneself as a kind of equal, not just as a reverent auditor. I began to write bad adolescent poems myself about the hopelessness of adolescent love.

After a similar interval of fifty years Noël Annan remembered as an eighteen-year-old schoolboy 'construing ... Auden's 1934 sonnet "Sir, No Man's Enemy, Forgiving All" as if it were Vergil with a much cleverer contemporary who later joined the Party'. Auden was a meeting-ground for young people: enthusiasm for his work seemed a measure of intelligence as well as an indicator of literary or socio-political seriousness. 'I should be interested to hear what you think of Stephen Spender – and Auden – who are objects of discussion here just now,' Elizabeth Bishop wrote from Vassar to a graduate student at Harvard in 1934. 'For six or seven years I was intoxicated by Auden,' Bishop's fellow American Frederic Prokosch wrote of this period. 'I kept muttering his lines in darkening woods and distant cities, in dim Gothic transepts, in evil-smelling alleys. He hung over my mind like a pale, impenetrable presence, both eerily intimate yet strangely antagonistic ... hinting at all the things I might have been and wasn't, that I might have done and didn't, that I could have endured but didn't.' The cult figure for literate young people was also a bugbear of his testy elders. 'Auden is not a poet,' insisted Humbert Wolfe. 'Random House continues to print beeyutiful volumes of shit by Spender and Auden,' Pound told Zukofsky. The intensity of feelings invested in Auden was not just metropolitan preciousness: emotions about him ran high in the provinces too.

When the mountaineering play which he had begun writing in Portugal with Isherwood was staged at Birmingham Repertory Theatre in March 1938, 'contrary to managerial expectations, the play packed the theatre' and there was a furious sequel when Thomas Kemp, the *Birmingham Post*'s theatrical reviewer, hailed the plot as 'an exciting dramatic adventure' but demurred at the patronising depiction of the lower-middle class: 'Why do our highbrows so often pity the masses, who don't need it?' A heated correspondence ran daily in the *Birmingham Post* for ten days, and resumed when the play was revived in November. 'The cynical pessimism of the play is typical of the outlook on life of all too many of the young university men of to-day,' fulminated F. J. of Handsworth on 4 April. 'Many of them are like spoilt children. My own attempt to give serious consideration to the play was hampered by the guffaws of many of them in the audience at cheap sneers which they would have recognised as hackneyed if they had been more seasoned playgoers.' The contrary case was put by Geoffrey Mears on 6 April:

the play goes a long way to smash the accepted conventions and clichés of a world that, to quote a poem of Auden's, 'has had its day', and that it exposes the petty principles and motives of the Sir James Ransom and Lady Welwyn class as being but the selfish prejudices and self-interestedness that are leading the world to ultimate chaos and destruction.... in the present state of things a regular job is slavery, pure and unadulterated. It is devoid of meaning and utterly purposeless. There is nothing more soul-destroying than the continual useless grind to eke out a living in a world that offers no hope, no joy, no ultimate aim.

Auden then was being appropriated for causes. He became the pretext for vendettas between newspaper columnists of irreconcilable politics. 'That famous roarer for old ladies, St John Ervine, has been filling the *Observer* for weeks with his violent abuse of that vital and interesting school of young poets headed by Wyston [sic] Auden, who are beginning to accept communism as their philosophy of life,' reported the *Daily Worker*'s Ralph Fox in 1936 after Ervine had called Auden 'a renegade ... hunting with the Bolshy-minded planners'. The left's special claims on Auden were strained when, at the instigation in 1937 of the Poet Laureate John Masefield, King George VI during a ceremony at Buckingham Palace awarded Auden the King's Gold Medal for Poetry in recognition of *Look, Stranger!* When Auden and Isherwood left for China in 1938, journalists and photographers massed at Victoria Station to record their departure. Inquisitive publicity was increased by the publication in 1938 of Isherwood's memoirs, in which Auden figured under the name of Hugh Weston.

'To love fame one must set much store by people in general; one must *believe* in them,' Valéry once wrote; but in youth Auden believed in machinery more easily than people, and still had no crude need of fame. Spender suspected that 'Auden understood people according to doctrines in books, but didn't really understand them as individuals he knew.' It was perhaps partly because of this isolation that Auden in adolescence and manhood felt that he needed visionary experiences. An ungenerous way of looking at ecstasy – experiences like Auden's vision of agape in 1933 – would be as a form of self-deception or spiritual intoxication by which people try to make themselves superior to circumstances. A visionary experience can be a device to exclude as much as possible of the hostile world from one's system, or to cheat the world of its triumphs. But at its most authentic the visionary experience illuminates what is excellent in the world without excluding or denying what is bad. Auden's vision of agape had changed his life, but it was incomplete, it showed only love as fruitful, perspicuous, intensifying and lucid. Yet long before Freud it had been recognised that hate is the necessary counterpart of love: there was the passage from Catallus beginning *Odi et amo* ('I hate and I love ... therefore I am in anguish'), so commonplace that it was taken as the armorial motto of an English peer, Viscount Norwich, a man whose ideas Auden thought 'would be no credit to a 12 year old'. Hate is a primal source too: strong, furious, annihilating and sometimes more pervasive than love. At the end of the decade Auden jotted down a maxim of Lavater: 'Thousands are hated, whilst none are ever loved, without a real cause.' He knew it would have been an act of hysterical and selfish denial to live from 1936 until 1946 as if that evening on the Downs lawn in June

1933 was all that counted. 'Europe lies in the dark,' he wrote in 1937. 'The will of love is done.'

Victorian Christians like Auden's clergymen grandfathers had regarded pugnacity and violence as expressions of original sin, and therefore as inescapable parts of human nature. This outlook, it seemed to many people who lived through the First World War, had led to an easy acceptance of human ferocity in public policy. Most progressive people after the war insistently denied what their Christian grandfathers thought self-evident. As Auden said in 1938, a fundamental principle of 'Liberal Democrats' was 'that man is born free, that the child is always by nature good and is made bad by society': in other words a denial alike of innate aggression and original sin. Though cruelty and calamity were exceptionally tangible and visible in the 1930s, they were perhaps no more prevalent than usual. But they moved centrally into Auden's conscience in 1936, accompanied by a faint but increasing sense that modern secular faiths gave no more convincing explanations than his grandfathers' doctrine of original sin. Humanity's fall from grace was made more lethal by its harnessing of modern technology. A decade later his sense of this was strong enough for him to contrast 'Our international rout / Of sin and apparatus / And dying men galore' with the beatific happiness of a woman he saw lunching alone 'In Schraffts'.

Auden's realisation of the ubiquity of human horror came during a voyage northwards from Reykjavik in August 1936. As a Gresham's pupil, he had had a 'short, sharp' craze for whales shortly before his decision to become a poet in 1922. Now he was drawn to them again. Michael Yates, who was with Auden, has described the day:

> During our passage to the far north on the *Dettifoss* we berthed for one day at Patreksfjordur for moving cargo. We had the crazy idea of walking in gum boots sixteen miles over the lava-strewn headland to a whaling station. The very long tiring toil brought us to the top where the view of the deep blue fjord was unsurpassed. No good. We continued wearily down to the scene of carnage. To Wystan whales were one of the most beautiful sights. Having watched the brutal destruction on the slimy slipway he remarked: 'It is enough to make one a vegetarian for life. It gives one an extraordinary vision of the cold, controlled ferocity of the human species.' We turned away and sought food and coffee but were refused. We were numbed and left

in disgust. I behaved very badly, refusing to speak for three hours. At the top of the watershed he turned and said: 'Picture of a person in a fucking awful temper.'

Now, beside Yates, when Auden was hungry, tired and shocked, he saw another 'vision' which was the necessary counterpart to the love in 1933. His susceptibility to violence was known to his friends – Auden's politics, Spender had written in 1935, contained no statement 'except perhaps a certain violence' – though he was never its perpetrator. 'It seems to me,' Isherwood wrote of this time, 'that Wystan was incapable of cruelty but that he had a streak of masochism in him which could invite it from others.' Yates's sulk on that afternoon in Iceland was violent in its intensity; it heightened the emotional pitch in a way that honed Auden's insight into cruelty.

Auden's photographs of the flensing of a whale by steam-winch, and of the gory debris on the slipway, were printed in *Letters from Iceland* opposite this text of a letter to Erika Mann:

There was a selfish little Englishman at Akureyri who said, apropos of Spain, 'Why can't these foreigners behave themselves. It's sickening. You can't travel anywhere nowadays without running into trouble,' and told me the French had no sense of discipline. There were delicious pickled pigs' trotters to eat at dinner. And that's about all I remember except the whaling station at Talknafjordur. O no it isn't. I had a nightmare after reading a silly book on spiritualism. I woke up sweating and wrote it down there and then in the middle of the night, but now I can hardly decipher what I wrote.

He recounts his nightmare: the only one in his life that he thought worth recording, he republished it thirty-five years later in the coded autobiography of his commonplace book, *A Certain World*, where he confirmed its date as August 1936. In 1970 he prefaced the dream with a quotation, 'Dreaming permits each and every one of us to be quietly and safely insane every night of our lives.' Auden added that (with this exception in 1936) he always experienced his dreams as 'boring in exactly the same way that lunatics are, that is to say, repetitious, devoid of any sense of humor, and insanely egocentric'. Auden the dreamer in Iceland is fearful of being overpowered by the 'terrifying affection' of a green-eyed creature which amputates 'the arm of an old lady who was going to do me an injury'; he feels pursued by someone reminiscent of 'the long red-legged scissor man in *Shockheaded Peter*', and passively longs for the protection of a smooth-faced blond companion. Everyone seems selfish and menacing except his father, who gives some half-measure of help (and to whom *Letters from Iceland* is dedicated). Fear is stronger than knowledge: children and animals run in terror from a thing about which they know nothing except that it is frightening; even perfect love does not cast out fear.

That perhaps is as closely as the dream needs interpretation; for immediately after it comes the waking nightmare of the whaling station (specially marked on the map in *Letters from Iceland*) and its vision of ferocity and indifference.

> I wish I could describe things well, for a whale is the most beautiful animal I have ever seen. It combines the fascination of something alive, enormous, and gentle, with the functional beauties of modern machinery. A seventy-ton one was lying on the slip-way like a large and very dignified duchess being got ready for the ball by beetles. To see it torn to pieces with steam winches and cranes is enough to make one a vegetarian for life. In the lounge the wireless was playing 'I want to be bad' and 'Eat an apple every day'. Downstairs the steward's canary chirped incessantly. The sun was out; in the bay, surrounded by buoys and gulls, were the semi-submerged bodies of five dead whales: and down the slip-way ran a constant stream of blood, staining the water a deep red for a distance of fifty yards. Someone whistled a tune. A bell suddenly clanged and everyone stuck their spades in the carcass and went off for lunch. The body remained alone in the sun, the flesh still steaming a little. It gave one an extraordinary vision of the cold controlled ferocity of the human species.

Among contemporary reviewers, only Louise Bogan identified this passage's importance.

The first poetic mention of Talknafjordur is in Auden's 'Letter to William Coldstream' of 1936. 'Let me pretend that I'm the impersonal eye of the camera,' he wrote to his painter friend. He describes his holiday snapshots in the book:

> Now there is a whaling station during the lunch hour

> The saw is for cutting up jaw-bones
> The whole place was slippery with filth – with guts and
>   decaying flesh –
>   like an artist's palette.

Coghill had once called Yates that 'nice English schoolboy', and two lines in the Coldstream letter runs: 'The poet's eye is not one from which nothing is hid / Nor the straightforward diary of a nice English schoolboy really much use.' At the time it seemed that neither of Talknafjordur's English visitors was equal to making sense of its horror: still less to cope with the trivialisation of iniquity represented by the wireless tune, 'I want to be bad'. Auden's vision at the whaling station was nevertheless incorporated into his outlook. As late as 1958 he praised Sir Vyvyan Board, 'thanks to whose life-long fuss the hunted whale now suffers / a quicker death'. But otherwise his references were characteristically less explicit. 'Musée des Beaux Arts', written at Brussels in 1938, reminds us how often and easily we put aside other people's catastrophes to pursue our own petty quotidian comforts. Most of us daily stick our spades into the carcass while it is still steaming and go off for lunch. To pretend that we are only involved in love, rather than implicated in suffering, is a cheat. 'Musée des Beaux Arts' begins:

> While someone else is eating or opening a window or just walking dully along;
> About suffering they were never wrong,
> The Old Masters: how well they understood
> Its human position; how it takes place
> While someone else is eating or opening a window or just walking dully along;

or else a bell summoning workmen for lunch. Auden conjured a scene from Brueghel's painting of Icarus falling into the Aegean off Crete rather than a fjord off the Denmark Strait:

>   everything turns away
> Quite leisurely from the disaster; the ploughman may
> Have heard the splash, the forsaken cry,
> But for him it was not an important failure; the sun shone
> As it had to on the white legs disappearing into the green
> Water; and the expensive delicate ship that must have seen
> Something amazing, a boy falling out of the sky,
> Had somewhere to get to and calmly sailed on.

He returned to this idea in 'Memorial for the City', partly prompted by his visit to the post-war ruins of Hitler's Germany:

> That is the way things happen; for ever and ever
> Plum-blossom falls on the dead, the roar of the waterfall covers
> The cries of the whipped and the sighs of the lovers
> And the hard bright light composes
> A meaningless moment into an eternal fact
> Which a whistling messenger disappears with into a defile:
> One enjoys glory, one endures shame;
> He may, she must. There is no one to blame.

The wireless playing its callous ditty at Talknafjordur provided images in other poems too.

Auden believed that people should be more attentive. 'The primary function of poetry, as of all the arts, is to make us more aware of ourselves and the world around us,' he wrote in 1938. 'I do not know if such increased awareness makes us more moral or more efficient: I hope not.' Yet he wished people would do their duty by their moment. In October 1939, in the title poem of *Another Time*, he wrote:

> It is to-day in which we live
> So many try to say Not Now,
> So many have forgotten how
> To say I Am, and would be
> Lost if they could in history.

After his visit to the whaling station Auden was continuously puzzling how the poet should live without cheating his historical moment. Despite his boyhood fondness for whales, his reaction in 1936 was not the literal reaction of an animal protectionist; he resembled not Shakespeare, who, he wrote in 1939, 'thought of the non-human world in terms of the human', but Rilke, who depicted 'the human in terms of the non-human ... a way of thought which ... is more characteristic of the child than of the adult'. The whale stood as a metaphor for human concerns in an epoch of 'external disorder and extravagant lies', he wrote in 1936; and two years later:

> in every body
> The ways of living are disturbed; intrusive as a sill,
> Fear builds enormous ranges casting shadows,

Heavy, bird-silencing, upon the outer world.

His politicisation was a gradual and uneven process. As a schoolboy and undergraduate he had been apolitical. Gradually in the early 1930s his indifference became overlain with concern about the ineptitude of political leaders and sympathy with their victims. He read Edmund Wilson's *Devil Take the Hindmost: A Year of the Slump* (1932) – reportage by a bourgeois liberal who had believed in American capitalism but turned to Marxist formulae when confronted by the human cost of capitalism's failure – and recommended it to his brother John. 'Its difficult to know what we ought to do,' he told John in September 1932. 'Its wicked to try and keep the ship going; its conceited to join the "We're doomed" gang, and cowardly to jump into the sea.' He sent money to Lancashire strikers, and visited the Soviet trade agency in London in an effort to find his brother a job outside India. He regarded the British in India as one of those 'empires stiff in their brocaded glory, / the luscious lateral blossoming of woe' and judged Lord Willingdon, the Viceroy, as 'a weak shit'. Yet overall he held out from the increasing political commitments of his friends. 'No 1 am a bourgeois,' he wrote to Doone in 1932. 'I shall not join the C. P.' In the 1930s he thought 'the Russians have no talents for anything but Religion and diplomatic intrigue'. As to communism, 'the interest in Marx taken by myself and my friends', he judged from the perspective of 1955

> was more psychological than political; we were interested in Marx in the same way that we were interested in Freud, as a technique of unmasking middle-class ideologies, not with the intention of repudiating our class, but with the hope of becoming better bourgeois; our great error was not a false admiration for Russia but a snobbish feeling that nothing which happened in a semi-barbarous country which had experienced neither the Renaissance nor the Enlightenment could be of any importance: had any of the countries we knew personally, like France, Germany or Italy, the language of which we could speak and where we had personal friends, been the one to have a successful communist revolution with ... the same phenomena of terror, purges, censorship, etc., we would have screamed our heads off.

He was less committed than Day Lewis or Spender to specific political causes, but the love he tried to feel for his neighbours after June 1933 made him susceptible to the din and jargon of political dissent. As one example, in 1933 there was a proliferation of books and pamphlets which argued that wars were fomented by private manufacturers of armaments who made their profits in mass slaughter. With the ruin of the Disarmament Conference by Hitler's withdrawal of German participation in 1933, 'armaments manufacturers commonly known among us as merchants of death – were a godsend in the way of providing us with an identifiable villain', Malcolm Muggeridge recalled. Fellow travellers saw this campaign as a way of surreptitious state-control of companies such as Vickers, to whom Auden and MacNeice later bequeathed 'The Balkan conscience and the sleepless night we think / The inevitable disease of their dangerous trade'. When in 1933 Auden wrote a monologue of manichaean amorality, he responded to this propagandist panic by entitling it 'Sermon by an Armaments Manufacturer'.

Auden's political outlook was always mediated by his reading, and in the 1930s he was influenced by authors as catholic as Lawrence and Kafka. He disbelieved in the virtuous power of intellect. Reviewing Bertrand Russell's *Education and the Social Order* in 1932, he insisted:

> that man's nature is dual, and that each part of him has its own conception of justice and morality. In his passionate nature man wants lordship, to live in a relation of power with others, to obey and to command, to strut and to swagger. He desires mystery and glory. In his cerebral nature he cares for none of these things. He wants to know and to be gentle; he feels his other passionate nature is frightening and cruel.

By 1935 he saw his position in terms both of a Kafkaesque quest and Christian symbolism:

> The task of revealing the hidden field of experience, of understanding and curing by love, is a very slow, but ultimately the only satisfactory, one. 'The chief sin', wrote Kafka, in one of his aphorisms, 'is impatience. Through impatience man lost Eden, and it is impatience that prevents him from regaining it.' People take to violence because they haven't the strength and nerve to be absorbent.

In 1936, in Iceland, he went for a country walk, 'thinking about a picture . . . I saw in some book' of 'a girl playing a flute to a young man, two infants wrestling in a meadow, and an old man staggering to a grave'. As he told Erika Mann, 'after tea the thoughts developed into a poem'. The picture sounds like the Duke of Sutherland's Titian known as *The Three Ages of Man* (c. 1512), although, as Titian's infants are sleeping intertwined, Auden's visual memory that they are fighting is a distortion which points to his distress at the time. The poem is a sad, reflective piece which begins by asking 'Who can ever praise enough / The world of his belief?' In the first verse Auden pictures a man's 'harum-scarum childhood' with its happy play 'in the meadows near his home' and its placid, safe experiences of love and phantasy. The second verse addresses his adult belief: 'to create it and to guard / Shall be his whole reward'. Auden suggests that to reach mature beliefs a man must deny his loves and relinquish the illusion of safety, must make choices that bring weeping. Later Auden entitled this poem 'The Price', for to him the price of understanding was high. The mature man:

> shall be
> Bride and victim to a ghost,
> And in the pit of terror thrown
> Shall bear the wrath alone.

The suggestion in 'The Price' that sentient, discriminating people are bound to feel scared and isolated accords with Auden's situation in the late 1930s: every European, it could seem, was caught, as he and MacNeice wrote in 1936, in 'madness, and the intolerable tightening of the mesh / Of history'. He had no doubts about 'all the hate that coercion must produce' or the outcome of the European crisis. He had been with Michael Yates and Peter Roger in Germany during the plebiscite campaign of August 1934 which had permitted Hitler to hold the posts of Chancellor and President simultaneously. He noted the terrorism as they motored from Cologne on 17 August:

All rather subdued this morning and no wonder in this country which is being run by a mixture of gangsters and the sort of school prefect who is good at Corps. Voting for the Reichskanzler on Sunday. Every house waves a flag like a baby's rattle.... Each shop has pasted a notice, 'We are all going to vote yes.' Slogans hang screaming above the cobbled streets of tiny hamlets, 'One Folk: One Leader: One Yes'.... In a furious temper for some reason or other (O, Mr Censor), skidding round corners on two wheels through pretty wooded hills.... Reached Eisenach, Bach's birthplace.... Talked to hotel proprietor who suddenly stopped and rushed to open the window. The Labour Corps were passing and one must be keen. After they had gone he closed it with a sigh of relief. Sat in a cafe in the market square listening to Hitler shouting from Hamburg. Sounded like a Latin lesson. Peter ate an ice out of his handkerchief.

This was only an early incident in the world's deterioration. During March 1936 Germany reoccupied its demilitarised border zone and in May Italy annexed Abyssinia. The Spanish Civil War raged from July 1936 until April 1939. Japan attacked China in July 1937. Austria was annexed by Germany in March 1938. 'Violence successful like a new disease,' Auden wrote a few months later, 'And Wrong a charmer everywhere invited.' In Iceland, writing 'Letter to Lord Byron', he described how the nineteenth-century writer had become a free-standing bourgeois instead of a nobleman's skivvy; yet just as the bourgeoisie hope for decorations or knighthoods, so writers aspire to nobility. Fortitude is the quality that aristocrats most value, and fortitude is more easily shown in action than ideas. When Byron could endure his circumstances no more, he buckled on his breastplate and went to his death in a Balkan insurrection.

Another study of a man submitting to pressure with fatal results is the central figure in the penultimate Auden–Isherwood play, *The Ascent of F6*, which the two friends had begun while staying together in Portugal in 1936. At the time their draft seemed 'a cross between Peer Gynt and Journey's End', so Auden told Spender: Peer Gynt being one of those 'scoundrels' like Faust 'especially favoured of God and men because they are faithful to the motto "To thyself be true", because they regard the Arbitrary in themselves as the Necessary'. The play underwent continuous revisions, about which Auden consulted several people. In November 1936, for example, he dined with Keynes, who had recently founded the Arts Theatre in Cambridge (where the play was eventually produced in April 1937). 'He was most charming, intelligent, straightforward, youthful, a sort of senior undergraduate; altogether delightful, but but but

– his finger nails are eaten to the bones with dirt and wet, one of the worst cases ever, like a preparatory schoolboy,' Keynes reported to his wife Lydia Lopokova. 'So the infantilism is not altogether put on.... all other impressions so favourable. But those horrid fingers cannot lie.'

The Peer Gynt figure in *F6* is a mountaineer called Michael Ransom, whose choices seem to parable those of any intellectual contemplating action. 'Ransom is by nature a leader of men, who hates the motives that cause others to accept his leadership and praise his achievements,' Charles Morgan wrote. 'When he is invited by his brother, a prosperous member of the government, to lead an expedition to F6, his intuition is to refuse, for he distrusts the political motives underlying the invitation and fears his own corruption by the idea of power. He goes nevertheless, and achieves what is, for him, a success spiritually barren.' While climbing the mountain, Ransom meets an abbot who warns him of the vanity and peril of achievement, and like the airman in *The Orators* offers submission as an alternative. It is unclear whether the dramatists were recommending a surrender of individual or collective will; but, in any case, Ransom's pride prevents him from following a contemplative life as the Abbot adjures. Ransom continues with his fatal expedition and thus causes the death of his followers. 'My minor place in history is with the aberrant group of Caesars: the dullard murderers who take the gentle from their beds of love and with a quacking drum, escort them to the drowning ditch or the death in the desert.' Ransom's predicament has real consonance with that of Auden. '*F6* was the end,' Auden told a BBC interviewer in 1963. In the weeks after its publication he recognised that its 'success had nothing to do with what I really cared about, and of course one would have to pay for it later'. With the publication and production of *F6*, emigration became his necessary choice, 'because I knew then that if I stayed, I would inevitably become a member of the British establishment'. He was right to anticipate his absorption by cultural and political authorities if he remained in Britain: many of his associates at this time like Britten, Coldstream and Spender duly collected their pecrages and knighthoods after the war.

Between the publication of *F6* in September 1936 and its production four months later, Auden made a choice which seems like a reworking of Ransom's predicament. In July 1936 General Franco's nationalist forces had rebelled against the Popular Front, the government of Republican, socialist and communist allies which had won the Spanish elections of the preceding February. Auden heard the news while in Iceland, and followed developments keenly. The early months of the war were ferocious. There was a massacre at Badajoz, Madrid was bombarded and Guernica razed by bombs from the air. Fascist governments in Germany and Italy came to the aid of Franco's nationalists; the Soviet Union and communist parties backed the republicans. The Comintern agent Willi Muenzenberg coined a slogan for Spain, 'We must organise the intellectuals,' although Auden in 1939 responded with a cautionary aphorism: 'That movement will fail: the intellectuals are supporting it.' Within a short period young intellectuals like John Cornford, with whom Auden had corresponded, and Christopher Caudwell, whom Auden ranked with I. A. Richards as a critic, enlisted in the International Brigade and were killed. Malraux organised a volunteer fighter squadron and wrote a novel about the war, *L'Espoir*. Other outsiders cut sillier figures. 'Bloomsbury and Greenwich Village went on a revolutionary junket; poets, novelists, journalists and art students flocked across the Pyrenees to attend writers' congresses, to bolster morale on the front by reading their works from mobile loud-speaker vans to the militia-men, to accept highly paid, though short-lived, jobs in one of the numerous radio and propaganda departments, and "to be useful", as the phrase went, on all kinds of secret, undefinable errands,' in Arthur Koestler's description. 'Louis Aragon threatened to resign from the War because another writer, Gustave Regler, was appointed to drive the culture-dispensing loud-speaker van, but became reconciled when Regler joined the International Brigade and was shot through the stomach.' The passage in *L'Espoir* where Malraux caricatured this pettish opportunism must have caught Auden's attention when he read the novel in 1938 for its central speaker is an airman–poet who has also written saga-novels and boasts how he cheats his readers. In reality Lord Antrim, Sir Richard Rees and others did humanitarian good, and it would be mean-spirited to be too cynical about the foreign involvement in Spain. As Day Lewis wrote of his flirtation with communism, 'there was generosity as well as absurdity in this, for my friends and I did at least make some attempt to imagine the conditions we did not share ... and we were prepared to help destroy a system that perpetuated itself by such hideous human wastage, even though our own pleasant way of life would be destroyed in the process'.

It was hard to stand aside without feeling ignoble. 'All intellectuals, scholars or artists, are temperamentally shy and introverted, and one of the chief deficiencies in their training, seems to me that they are never put on their guard against themselves,' Auden wrote to Professor Dodds in early December 1936. 'I have decided to go out in the new year, as soon as the book is finished, to join the International Brigade in Spain,' he announced. 'I so dislike everyday political activities that I wont do them, but here is something I can do as a citizen and not as a writer, and as I have no dependants, I feel I ought to go; but O I do hope there are not too many Surrealists there.' When challenged by Dodds about this decision, he explained that he had been 'seduced' by the example of Wilfred Owen. His allusion was to Owen's preface to his poems written before his death in action in 1918: 'I am not concerned with Poetry. My subject is War, and the pity of War.' As Samuel Hynes has shown, this preface had a huge influence in the 1930s. 'War's greatest appeal, at least for artists, intellectuals and introspective men, is that it makes the nature and urgency of action clear,' Hynes wrote in *The Auden Generation*. 'In the years between the wars, when young men wondered whether to act, and if so, how, they looked back with admiration to the examples of those earlier poets, who had acted.' Auden himself did not 'believe that poetry need or even should be directly political, but in a critical period such as ours, I do believe that the poet must have direct knowledge of the major political events', he told Dodds. He had no illusions that he would be much help to the Spanish. He told Dodds, 'I shall probably be a bloody bad soldier but how can I speak to/for them without becoming one?'

Before leaving he wrote 'Danse Macabre', which mocked his heroic posture. Yet for all his derision he was apprehensive. Shortly before his departure he went to his schoolfriend Tom Garland for a warm coat and a supply of painkillers. As Garland's wife Peggy recalled, 'Wystan ... was terrified at the thought of seeing wounded people in pain and thought he would be able to help if he could give them a shot of morphine or whatever it was.' He also saw Britten. 'He goes off to Spain (to drive an ambulance),' Britten noted on 8 January. 'I feel ghastly about it, tho' I feel it is perhaps the logical thing for him to do.' It is significant that Auden hoped to drive an ambulance: he remained to the end of his life so much the son of a doctor and nurse fascinated by medical life.

Auden visited Isherwood in Paris on his way. When Auden boarded his train for Spain on 13 January, 'despite all their jokes', as Isherwood later wrote, their parting:

> made them aware how absolutely each relied on the other continuing to exist.... They had been going to bed together, unromantically but with much pleasure, for the past ten years, whenever an opportunity offered itself.... They couldn't think of themselves as lovers, yet sex had given friendship an extra dimension. They were conscious of this and it embarrassed them slightly.... the adults were trying to dismiss the schoolboys' sex-making as unimportant. It was of profound importance. It made the relationship unique.

Isherwood returned to London, where the first night of *The Ascent of F6* was staged on 26 February. 'It went very well, every seat sold, & quite an appreciative audience,' recorded Kathleen Isherwood. Yet, for all the success of the evening, she had a mother's wistful anxiety about the outsiders who threatened her happiness. 'Wystan ... had gone to the Front in Spain ... & C wished he could go too, & hopes to later. If only Spain (from the start) could have fought out its own revolution.'

Auden's activities in Spain are hard to pinpoint. By mid-January he reached Barcelona, a Republican stronghold where the authorities were riven by factionalism and weakened by a food crisis. He was apparently travelling under the auspices of the Spanish Medical Aid Committee, a British group supplying physicians, orderlies and ambulances to the Republican side, but he seems to have done little for them or the Republican propagandists. He travelled to Valencia, from where he sent a pictorially vivid but politically obscure report that was published in the *New Statesman* on 30 January. Auden spent one night in Valencia drinking in a hotel with Koestler, a dissolute young war correspondent named Basil Murray, a lame Romanian pilot from Malraux's squadron and several others. The party was dominated 'by the pilot who, when we all got a little drunk, kept repeating that he knew he was going to die, hopped around excitedly on his game leg, and had to be carried to bed', but they were all in miserable disenchantment. As Auden wrote years later, in 1955, 'Nobody I know who went to Spain during the Civil War who was not a dyed-in-the-wool stalinist came back with his illusions intact.' The pilot was killed a few days later, Koestler was captured and condemned to death shortly afterwards, and Murray died of a drugs overdose on board a hospital ship from Alicante on 31 March. By contrast, Auden was lucky. He made a brief foray to the front near Zaragoza, but, like many other men in wartime, he spent his days drinking, waiting for action that never came, dispirited by the drift and bungle of events. He was thrown back on 'makeshift consolations' and returned to London months ahead of his schedule.

In Spain the conflict was between the Republican forces and fascism, the new European creed combining barbarism with technological innovation and respect for property rights. Fascists sought to destroy intelligible experience between men, and to overthrow the old order in heaven and earth. 'One cannot walk through a mass-production factory and not feel that one is in Hell,' Auden wrote in 1939. 'No amount of Workers' Control will alter that feeling.' Modern technology was weakening human powers of judgment, especially private judgments. The banal objects and lack of discrimination that characterised its accompanying consumerism were suppressants of the human power of choice, and hence advanced the abolition of conscience. In his article 'How to be Masters of the Machine', written for the socialist *Daily Herald* in 1933, Auden had warned that 'the machine ... tends to dictate that the particular desire it satisfies is like it, unique and ever active, and to suppress those for which it is not constructed, unless you, the owner, are quite certain exactly what you want it for, e.g. I want this wireless set to listen to the concert next Wednesday.... I do not want it to be turned on all day while I read.' Auden was crisp and didactic with his readers: 'Find out what you want first of all, and then if a machine will help you, use it.' Otherwise mechanisation would deprive people of everything that had defined humanity to itself as human. The wireless is a symbol which recurred in his writing, particularly after he had heard the whaling station's set emitting its inanities. For the protagonists who met in a bar in *The Age of Anxiety* (1944–6), 'the radio, suddenly breaking in with its banal noises upon their separate senses of themselves, by compelling them to pay attention to a common world of great slaughter and much sorrow, began, without their knowledge, to draw these four strangers closer to each other'. When it has served its purpose, and is just a stupid distraction, one of the quartet quells it by mental will-power: 'Quant pointed a finger at it and it stopped immediately.'

When Auden came to write his rallying-cry 'Spain 1937', one strand of the poem was its stress of the need for individual acts of conscience in defiance of technology's amorality: 'I am your choice, your decision: yes, I am Spain.' This call to arms was first published by Faber in May 1937 in a pamphlet of five printed pages (all Auden's royalties from its sale went to Medical Aid for Spain). For all its grandeur some phrases now sound like shrill falsehood: 'the poets exploding like bombs' ought to be a misprint, for exploding is what some poems should do. As Nicholas Jenkins has noted, 'the sheer sense of will, the sense of great literary powers placed, decisively but without full conviction, in the service of a just cause, is essential to the effect of Auden's poem'. It is altogether more rousing than, say, Neruda's contemporary 'The International Brigade arrives at Madrid' or other propagandist works, and also superbly unbigoted. Its justification is that it made people think intensely. In July 1937, for example, Maynard Keynes published in the *New Statesman* a commentary on the political message of this poem, 'fit to stand', as he wrote, 'beside great predecessors in its moving, yet serene expression of contemporary feeling towards the heart-rending events of the political world'.

Keynes quoted two lines:

To-day the deliberate increase in the chances of death;
The conscious acceptance of guilt in the necessary murder;

with the comment, 'in this he is speaking for many chivalrous hearts'. These lines seem to have troubled Auden almost immediately, for he referred to them obliquely a few months after the poem's publication in his lecture 'The Craft of Poetry' given at Queen Mary Hall on 5 November 1937. As Kathleen Isherwood noted in her diary, he 'maintained that poetry could never be taken quite seriously though it reflects on human behaviour or it can tell a story': in other words it deals with parabolic and not literal truths. 'The patience, character & will power necessary to the novelist is not to the poet.... to express what you would say, you must have had parallel emotions, if not the same – to write of murder you need not necessarily have murdered anyone, but can go through the sensation in killing a fly that you might feel in killing your Mother-in-law.'

In 1940 Auden amended 'the necessary murder' to 'the fact of murder' and 'deliberate' to 'inevitable'. By then Eric Blair, writing under the pseudonym of George Orwell in *Adelphi* in December 1938, had misquoted Auden's line as 'the acceptance of guilt for the necessary murder', a sentiment which epitomised (so he jibed) the collaboration of 'the gangster and the pansy'. This sexual rubbishing of Auden has particular significance: 'Often thoughts of hate conceal Love we are ashamed to feel, Auden wrote in 1939; Rayner Heppenstall in 1936 had complained to Richard Rees of 'Eric Blair, who got a bloody homosexual crush on me, stifled it, let it fester and then, when he had me helpless, went for me with a metal-bound shooting stick'. In 1940 Orwell revived his attack on Auden as an abettor of totalitarian cruelty. 'Mr Auden's brand of amoralism is only possible if you are the kind of person who is always somewhere else when the trigger is pulled': Auden notoriously was in the United States at this time while many of his contemporaries were fighting in the European war. 'So much of left-wing thought is a kind of playing with fire by people who don't even know that fire is hot.' Though this exchange is often upheld as an example of Orwell's uncompromising clearheadedness, it actually reads like a piece of Etonian bullying, or 'densely unjust', as Auden wrote on 11 May 1963:

I was *not* excusing totalitarian crimes but only trying to say what, surely, every decent person thinks if he finds himself unable to adopt the absolute pacifist position. (1) To kill another human being is always murder and should never be called anything else. (2) In a war, the members of two rival groups try to murder their opponents. (3) *If* there is such a thing as a just war, then murder can be necessary for the sake of justice.

Auden did not hold a grudge against Orwell, writing generously of him in 1971. He also came to regret the final lines of 'Spain':

> time is short, and
> History to the defeated
> May say Alas but cannot help or pardon.

These lines 'equate goodness with success', he wrote thirty years later. 'It would have been bad enough if I had ever held this wicked doctrine, but that I should have stated it simply because it sounded to me rhetorically effective is quite inexcusable.' The importance of 'Spain 1937' is as a necessary preliminary to the poetry written by Auden after his visit to the Sino-Japanese war in 1938. The sonnet sequence 'In Time of War' has been called by Mendelson 'Auden's most profound and audacious poem of the 1930s, perhaps the greatest English poem of the decade': it has altogether greater stature, moral cohesion, imaginative power and poetic significance than 'Spain 1937', yet Orwell and Auden's other critics have little to say of it.

Auden's Spanish visit is the least documented episode of his adult life. 'Exigence is never an excuse for not telling the truth,' he told Spender in August 1937, but he was reluctant to disavow progressive people's idealisation of the Republicans. His most revealing contemporary comments were in a review of Malraux's *L'Espoir* (published in Britain as *Days of Hope*). Auden's review is more revealing of his own state of mind than of its ostensible subject. He fastened on the need for a transcendent faith to make sense of things. 'This rare combination of the sensibility of the writer with the experience of the man of action has produced an epic which, in my opinion, is likely to emerge as one of the greatest books of our generation,' Auden wrote of Malraux's book in October 1938. Like Violet Clifton's love that made the fragments of life cohere, Malraux has 'faith that binds all the different scenes and characters into an attractive whole'. Although *Days of Hope* 'was written by an active fighter for the Spanish Government, you must not think that the Government is painted in sham snow white. Inefficiencies, cruelties, intrigues, the conflict between Anarchists and Communists, between those who want to be something and those who want to do something, are not glossed over, but through all the mess and muddle, the amazing courage and determination of the Spanish people shines out.'

Auden had seen all the mess and muddle in Republican Spain, but he had seen something that had made him flinch more deeply. He had gone there under the influence of Owen's phrase, 'The Poetry is in the Pity', and it was on this word that he later choked in disgust. 'Behind pity for another lies self-pity, and behind self-pity lies cruelty,' he wrote. Pity as a 'corrupt parody of love and compassion' led 'to the torture chamber and the corrective labor camp'. He had seen this mentality on the Republican side in Spain. Like Simone Weil, who returned from a Catalonian tour in 1936 having undergone religious conversion but preferring not to speak of her civil war experiences, Auden was shocked at the demolition, despoiling and enforced closure of the churches in Barcelona, revolted by the maltreatment of priests, knew in time that ten bishops and thousands of priests were murdered by Republican supporters. This began a process of thought that led to his reversion to Christianity. 'I could not escape acknowledging that, however I had consciously ignored and rejected the Church for sixteen years, the existence of churches and what went on in them had all the time been very important to me. If that was the case, what then?' There is a reference to Christian prayer in 'Spain' which few people have chosen to notice. Auden describes humanity calling out to the Creator:

> And the nations combine each cry, invoking the life
> That shapes the individual belly and orders
>   The private nocturnal terror:
> 'Did you not found the city state of the sponge,
> Raise the vast military empires of the shark
> And the tiger, establish the robin's plucky canton?
>   Intervene. O descend as a dove or
> A furious papa or a mild engineer, but descend'.
> And the life, if it answers at all, replies from the heart
>
>   . . .
>
> 'O no, I am not the mover;
> Not to-day; not to you'.

He was not ready, in the spring of 1937, to be moved by an act of faith.

In the few months after 'Spain 1937' Auden wrote a series of bitter ballads like 'Miss Gee' and 'Victor' which suggest a cankered mood. Then in July he visited Oxford. There, 'in a publisher's office, I met an Anglican layman, and for the first time in my life felt myself in the presence of personal sanctity', he wrote in 1956. 'I had met many good people before who made me feel ashamed of my own shortcomings, but in the presence of this man – we never discussed anything but literary business – I did not feel ashamed. I felt transformed into a person who was incapable of doing or thinking anything base or unloving.' The man was Charles Williams, a poet and religious writer who worked for Oxford University Press. He had a similar effect on people other than Auden. 'Behind the amiability, behind the evident modesty and simplicity, was ... such humility as, in any company, can charm and put at ease the most exalted, and subdue the most shameless,' T. S. Eliot wrote of their meetings. Williams joined a passion for poetry with a retentive memory so that he could quote at length from favourite masterpieces like *Paradise Lost* or Wordsworth's *Prelude*.

'At ease in human society, I am sure that he would have remained equally composed if a ghost, an angel or an evil spirit had entered the room. He would have known how to receive any kind of supernatural visitor, for he took the other world as simply as this one.' Quant quelling the radio by telepathy, or other bizarre moments in *The Age of Anxiety*, would have been credible to Williams. Eliot celebrated him as 'a man of unusual genius' for the way in which 'seeing all persons and events in the light of the divine, he shows us a significance, in human beings, human emotions, human events, to which we have been blind ... he writes about good and evil, about the inevitable progress of every human being to heaven or hell, simply because these are the most exciting things to write about.' Like Auden he had a serious view of the purpose of frivolity. He hailed for instance P. G. Wodehouse's butler-hero Jeeves as 'the Don Quixote of the twentieth century'. C. S. Lewis knew no one 'more playful' than Williams. He enjoyed 'high pomps', but always:

> as a game: not a silly game, to be laid aside in private, but a glorious game, well worth the playing. This two-edged attitude, banked down under the deliberate casualness of the modern fashion, produced his actual manners, which were liked by most, extremely disliked by a few.... Williams' manners implied a complete offer of intimacy without the slightest imposition of intimacy. He threw down all his own barriers without even implying that you should lower yours.

Williams's theory of belief had an echo almost of Coué's formula for self-mastery. He believed like Auden in choosing what one willed. It was in this direction that Auden's ideas moved during 1937.

Meanwhile he planned more travel books. A lecture tour of the USA with Spender, to be followed by a joint book along the lines of his Iceland collaboration with MacNeice, was mooted in May 1937, before Faber and Random House agreed to commission Auden and Isherwood to write a travel book. The authors decided that their subject would be the war which had been provoked by the Japanese in July with Marshal Chiang Kai-shek's nationalist forces in China. Isherwood's meticulous reportage was to provide a prose commentary on China and its war, while Auden would write about the war parabolically to provide a theory of human violence. After contracting with Faber, Auden spent part of August and

September 1937 living at Dover, where he befriended E. M. Forster – 'our greatest living novelist', he called him a year later. The dedicatory sonnet to *Journey to a War* is written for Forster:

> As we run down the slope of Hate with gladness
> You trip us like an unnoticed stone,
> And just as we are closeted with Madness
> You interrupt us like the telephone.

Isherwood was with Auden in Dover, and together they began their final play, *On the Frontier*, which was published by Faber in October 1938 (with a Group Theatre production following in November in Cambridge, and a performance in London in February 1939). The play centred on the infatuated, love-crossed children of the Vrodny family in Ostnia and the Thorvalds in Westland. As a counterpoint to their disrupted domesticity, there is a plot of high politics featuring an armaments manufacturer called Valerian who manipulates the fascist leader of Westland. The leader's craziness reflected the Kafka-like horror of European political reality, but the supreme aim of Auden and Isherwood was to disinter the human experiences that had been buried under the debris of slogans and false description. Some unsuccessful last-minute revisions and the pressing, grim horrors of the European crisis overtaking the details of the plot meant that *On the Frontier* was the least successful of their plays, though it had some powerful moments. 'There is no *inner* development in the course of the acts,' judged the *Times Literary Supplement*. 'We might parallel it in some ways with the morality play. The response to be evoked is "This is wicked. It ought not to be." It is also like a superb parody of public life, where Truth is borne through the theatre on a placard.' Privately the audience were more critical. 'Lord how bad the Auden Isherwood play was,' Virginia Woolf wrote to V. Sackville-West. 'Unquestionably it was a failure,' Keynes reported to Raymond Mortimer. 'They are getting too old for so much infantilism and amateurism.'

During the autumn of 1937 Auden prepared his anthology *The Oxford Book of Light Verse* (for which he received an advance of £100). It was the discussion of this project that had brought him into contact with Charles Williams. The anthology was published in England in October 1938 and in the States two months later. Like *The Poet's Tongue*, it was marvellously eclectic: carols, nonsense rhymes, Irish ballads, black spirituals, 'Casey Jones' and 'The Man on the Flying Trapeze' were mixed with Chaucer,

Shakespeare, Dryden and Blake. Light versifiers such as Barham and Praed were included with modern masters like Hardy, Lawrence and Yeats. In a characteristically astute review, Louise Bogan quoted Yeats to convey the mood of the book: 'Only that which does not teach, does not cry out, does not persuade, does not condescend, does not explain, is irresistible.' There was nothing sterile or hack about Auden's work on the book (although admittedly he delegated the dullest slog of compilation because of his absence abroad). Grey Gowrie has compared Auden's anthologising to the doodlings of Picasso: a necessary preliminary to great art which, because it is casual, unemotional, mongrel and playful, is perhaps the easiest way 'to show the fly the way out of the fly bottle'.

Auden and Isherwood left for China at the start of 1938. On 18 January a leaving party was held for them at Julian Trevelyan's studio in Hammersmith. Sir Edward Marsh, Rose Macaulay and Forster were among the guests. '"Benjie" Britten played & Hedley [sic] Anderson sang, & there were refreshments, & dancing & a buffet & think someone playing the concertina & *great* crowd of Wystan and C's friends,' noted Kathleen Isherwood. Brian Howard and Eddie Gathorne-Hardy started a brawl. 'Do not think C & W enjoyed it very much.' They left next day and reached Egypt on 25 January for a reunion with their Berlin friend Francis Turville-Petre. Together they were keeping notes, which Isherwood later reworked into the prose sections of *Journey to a War*. An early draft describing the voyage eastwards, with Auden's phrases more distinct in it, was published in *Harper's Bazaar*:

> CAIRO: that immense and sinister Woolworth's, where everything is for sale — love, lottery tickets, clothes hangers, honor, justice, indecent postcards, bootlaces, disease — as much and as cheap as you like, till the buyer goes mad with boredom and guilt. And behind it, at the end of a tram ride, the three Pyramids, looking ugly and quite new, like the tip-heaps of a prosperous quarry. For a long time, we couldn't find the Sphinx at all. Stumbling over the litter of recent excavations, we came upon it suddenly, smaller than its photographs, in a pit … it lies there mutilated and sightless, its paws clumsily bandaged with bricks, its mane like an old actor's wig, asking no riddle, turning its back upon America — injured baboon with a lion's cruel mouth, in the middle of invaded Egypt.

Afterwards Auden reworked some of these phrases into a sonnet ending, '"Am I to suffer always?" Yes.'

Their journey soon resumed. 'Wystan endured the voyage glumly, sometimes grumpily; he disliked being at sea, deplored the tropics, felt uprooted from his chilly beloved North,' Isherwood wrote. On 16 February they arrived in Hong Kong, where they were entertained by officials and tycoons. Auden remained disgruntled – 'the oxtail soup wasn't oxtail', he complained, 'the women were cows and wore mermaid dresses' – and later, in Brussels, wrote his poems 'Hong Kong' and 'Macao'. In this British colony they also befriended the Ambassador to China, Sir Archibald Clark Kerr, whom they met again in Hankow and stayed with in Shanghai. Clark Kerr had read some of Auden's poems, had enjoyed Isherwood's Berlin novels, and showed other signs of heterodoxy. He liked Auden and Isherwood because they went to China as lively, receptive travellers rather than committed ideologues. 'Looking for the war in China is like a novel by Kafka,' Auden wrote to Dodds on 20 April from the British Consulate at Hankow. Bulletins contradicted the evidence of their eyes; fighting eluded them. Taking 'a Lewis Carroll walking tour' on their first evening in Canton, they found 'two old men trying to put a rat into a bottle, a woman pouring water into a sieve'. Elsewhere they saw green horses which turned out to be white horses camouflaged against aircraft and met an old women who lived in a bee-hive. As in Spain, or any war, there were desultory days in which the two men waited for other people to make decisions about their fate. On 11 May they were at Tunki waiting for permission to go to the front. Mah-jongg players made a perpetual clatter of their pieces at the hotel, at breakfast there were patriotic songs, and, when the Englishmen returned from killing time in the shopping district, a Chinese acquaintance told them, 'I have spent the morning with the dictionary and learnt two new words – Jingoism and Rumour.'

There were also moments – not the most active or physically exciting – that had momentous significance. One lazy sociable day at Hankow raised all the great questions for Auden: cultural identity, phoniness and cheating, violence and faith. It was 23 April, St George's Day as Isherwood noted. First he and Auden went to a lunch-party at the British Consulate where they were staying.

Lunch was argumentative and political. Somebody present believed that Franco was a gentleman and a sportsman, because he played a good game of golf, and had attended the British Consul's funeral in the Canary Islands on his way to start the rebellion in Morocco. Somebody else gave an interesting analysis of Chiang Kai-shek's Easter Speech ... the Chiangs' Christianity will prove an increasingly effective political weapon to counter the propaganda of the Anti-Comintern Pact. The old accusations against the Communists and their allies of 'godlessness' are getting more and more difficult to sustain. Mao Tse-tung himself is said to have attended Mass.

Afterwards the two men went to a cocktail party at the Race Club. It seems to have reminded them of their prep school at Hindhead.

Not only the Race Club buildings but even the grounds surrounding them might well be in the heart of Surrey. Here, as Auden remarked, all trace of China has been lovingly obliterated. We drank to 'St. George's Day – England's Day', and looked forward to 'the match tomorrow with our brother Scots, and an excellent tiffin with the St. Andrew's Society'.

In the evening they attended a supper party at a Russian dance restaurant known to British officers as 'The Dumps'. It was not only St George's Day but, as Isherwood recorded,

also the eve of the Russian Orthodox Easter. Just before midnight we joined the group of onlookers at the doors of the Russian church, which stands a little way down the road from the British Consulate. The church itself was crammed. From the interior came whiffs of incense and hot leather – the nostalgic perfume of exile. Nearly the whole of the White Russian colony must have been assembled, including the taxi-girls from 'The Dumps'. Their high-boned faces, illuminated by the candles which each member of the congregation held in his or her hand, looked beautiful and cold and pure. Many of the taxi-girls were accompanied by their men friends, heavy, blue-chinned figures in dinner-jackets, waiting, somewhat impatiently, for midnight, when custom would permit them to exchange the ambiguous Easter kiss.

The contrast between the starchy, phoney, materialistic English, whose transplantation of Home Counties proprieties to China seemed so crassly outlandish, and the Russian exiles, who were so much less outlandish because, like Malraux in *L'Espoir* or Violet Clifton's *Book of Talbot*, their faith bound everything into a cohesive whole, was perhaps another episode in Auden's return to Christianity. It moved him towards believing the message that he found in Kafka: 'To be saved is to have Faith and to have Faith means to recognise something as the Necessary. Whether or not the faith of an individual is misplaced does not matter; indeed, in an absolute sense, it always is.' Several of the sonnets that he wrote refer to Christian beliefs like the Fall or Incarnation. The Chinese war was 'one sector and one movement of the general war' which for humankind 'in essence is eternal', Auden wrote, before rehearsing the doctrine of original sin in a section beginning 'And, if we care to listen, we can always hear them.'

'Spain 1937' was a rallying cry written by a poet who was trapped as the servant of his celebrity, but its glib, ingenious servitude to a political cause was cancelled by this sonnet sequence written a year later and called 'In Time of War'. In Spain Auden had relished the poets exploding like bombs, but Chinese searchlights raking the night sky during a Japanese air-raid take Auden into analogies which have no political opportunism about them. It is as if the searchlights reveal 'the little natures' – the personal hatreds which his grandfathers would have attributed to original sin – 'that will make us cry':

> Behind each sociable home-loving eye
> The private massacres are taking place;
> All Women, Jews, the Rich, the Human race.
>
> The mountains cannot judge us when we lie:
> We dwell upon the earth; the earth obeys
> The intelligent and evil till they die.

These sonnets, and the accompanying 'Commentary', attempt nothing less than a synthesis of human nature: they comprise a counterpart to Pope's *Essay on Man* written in an epoch of tyranny and violence. His intentions were so ambitious that, as he confessed at the time to Mrs Dodds of the 'Commentary', 'I am very uncertain this kind of thing is possible without becoming a prosy pompous old bore.' For a biographer, perhaps, the only way to convey the importance of 'In Time of War' is by showing its importance to readers at the time. 'Since Yeats's death he has taken his place as the first poet writing in English,' Lincoln Kirstein wrote of Auden in August 1939 after reading the Chinese sonnets. 'He is always suspect – a really dangerous person, in so far as anyone is dangerous – for he threatens even our most recent and difficulty intrenched [sic] ideas. He also employs pragmatic treachery to every conceived poetic formula. In this treachery he uses as forced allies any English poet from Beowulf to Byron. He scraps these allies, one after the other, to found a new front which may have certain special uses ... He can be hateful. He is the relentless adversary of the kind of weak conscience-money conspiratorial optimism which now identifies so many of us within the fringes of protest and action – where we have our precarious moral safety just under the angle of the guns of our real defenders.' The sonnets were difficult to read, Kirstein warned, because 'the thought they embody is hard for all of us to comprehend. Once they are understood, they make it even more difficult to proceed with that understanding in us ... The reason Auden is writing the greatest poetry of our speech is because his one subject is personal responsibility. He assumes for himself, as a man, the entire load, the whole blame.'

With Isherwood he sailed from Shanghai on 12 June, travelling via Japan to Vancouver, and then entraining to New York, which presented an attractive mixture of erotic pleasure and flattering attention: *Harper's Bazaar*, for example, published extracts from Auden and Isherwood's travel diary, which would have been unthinkable in an equivalent English magazine (though *Harper's Magazine* in London later reprinted the piece). Yet there was a trace of masochism in Auden's attraction to New York City. Years later he was 'reported to have told Professor Theodore Spencer he preferred to live in New York because the things he hated most were there more obvious and he was therefore in no danger of succumbing to their neon lures'. Although Auden and Isherwood returned to Europe after a fortnight in New York, the former lived mostly abroad until the end of September. 'He had already decided by August 1938, when I was staying with him in Bruxelles, to become an American citizen,' his brother John told Evelyn Waugh in 1951. He spent most of October 1938 living at his parents' house, where he completed the sonnet section of *Journey to a War*, although by mid-October he was also contributing book-notes to a leftist Birmingham workers' newspaper, the *Town Crier*, and was inveigled into propaganda work. On 6 November, for example, he and Isherwood lectured at the Group Theatre on China in wartime; on 28 November at Dulwich; and again on 2 December at Bedford College in Regent's Park. 'I get very depressed about running all over the place chatting about China,' he reported to Mrs Dodds in late 1938. 'Does it do any good? Should I be better employed on my own work? If so am I being immoral? Or is this just selfish? VERY TIRED of train journeys.'

The publicity included broadcasting too. 'Wystan Auden ... to the Alexandra Palace for the Television Programme this evening,' Kathleen Isherwood recorded in her diary on 12 October:

> The screen is very small & does not always focus quite clearly. It was a regular programme like cinema – with an announcer one sees as well as hears – Wystan & Christopher did a talk, & there they were, Wystan leaning back rather nervously in an arm chair & Christopher standing at one side against a bookcase. They talked on the drama in turn. Christopher was the clearer but both their voices were perfectly recognisable & the vision of them moderately clear – it was extraordinary to think that they were away at the Alexandra Palace – A Grierson Post Office film followed.

Auden also spoke on the Midland service of BBC radio about the Chinese war. 'Publicity is inescapable in any profession which aims to influence the public directly,' wrote Denis Healey, who as a young man in the 1930s was an intent reader of Auden's poetry and forty years later as Deputy Leader of the Labour Party retained his admiration. 'Auden', Healey wrote, 'understood the politician's problem because he too was a public figure':

> These public men who seem so to enjoy their dominion
> With their ruined faces and voices treble with hate,
> Are no less martyrs because unaware of their fetters.
> What would you be like, were you never allowed to create
> Or reflect, but compelled to give an immediate opinion,
> Condemned to destroy or distribute the work of your betters?

Auden had to escape this. 'We're VERY, VERY tired of admiration,' he wrote after settling in the US.

Shortly after emigrating, in the summer of 1939, Auden drafted a semi-autobiographical retrospective. 'Few of the artists who round about 1931 began to take up politics as an exciting new subject to write about, had the faintest idea what they were letting themselves in for,' he wrote. 'They have been carried along on a wave which is travelling too fast to let them think what they are doing or where they are going.' He and his friends had been political failures. 'If one reviews the political activity of the world's intellectuals during the past eight years, if one counts up all the letters to the papers which they have signed, all the platforms on which they have spoken, all the congresses which they have attended, one is compelled to admit that their combined effort, apart from the money they have helped to raise for humanitarian purposes (and one must not belittle the value of that) has been nil.' Auden saw the failure of the intellectuals as a failure of will. 'No one can succeed at anything unless he is not only passionately interested in it, but absolutely confident of success,' he wrote, with some echo of the maxims about personal resolve of Rivers and Coué whom he had studied in the 1920s. Artists were more futile politically than intellectuals. 'If the criterion of art were its power to incite to action, Goebbels would be one of the greatest artists of all time,' he wrote in 1939. 'Art makes nothing happen.' These views were unforgivable to some of his 1930s admirers, especially those who had thought him more *engagé* than he himself would have conceded.

But Auden made another choice at this time that proved embittering to some of his admirers. He left England. His decision partly reflected his lifelong wish for the strictest working routine and his settled dislike of the London literary life. He had always found his parents' house in Birmingham was better accommodated to hard-working seclusion than any of the flats or houses of his metropolitan friends. But in any case he wanted to keep clear of all the envy, rancour and indignation that surround disputed authors. Grigson in 1936 had depicted London as the place where 'the Great Game of Literature is being played', a miserable terrain on which 'the littlest men, the Herbert Reads for example, terrified that one day they may be out of things, are forming their Front'. Auden skirted these manoeuvrings, and had Grigson's respect for this. 'Integrity is the scarcest quality in young English writers, a meditated purpose is still more scarce. His toughness, his curiosity, his love, his versatility, his plain cleverness as a writer still lift W. H. Auden above everyone else.' It was Auden's integrity, toughness and meditated purpose that took him abroad. Early in December 1938 he went to Paris to lecture on poetic drama at the Sorbonne; he then spent about three weeks in Brussels with Isherwood, during which time he wrote a dozen poems of superb diversity.

Auden and Isherwood had contracted to write for the Hogarth Press a travel book on the United States with the preliminary title of *Address Not Known*. They returned to London early in January to prepare for what both of them intended to be their emigration to the United States. It was the culmination of so many of Auden's ideas since his journey to Iceland. About twenty years later he explained his decision to emigrate to a fellow literary exile, Robin Maugham.

> England is terribly provincial – it's all this family business. I know exactly why Guy Burgess went to Moscow. It wasn't enough to be a queer and a drunk. He had to revolt still more to break away from it all. That's just what I've done by becoming an American citizen. You can become an Italian or a French citizen – and that's all right. But become an American citizen and you've crossed to the wrong side of the tracks.... I also find criticism in England very provincial. In the literary world in England, you have to know who's married to whom, and who's slept with whom and who hasn't. It's a tiny jungle. America's so much larger.

In 1971 he quoted a phrase of Maugham's uncle, the novelist, 'In order to understand one's own country, one should have lived in at least two others,' and then told Geoffrey Gorer, 'I am much more conscious now of being British and Upper Middle Class Professional than I ever was when I lived in England.'

His departure was hurtful to his admirers, for whom it seemed a cruel example of how 'clever hopes expire'. The novelist Michael Nelson recalled a former Bryanston pupil (afterwards killed in the war) weeping in a café when he heard the news. Some reactions were more snide. A few days afterwards, Kathleen Isherwood was telephoned three nights running by a 'strange young man' who engaged in 'resentful' conversations which she summarised in note form:

> rather inclined to consider W C & Stephen were very lucky to have so caught the public fancy, some people hadn't such luck who also wrote, he & his friends etc! – asked what he had written? so far only

in a school magazine! but evidently felt that this was because merit
was not properly recognised – said very convenient for them to be in
N York now when bombs might be falling on England.

The carping did not abate; indeed the hardships of the war, and the
discomfort of cold, hungry, semi-bankrupt post-war Britain, often
increased the resentment. English reviewers of Auden's work in the 1940s
showed their grudge. Evelyn Waugh, reviewing Spender's memoirs in
1951, claimed that Auden had fled to the USA 'at the first squeak of an air-
raid warning'; the charge of cowardice was misplaced, since Auden in
China had proved 'obviously a brave man physically' neglecting 'his fear
under gunfire'. Nevertheless in a few cases the animosity became a feud to
the grave. Anthony Powell, whose squib on Auden and Isherwood
published in the *New Statesman* in 1940 provoked Kathleen Isherwood to
call him 'A Viper', was breakfasting with Kingsley Amis in 1973 when the
morning obituaries sent him into a paroxysm of glee. 'No more Auden,'
Powell announced. 'I'm delighted that shit has gone.' His loathing was
emphatic. 'It should have happened years ago … scuttling off to America
in 1939 with his boyfriend like a … like a …' Powell felt too violently to
finish his sentence. It was hard for some English to forgive Auden for
settling in the USA on the eve of war because that war so firmly settled
Britain's pretensions to cultural and political hegemony of the English-
speaking world. Those who considered him to be a military deserter were
often those who resented Britain's eclipse as a world power after 1945, and
were most reluctant to admit that the greatest English-language novelists
and poets in the 1950s and after were not British-born or British-resident.

Auden arrived in New York by ship on 26 January 1939. Isherwood
travelled with him, though their reasons for emigrating were not identical.
It was for Auden another act of self-mortification. 'An artist ought either
to live where he has live roots or where he has no roots at all,' he told
MacNeice in 1940. 'In England to-day the artist feels essentially lonely,
twisted in dying roots, always in opposition to a group … in America, he is
just lonely, but so … is everybody else; with 140 million lonelies milling
around him he need not waste his time in conforming or rebelling.'
Though Auden had left the European war zone, he was not running away
from the cold, controlled ferocity of the human race. 'He could have gone
to more terrible places, Rome for instance, but he wanted a place he could
not romanticize,' as Guy Davenport says of Auden's arrival in New York.

'He came to ensure that he was among humanity at its worst in this century.'

CHAPTER 7

'Mr Right has come into my life'

On their arrival in New York Auden and Isherwood took rooms in the George Washington Hotel, which provided low rates for long-stay guests. They stayed there until early in April, when they rented a cheap apartment on East 81st Street in the Yorkville district of Manhattan. Auden was poor, impressionable, eager for work but uncertain what to do; his situation was full of possibilities, which he approached with a mixture of apprehension and zest. He and Isherwood renewed friendships from their visit in July 1938, and were pitchforked into a hectic social round partly intended to bring them moneyed contacts. 'Auden is in NY and dined here last night, very energetic and amiable,' Glenway Wescott noted on 8 February. Paul Bowles saw him several times during 1939: 'he's pretty eccentric and does strange things like picking his nose and eating what he finds,' Bowles reported: 'however he's very bright and fun to talk to.' Some authors declined meetings. 'Just a note to ask you *not* to bring Auden and Isherwood to see me,' Louise Bogan wrote to Edmund Wilson on 22 March. 'I have no interest in seeing them, in their present phase, and ... can't say I want to spend an evening being examined by two visiting Englishmen, as a queer specimen.'

Her aloofness was in contrast to the excitement of Frederic Prokosch, who had printed some of Auden's poems. 'He looked youthful and alert, uncouth and yet sprightly,' Prokosch recalled of their early meetings. 'There was always a certain shyness and remoteness about Auden, as though he yearned for friendship but shrank from a deeper intimacy, and the enigma of his character lay in this remoteness, which eventually led him into the swamps of self-torment.' This judgment reflects the fact that, despite considering Prokosch to be one of his best critics, Auden rejected his proffered friendship, though for a time Prokosch took the snubs as if they were honourable scars. Auden was never avid, gullible or undiscriminating about admiration, although in New York he became accustomed to the explicit compliments and attentive respect of Americans and by the 1950s could feel hurt by the more oblique style of the English.

Auden and Isherwood were shamelessly on the pick for patrons. One evening they went to the 'immense Park Avenue apartment' of a rich old lady, Mrs Curry Maine. As they were leaving they met the impecunious left-wing English intellectual Esmond Romilly and his wife Jessica Mitford arriving. 'Esmond had known them quite well in London, but as though by common consent both they and we confined our greetings to a distant bow,' Mitford recalled. '"Trying to muscle in on our racket! They've got a hell of a nerve," Esmond muttered. Judging by their expressions, the thought was fully reciprocated.' Auden came to believe that 'the most striking difference' between Americans and Europeans was 'in their attitudes towards money'. His explanation of this helped to make his use of American patrons seem unexceptionable. Europeans recognised as an historical fact 'that, in Europe, wealth could only be acquired at the expense of other human beings, either by conquering them or by exploiting their labor'. There were few chances of great self-enrichment. It was a humane consequence that 'no European associates wealth with personal merit or poverty with personal failure'. But in the United States, 'the real exploited victim was not a human being but poor Mother Earth and her creatures who were ruthlessly plundered'. Auden thought that every American male could reasonably expect to make more than his father. 'What an American values, therefore, is not the possession of money as such, but his power to make it as a proof of his manhood; once he has proved himself by making it, it has served its function and can be lost or given away.' In his adopted country Auden was shocked by the waste: 'The great vice of Americans is not materialism but a lack of respect for matter.'

In the early months in New York Auden often saw his wife Erika Mann and her brothers Klaus and Golo. 'His manner was appealingly awkward, but at the same time self-confident,' Golo wrote in 1973. 'He had the air of one who was used to being *primus inter pares*, one might even say a triumphant air, so long as this does not suggest anything exaggerated or theatrical.' Mann added: 'He was the most intelligent man I have known, or rather, because "intelligence" only suggests insight and understanding, the cleverest, with a cleverness which was essentially creative. He thought truths out for himself. Many of them could have been expanded into whole books.' In August 1940 Auden visited Thomas and Katja Mann in California. Golo Mann later told Humphrey Carpenter that there was 'a slight erotical touch' in Auden's relations with his sister: he thought Auden's high valuation of the relationship was indicated by his visit to her parents in Switzerland in 1935. Auden afterwards became an editorial adviser to a cultural review, *Decision*, conceived by Klaus Mann. Auden contributed reviews, translations and poems in the first six months of 1941, and during March that year the two men collaborated in a radio discussion of the writer's functions in wartime.

Thomas Mann had been lent a summer house on Rhode Island by a rich spinster, Caroline Newton, to whom Auden was introduced early in 1940. She had been psychoanalysed by both Freud and Karen Horney, but despite setting up in psychiatric practice herself she remained a neurotic and even risible figure. To Auden she was a generous if emotionally exacting patron; she gave him cash, hospitality and gifts but was self-absorbed, histrionic and self-important. In 1942 he suspected her of having 'tried to poison me mildly' after he had taxed her with stealing some letters and wrote of her, 'Ladies who were meant to be unselfish maiden-aunts should not read Freud.' He broke with her in 1944, by which time he was bored with her clumsy demanding infatuation and perhaps ashamed of his cadging.

Auden was introduced by the Manns to other refugees from Nazi Germany, notably Wolfgang Kohler, one of the originators of gestalt psychology, 'a great man with quite a lot of neuroses', as Auden warned a friend; 'death is a subject which must never be mentioned in his presence and even age is risky'. Kohler had earlier been with Lane, Freud and Groddeck one of the psychologists whose ideas were used in *The Orators*. His work examined how the characteristics of things were altered by their environment, and emphasised how visual and auditory perceptions of an object were interactive with its surroundings. Auden had always liked symbolic correspondences because they were 'never one to one but always multiple, and different persons perceive different meanings', and absorbed Kohler's ideas into his growing religious sense. Kohler also appealed to Auden's detective instincts. The accumulation, classification and analysis of facts by Kohler, or by Auden's other father-figures like

Gerald Heard and later W. H. Sheldon and Eugen Rosenstock-Huessy, resembled the methods of Sherlock Holmes, an 'exceptional individual', as Auden wrote, 'who is in a state of grace because he is a genius in whom scientific curiosity is raised to the status of a heroic passion'. Auden had Holmes's urge for elucidation. He studied relations between people and things, involved himself in a maze of intricate detail, listing the congruences and incongruities, always defining and commenting. His words resembled the suspicious tricks of the public prosecutor whose speech opened his obituary of Yeats in *Partisan Review* of 1939: he knew that there was 'a connection between these facts' which would prove the guilt. 'We can repress the joy, but the guilt remains conscious,' he wrote in 1942, and twelve years later, 'The prosecutor knows the defendant will hang.'

From March 1939 onwards Auden earned fees by publishing book reviews or his new poems in magazines like the *Nation*, the *New Republic* and *Common Sense*, together with smaller, impoverished periodicals like the religious journal *Commonweal*. He avoided reviewing near-contemporaries (Louise Bogan and Theodore Roethke were exceptions), and reviewed only what he could praise (Lewis Mumford was an exception in 1944). 'Pleasure is by no means an infallible critical guide, but it is the least fallible,' he later wrote. He often seemed to be contending with the ideas of his subjects – in 1939 they included Matthew Arnold, de la Mare, Rilke, Rimbaud, Shakespeare, Voltaire and Yeats – and his prose continued to be a fascinating commentary on the poetry that he was simultaneously writing. 'Auden never argues with himself, never amends or modifies what he wishes to say … yet his style is never dictatorial; on the contrary it is intimate and friendly,' Golo Mann wrote of these articles. 'Nine out of ten of his pronouncements, taken at random, are so illuminating that to the reader it is as if the scales had fallen from his eyes.'

Auden was in demand as a public performer. 'Poets here are orators – have to be so, since the public is their paymaster and ready to pay them handsomely if only they will desert their caves of solitary personal feeling and come out and work for their affectionate generous masters' – so John Butler Yeats, the poet's father, had written from New York in 1910. Auden too was drawn from his cave. His speech on the European crisis to the Human Relations Institute of the University of North Carolina was reported in the *New York Times* and like MacLeish he might have made a career in punditry if he had wished. His decision to abandon political activism 'came after making a speech at a dinner in New York to get money for Spanish Refugees' on 16 March. 'I suddenly found ... I could make a fighting demagogic speech and have the audience roaring,' he reported to Mrs Dodds. 'So exciting but so absolutely degrading; I felt just covered with dirt afterwards.' He however continued to teach courses, for example giving weekly lectures on poetry to the pro-Soviet League of American Writers in the autumn of 1939 and to the New School for Social Research in the spring of 1940.

'New York is awful; we have no money, and few prospects of getting any,' he wrote to John Auden in April. 'If you ever get that depressed unable-to-concentrate feeling, try taking Benzidrine [sic] Tablets, but not too many.' He had been introduced to Benzedrine on his earlier visit to New York in July 1938, and for some twenty years used the drug to give him mental energy in the mornings. He supplemented it with the barbiturate Seconal at night. This was a human expression of his lifelong attraction to efficient machinery. He always admired people fulfilling their vocations, finding it 'beautiful' how they wore 'the same rapt expression, forgetting themselves in a function'. The 'inefficiency' of Rimbaud's later years, after he had abandoned his creative vocation for the life of an African chieftain, was, he wrote in 1939, 'pathetic'. Efficiency was a sign of vocation, and drugs seemed to make him more efficient: Benzedrine enabled him to start work when he willed. Like 'alcohol, coffee, tobacco' it was one of the 'labor-saving devices' in 'the mental kitchen', he wrote in 1948; 'but these mechanisms are very crude, liable to injure the cook, and constantly breaking down'.

Benzedrine (first synthesised in 1887) is an amphetamine which had been mass marketed since 1927 as a bronchial dilator. In the 1930s and 1940s it was prescribed for a multitude of conditions – night blindness, seasickness, migraine and impotence – and had no illicit connotations. Psychiatrists enthusiastically prescribed it to treat obesity and depression. It was dispensed to troops in the Spanish Civil War to combat battle fatigue; 72 million tablets were issued to British forces during the Second World War; the British Prime Minister Anthony Eden was sustained by Benzedrine during the Suez crisis; and it was given with official sanction to US troops in Korea and Vietnam as it could engender a disregard of danger. It was also used as a 'pep-up' pill by some American athletes and coaches. In 1956 it was confined to physicians' prescription in Britain, although its possession was criminalised only in the 1960s as part of the reaction against youth culture. Auden took his pill openly at breakfast as in the 1990s one might take vitamins. Benzedrine brings 'elation, confidence and a desire to communicate fine new insights', often raising libido though possibly rendering erogenous zones less responsive; but with time the exhilaration and sense of mastery fall away into anxiety. Increasing doses are needed to maintain its effect, but 'a single large dose', concluded an expert study in the 1950s, 'may cause psychotic symptoms'. Auden came off Benzedrine by the early 1960s; coincidentally or otherwise, his withdrawal was marked by the increased repetitiveness of his monologues, and the receding brilliance of his social techniques.

In Brooklyn at the end of March 1939 an eighteen-year-old called Chester Kallman stood in front of a mirror combing his hair, and said to his friend Harold Norse, 'Did you know that Auden and Isherwood are reading on West Fifty-second Street next week? Let's sit in the front row and wink at them!' Norse has described Kallman at this time:

> Both sexes merged with androgynous appeal: willowy grace combined with a deep, manly voice. Not at all effeminate, just young and blond, he was tall, unathletic, with slightly stooped shoulders, a spinal curvature, and a heart murmur from rheumatic fever in childhood. He disliked all physical exercise except cruising, which developed his calf muscles. He picked his nose with long spatulate fingers, dirt-rimmed, and thoughtfully examined the product – a sure sign of a Brooklyn intellectual.

On reaching the meeting on 6 April, Kallman and Norse sat in the front row. Auden, who arrived with MacNeice and Prokosch as well as Isherwood, was typically dishevelled, and Kallman hissed, 'Miss *Mess.*' The writers were due to talk on 'Modern Trends in English Poetry and Prose', but instead Isherwood gave excerpts from *Journey to a War*, MacNeice read from the manuscript of his 'Autumn Journal' and Auden recited his elegy to Yeats. Auden 'was the star, the gauche comedian, the mad genius', Norse recounted. 'He stole the show. Overcome by the situation, we stifled giggles and continued to flirt outrageously with Isherwood, winking and grinning, and he grinned back.' Auden thought the meeting 'awful' and did not see the front-row antics; as he once said, 'a man whose true world opens inward tends to develop a voluntary blindness toward outward things'. Afterwards he ignored an attempt by the two Brooklyn boys to interview him, but Isherwood gave Norse a card with his address and telephone number.

Kallman appropriated the card, and on 8 April visited Isherwood. Auden opened the door, hoping to find an athletic student who had been at the meeting; he whispered to Isherwood, 'It's the wrong blond.' Yet their first conversation was a success, and when Kallman returned to the apartment a second time, they became lovers. On this occasion Auden gave him a volume of William Blake inscribed with the last stanzas of a cabaret song 'O Tell Me The Truth About Love' written by him in 1938 for MacNeice's future wife, Hedli Anderson:

> When it comes will it come without warning
> Just as I'm picking my nose?
> Will it knock at my door in the morning,
> Or tread in the bus on my toes?

Kallman had never before received such attention and was proportionately inflated. In the next few weeks Auden was 'mad with happiness', he told Britten. To his brother John he wrote in May:

> Just a line to tell you that it's really happened at last after all these years. Mr Right has come into my life. He is a Roumanian–Latvian—American Jew called Chester Kallman, eighteen, extremely intelligent and I *think*, about to become a good poet. His father who knows all and approves is a communist dentist who would be rich if he didn't have to pay two sets of alimony.
>
> This time, my dear, I really believe it's marriage. The snag is I think I shall have to become an American Citizen as I'm not going to risk separation through international crises. I write letters every day when I am away and so does he, have given up biting my nails and feel all warm and soft inside like a housemaid. Not only can I talk to him as an equal but he understands sex like no one I've ever met.

This last phrase suggests an early stage of infatuation, for it soon became evident that the two men were not sexually compatible.

It was impossible to be indifferent about Kallman. He resembled

Auden's English friend, Brian Howard, immortalised by Evelyn Waugh as Ambrose Silk in *Put Out More Flags* and as Anthony Blanche in *Brideshead Revisited*. As a youth Howard was as bright as a kingfisher flashing its fire; but he had always a tendency to pampered caprice, and was turned by drink into an egocentric abyss. He was charming; but on provocation might become a festering mass of resentment; and, like all vindictive people, he loved a fight. 'Perhaps it was just as well for both of them, that it was I, and not Brian, who met Chester,' Auden wrote in 1942. '*Think* of the scenes.' Auden was one of the few friends with whom Howard did not quarrel ('I'm the only person who can at all manage him'), and they maintained a prized intimacy until Howard's suicide in 1958. Kallman, too, was precocious, wayward, wilful and perpetuated his childhood resentments into adulthood; he had a sardonic Jewish wit of the kind known as gallows-humour. Both men were alert, amusing reviewers and proficient poetic amateurs without the stamina for solitary work. Neither man was fastidious about money. Each enjoyed 'the power that corrupts, that power to excess / The beautiful quite naturally possess'. In the assessment of Lincoln Kirstein,

> Chester was cast, or cast himself, in an 'impossible' role. He was competitive, although he knew perfectly well that he hadn't much right to be, but he insisted on the pose out of pure orneriness. On one level Wystan took him as a sort of hair-shirt and put up with him as an article of undoubting faith. But there was a lot of romance, and perhaps romanticism, involved.... Chester was always – as far as I can recall – extremely witty. The horrors of life struck him with an ancestral expectation of the worst, and he could turn the worst off by camping. He reigned over this province of formalized sensibility by appropriating the emotional world of 19th century Italian grand opera. But he was not a screaming queen; his tone was moderate and, for this, much funnier.
>
> He also, of course, had a real musical knowledge, sense and understanding. He broadened Wystan's taste and information. He had a very good ear, and his own light verse, often dirty but often brilliant, was original and skilful. He was a real pain in the ass on many occasions and caused Miss-Master plenty of trouble.... he assumed this was his obligation, and almost a service.... He could be very nasty, even about Wystan, which did not make one love him....

He was extremely intelligent analytically, and this, in addition to everything else, Wystan found useful.

Auden soon came to recognise that their similar need of pain was a stronger tie to Kallman than homosexuality. 'What the "neurotic" individual compared with the "normal" individual, or the Jews collectively compared with the "Aryans" collectively, see clearly is that suffering has value,' he told Delmore Schwartz in 1942 in a passage that reflected his deteriorating relationship with Kallman. 'For this reason qua neurotic and qua Jew they are tempted to desire suffering; – hence the tenacity with which the neurotic clings to his neurosis and the Jew to his race-consciousness.'

Kallman's adoration of the opera reflected his tendency to operatic antics. He described an evening with his father and grandmother to Auden in a letter of 11 May 1939: 'After about an hour and a half of rowing I got to a semi-hysterical state wherein I ran my hands through my hair and shouted "I hate him" like a third Act ... If I start out being responsible for all the mud that clings to my trousers I shall never become clean.' But his love of music enriched Auden's life immeasurably, and the two men collaborated in writing seven operatic libretti in the years after 1947. Kallman's literary judgments were also influential. After emigrating to America, Auden wrote essays celebrating his two British poetic fathers, Yeats and Hardy, in a way which also served as a personal interment. He needed a new literary master for America. Kallman (whom he met a few months after Yeats's death) often spoke as a young man of Flaubert, Proust and Henry James. This provided Auden with a new archetype of the hermitical, self-sustaining migrant artist. A sonnet written in 1940 ends with an image from the conclusion of James's short story 'The Jolly Corner' about a successful, self-sufficient, loveless man who has moved to the loneliness of New York and feels himself 'the king of all creatures' until he sees:

> Approaching down a ruined corridor,
> A figure with his own distorted features
> That wept, and grew enormous, and cried Woe.

This parable of the artist's doubleness was only a part of James's inspiration for Auden. In 1941 – the year Auden regaled Louise Bogan with 'charming anecdotes' of James after she relented in her refusal to meet him – he wrote a superb elegy, 'At the Grave of Henry James'. In it Auden admires the way that James 'fastidious as / A delicate nun remained true' to his gifts and did not sully himself like all those other writers 'whose works are in better taste than their lives'. It ends with Auden beseeching James. 'Preserve me, Master,' he implores.

> Yours be the disciplinary image that holds
> Me back from agreeable wrong
> And the clutch of eddying Muddle.

But for Auden the chief excitement was that James's characters were 'concerned with moral choices; they may choose evil, but we are left in no doubt about the importance of their having chosen it'. *The Beast in the Jungle* was 'the most terrifying' of James's stories because its central character John Marcher vests all his emotions in an excessive spiritual anguish about some secret shame, and only experiences a vision of love, which makes sense of the world outside himself, when it is is too late to act on it. In Auden's reading, '"The Beast in the Jungle", the ultimate annihilating horror, is no external creature of nature or fate, no perturbation of nations or restraint of princes, but the shrinking of the subject's sovereign will from decisive choice.'

Love for Kallman was such a choice. His chief significance is that he fulfilled a poetic need. 'The experience – the sight, that is, of the beloved – arouses a sense of intense significance, a sense that the explanation of the whole universe is being offered, and indeed in some sense understood,' Charles Williams had written in 1938 of Dante's description of Beatrice. 'The extraordinary vision is that of the ordinary thing *in excelsis* ... no one yet discovered the light of glory in any man or woman by hunting for it; it seems that it may exist where it is not wanted.' Auden in 1940 quoted Dante's description of love as 'an accident occurring in a substance', and in 1963 described the vision of Eros to David Luke as 'an indirect manifestation of the glory of the personal Creator through a personal creature'. In his poetry as early as 1940 he celebrated how:

> anytime, how casually,
> Out of his organized distress
> An accidental happiness
> Catching man off his guard, will blow him
> Out of his life in time to show him
> The field of Being.

Meeting Kallman was such a moment: an occasion of accidental happiness and transcendent discovery. Though Auden celebrated the power and beauty of the ordinary person seen *in excelsis*, he recognised the transience even in the poems written in his early raptures over Kallman: 'Like love we seldom keep,' he wrote in September. He also knew the isolation in Dante's depiction of love: its inevitable descent, in Williams's words, from 'that thrilling indulgence of a mutual concentration' to 'the indulgence of single and separated concentrations'. Auden later told Howard Griffin in phrases recalling the ideas of both Kohler and Williams, 'The young lover resembles a figure in a Rouault; a thick black line separates him not only from his environment and his family but even from his partner.'

There was something self-consciously purposive about Auden falling in love; as Dr Auden wrote to Elizabeth Mayer, 'You know what a sense of Mission there has always been present in Wystan's plan of life from the time when he decided to leave England for America.' In 1939 Auden needed Kallman, as one object needed another in Kohler's gestalt psychology, to give him unitary sense. 'Now I have the answer,' he wrote in May; 'A Mission is going to find a performer,' he wrote a little later in *Paul Bunyan*; 'The person you really need will arrive at the proper moment to save you,' he told Charles Miller in 1941. When Kallman came to his door, Auden chose him as a precious object to concentrate on completely.

Shakespeare as much as Dante provided the imaginative antecedents for Auden's experience of Kallman. In the 1920s he had turned to Shakespeare's sonnets to make sense of his feelings for Bill McElwee and later Gerhart Meyer. Later he said of Shakespeare:

> in the *Sonnets* he desperately tries to do that which is forbidden: to create a human being ... he mixes words as if they were chemicals that might bring forth a homunculus.... He wants to make an image so that the person will not be a dream but rather someone he knows as he knows his own interest. He wishes the other to have a free will yet his free will is to be the same as Shakespeare's. Of course great anxiety and bad behavior result when the poet's will is crossed as it is bound to be.

This seems like a parabolic version of his own early relations with Kallman. Alan Ansen has described an evening in 1947 when he and

Auden went to listen to records at Kallman's flat with some other men. Auden got up to leave.

WYSTAN: 'Are you coming over to my place, Chester?' CHESTER: 'No thanks, I think I'll stay here.' WYSTAN: 'But, Chester honey, you can get a bath over at my place; it'll be ever so much more comfortable.' CHESTER: 'I have a very bad cold, Wystan; and I think I'd be better off staying where I am.' WYSTAN: 'Now, honey, that's all very well but you could still come over. After all, darling, you can bathe much more comfortably there.' CHESTER: 'I'm sorry, Wystan, but I think I'd really better stay here. I'd just like to talk to these fellows for a while.' WYSTAN: 'But it would be so much more sensible for you to come along with me. Come along now. You won't? All right.' Vox et praetera nihil: 'What a shame, Wystan, that God invented free will.' ... Wystan, having got his suit coat and raincoat: 'Are you sure you don't want to change your mind, Chester honey?' CHESTER: 'I'm afraid not.'

Another, earlier squabble was recorded by Norse. Auden and Kallman were travelling by subway to lunch with the latter's grandmother. 'The passengers stared in disbelief' as the two men argued about the parental symbolism of their sexual need for one another. 'We were yelling above the roar of the train, my dear, completely mad!' as Kallman said.

WYSTAN: I am *not* your father, I'm your *mother*.

CHESTER: You're *not* my mother! I'm *your* mother!

WYSTAN: No, you've got it all wrong. I'm *your* mother!

CHESTER: You're not. You're my *father*.

WYSTAN (screaming): But you've *got* a father! I'm your bloody mother and that's that, darling! You've been looking for a mother since the age of four!

CHESTER (shouting): And you've been obsessed with your mother from the womb! You've been trying to get back ever since, so I *am* your mother! And you're my father!

WYSTAN: No, you want to replace your father for marrying women who rejected you, for which you can't forgive him. But you want a mother who will accept you unconditionally, as I do....

CHESTER: *I'm your goddam mother for the same reason*! You're always sucking on me as if I were one giant tit.

WYSTAN: I must always have something to suck.

CHESTER: Not now, Wystan, not now.

This foolish scene was the result of amateur Freudianism, which enriched Auden's poetry with its myths, symbols and unresolved complexes, but which if taken too literally in life over-preoccupies people with childish needs, and arrests their emotional development.

After three weeks of intimacy with Kallman in New York, Auden was briefly separated from him. In an interview with the *New York Times* in March 1939 Auden had mentioned that he hoped to research his US travel book (projected with Isherwood) by teaching in private schools. This remark was noticed by Richard Eberhart, who taught at St Mark's School in Massachusetts, and he instigated an invitation to Auden. In May Auden went to St Mark's for a few weeks. Eberhart often celebrated this time: Auden covering the floor of his room with books; taking Benzedrine to speed up his mind; writing poems in company, always receptive to suggestions for their improvement; wolfing his food; backseat-driving when they went motoring in Eberhart's old green Pontiac; playing Berlioz records, 'vastly resonant, full of braggadocio'. Auden found his pupils nice but dull; the school itself anti-semitic and over-exclusive. 'The staff', he complained to Mrs Dodds, 'are treated like beasts. A small bed sitting-room, no alcohol allowed in the building, and stiff collars and two services on Sunday.' But the worst of St Mark's was his enforced separation from Kallman. In 'Love Letter', which he wrote to Kallman at this time, he exclaimed:

> O but I was mad to come here, even for money:
> To put myself at the mercy of the postman and the daydream,
> That incorrigible nightmare in which you lie weeping or ill
>   Or drowned in the arms of another.
>
> To have left you now, when I know what this warm May weather
> Does to the city; how it brings out the plump little girls and
> Truculent sailors into the parks and sets
>   The bowels of boys on fire.

After leaving St Mark's, Auden made arrangements to go away with Kallman. He had the consent of the boy's father, Edward Kallman, who showed a cheerful complacence about Auden's love for his son. 'Wystan calls it our honeymoon,' Kallman told Norse. '*Such* a romantic girl.' There seems to have been a proposal, or the exchange of marriage vows, which for Auden had sacred or sacramental meaning. He began wearing a ring, though this apparently was soon discarded. Leaving on 20 June, Auden and Kallman travelled by bus to New Orleans, and from there to Taos in New Mexico where D. H. Lawrence's widow Frieda lived. According to Norse, who was upset at Kallman leaving him, 'Wystan's state of bliss was somewhat marred by evidence of Chester's attempts' on the journey south 'to establish closer contacts with sundry youths on the bus or at stops'. There are hints that, like other honeymoons, it had disappointing moments. Auden, at least, seems to have been irritable in the company of others; but possibly they bored him, or he disliked sharing Kallman's attention with them. There was a more serious insecurity to his happiness. 'Paradise is a state of harmony of understanding,' he wrote while he was on the New Mexico honeymoon.

> We are always entering paradise but only for a moment, for in the instant of achieving a harmony we become aware that the whole which had previously seemed the limit of our consciousness is in its turn part of a larger whole and that there is a new disharmony to be reconciled. This awareness that paradise must continuously be lost, that if we try to remain in it Paradise will turn into Hell, is the pain of Purgatory, *La nostalgie des adieux*.

The harmony of his first weeks with Kallman was unsustainable. 'The memory of the bliss of Paradise is what gives us the courage to enter Purgatory again with hope to regain it,' Auden wrote in Taos. 'If we never experienced that happiness, we could not have faith.'

The preceding quotations are from *The Prolific and the Devourer*, a prose work on which he worked from May until September 1939. Its title and some of its themes were taken from Blake's *Marriage of Heaven and Hell*, but the greatest influence were the *Pensées* of Pascal, whom Auden studied at this time and about whom he wrote a long poem in August. Auden did not yet in the summer of 1939 admit the existence of God as 'an omnipotent free-willing immaterial agent', but he praised Christianity for its secular virtues. 'Industrialism is only workable if we accept Jesus's view of life, and conversely his view of life is more workable under industrialism than under any previous form of civilisation ... Epicurianism is only possible for the rich, Stoicism for the highly educated. Buddhism makes social life impossible; Confucianism is only applicable to village life;

Mohammedanism becomes corrupt in cities.' Auden thought 'the teaching of Jesus is the first application of the scientific approach to human behaviour – reasoning from the particular to the universal'. He quoted Kafka: 'Only our concept of Time makes it possible for us to speak of the Day of Judgment by that name; in reality it is a summary court in perpetual session.' This stimulating but eccentric study of Christianity and heresy was abandoned after the outbreak of war, and published posthumously.

At Taos the two men met Frieda Lawrence, whom Auden described as 'the original Earth-Mother' in a letter to Edward Kallman on 5 July. He continued in characteristically protective tones:

> C is getting rested by degrees I think, and his appetite is enormous. I'm a shade worried by his heart at this altitude but am going to have him vetted by a doctor.... Please excuse my impertinence, but if you could find time to write him a long, chatty letter, he would be so pleased. I wish you could have seen his face when he saw there was a letter from you, but he *was* a little dashed at its shortness. He misses you, you know, a great deal as I should if I were him.

In mid-July he also wrote to Mrs Dodds: 'The country here is dotted with the houses of second rate writers and painters. It's curious how beautiful scenery seems to attract the second rate. For me, I like it for a holiday, but I'd rather die than live permanently in a beauty spot, at least till I'm much older.' His impatience with the second-rate was shown a few weeks later when he was taken to the richly ornamented Santa Fé house of an American poetaster called Witter Bynner, who 'dressed for the occasion in a Mandarin's costume – an over-blouse in pale gray edged with a brocaded soutache, and black silk trousers'. According to a fellow guest, Margaret Lefranc,

> Auden was insufferable. He went snooping about the house, drink in hand, examining books, sniffing at antiques, and making loud asides about his disgust. Finally, I took him into the garden, thinking to remove him from earshot until he calmed down. But in the garden he became more obstreperous than ever and threatened to smash all the statuary. 'No one should have all these material possessions,' he complained, lashing out with an arm at one of the pedestals....

Dinner was nothing short of an ordeal. Auden continued to be nasty as a tomcat, making incessant thrusts at Bynner, who fortunately was at the other end of the table, out of earshot. The rest of us tried to talk loudly enough to drown out his sarcasms and derogation of Bynner's poetry. His appetite, however, was not in the least affected.

Lefranc's 'initial impression' of Auden, 'unchanged by longer acquaintance, was of an aloof, reclusive personality at the center of which was massive loneliness'. The honeymoon with Kallman does not seem to have mitigated this isolation. On 23 July Lefranc was asked by Frieda Lawrence to take some eggs to Auden.

We had seen the two men only infrequently, since we were given to understand they were cloistered with their work and preferred to be left alone. It was late in the morning when I arrived with Frieda's gifts, but both Auden and Chester looked as if they had just gotten out of bed. The house was in utter disarray. As though in tacit apology for the chaos, Auden said he and Chester had been working very hard. No doubt they had, but it was obvious that they also had been drinking red wine with some industry; I have an indelible memory of an open bottle on the table and Auden's wide mouth stained red.... Auden never wore anything but the trousers he had on when we met him: a slate-blue shirt, dirty beige trousers, espadrilles and a navy beret. The trousers had become so baggy as to look like a pair of Dutch breeches. We knew it was one and the same pair because of a large hole torn high up on the left leg at a rather critical spot which constantly threatened embarrassment to onlookers, if not to Auden. Another of Auden's idiosyncrasies was his steadfast refusal to wash himself in anything but a bathtub. Since the only running water was in the brook behind their cottage, the conclusion was inescapable.

Lefranc mentioned that she and another woman were motoring to California in a few days, and was astonished when Auden suggested that he and Kallman accompany them and share expenses: 'in earlier conversations Auden had made it clear that he hadn't much use for the company of women'. His love of economies was stronger than his misogyny. Predictably the travelling-party was strained, although parts of the journey excited Auden. He was 'perceptibly tense' when on 1 August they reached the Grand Canyon. He walked to the edge of the chasm, asked the others not to speak to him, perched himself on a rock and gazed without moving for almost an hour. Lefranc finally suggested that they stay the night. 'No,' he replied, 'there are only two ways of looking at a thing. One way is to have a fleeting impression, which may have its own kind of validity. The other is to see it for a very long time. If we leave now, my impressions will be cinematographic.' Auden summarised this journey to Mrs Dodds in a letter from Laguna Beach in California on 7 August: 'Arizona and Nevada really are quite astonishing; the mountains *really* look like those in fairy stories. I was always disappointed before with the reality. Boulder Dam gives one hope for the human race and is the most wonderful thing I've seen in America so far.' (He was very conscious at this time of the Rilkean device of expressing 'human life in terms of landscape'.)

By the end of the month the European war was looming. On his way from California to New York on 28 August he wrote again to Mrs Dodds as he and Kallman neared Kansas City: 'There is a radio in this coach so that every hour or so, one has a violent pain in one's stomach as the news comes on. By the time you get this, I suppose, we shall know one way or the other.' Hearing similar radio announcements in Britain Naomi Mitchison reflected, 'We all kept on noticing how these last two days have been a parody of all the Auden, Isherwood stuff; we might have been "on the frontier." I suppose the announcers just can't help parodying themselves.' On reaching New York Kallman had a reunion with Norse, with whom he went to Dizzy's Club in the jazz strip on West 52nd Street. 'The dive was the sex addict's quick fix, packed to the rafters with college boys and working-class youths,' Norse recorded. 'Amid the laughter and screaming and ear-splitting jukebox music, it was like an orgy room for the fully clad.' They recommended it to Auden. On the following evening of 1 September, hours after Germany invaded Poland, Auden went there alone. 'With floppy shoelaces, creased suit and tie, ash-stained, he must have looked out of place,' as Norse has imagined. 'Aware of the age difference and quite shy, he would have selected one of the two unused corner tables at the rear of the bar, which was usually deserted except for those too drunk to stand, from which he could observe boys kissing and groping under the bright lights ... Surely he jotted notes, or even the first stanzas, for it begins with the immediacy of composition in situ.'

Margaret Marshall at Dhakuvia Lake near Calcutta in the monsoon season of 1931. She confirmed Auden's interest in Coué, possibly gave him half-baked psychoanalysis and disastrously married his brother John.

Auden as a schoolmaster in the 1930s. 'Lucky, this point in time and space is chosen as my working place.'

Auden as sketched by
Mervyn Peake in 1937.
'O look, look in the
mirror, O look in your
distress; Life remains
a blessing, Although
you cannot bless.'

Auden in London in 1938.
Still imagining himself as a predatory Baron de Charlus.

Auden and Isherwood: '. . . how absolutely
each relied on the other continuing to exist.
They couldn't think of themselves as
lovers, yet sex had given friendship an extra
dimension. It made the relationship
unique.'

Auden in Central Park during his first visit to New York.
'He's very bright and fun to talk to,' Paul Bowles noted around this time.

The only friendship of Auden's life that ended bitterly
was with Benjamin Britten, pictured here in 1941 during rehearsals
for their critically unpopular collaboration, *Paul Bunyan*.

Chester Kallman and Auden stayed together at Caroline
Newton's house at Jamestown, Rhode Island, in the summer of
1941. When the two men were together, a friend said of such
moments, Auden was 'like an angel . . . still and lifted and lit by
extraordinary and sustaining joy'.

Auden at Jamestown with Isherwood and Kallman, to whom he
later jointly dedicated his *Collected Poems*. 'We're something
more exciting than just friends.'

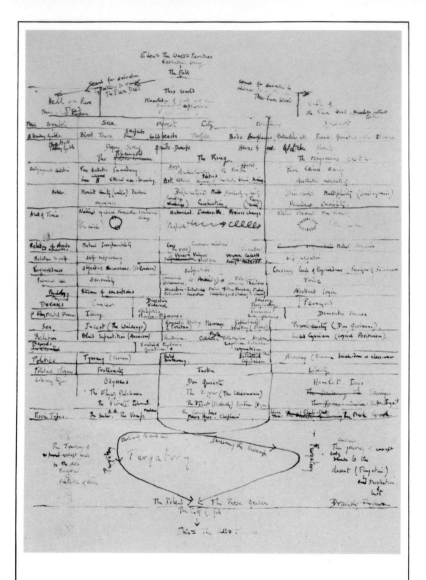

A chart prepared by Auden in 1943 for a
seminar on romanticism at Swarthmore College.
It traces the forms of human experience from the
Garden of Eden to Purgatory and beyond.

Rhoda Jaffe on the Atlantic beach at Fire Island
with Auden. 'Lots & lots of love,' he wrote to
her. 'You are <u>so</u> good, and I'm a neurotic
middle-aged butterball.'

Stephen Spender and Christopher Isherwood with Auden in 1947 on Fire Island, 'this outpost where nothing is wicked but to be sorry or sick'.

The only known photograph of Auden together with Day Lewis and Spender was taken at Venice in 1949.

His poetic reaction to the imminence of war begins in this way:

> I sit in one of the dives
> On Fifty-Second Street
>
> Uncertain and afraid
> As the clever hopes expire
> Of a low dishonest decade.

He spoke of the radio broadcasts that he and Naomi Mitchison and millions of others had heard:

> Waves of anger and fear
> Circulate over the bright
> And darkened lands of the earth,
> Obsessing our private lives;
> The unmentionable odour of death
> Offends the September night.

'September 1, 1939' was a poem which Auden later disowned: a line in the eighth verse – 'We must love one another or die' – seemed to him particularly mendacious, but whether the phrase is a muddling of the importunate demands of lust with the voluntary gift of love, or whether, as the poet Joseph Brodsky suggests, it should be read as meaning, 'We must love one another or kill,' the poem is neither contemptible nor insignificant. Its opening stanza is the most famous epitaph on the 1930s, it was the first poem of the Second World War, and less modish or corrupt than it later seemed to Auden. In his brilliant commentary on 'September 1, 1939' Brodsky stresses that it is pre-eminently about shame, which Auden presents with all-encompassing irony. The setting of the poem affected Auden's tone, for like anyone who is surrounded by people getting drunk faster than himself, he shifted from sympathy with 'faces along the bar' to estrangement and a sense of superiority over 'the sensual man-in-the-street'. The habitués of Dizzy's Club 'groping' one another, in Norse's word, may have suggested to Auden his image of the New York skyline, where 'buildings grope the sky' and are magnificent in their indifference to suffering. Auden's stress on 'the lie of Authority' shows a man who has already repudiated political organisation, and all the deceits of partisan life. The poem concludes, says Brodsky, with 'a self-portrait' of 'a stoic who prays', which is the goal but not yet the definition of the human species.

There was one pleasant interlude for Auden in the fall of 1939. Peter Pears and Benjamin Britten were living at Amityville on Long Island, where Auden visited them on 4 September, the day after the declaration of war. This visit broached a new and important friendship for Auden with their hostess, Elizabeth Mayer, a German Lutheran refugee aged fifty-six who resembled Constance Auden in appearance. 'Elizabeth was handsome and stately,' wrote Charles Miller, 'her brown hair silver-laced, braided and coiled with a crown'. At this time her husband (a Jewish psychiatrist) was working in a subordinate position at a small nursing home, and they were short of money, but she nevertheless acted as a mentor to young artists like Britten and Auden. She was a highly musical woman with many graces of intellect, though some found her demanding. Auden dedicated to her *The Double Man*, which he began writing a few months after their first meeting, and its central poem 'New Year Letter' is addressed to her. 'There are days', he wrote to her in 1943, 'when the knowledge that ... there will never be a person with whom I shall be one flesh, seems more than I can bear, and if it wasnt for you, and a few – how few – others, I dont think I could.' Elizabeth Mayer's friendship with Auden was lifelong. Later in New York City she lived at Gramercy Park, but she was not one of those society women who are no more than a smart address. In the 1960s she and Auden together translated Goethe's *Italian Journey*; in 1964 he celebrated her eightieth birthday with some verses; and 'Old People's Home' in 1970 was occasioned by riding the subway to visit her in miserable decrepitude: 'I revisage / who she was in the pomp and sumpture of her heyday / when week-end visits were a presumptive joy.'

Auden had another momentous experience in the weeks after the outbreak of war. In November 1939 he went to a German-language cinema in the Yorkville district of Manhattan. The proprietors were showing a Nazi propaganda film about the invasion of Poland. When Poles appeared on screen, some of the audience yelled, 'Kill them.' This moment of ugly human ferocity filled Auden with a sense of evil that was irresistible by any secular power. To Golo Mann he explained, 'the English intellectuals who now cry to Heaven against the evil incarnated in Hitler have no Heaven to cry to; they have nothing to offer and their protests echo in empty space'. A few months later, in his sermonising Commencement Address at Smith College, he declared, 'Jung hardly went far enough when he said, "Hitler is the unconscious of every

German"; he comes uncomfortably near being the unconscious of most of us.' He was now caught in horrified loathing of both rational disciplines and irrational creeds. Though he admired Nietzsche for flaying 'the arid prudence' of 'so-called Rational Man / That made envy the one basis of all moral acts', he recoiled from the Nietzschean Superman of the 1930s, 'this tenement gangster with a sub-machine gun in one hand', the types who had cried 'Kill them' in the cinema at Yorkville. For years he had been studying psychology, anthropology and other materialist or scientific doctrines in his effort to understand his nature and find an authenticity of feeling. But personal preoccupations like self-development seemed despicably indulgent set against the incarnation of evil that was Hitler; Auden felt that he needed to put himself under a more impersonal discipline. He felt there was such a schism in the universe as could only be reconciled by atonement and the Christian forgiveness of sins. It was after his experience at Yorkville that he resumed going to church.

The effects of his crisis were visible. 'Auden gave a Lecture here – very crowded audience, 300 seated, 20–30 *standing* throughout – and began by saying how proud he was to speak to the 1st University in the country in which he hoped to become, in a few years, a citizen,' I. A. Richards wrote to T. S. Eliot in December 1939 from Harvard. 'He is an utterly changed man ... thin, white, shrunk and tortured by something.' His state of mind at this time is conveyed in a magnificent review of de la Mare's *Behold the Dreamer*: 'We are confronted today by the spectacle, not of a utilitarian rationalism that dismisses all that cannot be expressed in prose and statistics as silly childish stuff, but rather by an ecstatic and morbid abdication of the free-willing and individual before the collective and daemonic. We have become obscene night worshippers who, having discovered that we cannot live exactly as we will, deny the possibility of willing anything and are content masochistically *to be lived*, a denial that betrays not only us but our daemon itself.' Yet this passive, masochistic suffering must be sharply distinguished from Auden's desire to suffer in choice. As he said, 'After a labyrinth of false moves and losses, you come at last to the place that you know is for you, unfortunately – the place you must learn to suffer; this has no kinship to masochism.'

His return to Christianity was not an abrupt severance with his past. He had been using Christian imagery and ideas since Iceland in 1936; Christianity had been attracting him since his visit to Spain in 1937; he had attended the Russian Orthodox Easter service in China in 1938. In his receptivity to religious ideas, he reflected other cultural tendencies of his age. Since the 1890s, when Nietzsche finished his work and Freud turned to psychoanalysis, there had been a devaluation of the intellect as artificial and unreal. Auden lived in an intuitive epoch, among a set of people who (even if they were irreligious) valued intuitive revelation. His own sympathies were polymathic, and to some extent his disillusion with the intellect was a result of increasing intellectual specialisation with its consequent fragmentation of vision and difficulties in framing unitary truths. 'Christianity' – so Auden in 1941 quoted Nietzsche as writing – 'is a system, a view of things, consistently thought out and complete. If we break out of it a fundamental idea, the belief in God, we thereby break the whole into pieces.'

As a boy he had thought his lack of faith was a personal and creative defect; in 1939 he still thought so. 'Lack of faith, hatred, are lethal to intelligence, and so for an intelligent animal, to survival,' Auden wrote in Taos. After hearing the Germans in the cinema shouting for death, he made an arbitrary resolution. 'I can be an object to myself and decide against any part of my personality, for whatever its social origin, it is mine now to do what I like with,' he asserted in 1944. 'The whole secret lies in arbitrariness,' he quoted from Kierkegaard. 'People usually think it is easy to be arbitrary, but it requires much study to succeed in being arbitrary so as not to lose oneself in it, but so as to derive satisfaction from it. One does not enjoy the immediate, but something quite different which one can arbitrarily control. You go to see the middle of a play, you read the third part of a book ... The more rigidly consistent you are in holding fast to your arbitrariness, the more amusing the ensuing combinations will be.' Auden found a new literary master in Kierkegaard, whom Charles Williams had lately commended for having few of the twentieth-century tendencies towards intellectual specialisation. Like Williams, Auden warned against turning Kierkegaard into a cult leader. 'The fatal follies of Marxists and Freudians should forewarn us from becoming Kierkegaardians, even if we will not listen to his own repeated warning, which Marx and Freud conspicuously fail to give, that he is a genius, not an apostle.' In Kierkegaard's view humanity was made up of conscious beings who had constantly of their own free will to choose out of an infinite number of foreseeable possibilities. The consequences of these choices could never be undone, which was the source of contemporary anxiety. The power whereby a man, 'without blinding himself to his anxiety ... is nevertheless still able to choose, is religious faith', Auden wrote in summary of Kierkegaard. Religious suffering was passionate; religious submission was redemptive. 'One must never desire suffering,' but instead 'remain in the condition of praying for happiness on earth', Auden quoted from Kierkegaard in a letter to Delmore Schwartz. 'If a man desire suffering, then it is as though he were able by himself to solve this terror: that suffering is the characteristic of God's love. And that is precisely what he cannot do: it is "the spirit" which witnesses with him that it is so; and consequently he must not himself have desired suffering.' This idea was incorporated in some of the most important passages of his poetry. As Sebastian says in 'The Sea and the Mirror', 'It is defeat gives proof we are alive.'

Though Kierkegaard was the greatest influence in this period, Auden also read deeply in the works of Reinhold Niebuhr, who with his wife Ursula became a close friend. To the Niebuhrs he dedicated one of his finest volumes of poetry, *Nones*, published in 1951. Charles Williams had recently published a theological history, *The Descent of the Dove*, which Auden read with delight and praised in two letters to him. Auden also re-read 'many times' C. N. Cochrane's study of thought and action from Augustus to Augustine, *Christianity and Classical Culture*. His public interest in theology intrigued some academics and clergy, 'but they were puzzled by his free use of theological categories', as Ursula Niebuhr recalled. 'For them these were supposed to be kept in their proper place, in their pigeon-holes, or indexed in their files, in the same way that the clothes that they wore to church on Sunday were kept for their proper use. But Wystan was taking them out, and scattering the terms – and was wearing Sunday clothes on weekdays.' He started going to Anglican Mass, although he did not return to the Anglican communion until October 1940.

The first great poetic expression of Auden's reversion to Christianity is in the book (mainly written between January and October 1940) published in the USA by Random House in March 1941 as *The Double Man* and by Faber in May as *New Year Letter*. In it he synthesised ideas of Kierkegaard, Kohler, Kafka, Williams and others to seek 'A true gestalt where indiscrete / Perceptions and extensions meet.' His 'Prologue' is followed by his 'New Year Letter' addressed to Elizabeth Mayer and running in couplets for over 1700 lines – 'much the best thing he had written', it seemed to Edmund Wilson on reading it first in the *Atlantic* in 1941 (at a time though when Delmore Schwartz 'was denouncing the poem to everybody'). This poem, as Spears says, 'hesitates on the edge of belief in Christianity, as in the beautiful concluding prayer to a deity who has been demonstrated to be a necessary cultural and philosophical hypothesis'. Auden's friend Bishop Peter Walker writes of this prayer (beginning 'O unicorn among the cedars / To whom no magic charm can lead us'): 'In its succession of Christian images, their subtlety, their sureness of reference at every point ... this is a masterly sequence of digested Christian sophistication, and delightful in the mastery of it.' It typified the personified form in which Auden accepted Divinity that, following the unicorn prayer, he concluded 'New Year Letter' with praise of one of God's creatures, Elizabeth Mayer, 'dear friend ... with your learned peacefulness'.

Auden's 'Letter' was followed by eighty-one pages of prose notes and extracts, aphoristic quotations and shorter poems or doggerel by Auden which supplement or gloss the title poem. Their breadth of subject – anthropology, cosmology, embryology, history, metaphysics, psychology and sociology – provoked the specialists whom he believed were fragmenting human vision. Randall Jarrell, who admired 'New Year Letter', was sceptical about this section of *The Double Man*. 'Some notes are valuable in themselves, some amplify or locate the poem's ideas; but these water a positive desert of Good Sense: machine-made parables, forced definitions, humorless half-truths, with which we wearily dissent or impatiently agree ... To the question, "What is the only thing that always remains work," Auden replies, *the ethical*; the victims of his insistent raids on the Moral can ruefully agree.' The final section of the book comprises twenty sonnets entitled 'The Quest' with an epilogue. The sonnets, thought Louise Bogan, were in Auden's 'former manner and sound a little composed'. They do not compare with the sequence 'In Time of War' written after his return from China in 1938; but they are all elegant, accomplished and some like 'The Third Temptation' are magnificent. They are a mixture of fairy tale, spiritual travail and striving for existential authenticity: *Alice in Wonderland*, Rilke, Kafka, Kierkegaard are obvious influences, but novelists like Proust and James as well as theological historians like Cochrane and Williams contribute to the images and arguments of different sonnets.

American reactions were generally more favourable than British. The *New Statesman* reviewer was begrudging both personally ('the more poets who can save their skins in this war, the better perhaps') and poetically. He thought much of 'New Year Letter' was 'mumbo-jumbo', disliked the 'encyclopaedism of the notes', despised the influence of a 'culture-germ' like Groddeck, and was shocked by the importance to Auden of Charles Williams. But he recognised the greatness of the prayer 'O Unicorn among the Cedars'. It is not surprising that the British – involved so desperately in the world war – were exasperated by Auden's apparent detachment. In fact, he followed events closely, though his few direct public comments on the war – for example his 'Open Letter to Knut Hamsun', the Nobel Prize-winning novelist who had become a spiritual collaborator with the Nazi invaders of Norway – are inevitably pompous. He knew very well that 'in the war years a poet had to be other-worldly', as he said in 1947. 'At any rate, I did. There was just nothing to say about the chaos of this world. All that could be said had been said. There was no point in my saying it again, a little more hysterically.' The war was an incident in the history of shame. In 1942, following the assassination of the Reichsprotektor for Bohemia and Moravia by Czech patriots, the Nazis murdered all of the men and fifty-six of the women of a mining village called Lidice, sent all its children to correction camps, demolished every building and abolished its name. This atrocity inspired a 'mass of versified trash' which prompted Auden to conclude, 'that what was really bothering the versifiers was a feeling of guilt at not feeling horror-struck enough'. A good poem, he thought, could possibly have been written about Lidice: 'One that revealed this lack of feeling, that told how when he read the news, the poet, like you and I, dear reader, went on thinking about his fame or his lunch, and how glad he was that he was not one of the victims.' He had already written this poem, in 1938 ('Musée des Beaux Arts'); had lived with this knowledge since the workmen had gone off for lunch at the whaling station in 1936.

While he was writing *The Double Man* in 1940, Auden, who had registered for the draft in the USA, became the target of an ebullition of English anti-intellectualism. It began early in the year after an indiscreet letter from Isherwood declaring that he would not return to England was leaked to Auden's old Oxford friend Tom Driberg, who quoted it in his newspaper gossip column. Isherwood's declaration was provocative of the national mood. John Lehmann, whose publishing contract had encouraged Auden and Isherwood to leave Britain, has described how some politicians, bureaucrats and military leaders felt antagonistic towards intellectuals after the outbreak of war. They thought highbrows were too individualistic for the good of a united war effort; indeed they regarded them almost with the words of Auden's 'Address for a Prize-Day': 'Anaemic, muscularly undeveloped and rather mean ... Give them regular but easy tasks and see that they do them properly. Hit them in the face if necessary. If they hit back you will know they are saved.' Lehmann 'sensed an only just undivulged wish to put us in front of a firing squad, or at least to clap us into prison for the duration under regulation 18B' which finally erupted in a furore over Auden and Isherwood. As one example in June 1940 Cyril Connolly was detained by ten policemen in Oxford on the feigned suspicion that he was a spy. One policeman remarked sniffily as he leafed through a copy of Connolly's magazine, *Horizon*, 'Nude figures.' When Connolly interposed that the plate was a Burne-Jones reproduction, the policeman retorted that he didn't care if it was 'Epstein or Einstein' (he *was* an Oxford policeman). After Connolly was released from their bullying, a military policeman protested to the inspector in charge, 'You mean to say you've got no charge against him, you can't even put him in the Coop for the night – what's the good of us fellows doing our job if you won't back us up?' Even so Connolly next day received an intimidating visit from a detective in London. It was as part of this national mood to put intellectuals in the Coop for the night that, in Lehmann's words, 'Christopher and Wystan were suddenly branded as traitors and cowards in a campaign that was waged with the utmost fury against them in dailies and weeklies.' The force behind the campaign was a loathing of mental or sexual heterodoxy. Significantly the offensive parliamentary question of 13 June 1940, which accused Auden and Isherwood of 'seeking refuge abroad' and demanded their compulsory repatriation and military conscription or their expulsion from British citizenship, was put by Sir Jocelyn Lucas, a backbencher who was a breeder of Sealyham terriers and author of *Simple Doggie Remedies*. Lucas was a great enforcer of conventions and once gave a public dressing-down to a fellow Conservative MP for wearing suede shoes.

Auden wrote of these 'minor personal unpleasantnesses' to his brother John that 'since the British Embassy has been instructed to discourage those without technical qualifications from returning, I dont see the point of writing in a cottage waiting for the parachutists ... all that we can do, who are spared the horrors, is to be happy and not pretend out of a sense of guilt that we are not, to study as hard as we can, and keep our feeble little lamps burning in the big wind'. Looking back on this time MacNeice noted, 'the Left Wing movement in the thirties encouraged us to try to be normal, and all that affectation of the Normal only led to sterility'. (Auden in Iceland had identified 'Normality' as 'the goddess of bossy underlings'.) English radicals were just as keen as philistine Tory baronets to discipline and curb and sterilise. When Auden's 'At the Grave of Henry James' was published in *Horizon* in 1941, the *New Statesman* described it as 'a long, delightfully clever, deplorably ramshackle affair', and then jeered, 'Auden and James have at least one thing in common: they both changed nationality for the same reason – the neutrality of the United States' (which was not only 'the dirtiest witticism' that Grigson 'ever read,' but inaccurate, for though Auden had applied for US citizenship in 1940, he remained a British national until 1946).

In October 1940 Auden moved into a brownstone house at 7 Middagh Street in Brooklyn rented with the help of Lincoln Kirstein by George Davis, the fiction editor of *Harper's Bazaar*. Davis was a resourceful man whose escapades gave his friends pleasure. 'George's account of his weekend reads positively like Kraft-Ebing [sic] – and I do mean the parts in Latin,' Kallman wrote on one occasion to Auden: 'Really that boy gets into outlandish places.' Other tenants included Paul and Jane Bowles, Britten and Pears, MacNeice, Carson McCullers, Oliver Smith, Golo Mann in the attic, and the striptease queen Gypsy Rose Lee, who was writing a mystery entitled *The G-String Murders*. Paul Bowles recalled:

Richard Wright eventually moved into the basement with his wife and child, with Auden ... on the top floor, after Britten and Pears had gone elsewhere ... Practically everyone I knew came at one time or another, including Virgil Thomson and Aaron Copland ... Denis de Rougemont, Tchelitchew, Dali, and Genia Berman, Bernstein, Kirstein and Blitzstein ... it was full of people always ... and it worked very well, except for a few terrible rows, which were inevitable.

This household has fascinated students of bohemian living. For Golo Mann only Auden counted:

> He kept order in the house. There were two coloured servants, who cleaned and cooked the meals – formal, heavy meals which were eaten in a gloomy basement with plush-covered furniture. If anyone was late, Auden did not conceal his disapproval. Expenses were covered in accordance with a complicated system thought out by Auden ... Once a week there was a 'bill-day', announced with a certain satisfaction by Auden at breakfast time; afterwards he went from room to room collecting payment. He ate enormously, and also drank a good deal, but only wine – a cheap Chianti or something of that kind.

Auden was neither an equable companion nor a sympathetic, imaginative, soothing lover. His admiration of others was often possessive. Margaret Lefranc, who met him in 1939, noted: 'He could be charming and brilliant at one moment and in the next erupt in a childish rage, usually at some trivial matter: a bad meal, or his failure (which ought not to have surprised him) to find his favorite English cigarettes.' At New York and Princeton that year Golo Mann rejoiced in Auden as a 'striking and provocative' conversationalist, but his monologues were 'one-sided, and any remark one might try to interject was brushed aside with a "Quite"'. He was prone to oracular remarks which on examination could seem trite: 'one of the symptoms of happiness is a lively curiosity that finds others as interesting and worth knowing as oneself,' he declared of Voltaire in 1939. He misjudged people's reactions to his advice. At Christmas of 1939 he sent Norse a 'preachy' letter exhorting him 'to accept all that I had suffered as the true gifts of life, and to reject worldly values'; it had a 'shattering' effect on Norse, who later described Auden as 'a dogmatic tyrant' who was 'rude and unfair'. Early in 1942 Auden sent a similarly bossy and crushing letter to Britten accusing him of 'playing the lovable, talented little boy' which offended the recipient irreparably. In August 1942 after being consulted by a young admirer, Delmore Schwartz, about his long-gestating epic poem 'Genesis', he replied with a long, partly irrelevant, sermonising letter which showed a failure of imagination about Schwartz's feelings and needs: it turned Schwartz into a critic who in 1947 stood against other reviewers by indicting *The Age of Anxiety* as 'the most self-indulgent book Auden has written'. On a later occasion in New York, after he had criticised Spender, who then promised to amend, Auden groaned and held his head in his hands. 'Why do you take me seriously?' he asked Spender. 'My only complaint about Americans is that they will take me seriously. I did trust my English friends not to take me seriously.'

Auden did not understand (or chose to forget) what a youth of Kallman's age could bear. He tried to 'drive a wedge' between Kallman and 'everyone close to Chester', according to Norse, and treated the set of Brooklyn boys as if they were his pupils. At St Mark's in May 1939, as Eberhart heard, 'instead of asking boys to paraphrase a quatrain of Gray's Elegy, he will excise key words, put in odd or nonsense words in their places, then ask the boys to hit the meaning of the original as nearly as they can'. Similarly, when Kallman first took Norse to visit him, Auden set them an intimidating test: he would name a word, and expect them to supply the antonym. Kallman grimaced in mock alarm, and Norse suffered a mental paralysis until Lincoln Kirstein took him home. 'Auden's look was quite relentless, penetrating, dispassionate, like a family doctor whose hobby was metaphysics,' Kirstein commented. They had both been born in 1907, but Kirstein 'always felt – then and later – that he was a generation older than myself, and I sensed from the first an omniscience and ... authority that was never false ... The pressure and quality of his energy – physical, mental and emotional – demanded something approaching an equal expenditure to support or resist. He'd known more, read more, seen more.'

This intensity must have been brutally intimidating for a youth even as gifted and ambitious as Kallman, who required strength, will and ingenuity to withstand Auden's stifling demands. The strain was intellectual as well as emotional. In these early years Auden could be tetchy if Kallman did not endorse his aesthetic opinions (though later, in the 1950s, the roles he had inflicted on them were reversed, and Auden was dependent on Kallman's critical judgments). Thus he was annoyed on their honeymoon in 1939 by Kallman's repeated quotations from Hart Crane, whom Auden despised as 'a crooked immoralist'. His self-centred and adamantine hectoring was a potentially disastrous form of Pygmalion-ism. He had the tactlessness of someone who inhabited, as Spender suspected, 'an entirely verbal world'. Randall Jarrell suggested that Auden 'always made such impossible exacting demands on himself and every-body else partly because it kept him from having to worry about the more ordinary, moderate demands', and there is a sense that Auden was striving hard to be exceptional. In a review of Carl Sandburg's biography of Lincoln in 1940, he wrote in terms of Great Men that may seem complacently self-referential:

> The one infallible symptom of greatness is the capacity for double focus ... knowing themselves, they are skeptical about human nature but not despairing; they know they are weak but not helpless ... They are unconventional but not bohemian; it never occurs to them to think in terms of convention ... Objective about themselves with the objectivity of the truly humble, they often shock ... knowing that the only suffering that can be avoided is the attempt to escape from suffering, they are funny and enjoy life. And the half-men and the half-women, the little either-or people, hate them when they are alive and insult them when they are dead by trying to imitate their mannerisms.

This is written by someone trying to live a pitch above the ordinary and making assumptions of superiority to maintain his level.

Auden's emotional pedagogy in his friendships partly arose from his tendency to explain people's lives according to childish origins and juvenile models. 'Freud,' Empson wrote in his review of *Another Time* in August 1940, 'is largely responsible for this idea that people are best understood by seeing them as children.' Auden was susceptible to this Freudianism. Thus in 'New Year Letter' he wrote that the typical human state is 'half angel and half petite bête', which describes not only Kallman but (as James suggests in *The Turn of the Screw*) most children too. Auden wrote in 'Montaigne' (1940), 'Love must be re-grown from the sensual child,' and admired Rilke at this time for thinking in ways 'more characteristic of the child than of the adult'. His advice to young writers – given in his essay on Henry James's *The American Scene* – was 'do not write your biography, for your childhood is literally the whole of your capital'. But though an interest in childhood can stimulate poetic creativity, childish concerns are a confusing source of advice for lovers; and Auden's love for Kallman was further confused by the discrepancy in their ages. In 'Heavy Date' (1939) Auden concluded that lovers 'In their loves are equal', but this was a muddled idea, for he was really writing of lust: 'Sophomores and peasants / Poets and their critics, / Are the same in bed.' Equality in love is more elusive than an equality of lusts. It is easy to understand a man in his thirties lusting after someone about fifteen years younger; but love is less comprehensible. Years later Auden himself quoted Saint-Exupéry: 'Love does not consist of gazing at each other but in looking together in the same direction.' The visions of a thirty-two-year-old and an eighteen-year-old gazing in the same direction are likely to be irreconcilable, as he painfully discovered. Part of the nightmare envisaged by Herod (in Auden's 'For the Time Being' of 1942) was that 'Life after death will be an eternal dinner-party where all the guests are twenty years old' – a characteristically adolescent prefiguration of Sartre's *Huit Clos*. Yet in his poem 'Schoolchildren' of 1937 Auden had seen the difference between children and adults, writing of the former 'these dissent so little ... weak like the vows of drunkards', and of the latter, 'tyranny is so easy'. As early as his visit to Iceland he had recognised the temptations to tyrannise: 'Like a child that feels neglected, / Our proof of goodness is the power to punish, / We recognise them when they make us suffer.'

The need for tests in love is one theme of Auden's great, gloomy epithalamium of 1940, 'In Sickness and in Health'. In it he represents lust as 'a land of condors, sick cattle, and dead flies' where 'goods are smashed that cannot be replaced' and 'figures of destruction unawares / Jump out on Love's imagination / And chase away the castles and the bears'. Don Juan ('so terrified of death') is an example of lust in action:

> he must find
> Angels to keep him chaste; a helpless, blind
> unhappy spook, he haunts the urinals,
> Existing solely by their miracles.

Those who try to repress their lusts with political violence are as unmeritorious as those who 'commit / That sin of the high-minded, sublimation'. Still there is reason to 'rejoice' in lust, and Auden prays that Eros be channelled into acts of veneration:

> Force our desire, O Essence of creation,
> To seek Thee always in Thy substances,
> Till the performance of those offices

>Our bodies, Thine opaque enigmas, do,
>Configure Thy transparent justice too.

Yet we must not be smug about 'this round O of faithfulness we swear' or let 'Mere habits of affection freeze our thought / ... And take our love for granted'. He enjoins, 'Love permit / Temptations always to endanger it.'

The temptations that threatened Auden's love were all too pressing. The incompatibility between Auden and Kallman's sexual preferences was lethal to their marriage. 'To me the act of fucking, whether heterosexual or homosexual, seems an act of sadistic aggression, to submit to it, masochistic, and neither actively nor passively have I ever enjoyed it,' Auden once wrote (in this he resembled Wagner, whom, he thought, 'regarded sex as a torment'). 'Those who practice sodomy, whether active or passive, have a certain feeling of superiority to those who like myself are only cock-suckers. They consider us a bit sissy, and I expect they are right.' Kallman, by contrast, then aged nineteen, wrote to Norse in July 1940 that he was bored staying with Auden at the Massachusetts country home of Kirstein's sister: 'When I do get back to the city I expect to spend $\frac{3}{4}$ of my time flat on my stomach biting into pillows, listening to the music ... of the bed-springs.' On a visit to Isherwood in November 1941 he complained to Auden that there were not any 'real men' in Los Angeles: 'Just the other night I picked up a 6 ft $2\frac{1}{2}$ in merchant sailor from Brooklyn. Wildly attractive, young, strong, perfectly built and large. I was all prepared for an absolutely relentless fucking, – but – as it turned out in the end, that is what I had to provide him with.' Spender thought that Auden wanted Kallman as his 'court jester' but expected a fidelity and steadiness that were impossible in so seductive a jester. As Auden said (too pessimistically) in 1948, 'Sexual fidelity is more important in a homosexual relationship than in any other; in other relationships there are a variety of ties, but here fidelity is the only bond.' And it was by infidelity that Kallman broke the bonds in which Auden was confining him. It was for Kallman in every way a necessity.

Late in 1940 Auden invited a tall, handsome, athletic, well-educated young Englishman named Jack Barker to stay at the house on Middagh Street. This Englishman was working on merchant ships crossing between Britain and the United States. Auden introduced him to Malcolm Cowley, who commissioned an article from him for the *New Republic*. As the

Englishman later wrote to Dorothy Farnan (who eventually married Edward Kallman and became Chester's stepmother):

> I was fascinated by Chester's scintillating and witty conversation. He and Wystan obviously enjoyed tremendous intellectual rapport. But the fact that Wystan and Chester had pledged their eternal troth I had no earthly way of knowing. This was, in fact, Wystan's Achilles' heel. He had consummated a marriage *dans les yeux de Dieu* and was not even living with his partner for life. He was so blindly in love with Chester that he believed implicitly in his 'innocence' and fidelity to his marriage vows. I was staying with Wystan; yet he never hinted to me ... that Chester was his lover who must not be touched. Certainly I thought that there might be an affair, but scarcely a very active one.

He and Kallman began an affair which soon had them both in an emotional thraldom. Its pleasures and tensions were probably heightened by the interruptions when the Englishman left New York on trans-Atlantic runs on his merchant ship dodging German submarines. For the first few months in 1940–1 the affair was a secret. Its surreptitiousness was doubtless exciting; Kallman was not the first man to find power and fun in dodging, plotting, sneaking and lying, and Auden in his early despair was determined to be deceived. The affair seems to have been known to him by the spring of 1941. 'Many people have the experience of feeling physically soiled and humiliated by life; some quickly put it out of their mind, others gloat narcissistically on its unimportant details; but both to remember and to transform the humiliation into something beautiful ... is rare,' he wrote in April, consoling himself with the idea that 'an artist is someone who is able to express his human development in a public medium'. Rolfe Humphries at a meeting in May found him 'full of ideas about moral character and what-not'. In June, possibly hoping to get Kallman away from New York, he arranged for Caroline Newton to pay for 'Chester ... to get educated'. His review at this time of Denis de Rougemont's *Love in the Western World* also contains hints or fractions of knowledge.

Yet though he tried to tell himself that Kallman's imperfections were lovable, his power of submission was limited. In July 1941 he erupted in frustrated recriminations. 'Chester retired to his room in a fit of pique, threw himself on the bed, and went to sleep,' Dorothy Farnan has recorded. Auden felt 'a violent impulse to murder ... and during the night that followed he put his large, thick fingers round Chester's throat and pressed hard'. Kallman woke, pushed Auden away and fled. Years after this crisis Auden still referred to the Englishman as 'evil', which was so wild a misdescription that Spender thought Auden was unbalanced on the subject. Auden told Spender (and apparently others) that he had contemplated murdering his rival. In conversation in 1950 he declared that *crimes passionels* occurred 'because an individual confuses a human being with a thing', and added, 'courage is required to pursue love to its logical violence'. He referred to these emotions publicly too: 'Providentially – for the occupational disease of poets is frivolity – I was forced to know in person what it is like to feel oneself the prey of demonic forces, in both the Greek and the Christian sense, stripped of self control and self respect, behaving like a ham actor in a Strindberg play.' As late as 1947 he spoke of consulting witch doctors from Dahomey as a way 'to make Chester love him faithfully and exclusively again'. Hearing this, Alan Ansen said, 'You can be very frightening,' and Auden replied, 'Oh, I know I'm crazy on some subjects.' Kallman encouraged crazy excitement. 'It was Chester's nature to create jealousy, misery, and rage in his lovers,' the Englishman recalled. 'He would cuckold them to their faces. The reason was a longing to be mastered. He was thrilled when I threatened to throw him out of the window and walloped him in the face. But even when he was tired of his lovers, Chester wanted to continue to bind them to him and had this incredible magnetic capacity of doing so, even after he had lost his looks.'

In mid-July 1941 Auden went to teach briefly at Olivet College in Michigan. 'For a combination of reasons, personal, artistic and climatic, I have felt very lonely and low here,' he wrote at this time to the Niebuhrs. 'If I stay here any longer I shall either take to the mysticism that Reinhold so disapproves of, or buy a library of pornographic books.' He went in August to stay with Kallman at Caroline Newton's house at Jamestown, Rhode Island. There another grief befell him. The house-party was due to dine at Newport with Admiral Ernest King, then commanding the Atlantic Patrol Force of the US Navy. A telegram was read over the telephone to Caroline Newton bringing news from England which she asked Kallman to tell Auden. He went to Auden and announced, 'We're not going to King's.' Auden replied, 'Goody, goody.' Then Chester said,

'The reason is your mother has died.' Auden sat in silence, then made a wry remark and wept. A few days later a letter arrived from his mother, but he burnt it unread. Afterwards Dr Auden described his wife's last months in a characteristic letter to a former employee:

> She had been in failing health for some time & had a bad heart attack on Whit-Tuesday, but made a wonderfully good recovery & was soon active. We have had no maid since Maggie married eighteen months ago & later only a woman coming in for 3 hours more or less daily. She went down to stay at Monmouth at the beginning of August & came back very much improved, with her sister Mildred. She went to bed comfortably & chatted with Mildred till she felt inclined to sleep. I was out on Home Guard duties & had told her that I wd not disturb her. However I spoke at her door about 10.40 and again at 11 but received no answer, & I have no doubt that her silence was not that of sleep but of death, though it was only when I took her tea (which I always made myself) at 6.45 the next morning that I knew the truth. We are both strongly in favour of cremation and I took the mortal elements up to Wesco and there scattered them in a churchyard.

In the spring of 1941 Auden had written a lucrative article for *Harper's Bazaar*. In it he expressed his hope for 'the good fortune to die in bed,' so it was perhaps consoling that his mother had done so. The article (unfortunately published shortly after her death) was a genial, elegant survey of the deathbed remarks of the famous and obscure. One of his concluding quotations – 'Bert Savoy, the famous female impersonator, was watching a thunderstorm with some friends, "*There's Miss God at it again*," he exclaimed and was instantly struck by lightning' – is his first traceable use of the phrase 'Miss God', which he increasingly adopted. 'I'm afraid that Miss God insists that I go to bed early,' he told younger friends; 'of course it's a sin,' he would say of homosexuality. 'We just have to hope that Miss God will forgive us.' He also wrote an affectionate squib on Wallace Stevens beginning 'O my dear, more heresy to muzzle', entitled 'Miss God on Mr Stevens'.

In the autumn of 1941 Auden started work as Associate Professor of English in the University of Michigan at Ann Arbor. 'I'm fairly settled in now; and getting down at last to some work,' he wrote to Caroline Newton in October. 'Happy I can't pretend to be: I miss Chester; I miss New York.... "Il faut payer" for the happiness of the last $2\frac{1}{2}$ years; alright, but what is harder is that one must not only pay but like the paying.' His unhappiness was aggravated by the cruelly self-centred letters he was receiving from Kallman, who had gone to Los Angeles in search of work. 'But there are simply no jobs for an inexperienced girl,' Kallman complained on 3 November. 'Sex has been spotty and silly consisting of quick ones and morceaux de commerces who decide that I'm their dear one, – and have to be dropped discretely [sic] before the whole business, – the jealousy, the affection, the conversation, – becomes too violently tiresome – and God it's such a bore, bore, bore.' Auden agreed to pay Kallman's fees for secretarial training, but the latter was soon complaining about his lack of money in what must have been a peculiarly hurtful way. He had met a 'divine soldier and his friend' who 'just want to fuck all night long', he wrote on 7 December, but 'having no money' he had 'no place to take them'. This letter was written on the day of the Japanese attack on Pearl Harbor: 'It's all very depressing – and now war.' His reaction to the catastrophe in Hawaii was centred on his sexual deprivation. 'It really isn't fair,' he wailed to Auden. 'I feel bitter, vindictive, half-immersed in "circular madness", and up to my scalp in roaring hatred, and then to have these days of sheer sexual frustration. Is it asking so much to be fucked or even to indulge in the simplest of childhood experiences with a more dangerous engine?'

Later in December Kallman arrived in Ann Arbor, and he and Auden travelled together to California, where they visited both Isherwood and the Manns. Kallman had been complaining of Isherwood's attitude earlier ('Christopher having said that he was a fool to take me seriously since no one he knew besides you did, and that was just an eccentricity permissible to a great man'), and the Manns' hostility to Kallman led to a permanent chilling of relations by Auden. He attributed their attitude to jealousy of Caroline Newton's patronage and to anti-semitism about Kallman; but perhaps they found traces of an escapade about which he boasted on his return to Ann Arbor: 'At the Manns', we took turns screwing a friend on Thomas's big bed when the family was away.' Certainly his relationship with Kallman was disrupting his other friendships. The next month, in January 1942, Auden severed relations with Kirstein's sister Mina Curtiss because she regarded Kallman as 'just a Brooklyn kike'. It was at this time that Auden wrote of him to Caroline Newton, 'He makes me suffer and commit follies, without which I should soon become like the later Tennyson.' He saw the artist as a masochist ('Suffering is not the cause of genius but its guardian angel, the means by which its possessor is compelled to make the use of his talent a serious matter, the limits which make his freedom a reality') whose work was passive before the power of its audience ('an artist, the one worldly calling which by its nature can force its help on no one, for whatever pleasure and profit one derives from a work of art depends upon what one brings to it'). Yet he had heard too much pretentious talk of suffering by third-rate dabblers wanting a reputation for spiritual superiority, so also insisted to an Ann Arbor student, Charles Miller, 'If one says, "I am a lonely poet, I suffer more than John Jones of the Elks Club," one has a false concept of suffering and sensitivity. We are all basically the same, we all suffer equally.' He wrote to James Stern in 1942, 'because one thinks one has had a vision in which suffering is turned into joy, one wants to share the joy with others'.

Miller came from a poor rural family, and had moved into Auden's house as his cook. Visitors like Elizabeth Mayer and Erika Mann constantly urged on Miller his duties of subordination. He was an observant young man, understandably awed by his companion, and kept a reverent but informative journal. 'Charlie, it's *amazing* that no one has really written about the true America, the land of the lonely!' Auden said on one occasion. 'The land of eccentrics and outcast lonelies.' Auden was troubled at Ann Arbor by local anxieties about homosexuality: 'My chief worry is gossip which means that every time I ask anyone in pants to the house, they are either hoping or dreading that I shall make a pass.' In February 1942 Kallman entered the graduate school at Ann Arbor at Auden's expense, but Auden left Michigan after the spring semester of 1942 and spent part of the summer as Caroline Newton's guest in Pennsylvania. He wrote to James Stern in April 1942, 'I never really loved anyone before, and then when he got through the wall, he became so much a part of my life that I keep forgetting that he is a separate person, and having discovered love, I have also discovered what I never knew before, the dread of being abandoned and left alone.'

Yet he had wide interests beyond Kallman and was always developing his ideas. One important friendship was with Louise Bogan, whom he first met in January 1941 at the apartment of Cyril Connolly's first wife, Jean.

He arrived with 'a whole cloud of mysterious little male presences all looking ... like pressed flowers', Bogan reported. 'He is very homely, with a large mole on one side of his face; and looks lined and concentrated: much older than I expected.' They talked of poems and critics, and agreed to meet again. 'He said he lives very quietly in Brooklyn, not seeing anyone for weeks at a time (I think this is unlikely; but maybe he doesn't think the little pressed flowers anybody).' They had another successful meeting in July 1941. 'We had a grand evening, just *crammed* with Insights and Autopsies, and Great Simple Thoughts, and Deep Intuitions,' Bogan told Morton Zabel. 'He gave me some Profound Advice (in a rather oblique way) just before he left; and I do think him a real and natural person. Complicated as hell, of course; and I should hate to cross him; but fundamentally sound, tender and full of Recognitions, and AMOR.'

Auden regarded Bogan's columns in the *New Yorker* as proof that she was 'the best critic of poetry in America' and he ranked her with Eliot, Moore and Riding as the only important American poets. His review in 1942 of Bogan's *Poems and New Poems* for *Partisan Review* was a shrewd assessment of her work as well as self-revealing. 'The first successful poems of young poets are usually a catharsis of resentment,' he wrote. 'The poet who escapes from the error of believing that the reflection of his life to his work is a direct one, that the second is the mirror image of the first, now falls into the error of denying that there need be any relation at all, into believing that the poetry can develop autonomously, provided that the poet can find it a convenient Myth.' Some poets 'fashion an image out of the opposites of puritanical parents or upper class education' but 'still the personal note appears, only now in the form of its denial, in a certain phoney dramatisation, a "camp" of personality'. Yeats, 'the romantic rebel against the Darwinian Myth of his childhood with its belief in The Machine and Automatic Progress', instead adopted 'woozy doctrines like the Aristocratic Mask and the Cyclical Theory of Time'. Comparison of Yeats's *Second Coming* with Eliot's *East Coker* showed how 'the adoption of a belief which does not really hold as a means of integrating experience poetically, while it may produce fine poems, limits their meaning to the immediate context; it creates Occasional Poems lacking any resonance beyond their frame'.

This was the credo with which Auden approached his next major pieces of work, the Christmas oratorio 'For the Time Being' (1941-2) and 'The

Sea and the Mirror' (1942–4), experiments in dramatic poetry which were both based on Kierkegaard's three categories of human experience, the Ethical, Aesthetic and Religious. He started the oratorio at Ann Arbor in October 1941. It was supremely a memorial to his mother: he intended to celebrate the musical pleasures and religious rituals shared by them in his childhood. But he was writing in the aftermath of the destruction of his marital hopes with Kallman, and he treated the Christmas story as an allegory of individuals personifying divine love. This was an experience that he visibly felt long after the crisis in his relations with Kallman in 1941. In the mid-1940s they once dined together with Helen and Herbert Sonthoff at Swarthmore. 'I saw Wystan sitting on the floor, beside you, looking through records in Herbert's study, his face lit, sweet, with a kind of glowing stillness I'd not seen before,' Helen Sonthoff told Kallman thirty years later. 'The words in my head were "like an angel" ... that big man ... still and lifted and lit by extraordinary and sustaining joy.'

Auden also wished to provide a libretto which Britten could set to music, but this was the least successful aspect of the work. His relations with Britten had become vexed. Following a suggestion from Britten's New York publishers that he write a piece for performance by high-school pupils, the two men had in late 1939 began collaboration on an operetta *Paul Bunyan* about the lumberjack hero of American frontier legend. The work was disrupted by Britten's illness, and the anticipated Broadway production by the Ballet Caravan of George Balanchine and Lincoln Kirstein never took place. It was finally performed by a mainly student cast on the campus of Columbia University in New York in May 1941. To Britten's distress it impressed few critics. 'The plot, as in the score, is a little of everything, a little of symbolism and uplift, a bit of socialism and of modern satire, and gags and jokes of a Hollywood sort,' recorded the *New York Times*. Virgil Thomson in the *New York Herald Tribune* called Auden's writing 'flaccid and spineless' and judged that whether *Paul Bunyan* was 'an allegory or a morality ... it is utterly obscure and tenuous'. He despised the libretto for pretending to praise the American frontier legends when Auden's overriding aim was to write ironically about the literary traditions of his newly adopted country. If these critical rebuffs were not hurtful enough, Britten was mortified by a bossy letter seemingly critical of his relationship with Pears which he received from Auden in 1942. He was further exasperated by the libretto of 'For the Time Being' sent to him after his return to Britain with Pears. Auden's structure was too long and complicated for a musical setting, despite his consultation of the models of Bach and Berlioz. Britten wrote only fragments of music for the oratorio, and after 1947 estranged himself from Auden.

'The relation of life to work is dialectical,' Auden had insisted in his Bogan review. 'Belief and behaviour have a similar relation, that is to say, that beliefs are religious or nothing, and a religion cannot be got out of books or by a sudden vision, but can only be realised by living it.' In 'For the Time Being' Auden examined issues of belief and behaviour, but his supreme purpose was religious rather than ethical. He wrote to Stern, 'In 1912, it was a real vision to discover that God loves a Pernod and a good fuck, but in 1942 every maiden aunt knows this and its time to discover something else He loves.' His oratorio is a protean Christmas pageant in which characters represent stereotypes as well as individuals. As he explained to his father in 1942, 'I was trying to treat it as a religious event which eternally recurs every time it is accepted.' The prose section of 'For the Time Being', in which Herod, speaking as a liberal rationalist, laments the need for the massacre of the innocents, is delectable in its ironies; it is incidentally a renunciation of the opinions offered by Auden during his public-speaking phase in 1938. Herod shows how absurd the Religious man seems to an Ethical man, but it is Herod's rationalism that really seems futile: Herod seems to sense this himself at the end, for his speech breaks down into panic, bafflement and self-pity. Auden partly represents himself in the character of Joseph, who is told by the Narrator, 'To choose what is difficult all one's days / As if it were easy, that is faith.' One of the finest passages is the Chorale addressed to God in which, with characteristic irony, Auden makes both his own vocational statement and an Augustinian declaration of *O felix culpa*:

> Though written by Thy children with
> A smudged and crooked line
> The Word is ever legible
> Thy meaning unequivocal
> And for Thy Goodness even sin
> Is valid for a sign.
>
> Inflict Thy promises with each
> Occasion of distress
> That from our incoherence we

May learn to put our trust in Thee
And brutal fact persuade us to
Adventure Art and Peace.

In August 1942 a military draft board summoned Auden, but he was rejected after an interview on 1 September with a 'psychiatrist who was both unpleasant and grotesquely ignorant'. He had prefigured this fate in *The Orators*, where the airman forewarns that the 'poor little buggers … won't get through the medical'. It was humiliating to be excluded because of his homosexuality. 'If I'd had a heart condition or something like that, a legitimate out, I should have been delighted,' he later told Alan Ansen; he resented his categorisation as a deviant on a par with public exhibitionists. Shortly afterwards he began teaching at Swarthmore College, a Pennsylvanian co-educational liberal arts institution, founded in 1864 by Quakers but which had been non-sectarian since 1911. '*Very* tired of reading "creative" mss., each more infantile than the last,' he reported to James Stern in November. 'At my last Thursday evening At Home, my room was packed to capacity with girls who wanted to know if I felt inspired when I write. How Yeats would have enjoyed himself. I didnt.' Initially he was supported by a Guggenheim fellowship, but after its expiry in 1943 he received a full-time teaching appointment as an associate professor. His students seemed to him victims of the invincible American matriarchy. 'For an Englishman coming over here to teach, the rudeness of the students is quite shocking,' he said in 1947.

> After all, he is more or less in the position of father; and the psychological background of the American student doesn't teach them obedience to a father image, which is too bad. It isn't that they shouldn't eventually find out the limitations of the father substitute and eventually discard him; that's quite as it should be. But they begin with the idea that they are the important ones to be pleased not taught and that their untutored reactions ought to be their final judgment on their instructor. They're so disobedient because of the way they've been brought up.

He found Swarthmore puritanical about alcohol and other matters. 'The more I think about it, the less I feel like facing another year at Swarthmore,' he wrote to James Stern on 5 July 1944: 'I am, after all, a crook, and need a more baroque and louche habitat to breathe in, than the

Quakers provide.' In the event he remained at Swarthmore until March 1945, when he was finally offered war work in association with Stern.

In the Swarthmore years Auden wrote 'The Sea and the Mirror', his epilogue to Shakespeare's *The Tempest*. It presents the Christian conception of art and traces the kinship between perfect divine love and imperfect human love. 'Art', Auden had written in 1943, 'is not Magic, i.e., a means by which the artist communicates or arouses his feelings in others, but a mirror in which they may become conscious of what their own feelings really are: its proper effect, in fact, is disenchanting.' The doubleness of *The Double Man* continues in the poems and lyrics of 'The Sea and the Mirror'. Each of its characters comments on the antagonism of opposites yet it ends by celebrating 'the sounded note' of 'the restored relation'. There is a necessary doubleness in every neighbourhood: 'the railroad above which the houses stand in their own grounds, each equipped with a garage and a beautiful woman, sometimes with several, and below which huddled shacks provide a squeezing shelter to collarless herds who eat blancmange and have never said anything witty'. Objects have their necessary counterparts: 'Gallows and battlefields are, after all, no less places of mutual concern than sofa and bridal-bed.' Auden's characters are like one another's manikins, but it is impossible to say which is the master or who depends on the other most. Auden treated his characters as if they were historical figures, whom he believed should never be seen as lost souls or irredeemably damned. 'Only fictional characters like Othello, who have no life outside our knowledge, can be so presented,' he wrote in 1946. 'We have no right to believe, far less to hope, that even Hitler is in Hell.'

One might say that Kallman's English lover of 1941 is parabolically represented by Antonio, the usurping Duke of Milan, who issues the taunt, 'As I exist so you shall be denied / Forced to remain our melancholy mentor / The grown-up man, the adult in his pride'; but that would miss the point of 'The Sea and the Mirror'. It is not 'about' Auden's private life or his homicidal feelings. 'On account of you,' Auden wrote to Kallman in 1941, 'I have been, in intention, and almost in act, a murderer.' His homicidal impulses against the Englishman, or his gesture in pressing his thick fingers round the throat of the sleeping Kallman, were real experiences which he turned into symbolic forms of violence. These experiences were necessary for him to write about destructiveness in new ways rather than the direct cause of anything in 'For the Time Being'. As Valéry wrote, 'all criticism has been dominated by the outworn principle that the man is the *cause* of the work – as in the eyes of the law a criminal is the *cause* of his crime. Much rather, they are the effects of it in each case.'

The blemishing of Auden's image of a perfect Kallman was like the death of Beatrice: it resulted not in the rejection of images, but allowed the arrival of a greater image. In 'The Sea and the Mirror' Sebastian speaks as someone who has excited himself with phantasies of killing: 'To think his death I thought myself alive / And stalked infected through the blooming day.' But the idea that everything can perish by the sword is a 'lie': all over the world there are examples of an absolute goodness which is concrete and not phantasy: a 'dearness' that 'is no lover's dream'. Sebastian is 'wicked', has coveted his brother's crown but rejoices in the 'bleak Exposure' of his plots. His failure has saved him. 'I smile because I tremble, glad today / To be ashamed, not anxious, not a dream.' The letter of Sebastian's brother Alonso King of Naples to his son Ferdinand is central to 'The Sea and the Mirror' in every way. 'Only your darkness can tell you,' Alonso warns,

> Which you should fear more – the sea in which
> A tyrant sinks entangled in rich
> Robes while a mistress turns a white back
> Upon his splutter, or the desert
> Where an emperor stands in his shirt
> While his diary is read by sneering
> Beggars, and far off he notices
> A lean horror flapping and hopping
> Toward him with inhuman swiftness:
> Learn from your dreams what you lack.

Whatever choices are taken, faith and gratitude must never be lost: 'Believe your pain: praise the scorching rocks.'

The culmination of 'The Sea and the Mirror' is the long prose speech of Caliban. In 1946 Auden judged that 'Henry James' *Prefaces* are the best stuff I know about the nature of the creative act'; he wrote Caliban's speech as an imitation of James's prefaces. It took him six months to plan and write; at the end of his life he remained as proud of it as anything he had written. He was right to be proud, for its magnificent prose introduces great, brave ideas that were essential to his poetry for the rest of his life.

Caliban begins by mocking the redemptive pretensions of Art. 'We should not be sitting here now, washed, warm, well-fed, in seats we have paid for, unless there were others who are not here; our liveliness and good humour, such as they are, are those of survivors, conscious that there are others who have not been so fortunate,' Caliban tells the audience:

> others whose streets were chosen by the explosion or through whose country the famine turned aside from ours to go, others who failed to repel the invasion of bacteria or to crush the insurrection of their bowels, others who lost their suit against their parents or were ruined by wishes they could not adjust or murdered by resentments they could not control; aware of some who were better and bigger but from whom, only the other day, Fortune withdrew her hand in sudden disgust, now nervously playing chess with drunken sea-captains in sordid cafes on the equator or the Arctic Circle, or lying, only a few blocks away, strapped and screaming on iron beds or dropping to naked pieces in damp graves.

It has often been said how universal is the appeal of Auden's love poetry. There is a similar universality in his treatment of shame. In 'The Sea and the Mirror' Sebastian has already represented the shame of the brother who thought to kill and usurp a throne; in this resoundingly important passage Caliban speaks of the guilt of the survivor. The gratitude, thanksgiving and avidity for life which are so often themes of Auden's later poetry derive from Caliban's rueful reflections on the privileges of survival. Auden is writing about accident and tragedy: the circumstances in the life of an individual which unavoidably cause some natural aim or desire to end in catastrophe when carried out. The poignancy of Caliban's speech in the mid-1940s, after a decade of totalitarian violence and usurpation, has been no less since the 1980s, when 'Fortune withdrew her hand in sudden disgust' from hundreds of thousands of people, who found they had been ruined by wishes they could not adjust. For those who survive world wars, or escape viral revolts, and feel ashamed to usurp the place and pleasures of better, bigger, braver people 'dropping to naked pieces in damp graves', Auden gives the great Christian message: 'Whatsoever thy hand findeth to do, do it with thy might; for there is no work, nor device, nor knowledge, nor wisdom, in the grave, whither thou goest.' This is formulated irresistibly by Alonso:

> How soon the lively trip is over
> From loose craving to sharp aversion,
> Aimless belly to paralyzed bone:
> At the end of each successful day
> Remember that the fire and the ice
> Are never more than one step away
> From the temperate city; it is
> But a moment to either.

Despite his admiration for James's prefaces, Auden thought after reading James's journals that, like Rilke's letters, 'there are times when their tone of hushed reverence before the artistic mystery becomes insufferable, and one would like to give them both a good shaking.' As he told Howard Griffin, 'out of their monstrous vanity human creatures want to be their own cause'. Caliban presents Ariel as the sprite of Aesthetics who gives the artist his inspiration; after a time, their partnership becomes stale, the artist loses his vision and gives Ariel his packing-orders. 'Striding up to Him in fury, you glare into His unblinking eyes and stop dead, transfixed with horror at seeing reflected there, not what you had always expected to see, a conqueror smiling at a conqueror, both promising mountains and marvels, but a gibbering fist-clenched creature,' Caliban says. 'This is the first time indeed that you have met the only subject that you have, who is not a dream amenable to magic but the all too solid flesh you must acknowledge as your own.' This is the climax to Caliban's Jamesian speech (and is inspired by the culmination of Henry James's story 'The Jolly Corner'). In Auden's climax, as Julian Symons first noted, Ariel turns into Caliban, who represents humankind in all its depravity. In Shakespeare, Ariel and Caliban are both children of the witch Sycorax, and have an inseparable doubleness as siblings. 'The point of this parable', wrote Symons, 'is that the artist does not produce with his eye upon the object. Ironically, he is able to interpret life only by becoming detached from it: but this detachment itself precludes a completely truthful view of the predicament and nature of man.'

After this climax the tone of Caliban's speech becomes less Jamesian, and its content changes too. Auden in the middle of the world's worst war would not limit himself to a discussion of sacrosanct aesthetics. Escapism leads to hell, or at least to an Audenesque hell where 'cones of extinct volcanoes rise up abruptly from the lava plateau fissured by chasms and pitted with hot springs'. Even if one does make a leap of faith, the religious experience cannot transcend 'the massacres, the whippings, the lies, the twaddle', still less 'our shame, our fear', Caliban concludes. 'It is just here, among the ruins and the bones, that we may rejoice in the perfected Work which is not ours.' Auden cannot mention God. As he had said in 1941, literary intellectuals' attitude to theology was the 'final prudery'. Yet he believed, so he told Dodds shortly after finishing the work, that 'the world problem now is a religious crisis'. This belief, which was scarcely disguised, left liberal and agnostic readers uncomfortable or aghast.

The oratorio and 'The Sea and the Mirror' were published together in a volume entitled *For the Time Being* (by Random House in September 1944 and by Faber in March 1945). Its critical reception varied on each side of the Atlantic. It was hailed as 'the most memorable book of poetry of the year' by Louis Untermeyer in the *Yale Review*. 'All of Auden's accomplishments – his restless wit, his bravura technique, his quick-probing mind, his passion for combining old forms with new experiments – are united in a brilliant and maturely satisfying work.' In Britain Julian Symons placed *For the Time Being* 'very high' among 'the impressive failures of literature ... on the same shelf with the *Essay on Man* and *In Memoriam*.' Symons was a craggedly independent critic who rebuked the modish meanness in London. 'If we compare it with the other poetic performances of our time, it far exceeds them in skill, subtlety, and in everything except that basic seriousness which is the prerequisite of a *great* poem. The ignorance and insensitiveness that have marked its reception in England reveal painfully the depth to which literary criticism has sunk.' It was as much the duty of a critic to review Auden's poems without bias about his emigration as to give an unbigoted review of Wilde after his arrest. Timid, fashionable vindictiveness is despicable in any generation.

'The two poems, taken together,' Louise Bogan wrote of *For the Time Being*, 'constitute the most minute dissection of the spiritual illness of our day that any modern poet, not excluding Eliot, has given us.' This achievement was the culmination of a process that had begun in 1936, when Auden had gone to Iceland and entered a new phase of ethical questing. He had wanted to settle his relations with other people, to scrutinise his influence on others and to test his capacity for good and evil. He wanted, in short, to check that he did not do harm. His position might have been summarised in the words of the Anglican Catechism, which he well knew: 'To do my duty in that state of life, unto which it shall please God to call me.' He would for many years express this sentiment from the Catechism in secular language, but after the death of his mother this inhibition was loosened. He chose a faith that made sense of his past and present experience, and seemed likely to make his future actions more coherent. By the publication of *For the Time Being* he was declaring himself as a religious writer. He closed the war period resembling Alonso:

> once King
> of Naples, now ready to welcome
> Death, but rejoicing in a new love,
> A new peace, having heard the solemn
> Music strike and seen the statue move
> To forgive our illusion.

CHAPTER 8

'Disgraces to keep hidden from the world'

'At the age of thirty-seven I was still too young to have any sure sense of the direction in which I was moving,' Auden once wrote. He was thirty-seven in 1944, the last year of his full-time employment at Swarthmore. It took a visit to the war ruins of Europe in 1945 and a more permanent settlement in New York in 1946 to bring him to maturity. In the ensuing four years Auden's sense of direction became sure. The finest expression of this maturity is the poetic sequence entitled 'Horae Canonicae', which he began writing in 1949 and apparently completed as late as 1954. But the early years of his resettlement in New York were perhaps the richest of his life. They were the time of his 'life crisis which, in various degrees of intensity, we all experience somewhere between the ages of thirty-five and forty-five', as he later wrote. He felt he had to maintain his incorruptibility in a new epoch of temptations: 'it is not madness we need to flee, but prostitution,' he warned in 1949. He so much admired Marianne Moore's poems 'because they convince the reader that they have been written by someone who is personally good,' and quoted with approval her remark, 'rectitude *has* a ring to it, I would say ... with *no* integrity, a man is not likely to write the kind of book I read'. The American psychoanalyst Erik Erikson once defined a state of mind which he called the 'Crisis of Integrity' in phrases that were cited by Auden.

It is a post-narcissistic love of the human ego – not of the self – as an experience which conveys some world order and some spiritual sense, no matter how dearly paid for. It is the acceptance of one's one and only life cycle as something that had to be and that, by necessity, permitted of no substitutions: it thus means a new, a different love of one's parents. It is a comradeship with the ordering ways of distant times and different pursuits, as expressed in the simple products and sayings of such times and pursuits. Although aware of the relativity of all the various life styles which have given meaning to human striving, the possessor of integrity is ready to defend the dignity of his own life style against all physical and economic threats. For he knows that an individual life is the accidental coincidence of but one life cycle with but one segment of history; and that for him all human integrity stands or falls with the one style of integrity of which he partakes.

These were the constituents of Auden's life after 1945, and they have their counterpoints in his work. 'Every ordinary man', Auden wrote in 1950, 'wanted desperately to become a conventional man; that is to say, to lose his humanity and become a mechanical doll.' By contrast poets must want desperately to be exceptional in their submission: to be so conscientious in their vocation – so full of Marianne Moore's rectitude – as to resemble a penitent seeking forgiveness. As Auden said in 1951, 'Poetry is reflective art, its existence is proof that man cannot be content with the outbursts of immediate sensation and that he wants to understand and organise what he feels.'

He had always used landscape to symbolise the instincts and experiences of human life: in poems like 'The Capital' (1938) or in such phrases as 'the mental mountains and the psychic creeks', 'the caves of accusation' and 'the canyons of distress'. But in the late 1940s many of his most important poems – 'The Age of Anxiety', 'In Praise of Limestone', 'Pleasure Island' and 'Ischia' – use the scenery of his daily life to exemplify himself as a conscious thinking individual. His four protagonists in 'The Age of Anxiety' are seeking, he states, 'that state of prehistoric happiness which, by human beings, can only be imagined in terms of a landscape bearing a symbolic resemblance to the human body'. His imaginary landscapes were used to express his renewed sense of thanksgiving at his survival: his happiness at being someone who, in Caliban's words, had not lost his suit against his parents, or been murdered by uncontrollable resentments, or failed to repel a bacterial invasion. As he wrote in 'Ischia',

> At all times it is good to praise the shining earth,
> Dear to us whether we choose our
> Duty or do something horrible.

The divine duty was to be happy. Pleasure and suffering were feelings which only had significance in relation to happiness. 'As a consequence of man's fall, the pleasure he finds in loving himself frequently conflicts with the duty to love in which lies his happiness, so that doing his duty involves accepting suffering,' Auden wrote in 1950. 'We must accept suffering if and when it comes, not because suffering is a morally superior condition we can pretend that we desire, nor that any pleasure is an illusion that we can pretend to despise, but because our duty to be happy is the only matter we have to consider.'

His visit to Europe in 1945 was a necessary antecedent to this final phase of his life. In April he was recruited to the Morale Division of the US Strategic Bombing Survey in Germany. He left for Europe in a flurry of disorder. 'If Wystan's home is usually in a chaos which looks as though a mythical beast had gotten drunk and had wandered through shitting books and soiled shirts, you can imagine what it looked like in the throes of packing,' Kallman reported. Auden first travelled to England, where he arrived at the start of May, declaring, 'My dear, I'm the first major poet to fly the Atlantic.' In London he offended friends like Lehmann and Spender by deploring English discomfort and praising American cultural vitality, and by telling Lucian Freud (who repeated the remark) that he was the only person he wanted to see in England. Perhaps his tactlessness was intended to forestall the hostility epitomised by a remark of Robert Graves at this time: 'Ha ha about Auden: the rats return to the unsunk ship.' But as Edmund Wilson wrote shortly afterwards to Mamaine Paget, 'In fundamental ways, he doesn't belong in that London literary world – he's more vigorous and more advanced. With his Birmingham background ... he is in some ways more like an American. He is really extremely tough – cares nothing about property or money, popularity or social prestige – does everything on his own and alone.' The antagonism to him in Britain was evident in the reception of his selection of Tennyson's work published as the inaugural volume of a series entitled 'The Poets on Poets'. In his introduction he wrote of Tennyson, 'In youth he looked like a gypsy; in age like a dirty old monk; he had the finest ear, perhaps, of any English poet; he was undoubtedly the stupidest; there was little about melancholia that he didn't know; there was little else that he did.' Such phrases were found inexcusably patronising when the book was published in London in 1946. Sir Desmond MacCarthy wrote a magisterial review mocking Auden's picture of Tennyson as a 'poor, congenitally morbid, empty-headed arrivist who sold his early poetic gift for riches.... How different from some poets and authors today, leaders of the young, champions of the oppressed, beacons of the future, thinkers, who, when civilisation and their fellow-countrymen were in danger, promptly left for Hollywood!' Auden's reaction was bemused. 'I became Public Cultural Enemy No I over the Tennyson preface,' he wrote to Dodds. 'I'm delighted that the English can get excited over poetry though it is a little comic seeing that T is one of my favorite poets.'

On his English visit of 1945 Auden spent a day with his father at Wesco, a hamlet in the Lake District with 'views of transcendent beauty' where Dr Auden had bought a small house in the 1920s. He then crossed the North Sea to Darmstadt, 'where there once was a town', as he wrote on 9 May to Elizabeth Mayer. An air-raid lasting fifty-one minutes on 11 September 1944 had created a firestorm in which 8433 human beings had been killed or burned to death, adult corpses shrivelling to the size of the babies in the heat. The psychological aftermath of this firestorm was one subject on which he was expected to report. Auden, like other Bombing Research Analysts of the Strategic Bombing Survey, interviewed German civilians selected at random. As he recalled in 1963, 'We asked them if they minded being bombed. We went to a city which lay in ruins and asked if it had been hit. We got no answers that we didn't expect.' Auden tried to be cheerful – 'We are very fortunate in our billets, the house of the leading local Nazi who committed suicide. There are real beds, *atrocious* pictures, a dull library, hot water and a very nice lot of people' – but the reality of Darmstadt's incineration kept breaking through. He told Elizabeth Mayer, 'I keep wishing you were with us to help and then I think, perhaps not, for as I write this sentence I find myself crying.' Together with James Stern, who has left an account of Darmstadt in his memoir *The Hidden Damage*, Auden undertook an upsetting tour of Bavaria. He met survivors of the concentration camps, and gave a hundred dollars to a woman from Dachau. More agreeably he met both Lincoln Kirstein and Nicolas Nabokov, and diverted himself with investigations that mingled Sherlock Holmes with Alfred Kinsey. In Munich he collected testimony on the July 1944 plot to assassinate Hitler; he also commissioned research into the effects of war conditions upon prostitution.

It is unfortunate that the report of his enquiry has not been traced for he was acerbic about the methods of the newly emergent generation of sexologists. He told Ansen in 1947, 'The Kinsey Report is very bad – too many male whores interviewed – 826 – in proportion to the total interviewed, and he paid too little attention to anal activities.' He agreed with Lionel Trilling that Kinsey's reports were an attempt by statistical science to reassure people that human solitude was imaginary and that physical contact was more than an expedient consolation. This reflected his own post-war outlook: 'I feel very guilty now about encouraging people to think I care more than I do,' he said in 1947. 'I don't care about the excitement of the chase one little bit. What I would really like would be a brothel where you simply go in, pay your money, and go home at a reasonable hour without any understanding on either side.' As Auden told Howard Griffin in 1950, 'Sexual experience never means a truly complete but always a broken and divisive way of knowing one another.' Years later, in 1963, he wrote, 'Loneliness waited / For Reality / to come through the glory hole.'

Auden returned to New York in August 1945, and kept busy with editorial assignments from publishers. He was appointed editor of the 'Younger Poets' series of Yale University Press, and in the next twelve years spotted incipient talents like John Ashbery and Adrienne Rich, whose early poems showed Auden's influence. Since December 1943 he had been working intermittently with Brecht on an adaptation of Webster's *The Duchess of Malfi*; from September 1945 until April 1946 the two collaborators applied themselves more concertedly to the text. They were not mutually congenial: indeed Auden called Brecht 'odious'. Brecht eventually withdrew for reasons unconnected with Auden from the Broadway production of October 1946, which flopped. During 1944–5 Auden also provided song-lyrics for James and Tania Stern's translation of Brecht's *The Caucasian Chalk Circle*. Hopes of a Broadway production proved chimerical, and although Auden enjoyed his collaboration with the Sterns, he treated these Brechtian interludes as unimportant. He taught the spring semester of 1946 at Bennington College in Vermont, and on 20 May was sworn into US citizenship. In the months that followed he intensified his sense of location: in August 1946 he took a lease on an apartment, made himself a New Yorker, used the city as a landscape of ethical tests.

He settled at 7 Cornelia Street in Greenwich Village and lived there until 1951. This apartment was the first home that he had to himself for any time. In the 1930s he had lived on school premises or at his parents' house in Birmingham with occasional intervals in the flats of London friends or in rented rooms in Berlin and Brussels. It was unusual for a man of his generation and class to lack a settled home of his own. Among his English friends of the 1930s perhaps only Isherwood and Brian Howard – who usually stayed with their mothers when they were not in Continental *pensions* or hotels – were similarly unsettled. People in the 1930s would lament, 'it's such a pity Wystan never grows up'; but for him, property and security were low priorities, and he did not wish to waste time and energy in growing up in ways that would not serve his vocation. His unsettlement was a choice, and an assertion of his wishes, rather than a sign of personal incoherence. Auden's rejection of continuous domicile also reflected his isolation. As he neither expected nor experienced an equal love, there was no one with whom he wished to live. He and Kallman did not live together in New York in a settled way until 1951, when Auden rented an apartment for them to share at 235 Seventh Avenue. Until then their longest uninterrupted time together seems to have been their honeymoon in 1939 and the spring semester of 1942 when they were together at Ann Arbor. Though Auden briefly in the autumn of 1939 rented a flat of his own in Montague Terrace, Brooklyn Heights, until he returned from the war in 1945 he lived in communities – the household on Middagh Street or rented college buildings – or in the homes of hospitable friends like Mina Curtiss, Caroline Newton and the Sterns.

The Cornelia Street apartment was, he wrote at the time, 'too expensive, too small, and in the village which I dislike but it is in a new building and really quite nice'. A different impression is given by Norse's description of his first visit there: 'New but drab building, sandwiched between sweet-smelling Italian bakeries and *salumerias* on the narrow street.' The apartment itself 'was small and squalid, boxlike, ill lit by garish overhead light bulbs in a tacky chandelier at the center of the dusty ceiling', Norse recalled. 'Against one wall in the untidy living room stood a smallish worktable, overflowing in monumental disarray; books, maga-zines, manuscripts, cigarette cartons and packs, ashtrays choked with butts, a portable typewriter.' Howard Griffin's account is similar. 'With its unmade army cot in one corner and the stacks of carelessly arranged books, there is a sort of conscious disorder about Auden's room. Rough planking on horsetrees forms a table, covered with bits of ms., books, photographs. The twelve volumes of an Oxford Unabridged Dictionary slant against the wall.' While talking to Griffin, Auden sometimes consulted his sources: 'with books his hands took on deftness and lost all the ineptitude that they had with plates and cups'. Afterwards Griffin reflected that Auden 'prides himself on his freedom from worldly possessions.... with him lack of a permanent habitation formed a humanistic release; he only wanted to search for men who actively believed in the things he did'.

An old Oxford friend of Jimmy Stern's, Harold Acton, who often saw Auden after his move to Cornelia Street, recognised his new delight in city life: 'He captured live images in mid-air, entranced by phenomena that irritated Evelyn Waugh – by the racy slang, the garrulous cab drivers, the jets of steam in the streets.' He impressed new acquaintances with a vitality that matched his surroundings in the Village. Vassily Yanovsky, who was introduced to him at this time, recalled: 'The most cherishable trait in Wystan was, for me, from the start, his specific, inexhaustible, I would say Russian, passion to debate a problem to its end ... willing to go to the very edge of an issue, camouflaging his eagerness with Anglo-Saxon "irony", yet never tiring, provided there was more wine in the bottle.' Yet at this time Auden equally relished the anonymity of New York. 'The city forces you to listen to other people's conversations,' he said in 1950. 'You become the public citizen. Whereas a large landscape diffuses energy, in the midst of a city you can concentrate.' The concentration and isolation were deliberate. Norse often saw Auden eating alone in a restaurant on Barrow Street. 'Barely looking up, he would grunt hello or merely nod and return to his book as if it demanded every precious moment of his attention.'

Auden's milieu on Cornelia Street is crucial to his creativity in the late 1940s. He chose to make it his Great Good Place. Caliban in 'The Sea and the Mirror' had presented a railway journey as a parable of life. The dirty human traffic in waiting-rooms, ticket queues and parcel offices provides the traveller with his chance: 'it is in those promiscuous places of random association, in that air of anticipatory fidget, that he makes friends and enemies, that he promises, confesses, kisses and betrays'. By contrast 'the main depot' of the railroad is only 'the Grandly Average Place'. The inspiration for Auden's railway parable is a short story 'The Great Good

Place' by Henry James which opens with an author named George Dane in his rooms, like Auden in Cornelia Street, engulfed by 'an immense array of letters, notes, circulars, that pile of printer's proofs', by 'periodicals of every sort', but above all by books, 'in wrappers as well as disenveloped and dropped again – books from publishers, books from authors, books from friends, books from enemies'. Dane, who is near to breakdown, changes place with an acolyte and is spirited away to a retreat which may be a sanatorium, or a sacred convent, or an hotel without noise, or a club without newspapers, or 'a sort of kindergarten ... of some great mild, invisible mother who stretches away into space and whose lap is the whole valley'. Here the persecuted author finds 'the vision and the faculty divine'. James, so Auden judged in 1946, was 'writing a religious parable' about 'a spiritual state which is achievable by the individual now'. There was a dialogue about the whereabouts of this Great Good Place which Auden quoted:

'Where is it?'
'I shouldn't be surprised if it were much nearer than one ever suspected.'
'Nearer "town," do you mean?'
'Nearer everything – nearer everyone.'

On this passage Auden commented,

Yes. Nearer everything. Nearer than James himself, perhaps, suspected, to the 'hereditary thinness' of the American Margin, to ... 'the torture rooms of the living idiom', nearer to the unspeakable juke-boxes, the horrible Rockettes and the insane salads, nearer to the anonymous countryside littered with heterogeneous *dreck* and the synonymous cities besotted with electric signs, nearer to radio commercials and congressional oratory and Hollywood Christianity, nearer to all the 'democratic' lusts and licenses, without which, perhaps, the analyst and the immigrant alike would never understand by contrast the nature of the Good Place nor desire it with sufficient desperation to stand a chance of arriving.

Auden in the late 1940s hoped that the coarse redolences of the city would bring him nearer everything. He thought that authors should lose their sacred interiors because their traditional immunity from common-place human pressures had been destroyed in the 1940s. 'The day of the Master's study with its vast mahogany desk on which the blotting paper is changed every day, its busts of Daunty, Gouty and Shopkeeper, its walls lined with indexed bookshelves, one of which is reserved for calf-bound copies of the Master's own works, is over for ever,' he wrote in 1948. 'From now on the poet will be lucky if he can have the general living room to himself for a few hours or a corner of the kitchen table on which to keep his papers. The soft carpets, the big desks, will all be reserved by the Management for the whopping liars.' Yet he was deeply ambivalent about his sacrifices in favour of disarray and *dreck* and urban hordes. He still retained the preferences of his boyhood. '*My* Great Good Place', he told Grigson, 'is the part of the Pennines bounded on the S by Swaledale, on the N by the Romans Wall and on the W by the Eden Valley.' He knew though that spiritual quietude was represented in different ways for different people at different times: 'Venice was for him the Great Good Place,' he wrote of Frederick Rolfe (Baron Corvo), 'a city built by strong and passionate men in the image of their mother, the perfect embodiment of everything he most craved and admired.' He loathed the degradation of Cornelia Street too. 'My Negro maid has left me,' he fumed in 1948. 'She didn't show up after that day she cursed at me. It's a disgrace that I have to live like this. It's so hard to get servants and accommodation in this country.... I don't see why I shouldn't have a nice house.' And in a New Year letter of 1948 to Alan Ansen, he counselled, 'BE MORE BOURGEOIS AS BEFITS A SCHOLAR AND A GENTLEMAN.' It was to Ansen too that he dedicated a book written in 1948–9 with a quotation from Baudelaire: 'Étude de la grande maladie de l'horreur du domicile'.

The Village in 1946 resembled Paris in the 1920s. Anatole Broyard, who lived round the corner from Auden in Cornelia Street, has written in his Greenwich Village memoir, *Kafka Was the Rage*: 'Rents were cheap, restaurants were cheap, and it seemed to me that happiness itself might be cheaply had. The streets and bars were full of writers and painters and the kind of young men and women who liked to be around them.' Auden was a familiar figure among the picturesque, battered buildings. 'I often saw him scurrying along with his arm full of books and papers. He looked like a man running out of a burning building with whatever of his possessions he'd been able to grab.' On one occasion in a stationery store on West

Fourth Street Broyard's lover, Sheri, collided with Auden. As she fell, she clutched Auden round the neck, and pulled him down on top of her. 'She clung to Auden, who was sprawled in her arms. He tried desperately to rise, scrabbling with his hands and his espadrilles on the floor. He was babbling incoherently, apologizing and expostulating at the same time, while she smiled at me over his shoulder, like a woman dancing.' For *Mademoiselle* magazine Auden described the situation of this young intelligentsia:

> She worries about her feminity and her boy friend is equally concerned about his masculinity. It is extremely probable, therefore, that she (and he) is paying visits to a psychiatrist or psychoanalyst.... The new novels she reads reflect this interest in the inner life; they are likely to be more fantastic than naturalistic and to show the influences of writers like Henry James and Kafka. At her parties existentialism has replaced Marxism as a conversational topic; her notions of what Kierkegaard, Heidegger, Sartre, et cetera, actually wrote are probably vague but she knows it has something to do with anxiety, guilt, and making choices.

Their circumstances were intensely bookish. 'Books steadied us; it was as if we carried a heavy bag of them in each hand and they kept us level,' in Broyard's words. 'If it hadn't been for books, we'd have been completely at the mercy of sex. There was hardly anything else powerful enough to distract or deflect us.'

Two bookish young men, Howard Griffin and Alan Ansen, helped Auden with his work at this time, and both compiled valuable accounts of his conversation. 'I thought over many of the things which Auden had quickly, offhandedly said,' Griffin noted after a long dialogue. 'In his mind, I saw, everything fitted together; there was nothing fortuitous. During our talk sections of his poetry that had puzzled me gradually became clear, interlinked, even inevitable, and I wondered how I could ever have questioned them. Even in his most casual remarks, a hard integration existed.... In a unique sense, everything *mattered* to him.' Auden's friendships were unsentimental, and though unlike Britten he did not repudiate friends and cut them out of his life, he never clung weakly to acquaintances. He quoted approvingly some lines of Edward Thomas,

> we were not friends
> But fellows in a union that ends
> With the necessity for it, as it ought.

He kept a strict routine, and turned away friends or casual visitors who bothered him during his work hours (his concentration was most intense from 7 till 11.30 in the morning). He told Griffin, 'I am compulsive in my work habits. If I've got an engagement at six, and work till 5.45 and my friend doesn't show up at the proper time, I can't go on working. Something breaks the connection…. Also my supposedly self-regulating needs, such as hunger, do not operate by themselves but according to the schedule. For instance: ordinarily I stop work at 5.30. At six I start getting hungry. One day a prankster set the clock back two hours and I worked till seven-thirty with no trace of hunger. In this apartment, you know, I'm not conscious of the city out there.'

One of Ansen's tasks was to check the metrical stresses in 'The Age of Anxiety'. This long poem (the last long poem Auden wrote) was conceived in the summer of 1944. It was perhaps as much as half-written by the end of 1945, although he worked on it throughout 1946 and did not finish until February 1947. It was published with the subtitle 'A Baroque Eclogue' by Random House in July 1947 and by Faber in September 1948. 'The Age of Anxiety' begins with four strangers meeting in wartime in a bar and talking against the background 'noise of the El on Third Avenue'. Their impersonality is just that of strangers in a bar and characterises them as city-dwellers: they are types who transcend personal identity. The bar, Auden wrote, is 'an unprejudiced space in which nothing particular ever happens'; its habitués make no choices, are passive in their anxiety and waste their lives waiting to live. Auden's four protagonists are Malin, a medical officer in the Canadian air force, personifying Thought; Rosetta, a Jewish department-store buyer, personifying Feeling; Quant, a weary clerk, who personifies Intuition; and Emble, a sexy young naval recruit, who represents Sensation. These four faculties had also spoken in a short dialogue in 'For the Time Being'. Malin desires Emble, who is attracted to Rosetta. Malin is the only one of this quartet to understand their predicament, but Rosetta is the strongest and leads the others. Emble's subjectivity means that he has the weakest will. Yet they are all fortunate: their chance meeting leads to an authentic, if brief, sense of community feeling; and Rosetta and Malin enjoy a rarer fortune still, for at the end of the poem, each receives a reward worthy of the hero of a quest: a moment of revelatory understanding in which, even if transiently, everything makes sense and their experiences co-inhere.

As usual there were a multitude of influences in Auden's poem: *Finnegans Wake*, Jung, Kierkegaard, Dante and Niebuhr are among the most important. The private phantasy worlds of his protagonists are treated with invincible and far-reaching irony. But Auden also declares, 'Human beings are, necessarily, actors who cannot become something before they have first pretended to be it; and they can be divided, not into the hypocritical and the sincere, but into the sane who know they are acting and the mad who do not.' This deeply depressing yet potentially liberating viewpoint is as central to Auden's outlook in this period as his Christian beliefs. It contributed to his bleaker moments of personal unhappiness. Thus the proof of Quant's sanity is that he knows what he has faked. Yet self-knowledge of his inauthenticity brings shame, grief and an acute sense of isolation:

> Who will trust me now,
> Who with broad jokes have bored my children
> And, warm by my wife, have wished her dead
> Yet turned her over, who have told strangers
> Of the cars and castles that accrued with the fortune
> I might have made?

The landscape frame for 'The Age of Anxiety' is New York City. When the poem was near completion Auden confessed his 'constant regrets that I am too short-sighted, too much of a Thinking Type, to attempt ... poetry which requires a strong visual imagination'. He dedicated the poem to Betjeman, and averred that he wished he had the powers to write Betjemanesque architectural poems, especially one commemorating the demolition of 'the most beautiful building in New York, the El station at Sands Street' near the naval yards in Brooklyn.* 'The Age of Anxiety'

---

* He wrote one poem about favourite New York buildings, Schrafft's coffe shops, but other private landmarks he wished to commemorate poetically included Stouffer's Teashop, the Brighton Beach Line, the General Theological Seminary on Ninth Avenue at Twenty-First Street, the Shakespeare garden in Central Park, the Portugese Jewish cemetery on West Eleventh Street, the Garibaldi house on Staten Island, Welfare Island, the Hotel Seville on Twenty-ninth Street, Sam's Umbrella Shop and the Museum of the American Indian.

begins on Third Avenue. After a dream sequence, it shifts to Rosetta's apartment, and closes with Emble asleep on her bed, Quant walking the city streets and Malin on a train crossing Manhattan Bridge. New York symbolises human existence, part of a 'stupid world / where gadgets are gods'. In 'The Prologue' Malin recalls the horror of a bombing-raid ('houses flamed in / Shuddering sheets'), and finds 'the new barbarian is no uncouth / Desert dweller' or savage from a fir-forest:

> factories bred him;
> Corporate companies, college towns
> Mothered his mind, and many journals
> Backed his beliefs. He was born here. The
> Bravura of revolvers in vogue now
> And the cult of death are quite at home
> Inside the city.

Malin develops some of the ideas from the 'New Year Letter' of 1940. Industrial civilisation had developed elaborate ruses to keep us from truth. Gutter journalism, demotic broadcasting, technology, speed were uprooting, destroying or trivialising all genuine contact with things as they really are. Modern conditions made it impossible to stop the hypocritical, insane acting which we delude ourselves into believing is anything but a fugitive panic. Auden's characters retreat further into private worlds of symbol which leave them uneasy and dissatisfied. Their anxiety is an expression of potential spiritual health. It shows awareness of the shallowness of their lives and the possibility of sailing out, in a favourite phrase of his from Kierkegaard, over a depth of 70,000 fathoms. Auden's protagonists use their private worlds of symbol to escape from a personal anxiety that is essentially religious. Early on Malin explains the source of this anxiety as the original sin in man:

> this guilt his insoluble
> Final fact, infusing his private
> Nexus of needs, his noted aims with
> Incomprehensible comprehensive dread
> At not being what he knows that before
> This world was he was willed to become.

The poem closes with a consummate declaration of Christian experience:

> In our anguish we struggle

To elude Him, to lie to Him, yet His love observes
His appalling promise; His predilection
As we wander and weep is with us to the end,
Minding our meanings, our least matter dear to Him.

Auden often wrote at his best when he was reacting against himself. His work was a public dialogue of private ideas; it was strongest when these ideas were not static. There was for him perhaps too little movement from 'New Year Letter' through 'The Sea and the Mirror' to 'The Age of Anxiety'. Alan Ross reviewing the latter in the *Times Literary Supplement* was bored by the 'appearance of recapitulation' and irked by 'the subconscious need for explanation which has developed into a neurosis'. He thought 'Mr Auden has written his one dull book, his one failure', which fails 'because it lacks a discriminating human sympathy ... its movement is the movement of a robot, faintly parodying its former self'. Patric Dickinson in *Horizon* was also bored. 'The purpose is to show what goes on in four separate minds. But what does go on is a re-hash of Auden's psychology divided by four, and multiplied by a great many of his older clichés.' Perhaps in reaction to such comments Auden a few years later himself wrote that any poet who had 'spent twenty years learning to be himself ... finds that he must now start learning not to be himself. At first he may think this means no more than keeping a sharper look out for obsessive rhythms, tics of expression, privately numinous words, but presently he discovers that the command not to imitate himself can mean something harder than that. It can mean that he should refrain from writing a poem which might turn out to be a good one, and even an admired one.'

Nevertheless in 1947 his new book had many admirers. Edmund Wilson 'thought *The Age of Anxiety* was wonderful – as an exploit in language and imagery, it really rivals *Finnegans Wake*'. Leonard Bernstein found it so 'fascinating and hair-raising' that he composed a symphony for piano and orchestra 'The Age of Anxiety (after W. H. Auden)', completed in 1949. Eliot thought 'that it was his best work to date'. A thousand copies were ordered by the US Navy, and in 1948 the book won a Pulitzer prize: this was a particular coup, for it was the first of his books eligible for the prize, which can only be awarded to American citizens. One appeal to naval men and the Pulitzer committee was perhaps its title, which seemed to describe (but had little directly to do with) the atmosphere of the Cold

War – 'times like the present / When guesses can prove so fatally wrong', as Auden wrote in 'The Managers' (June 1948). Nevertheless in the USA too this book drew Auden's most disobliging reviews in twenty years. '*The Age of Anxiety* is the worst thing Auden has written since *The Dance of Death*; it is the equivalent of Wordsworth's "Ecclesiastical Sonnets",' Randall Jarrell declared in the *Nation*. 'The man who, during the thirties, was one of the five or six best poets in the world has gradually turned into a rhetoric mill grinding away at the bottom of Limbo, into an automaton that keeps making little jokes, little plays on words, little rhetorical engines, as compulsively and unendingly and uneasily as a neurotic washes his hands.' Jarrell was an extremist, who resented that Auden had once been essential to him and feared that he could not continue to be carried on Auden's back. Jarrell's doubts perhaps also derived from a literalness, or failure of ironic recognition, in Americans, who seldom understand 'the basic frivolity in art', Auden thought. 'People don't understand that it's possible to believe in a thing and ridicule it at the same time,' he told an interviewer from *Time* in 1947. 'It's hard for them, too, to see that a person's statement of belief is no proof of belief, any more than a love poem is a proof that one is in love.' The poetic public, with its yearning for celebrity and trivia, could be disappointing.

'The ideal audience the poet imagines consists of the beautiful who go to bed with him, the powerful who invite him to dinner and tell him secrets of state, and his fellow-poets,' Auden wrote in 1948. 'The actual audience he gets consists of myopic schoolteachers, pimply young men who eat in cafeterias, and his fellow-poets. This means that, in fact, he writes for his fellow-poets.' In the 1940s his American poetic friendships proliferated. He seems always to have been disliked by Robert Frost, who was jealous of all rivals and perhaps chafed at Auden's mischievous but not factitious comparison of his poems to Cavafy's simple, cruisy lyrics. William Carlos Williams was antagonistic in the early 1940s, possibly because he resented Auden's greater success when they performed together at a poetry reading, but they were reconciled by 1952, when Auden offered the use of his house at Ischia for a holiday. These jealousies were exceptional. 'We drank and roared ... until 3:30 or 4:00,' reported Theodore Roethke after an evening at Bennington. 'I like him very much.... He's cockier than he used to be ... and damned smart.' Auden was best man at Roethke's wedding in 1953. Louise Bogan wrote, 'I want to talk to him; he has such piercing insights into the bare spots in one's spirit.' Despite the poetic tensions between them, Jarrell thought him 'awfully nice'. Older poets like St John Perse turned to him with gratitude too; Auden responded with the dedication of 'Winds' to Perse. 'Mr Auden is a blessing wherever he is,' Marianne Moore wrote to Elizabeth Mayer. 'To feel so intensely and so intelligently as he does, is to "suffer", but surely consolation will attend him. I would be happier if I could remove some of his burdens and secure to him certain joys.' (In turn he regarded Moore as 'one of the nicest people I have ever met', her poems as 'intelligent, sensitive and beautifully written'.) One can guess that 'love undying' was one of the joys she wished him.

His undying love was for Kallman. He remained, in Edmund Wilson's phrase, 'a homosexual chauvinist'. Wilson in 1946 found him 'homosexual to an almost fanatical degree – tells people that Eisenhower is queer and assured me the other day that Wagner's Tristan and Isolde were really a couple of Lesbians, because a man making love to a woman couldn't really get into that rapturous state – he would be "thinking about something else" '. Reading *The Bostonians* by Henry James in 1947, Auden announced, 'wonderful and extraordinarily daring, all about lesbians'; its character Verena 'is simply trade'. Some such remarks were teases – as when he told Ansen, 'I'd rather go to bed with Truman than MacArthur' – but they developed a nervous repetitive monotony: 'Auden appears to be infatuated with J. Edgar Hoover and Molotov, inquiring of all if they think these chaps are queens,' Delmore Schwartz observed. There was sometimes a fierce passion beneath such chatter, as when he said of 'that horrible Labouchere', a British politician who had initiated a calamitous extension of criminal sanctions against homosexuality, 'I should like to throw shit on his grave.' Yet even Auden's chauvinism was breachable. In 1944 he met a young woman called Rhoda Jaffe, who had been a Brooklyn classmate of Kallman. She was then working for a New York restaurateur, and married to another Brooklyn College contemporary, Milton Klonsky. She was estranged from her husband by late 1945, when Auden invited her to his apartment to type manuscripts. While she was typing, according to Kallman, Auden announced in his abrupt way, 'I think we ought to have an affair.' It was directly consummated.

Kallman and his set professed astonishment when the couple were seen together, and Auden (writing from Bennington in April 1946) evidently

relished the extravagance of 'current rumour' circulating about them in
New York. There was nothing strange or novel in Auden's heterosexual
activity. There had been other brief sexual affairs with women since 1926:
his Austrian landlady Hedwig Petzold was perhaps the first. Kallman
himself was supposed by Dorothy Farnan and some of her friends to have
been lightheartedly available: 'he slept with women ... and he never, never
told'. But this is all speculation, and Kallman publicly claimed an exclusive
homosexuality; he would rebuke Auden for his adventures with women by
remarking, 'But after all, *I'm* pure.' In an article for *Harper's Bazaar* on
femininity written during his affair with Jaffe, Auden identified his taste
for exciting, corrupting, captious women – Merimée's *Carmen*, Marguer-
ite Gautier in Dumas' *Camille* and Beerbohm's *Zuleika Dobson* were his
favourite fictional heroines – but this was partly ironic.

As to Jaffe, Ansen recorded after his first meeting, 'Rhoda turned out to
be terribly good-looking, golden haired, dynamic, somewhat dictatorial
(though pleasantly so).' Two topics fascinated her, 'psychology in general
and her own pychological condition in particular', Farnan found. 'One
learned very early that Rhoda and her sister had been in an orphanage; that
they resented their father for having put them there after their mother's
death; and that Rhoda had been in psychotherapy ever since she could
afford to employ a psychiatrist.' After finishing at Brooklyn College she
had worked as a waitress to pay her analyst, who was a Freudian: Rosetta in
'The Age of Anxiety', who is supposedly based partly on her, said, 'I hide
away / My secret sins in consulting rooms.' Jaffe analysed 'all her friends,
acquaintances, employers and lovers when she was not analyzing herself',
according to Farnan. 'She knew and used all the jargon of the profession,
then regarded by many as the panacea for the ills of Western civilisation.
Wystan ... took delight in mulling over with Rhoda all her dreams, all his
theories about cures, and all the facets of the psyche of Chester Kallman.'
Auden's letters to Rhoda Jaffe show that she mattered to him a great deal
until their contacts petered out in 1948; his seduction of her had little in
common with the anxious, guilty state of mind in which, twenty years
earlier, he had proposed marriage to Sheilah Richardson. Her conversation amused him, her company was consoling and their affair served a need
in his work at the time. Farnan's attitude was influenced by Kallman's
mockery, which covered an acrid jealousy. If Jaffe was resented by some of
Auden's acquaintances, she impressed friends like Ansen and the Sterns.

Poets, Auden knew, use people. They need them as the focus of the sensations about which they want to write. 'The girl whose boy-friend starts writing her love poems should be on her guard,' he wrote in 1948. 'Perhaps he really does love her, but one thing is certain: while he was writing his poems he was not thinking of her but of his own feelings about her.' Poets are not necessarily insincere, but they enlist or subordinate other people to serve their vocation: to illustrate this Auden in 1948 quoted St Augustine's admission after the death of someone he had loved, 'I would rather have been deprived of my friend than of my grief.' A year later he told Day Lewis that a poet's 'proper concern is with the object to be created – an object which, however much of himself goes into it, must end up as a not-self'. One of Auden's letters to Jaffe seems particularly suggestive. 'Miss God appears to have decided that I am to be a writer, but have no other fun, and no talent for making others as happy as I would like them to be,' he wrote in June 1947 in a letter which signs off, 'Lots & lots of love darling. You are *so* good, and I'm a neurotic middle-aged butterball.' Having declared himself as supremely an author, whose vocation isolates him from happiness and requires him to use his lovers as objects to help explore his feelings, he enclosed a 'love poem which I defy you to say is obviously written by a queer'. This 'Serenade' of June 1947 concluded:

> So my embodied love
> Which, like most feeling, is
> Half humbug and half true,
> Asks neighbourhood of you

– lines suggesting that he needed Jaffe to make his neighbourhood complete. He never lived in a ghetto, nor was a poet of the ghetto. 'I've come to the conclusion that it's wrong to be queer,' he told Ansen. 'In the first place all homosexual acts are acts of envy; in the second, the more you're involved with someone, the more trouble arises, and affection shouldn't have that result.' Yet he had long recognised the merits of comprehensive experience. 'One shouldn't confine oneself to queer society,' he said in 1947. 'You should look for the nice people in every group.' He foresaw perils for women who 'go around with a social group of queers. All right, the people are more amusing, the conversation wittier, but it does terrible things for the girls' egos because they find themselves in a society where they are not really needed.'

Auden's experiments in neighbourhood and sexuality and his submission to the duty of happiness were occuring in a puritan environment. In 1946 the literary editor of the *New York Times* was forbidden to publish a favourable review of Edmund Wilson's novel *Memoirs of Hecate County*, bookstores stocking it were raided, and it was suppressed after a prosecution in the New York courts. In New York there were legal sanctions against a bar-tender serving alcohol to any man suspected of homosexuality; movie censors prohibited stories depicting extra-marital sex without retribution; there was neither infallible contraception nor legal abortion. It was in this atmosphere that late in 1948 Auden wrote a long poem, 'The Platonic Blow, by Miss Oral'. 'Deciding that there ought to be one in the Auden Corpus, I am writing a purely pornographic poem,' he told Kallman on 13 December. 'You should do a complementary one on the other Major Act.' The poem has some importance. It bears the stylistic influence of Charles Williams, and Auden's punning use of the word 'corpus' indicates its purpose of corporeal celebration. It is most noticeably a hymn to pleasure; but it has other traits, which are less easy to recognise more than forty years later in a less inhibited time. The idea of sex in the poem is as exciting as the act; the poet's visual hunger is stronger than his sexual need; the predictable climax is less interesting than the foreplay. It is a poem written in an epoch of sexual repression rather than satiation.

'All American writing gives the impression that Americans don't really care for girls at all,' Auden reflected after reading Fitzgerald's *This Side of Paradise* in 1948. 'What the American male really wants is two things: he wants to be blown by a stranger while reading a newspaper, he wants to be fucked by his buddy when he's drunk. Everything else is society.' Auden was probably right about the feelings of the American male but wrong about the sexual acts. Homosexuality is not the issue but infidelity. 'As far as one can judge, Lawrence was by temperament monogamous,' he had noted a year earlier. 'The average man is not, and on him the effect of reading Lawrence has been, only too often, to send him (or her) off in a search for the perfect sleeping partner who, according to the doctrine, is most likely to be found among "primitive" or working-class types, one, in fact, who is, outside of the bed, an awful bore.' One result of contemporary 'secularization of belief, the mechanization of work, the atomization of society, birth control, and so on' was that 'the average man today is obsessed with sex ... partly because it seems to him the only sphere in which he is a free agent, in which his failures and his triumphs are really his; hence, if he fails here, he has achieved nothing with his life'. For Auden it was an *acte gratuite* to recognise the possibility of sexual choice, to make a choice, and then to lapse from that choice; the exhausting succession of affairs and infidelities practised by Kallman seemed to Auden not a real expression of freedom, but an abdication of true choice, and pettish rebellion against circumstances which he was not strong enough to resist. Kallman's inveterate cruising perhaps persisted because Auden's possessive love made him powerless. Edmund Wilson noted, 'Wystan has prevented him from having a life of his own', and Kallman himself admitted in 1950, 'I don't really know how to define myself these days.'

In 1946 Auden bought jointly with the Sterns a shack at Cherry Grove, a little seaboard settlement on Fire Island, which is a long, thin sandbank off the Atlantic coast of Long Island. It was his retreat from the stifling summer heat of New York City, from where it could be reached by train and a ferry ride from Sayville on Long Island; but also an arena in which he watched the debasement of Lawrentian ideals by average men. Their shack was named Bective Poplars in reference to James Stern's childhood home and to the Poplars at Horninglow, the gloomy Staffordshire house of Auden's paternal grandmother – a joke, for Fire Island was the antithesis of dingy and uncomfortable British provincialism. It was covered only with shrubs and small trees: its wide Atlantic beach looked out over vast, magnificent views: the Fire Island Hotel, which was reached from Auden's shack by a raised wooden boardwalk, was drunken and cruisy: and there was every sequence of sexual coupling to be had in the shacks, on the beach or in the dunes and copses. The island in summer was an incarnation of paradise as imagined by Ronald Firbank (who supplied an epigraph for 'The Age of Anxiety'). 'Firbank's extraordinary achievement was to draw a picture, the finest, I believe, ever drawn by anyone, of the Earthly Paradise, not, of course, as it really is, but as, in our fallen state, we imagine it to be, as the place, that is, where without having to change our desires or behaviour in any way, we suffer–neither frustration nor guilt,' Auden wrote in the *New York Times* in 1949. 'The first axiom of such an Eden is that it is a world of pure being; what people are or what they want or ought to be are identical ... The second is that there is no law and no super-ego; for few Firbank characters confine their affections to a single object, or a single sex, even fewer can say no, but nobody is shocked and nobody gets hurt. Religious exercises are practiced extensively but, since God is loving without being a judge, they are all, even those of mortification, pure fun.'

Auden wrote to Jaffe from Fire Island each week during his visit in the summer of 1947. His letters give a revealing picture of his emotional life there. On 10 June he reported: 'Chester came out on Saturday for one night, very fussed over his matelot and having to telephone constantly to NY. The latter, he tells me, is, what I suspected, *very* gentile and hard drinking. I hope he won't get too involved, poor thing, as I don't believe he can have a serious relation with anyone who is interested in baseball.' A week later, on 17 June, he wrote again: 'He's through with that matelot but is probably bringing out another one (he *says* it's platonic) next weekend. OK with me, but I will not have the sailor pick up a Sayville skirt at the bar and bring her to the house. If he does, I shall use the Flit gun.' On 25 June he consulted Jaffe about a former Bennington pupil who needed advice: 'a little vague, but I think she needs an abortionist'. He had been to a cocktail party, 'and was very flattered because *the* beauty of the island made eyes at me, much to the fury of the other queens. I fear, though, this only means that he has a notebook full of sonnets to his drugstore sweetheart which he is burning to show me.' On 2 July he thanked Jaffe for arranging the Bennington girl's difficulties. 'She is a terrible mess inside, and drinks far too much and needs a pappa, but is not hopeless.' His personal news showed that he remained a romantic optimist who still vested his discoveries with exceptional qualities. 'About the Beauty (who has the unromantic name of Bill Miller, Jr) there is a great deal to tell ... I was wrong and have had one of the most extraordinary experiences of my life. He departed Sunday Night but will return later in the season, having left his tent here. I have never before met someone who has never in his life known failure of any kind and yet is completely unspoilt.' His letters alluded to the self-inflicted mortifications of life with Kallman as his chief companion and love-object. 'Work has been rather difficult since Chester came but I think he is settling down now into a more regular life,' he reported to Jaffe on 14 July. 'The triple situation, of being sexually jealous, like a wife, anxious like a momma, and competitive like a brother, is not easy for my kind of temperament. Still, it is my bed, and I must lie on it.'

He could have avoided this suffering if he had wished, but his fidelity to his ideal of Kallman was proof of his free will; he needed pain as a reminder of the frivolity of art, that is, of art's inability to change people. 'People are born serious, selfish and honest,' he told Griffin. 'Through suffering, they must learn to become frivolous and insincere.'

An Oxford acquaintance, Maurice Cranston, has left a vivid account of a visit to Fire Island in the summer of 1947.

> The paths on the island were long wooden duck-boards over the sand. As we walked along a narrower plank towards his home, Auden said: 'I'm afraid the place is in a mess.'
>
> It was. The building itself was a ramshackle structure that had somehow survived a hurricane. It was made of wood and stood on several pillars. Underneath there were some empty bottles and cans in the sand. On the porch there was a tumbledown bed and an unexpected pile of rusty toys. Inside there was a muddle of books and furniture and food…. Auden surveyed the untidiness with fond contentment.
>
> 'I see that you live alone when you are here,' I said.
>
> 'Don't you think that,' Auden shrugged his shoulders, *'si vous avez la vocation de la vie intellectuelle mieux vaut rester célibataire.'*
>
> . . .
>
> We went out of the cottage discussing the theory of detection, and soon our talk turned to sin and theology, each of us being a species of Anglo-Catholic. This went on until the sun went down and it was time for me to cross the water to go to a dinner party.
>
> 'One week-end,' Auden said, as we stood at the dock, 'the bar on that island … incredible … you should see it.'

On the wall of the shack Auden kept ordnance-survey maps of Alston Moor in Cumberland and Heysham in Lancashire. Like his poems they were analogous good places to Fire Island. 'A poem is a witness to man's knowledge of evil as well as good,' he wrote in *The Dyer's Hand.* 'It is not the duty of a witness to pass moral judgment on the evidence he has to give, but to give it clearly and accurately; the only crime of which a witness can be guilty is perjury.' A poet must not fake his feelings; but recollected feelings are beyond judgment because 'the historical situation' in which they arose has receded into the past. 'Every poem, therefore, is an attempt

to present an analogy to that paradisal state in which Freedom and Law,
System and Order are united in harmony. Every good poem is very nearly
a Utopia. Again, an analogy, not an imitation.' It was on this basis that in
1948 Auden wrote a poem entitled 'Pleasure Island'. It begins:

> What there is as a surround to our figures
>   Is very old, very big,
> Very formidable indeed; the ocean
>   Stares right past us as though
> No one here was worth drowning, and the eye, true
>   Blue all summer, of the sky
> Would not miss a hiddle of huts related
>   By planks, a dock, a state
> Of undress and improvised abandon
>   Upon shadowless sand.

This Firbankian Eden is a beautiful place where nothing of importance
can occur:

> The coast is a blur and without meaning
>   The churches and routines
> Which stopped there and never cared or dared to
>   Cross over to interfere
> With this outpost where nothing is wicked
>   But to be sorry or sick,
> But one thing unneighbourly, work.

He describes the course of a typical day there, which does not resemble the
canonical hours of Easter Friday traced in his sequence 'Horae Canonicae'. Instead Pleasure Island seems associated with Ariel, the accommo-
dating, facile, destructive sprite of Aesthetics in 'The Sea and the Mirror'.
The timelessness of the island life becomes monotonous. A visitor lies on
the beach gazing at 'bosom, backside, crotch', or:

> surrenders his scruples
>   To some great gross braying group
> That will be drunk till Fall. The tide rises
>   And falls, our household ice
> Drips to death in the dark and our friendships
>   Prepare for a weekend
> They will probably not survive.

There seems to be little chance of these libertines finding any sense, but one of them – misused and misnamed as a sex object, deprived of what Auden would have called a Christian name – has a revelatory moment in spite of all the abuse:

> without warning,
> A little before dawn,
> Miss Lovely, life and soul of the party,
> Wakes with a dreadful start,
> Sure that whatever – O God! – she is in for
> Is about to begin,
> Or hearing, beyond the hushabye noises
> Of sea and Me, just a voice
> Ask as one might the time or a trifle
> Extra her money and her life.

The exclamation 'O God' has a doubleness – theological gravity as well as camp silliness – and reflects a Kierkegaardian existentialism. Auden recognised that seeming incompatibilities could in fact coexist; it was impossible to decide which had mastery over the other. It was like the great puzzle at the centre of Auden's emotional life. 'Looking at this young blond angelic and demonic boy, the Chester Kallman' of the 1940s, Vassily Yanovsky 'imagined that Wystan was destroying him … but gradually another thought insinuated itself: perhaps Chester was ruining Wystan. The truth probably was … each needed and abused the other.'

Certainly their relations remained turbulent. 'You either have to leave him alone or be as tough as leather,' Auden said of him in 1948. Spender felt 'that since Chester was a very competitive person, he had begun to believe that Auden had destroyed his personality'. Auden at moments of stress had used his book-reviewing as a public commentary on their relationship, and Kallman used his position in 1945–6 as operatic columnist of *Commonweal* to retaliate. Several of his articles contain digs at Auden. He opened a piece written shortly after Auden had taken up with Rhoda Jaffe with the remark that 'old men who want love are naturally comic'. Auden now looked older than his age, and was enforcing rituals in his life that seemed prematurely old. An article by Kallman on Wagner's *Die Meistersinger* took the figure of Hans Sachs and argued that this supposedly 'wonderful old gent' is really 'one of the most disheartening figures on the operatic stage'. Kallman's article was entitled 'Portraits and

Parables' and there can be little doubt of the subject of his parabolic portrait. Sachs, said Kallman, is a 'tired pedant, ashamed of his knowledge, bitter about his age, disappointed in love, unsatisfied with his art', but a master of concealment. 'He has learned, and learned with difficulty, the business of being the sympathetic personality that makes warm impersonal judgments. He has learned to take public approval as a substitute for inner satisfaction.' But Sachs 'betrays himself in his choice of causes to champion. Walter sings before the Mastersingers and Hans Sachs is taken with his youthful outburst. But Walter's song is frankly bad and ... *that's* the point Sachs is really interested in ... what a comfortable feeling of regained youth he can indulge in, without any threat to whatever artistic reputation he may have himself, by defending that impossibly self-satisfied young man and his inflated passions. Sachs is, indeed, the prototype of all professional anthologists.' (Auden was then writing an article on anthologising which was published in *Commonweal* a fortnight later and compiled a total of twenty-two volumes of anthology in his lifetime.) Kallman mocked the devious contortions of Sachs who, he wrote, 'if he can't have love' pretends to prefer 'the glories of the impersonal'. Kallman described Sachs's behaviour as 'the embarrassed heavy gesture of a recluse trying to be one of the boys. Naturally Sachs chooses an untalented young man to represent the "new" for him ... Sachs would be the first person to object to what was really new; and his objection would probably take the form of an objection to intellectuality.' The review concluded, it is not fanciful to think, with another dig at Auden's interest in Rhoda Jaffe and a complaint about some rebuke of Auden's to Kallman: Sachs's 'treatment of Beckmesser (who, at least, has the conviction to remain what he is) is shameful and sadistic'.

Kallman's review shows considerable self-knowledge, especially if he saw himself as Walter, whose songs were mediocre. His own poems were competent but irretrievably minor. In 1947, however, when his relationship with Auden had reached 'its lowest ebb', he was rescued from obscurity by Auden's insistence that they collaborate in the libretto for Stravinsky's opera, *The Rake's Progress*. At a stroke Kallman was given world stature as a librettist. The possibility of this arrangement arose from Aldous Huxley's suggestion that Stravinsky should ask Auden to write the libretto of a moral fable based on eight Hogarth engravings. The idea attracted Auden, whose hankering to write a libretto is discernible in the structure, songs and dialogue of the three long poems that he had written since 1942. A libretto could release him from the private, ironic modes which he had avowed poetically since 1939; he could be loud and declaratory and address a wide public. Opera also exempted him from being always judicious. Auden devised a preliminary scenario with Stravinsky on a visit to Hollywood in November.

Without consulting Stravinsky, Auden on his return to New York enlisted Kallman as a collaborator. This was not grotesque, for Kallman was passionate and discerning about opera: indeed personified it if, as Auden suggested, 'opera ... is an imitation of human willfulness ... rooted in the fact that we not only have feelings but insist upon having them at whatever cost to ourselves'. Stravinsky was disconcerted to find the names of Kallman and Auden appearing with equal prominence on the title-page of the typescript sent to him in January 1948 with an insouciant letter in which Kallman was introduced as 'an old friend of mine in whose talents I have the greatest confidence'. Stravinsky was advised by his attorney to withdraw from his agreement on the ground that he would be implicating himself 'in a sexual hoax'. This hostility diminished after Stravinsky met Kallman in New York in April 1949 and found him congenial: he and his two librettists continued in a spasmodic process of revision until March 1950. Auden was wont to insist that there was a fusion of selves in his literary collaborations, and that he and Kallman achieved 'a corporate personality' as librettists. This is a touching idea, but hardly sustained by the text, where the inequities of talent are plain. As Mendelson has written, 'The finished libretto displays Kallman's skill at local dramatic effects and his light but sharp-edged exuberance of tone, combined with Auden's structural intelligence and the anachronistic allegory that he had perfected in his longer poems.'

The première of *The Rake's Progress* took place at a music festival at Venice on 11 September 1951 with Stravinsky as conductor: 'really lovely music – such tunes, my dear', Auden wrote afterwards. He was understandably overwrought before the Venice performance. 'Wystan, finding his La Scala-financed accommodations at the Bauer to be bathless and viewless, flees to the I. S.'s [Igor Stravinsky's] over-upholstered and luxuriously uncomfortable Royal Suite and bursts into tears,' Craft recorded. Stravinsky summoned the manager to explain that 'Maestro Auden' was 'a kind of Guglielmo Shakespeare, who, moreover, had been received at Buckingham Palace by the King'. A better room was provided, 'but Wystan's tears, expressing so much frustration and wounded pride, have watered us all a bit, not because he is beyond the most appropriate age for them, but because of his vastly superior mind'. Dylan Thomas, who heard the Venice première on the wireless, said afterwards, 'Auden is the most skilful of us all.' A subsequent performance at the Metropolitan Opera in February 1953 elicited reviews which were 'wildly enthusiastic or violently anti', as Auden reported. *The Rake* is the only one of the six Auden–Kallman operas to have entered the repertory, and is the opera in which Auden's poetic power is best matched with the composer's strengths.

Auden–Kallman libretti teasingly draw on episodes from their lives: their *Elegy for Young Lovers* (1959–60) depicts a relationship between an egotistical, exploitative artist and an intense, possessive, suspicious, fretful, histrionically self-sacrificing elderly lady admirer which cruelly resembles the contacts of Auden and Caroline Newton in the 1940s. Rakewell in *The Rake's Progress* is a passive, self-destructive youth who is misled and ruined by his false servant and personal devil, Nick Shadow. Rakewell indulges in the corrupt choices that fascinated existentialists of the 1940s; his arbitrary decision is not a matter of imagination and spirit, like Auden's Kierkegaardian reversion to Christianity, but a weak, futile gesture. He foresakes his betrothed, Anne Truelove, to marry Baba the Turk, a bearded lady. The mortification of Truelove, and the endurance of her love, resembles Auden's professed attitude after he had been supplanted by Kallman's English lover in 1941. Rakewell's reconciliation with Truelove can be likened to a leap of faith, but it is not enough to save him and he is condemned to madness in Bedlam.

At the time of the Venetian première Auden wrote: 'The verses which the librettist writes are, so to speak, a private letter to the composer; they have their moment of glory when they suggest a melody to him; then they become as expendable as infantry to a Chinese general.' He enjoyed his role as Stravinsky's infantryman, and relished the librettist's exemption from some of the ethical constrictions of poetry: 'Self-deception is impossible in opera, because music is immediate, not reflective; whatever is sung is the case.' For Auden personally the most important feature of his work as a librettist was the happiness it brought him with Kallman; he was so keen to be seen publicly as Kallman's partner that, when the latter did not attend a performance, Auden avoided going on stage to receive applause by himself. Their collaboration in *The Rake's Progress* revivified – perhaps even saved from destruction – Auden's relations with Kallman. Their collaborations continued.

The writing of moral parables in the form of operatic libretti freed Auden to write other meditations. 'To hear people talk, you would think that in their free time, i.e. when not engaged either in action or directed thinking, they were concerned with nothing but sex, prestige and money,' Auden wrote in 1948. But the readiness with which such topics were discussed betrayed their superficiality. 'Underneath them our serious daydream carries on its repetitious, querulous life, and it too has its manifest and latent content. What it actually says over and over again is: "Why doesn't my neighbor love me for myself?", but this is a code message which, de-coded, reads: "I do not love my neighbor as myself and may God have mercy on my soul." About this, just because it is a serious matter, we quite rightly keep silent in public.' In June 1948 he wrote a 'Song' expressing this idea:

> Deftly, admiral, cast your fly
> Into the slow deep, hover,
> Till the wise old trout mistake and die;
> Salt are the deeps that cover
> The glittering fleets you led,
> White is your head.

> Read on, ambassador, engrossed
> In your favourite Stendhal;
> The outer provinces are lost,
> Unshaven horsemen swill
> The great wines of the Châteaux
> Where you danced long ago.

> Do not turn, do not lift, your eyes
> Toward the still pair standing
> On the bridge between your properties,
> Indifferent to your minding:
> In its glory, in its power,
> This is their hour.

> Nothing your strength, your skill, could do
> Can alter their embrace

> Or dispersuade the Furies who
> At the appointed place
> With claw and dreadful brow
> Wait for them now.

The first stanzas introduce two father-figures against a background 'of personal and national defeat, conveyed with Auden's usual brilliance of sinister suggestion', as John Bayley has noted. 'They are men of real accomplishment whom a calamitous period of history (which may still be going on) proved too much for.' Auden believed that 'one thing only, is serious: loving one's neighbor as oneself', so the lovers stand on a bridge connecting neighbouring properties and representing the possibility of loving one's neighbour as oneself. They show for a moment how great and curative love *might* be; yet their love is as evanescent as naval glory or diplomatic triumphs: they can enjoy their moments of passion or caritas, but the revelatory excitement goes stale, or they lapse into the self-destructive, post-lapsarian shame that brings the Furies down on them. Because the private domain is so prized – the holding open of a door for a stranger potentially so much more significant an act than any public tumult – the worst ravages of the Furies' claws are inflicted on private citizens. It is the private duty to love a neighbour which, if fulfilled, would stop the wars, annexations and spoliation more surely than diplomacy.

This 'Song' was written during the course of a visit to Europe in 1948. Auden arrived in England early in April with Kallman. Their visit was an equivocal success, for Kallman repeatedly felt affronted by English people. Cyril Connolly gave a party to honour Auden at which the guests included Betjeman, MacNeice, Elizabeth Bowen and Lucian Freud; but he spoiled the effect by asking Kallman, 'How does it feel to be the male Alice B. Toklas?' Kallman would have been equally indignant at the description by the anthologist Cicely Mackworth of a cocktail party later given by Nancy Cunard: 'Day Lewis was there, Connolly, Alec Waugh, Auden (with an atrocious little blond cockney boy-friend in tow, Chester by name, who called him darling at the top of his voice all the time. Really!)'. A visit to Auden's father at Wesco was equally fraught. The old man was disappointed not to have more time alone with a son whom he adored; anti-semitic remarks were made or imagined. Early in May Auden and Kallman went to Paris, where they met Isherwood, and then proceeded to Florence and Rome.

'My first image of Italy is associated with an aunt whose devotion to the country led her into building her dream Italian house in one of the wettest parts of England,' Auden recalled a few years later. (The aunt was Mildred Bicknell, and the house was the Benches at Monmouth, where his mother stayed just before her death.) 'It was dreadfully damp and draughty and the verandah shut out the sun; still I thought it beautiful.' The beauty in flaws, and the necessity of faults, are the subject of a great poem written by Auden soon after their arrival in Italy, 'In Praise of Limestone'. He had recently written: 'a society which really was like a poem and embodied all the esthetic values of beauty, order, economy, subordination of detail to the whole effort, would be a nightmare of horror, based on selective breeding, extermination of the physically or mentally unfit, absolute obedience to its Director, and a large slave class out of sight in cellars'. Later he explained that a poem should be both 'a verbal earthly paradise, a timeless world of pure play, which gives us delight precisely because of its contrast to our historical existence with all its insoluble problems and inescapable suffering; at the same time we want a poem to be true ... and a poet cannot bring us any truth without introducing into his poetry the problematic, the painful, the disorderly, the ugly'. Auden praises a landscape standing over limestone faults, a place with the imperfections of reality. In the brutality of New York City he had constructed a great good place where the flaws would help him to appreciate perfection; and by analogy he celebrates limestone terrain 'because it dissolves in water'. Auden's poem 'imagines a harmony that its own restlessness keeps dissolving and a way of life that runs away even as it is clutched', as Laurence Lipking says. Limestone 'represents not an escape from anxiety, but a moral reflection upon it'. The limestone is analogous with hidden relationships – 'a secret system of caves and conduits' – and its faults analogous with human frailty. Many modes are encompassed in the poem: the calm, the classical, the totalitarian, the randy, the mad camp. Differences do not exist to be overcome, but for emphasis and celebration; that is why the life of New York City could be analogous to a limestone terrain. It is this perception – half-hidden from consciousness in rich, mysterious yet disenchanting phrases playing a game of knowledge – that makes 'In Praise of Limestone', as Spender judged at the time, 'one of the great poems of this century'.

Later in May Auden went with Kallman to Ischia, an island in the bay of

Naples which was to remain an important locality in his life until 1957. He worked most mornings and achieved a prolific output: 'its such a relief not to have to think for a few months about hack work', he reported to Jaffe on 30 May. He and Kallman were accompanied by Brian Howard and his boyfriend. Initially they 'had one or two dreadful evenings' with Howard 'going on a drunk when he becomes paranoic, but that is over now and I am, anyway, devoted to him. Chester is well and enjoying himself. I make silly little scenes occasionally but otherwise life is harmonious.' Howard's letters to his mother at this time are some of the happiest of his life. 'We live in a rambling hotel, with huge *domed* rooms, white-washed, with blue and lime cornices, entirely alone. Right on the sea. There is a court-yard in the middle, with a vine-trellised roof ... My bath water is heated on a charcoal fire, and we eat octopi, eels, fish, veal, rice, eggs.' Auden wrote a long poem entitled 'Ischia – For Brian Howard', and managed to curb his friend's excesses. 'Wystan's influence is *really* good for me,' Howard told his mother. 'He is quite undeceivable, and he never flatters, lies or exaggerates ... He is an exceedingly *good* man, in the most serious sense, and his standards are ruthlessly high.'

Auden found Ischia so congenial that within two months of arriving he rented a house (in the Via Santa Lucia at Forio) at an annual rent equivalent to $230. It had three bedrooms, two reception rooms, a large kitchen, lavatory, two half-wrecked rooms (all with vaulted ceilings), a hot spring in its derelict basement and a fruitful garden surrounded by vineyards. 'The sex situation in Forio is from my point of view, exactly what it ought to be, i.e. the women never go into the cafes or bars, and if they do appear on the beach, are covered up to their ankles, very few of the men and boys are queer (the Town queen is the son of the Mayor) but all of them like a "divertimento" now and then, for which it is considered polite to give 35 cents or a package of cigarettes as a friendly gesture,' he wrote to Jaffe on 6 July. 'It is so nice to be with people who are never shocked or psychologically insecure ... Everyone of course knows who goes with whom within 24 hours.' A year later he told Jaffe, 'The women here are infinitely superior to the men who behave exactly like girls in a boarding school with their absurd little jealousies and gossip.'

Auden and Kallman left Ischia late in July and returned to London. Connolly arranged for them to use a flat in Paultons Square, Chelsea. There Auden had a lesson in the obstacles to loving one's neighbour, in this case an actress called Anne Valery who occupied the flat downstairs. 'Never far from his beloved bottle of booze, he joined us for a celebration drink while Chester banged about in the kitchen,' Valery recalled. She was a careless cook who continually slopped milk and soup over the burners of their shared gas-stove. For three days Kallman had 'suffered in silence, staring at me angrily as he hugged a tin of Vim' scouring powder, but she had missed the hint. Finally when her fudge boiled over, 'Chester came running out of the kitchen and shouting up the stairwell that he would not share his kitchen even if they had to starve. Poor Auden, who pretended that all he wanted was a quiet life, had tried to act as the peacemaker, but Chester would not be placated and stomped off to Chelsea Barracks where he had made a lot of friends.'

Auden returned to the USA while Kallman went to Ischia to put their new household in order. There was no question of Auden settling permanently at Forio. 'Italy may stimulate the imagination but there is nobody there from whom one can learn how to write,' he insisted. 'Nor anywhere else in Europe, for that matter. If exchange of ideas and contact with intelligent minds is what one wants, one had better stay in New York.' Nevertheless the separation from Kallman hurt Auden. He wrote on 1 November, 'All my love and kisses and do be nice and go on writing me, as I really feel very lost without you, even if a little less tormented.' There were nevertheless various troubles between them. Kallman resented a new, transient protégé of Auden's and threatened him with desertion. 'If I'm anxious for you to approve of Wayne it's not because you're the Beatrice for whom I cherish a grotesque passion, but because you are the one comrade my non-sexual life cannot do without,' Auden protested on his birthday, 21 February 1949. 'Expressions like "bowing out" and "disappear" are thrusts of the knife which, as you know only too well, you beast, hurt. Still, I adore you and I suppose you must deserve it.' There were also disagreements over money and the management of the Ischia household. 'I'm a little drunk and in a paranoic mood for which you must make allowances, but thinking over things I'm beginning to boil,' Auden fumed on 24 February. Yet for him there remained delectable aspects of life with Kallman. Some of them are indicated in a review written around this time of a biography of Wilde. 'Serious prophets are not ideal guests for a party, but a good playboy is always welcome, except to those who have murdered the child in themselves.' He reconstrued

Wilde's ethics in terms which show why Fire Island and Ischia could seem a version of Eden. Wilde was also a paradigm explaining both the vivacity and sexual vagrancy of Kallman: 'A person with this passionate need to be loved has constantly to test those around him by unconventional and provocative behavior, for what he does or says must be admired not because it is intrinsically admirable but because it is *his* act or remark.' Such a person, Auden thought, was 'frequently homosexual' because:

> the sexual act comes to play the same role vis-à-vis those with a lesser degree of consciousness, the young, the working-classes etc. that conversation plays vis-à-vis those with an equal degree; it becomes a magic role of initiation into worlds which one cannot approach on a conscious level. In a homosexual of this kind – corresponding to the test of eccentric behavior in the drawing-room – one usually finds a preference for 'trade', i.e., sexually normal males, because, if another homosexual yields to him, he is only one of a class, but if he can believe that an exception is being made in his case, it seems a proof that he is being accepted for himself alone.

There was much in Auden's life in 1948–9 beyond thoughts of Kallman. In March he delivered lectures on the iconography of the sea in Romantic literature at the University of Virginia, which were published under the title of *The Enchafèd Flood* by Random House in March 1950 and by Faber in February 1951. Another distraction was Auden's membership of the committee appointed under the auspices of the Library of Congress to award the first Bollingen prize for poetry (worth $10,000). The committee included Aiken, Bogan, Eliot, Lowell and Tate. After nervous deliberations between November 1948 and February 1949 they decided their preference for Ezra Pound's *Pisan Cantos* over William Carlos Williams's *Paterson (Book Two)*. They were apprehensive of an outcry, for Pound in 1945 had been forcibly repatriated to the United States from Italy to face a charge of treason, although the authorities had avoided a trial by consenting to the fiction that he was unfit to plead. Since then he had been incarcerated in a Washington asylum. The Bollingen committee's selection was wildly abused in the press. 'The whole Pound business has turned very ugly: I was misquoted in Congress and half-expected to be subpoenaed before a committee,' Auden complained.

Having taken Italian lessons, he left for Ischia early in April 1949. 'I work, am *very* chaste, and never wash,' he announced by postcard on 7 May to Jaffe. 'To my great delight,' he added ten days later, 'I find myself completely untroubled by sex; Chester, too, is quite changed, and in consequence, our relationship is, for the first time, a really happy one.' To his old schoolfriend John Hayward he wrote, 'there is no encircling gloom here – sunshine, fine company, lovely food and wine. Tonight the Opera and a birthday party'. At such moments they achieved the happiness promised by Camus:

> Sexuality leads to nothing. It is not immoral but it is unproductive. You can devote yourself to it for as long as you do not wish to produce. But only chastity is linked to a personal progress. There is a time when sexuality is a victory – when we free it from moral imperatives. But it then quickly becomes defeat – and the only victory is the one which we then wrest from it: chastity.

In June Auden wrote a major poem entitled 'Memorial for the City' (dedicated to the memory of Charles Williams) in which the Christian community is represented by the City. Auden had believed that versifying about wartime massacre had been demeaning, and had not rushed to turn the horrors of his visit to Germany in the summer of 1945 into clever poetics. But in 1949, writing 'Memorial for the City', he was free to mention 'the crematorium chimney' of a concentration camp, and to describe in part III a war-incinerated city like Darmstadt. When he writes that 'the humour, the cuisine, the rites, the taste, / The pattern of the City, are erased', he means Christianity is as 'abolished' as the wrecked city divided by barbed wire; similarly 'the Cathedral far too damaged to repair' is made of faith as well as masonry. The fourth and final part of the poem speaks of human weakness and of the Flesh with an allusive intimacy. The section begins, 'Without me, Adam would have fallen irrevocably with Lucifer; he would never have been able to cry, *O felix culpa*.' This sentences encapsulates Auden's thought in the late 1940s and 1950s, for the Christian sentiment *O felix culpa* (happy to err) is what the celebration of flaws in 'In Praise of Limestone' and much else is about. The section proceeds with disarming irony ('I was the missing entry on Don Giovanni's list; for which he could never account') showing again that

Auden is often most fun when most grave. He ends with the promise of Resurrection.

Auden's early metaphor for a poet had been the secret agent, a subversive who exists for the transmission of ideas across borders and whose pretences at being an ordinary person are mimicry. But in 1949 it struck Auden that the poet was more like a tycoon. Both poet and tycoon should be shrewd, dauntless, fresh, keen, acquisitive, constructive, calculating yet ardent and impulsive, with a furious self-centred energy about their plans and a childish naivety about their possessions. So Auden wrote a poem about a tycoon, who strikes the usual poses of his breed but knows he is an actor and a hypocrite – is, therefore, an exceptional man in his integrity. Auden's tycoon has exemplary sanity because he is not one of the mad, defined in 'The Age of Anxiety', who does not realise that his life is a pretence. He is someone who recognises that his outward life is mimetic: he needs his inner self-loathing to survive; he suspects that without suffering 'he would die'. This tycoon poem was written after Auden reviewed T. S. Eliot's *Notes Towards the Definition of Culture* in April 1949. 'Like most important writers, Mr T. S. Eliot is not a single figure but a household,' Auden's *New Yorker* essay begins. Eliot's household had three residents: 'First, there is the archdeacon, who believes in and practises order, discipline and good manners, social and intellectual, with a thoroughly Anglican distaste for evangelical excess'; but 'the poor gentleman is condemned to be domiciled with a figure of a very different stamp, a violent and passionate old peasant grandmother, who has witnessed murder, rape, pogroms, famine, flood, fire, everything; who has looked into the abyss and, unless restrained, would scream the house down'. (Twenty years later, lecturing in anti-semitic Vienna, he provocatively declared of Eliot, it was 'the Yiddish Momma who wrote the poems'.) The third resident of Eliot's household was 'a young boy who likes to play slightly malicious practical jokes. The too earnest guest, who has come to interview the Reverend, is startled and bewildered by finding an apple-pie bed or being handed an explosive cigar.'

This review led to a poetic idea. 'Don't tell anyone, but the poem in *Nones* entitled A Household is a self-portrait,' Auden explained in a letter to Monroe Spears of 11 May 1963. 'In it I tried to apply the same trinitarian analysis of personality to myself as I applied to Eliot in my *New Yorker* review.' Auden is not only the tycoon in 'The Household', but the old lady and the bad boy (henceforth he sometimes jokingly called himself 'the old lady' or 'your old mother'). As self-analysis, the poem is a terrifying example of estrangement and courage. As the most comprehensive self-description that Auden offered, it is a crucial text in his biography.

His trinitarian self-portrait of 1949 reads like this:

When, to disarm suspicious minds at lunch
Before coming to the point or at golf,
The bargain driven, to smooth hurt feelings,

He talks about his home, he never speaks
(A reticence for which they all admire him)
Of his bride so worshipped and so early lost.

But proudly tells of that young scamp his heir,
Of black eyes given and received, thrashings
Endured without a sound to save a chum;

Or calls their spotted maleness to revere
His saintly mother, calm and kind and wise,
A grand old lady pouring out the tea.

Whom, though, has he ever asked for the week-end?
Out to his country mansion in the evening,
Another merger signed, he drives alone:

To be avoided by a miserable runt
Who wets his bed and cannot throw or whistle,
A tell-tale, a cry-baby, a failure;

To the revilings of a slatternly hag
Who caches bottles in her mattress, spits
And shouts obscenities from the landing;

Worse, to find both in an unholy alliance,
Youth stealing Age the liquor-cupboard key,
Age teaching Youth to lie with a straight face.
Disgraces to keep hidden from the world
Where rivals, envying his energy and brains
And with rattling skeletons of their own,
Would see in him the villain of this household,
Whose bull-voice scared a sensitive young child,

Whose coldness drove a doting parent mad.

Besides, (which might explain why he has neither
Altered his will nor called the doctor in)
He half believes, call it a superstition,

It is for his sake that they hate and fear him:
Should they unmask and show themselves worth loving,
Loving and sane and manly, he would die.

CHAPTER 9

'I was glad I could be unhappy'

'Since the work of the artist is openly subjective, and "feigned" history, what matters is not what happened to him, but what he has made his experience into,' Auden wrote in 1955. His own situation, he suggested, mattered less than the purposes to which he put his feelings. Suffering continued to be a necessity for him. In 'Homage to Clio', the title poem of his collection published in 1960, he wrote, 'I was glad I could be unhappy,' for without grief and loss 'forgiveness would be no use'. Suffering provided the inconsolable feelings which in the 1950s characterised his best poems, such as 'The Shield of Achilles' in 1952, and 'Vespers' and 'Compline' in 1954. In them his spirit transcended the shame that had so much characterised him in the 1940s just as the poems themselves outreached the ironies of 'The Age of Anxiety'. In them, he seemed to suggest, art should be robust, for life was seldom tender. Their landscape was far removed from Auden's great good places of the late 1940s: the terrain of 'The Shield of Achilles' was:

> A plain without a feature, bare and brown,
> No blade of grass, no sign of neighbourhood,
> Nothing to eat and nowhere to sit down.

Yet if there was no solace in such places Auden himself attained that personal state of being to which, as Brodsky recognised, he aspired in 'September 1, 1939': he became 'a stoic who prays'. Auden's stoicism was that of someone who cannot be consoled by what is happening and does not want to be fobbed off with comforting half-truths or pretty phantasies. 'Nothing is lovely, / Not even in poetry, which is not the case,' he wrote in 1953.

As Auden grew older, his praise at being alive – signalled by Caliban's speech in 'The Sea and the Mirror' – was intense and unrelenting. He had no wish to revel in personal atrocities or lose himself in mean, sordid oblivion. In 1950 he praised Cocteau for his sense of gratitude and comeliness: 'The lasting feeling that his work leaves is one of happiness; not, of course, in the sense that it excludes suffering, but because, in it, nothing is rejected, resented or regretted.' He similarly enjoyed Aubrey's *Brief Lives* because it was so free of twentieth-century *schadenfreude*: 'One of our most contemptible traits is our belief that bad news is more real than good news,' he complained in 1958. By contrast he had trouble finishing a review of Santayana's memoirs for the *New Yorker*. 'I hate him so much, I dont know what to say,' he explained to Spender. What he disliked in Santayana was 'his inability to praise anyone wholeheartedly without some derogatory comment'. Often Auden expressed his good news in the language of raillery and irony: 'comedy', he wrote in 1957, 'is the noblest form of Stoicism'.

His frivolity was easily misunderstood. In 1955 he gave a poetry reading at Wesleyan University in Connecticut, and was afterwards challenged by Nikos Stangos, 'a committed modernist/experimentalist' Freshman, who thought the poems he had read were inexcusably 'frivolous'. Stangos demanded 'if he realized that that kind of poetry was silly and dead': Auden retorted to the effect that 'he didn't care what I thought'. He was now widely misunderstood as a reactionary coward who had reneged on the radicalism of his youth. In his poem 'Lakes' of 1952 Auden listed mellifluous words like piedmont and dimple describing types of water-pool, and then concluded, 'Just reeling off their names is ever so comfy.' He used the ugly slang 'comfy' to undermine the seductiveness of his earlier honeyed words and thus to be self-deflationary as a poet; but this irony was missed by several critics, who solemnly condemned his cosy smugness. The accusations of treachery to his old causes were given some odd, exterior strength by the changes in his physical appearance. His body seemed to have turned on itself. When aged only forty-eight he was described by Jarrell as 'no longer a lank, towheaded, slouching boy', but someone 'convincingly old, so irrevocably, inexorably middle-aged ... who looks at you with a lined, sagging, fretful, consciously powerful old lion's face'. People usually only noticed the superficialities. The important truth is that in the 1950s he was among the most implacable of counter-revolutionaries against the spirit of the times believing, as he later wrote, that 'Alienation from the Collective is always a duty.' During the 1930s intellectuals had followed authoritarian political creeds, chiefly Marxism, and in the 1940s many of them had reneged on their old beliefs, without much understanding of how they had erred. As Hannah Arendt wrote, 'Far from giving up their belief in history and success, they simply changed trains as it were; the train, socialism and communism, had been wrong and they exchanged it against the train of capitalism or Freudianism or some refined Marxism or a sophisticated mixture of all three. Auden, instead, became a Christian.' This was an honourable dissidence in what Arendt described to Prokosch as 'the disgusting, posturing fifties.'

In 1954 Auden quoted Camus: 'the real passion of the twentieth century is servitude'; but he did not mean this in the narrow sense of party slogans or bohemian catchphrases. The servitude was altogether more comprehensive. 'In 1914 a revolution was set in motion which has involved the whole world and is still going on,' Auden wrote in 1952 from ideas which originated from his reading of de Tocqueville.

> If every revolution can be represented graphically by a symbolic figure – the Papal Revolution by a twin Warrior-Priest, the Lutheran by a God-fearing paterfamilias, the English by a country-gentleman, the American by a pioneer, the French by an intellectual – then the contemporary symbol is a naked anonymous baby. It is for the baby's right to health, not for the freedom of any person or class to act or think, that the revolution is being fought everywhere in one way or another. A baby has to be controlled, it has to be indoctrinated, it cannot be told more of the truth than it can profitably understand, so the present revolution is authoritarian and believes in censorship and propaganda. Since its values are really derived from medicine, from a concept of health, it is hostile to any nonconformity, any deviation from the norm. It is precisely, therefore, the exceptional man, the man of talent, the man who works alone, the man whom the French Revolution liberated and admired, who has become the object of greatest suspicion.

The symbols of the mid-century world revolution were, he wrote, 'the naked anonymous baby and the tomb of the Unknown Soldier. The body knows nothing of freedom, only of necessities, and these are the same for all bodies. Hence the tendency of the revolutionary party in concentrating on this one goal to deny all liberty and all minority rights. In so far as we are bodies, we are or ought to be revolutionaries; in so far, however, as we are also souls and minds, we are or ought to be counter-revolutionaries.'

He had always been interested in the symbolism of the human body. In his Icelandic letter to Richard Crossman of 1936 he had asked,

> Isn't it true however far we've wandered
> Into our provinces of persecution
> Where our regrets accuse, we keep returning
> Back to the common faith from which we've all dissented,
> Back to the hands, the feet, the faces?

As his own body began a much remarked deterioration, attributable perhaps partly to his dependence on Benzedrine, tobacco and alcohol, the human body more than ever symbolised for him Christian reconciliation and unity. In Corinthians, for example, Christ is likened to a single body which has many parts like the hand or the eyes each with a distinct function; yet the body is undivided for all its different parts are united in the same concern for one another. By analogy all Christians are Christ's body, and each one is a part of it. Such ideas of bodily wholeness attracted Auden. In the 1950s, living under a Christian system of belief, he hoped for the forgiveness that follows from suffering, and wanted reconciliation and unity to replace persecution, accusation, shame and guilt. 'Every beautiful poem presents an analogy to the forgiveness of sins, an analogy, not an imitation, because it is not evil intentions that are repented of and pardoned but contradictory feelings which the poet surrenders to the poem in which they are reconciled,' he wrote in 1950. Examples of this sentiment are his beautiful love lyrics of 1953, 'The Willow-wren and the Stare' and 'The Proof', in which contradictory feelings are reconciled – in the first case with ironic equivocation, and in the second with two lovers remaining innocent and happy in a world of chaos and spite. In the 1950s Auden admired St John Perse for trying 'to express in every one of his poems ... the sacredness of being', and dedicated some of his most ambitious work to celebrating 'the sense of Nature declaring the glory of God and the holiness of the Flesh which the Christian doctrine of the creation and the Incarnation imply'. This was crucial. 'Wystan tries to convince me about the resurrection of the body, – but he will talk poetry – so I don't know *what*'s to happen,' Kallman wrote in 1950.

A feature of his interest in the body was his enthusiasm for the classification of human types as mesomorphs and endomorphs, about which he joked in his verses of 1950, 'Footnotes to Dr Sheldon'. But he recognised William H. Sheldon's work as 'pseudo-sciensy [sic] rubbish', and his impulse for personification was more richly satisfied by the quirky classifications of Isaiah Berlin's study of Tolstoy, *The Hedgehog and the Fox*. Berlin's book, which Auden reviewed for the *New Yorker* in 1954, provided him with the ideas for a parabolic self-analysis. Berlin divided human beings into hedgehogs, who 'relate everything to a single central vision, one system less or more coherent or articulate, in terms of which they understand, think and feel', and foxes, pursuing 'many ends, often unrelated and even contradictory, connected, if at all, only in some *de facto* way, for some psychological or physiological cause, related by no moral or aesthetic principle'. Dante, Plato, Lucretius, Pascal, Hegel, Dostoevsky, Nietzsche, Ibsen and Proust were Berlin's examples of hedgehogs (Auden surely was a hedgehog too); the foxes included Aristotle, Montaigne, Erasmus, Molière, Pushkin, Balzac and Joyce. Berlin's playfulness was a reaction to a phenomenon noted by Spender on a visit to the United States in 1953. 'Sometimes I have the feeling that in America no instinct or intuition is taken for granted,' Spender reflected. 'Everything is questioned and explained, with the result that there is a kind of low-level rationalization or intellectualization of every kind of behaviour. No-one is happy until the whole of life has been translated into pseudo-scientific jargon.' It was also as a reaction to this that Auden propounded an alternate schema derived from a passage in *Alice in Wonderland*:

She began thinking over all the children she knew that were of the same age as herself, to see if she could have been changed for any of them.

'I'm sure I'm not Ada,' she said, 'for her hair goes in such long ringlets, and mine doesn't go in ringlets, at all; and I'm sure I can't be Mabel, for I know all sorts of things, and she, oh, she knows such a very little!... I'll try if I know all the things I used to know.' *(Alice fails to remember anything properly, and starts to cry)*. 'I must be Mabel after all, and I shall have to go and live in that poky little house, and have next to no toys to play with, and oh, ever so many lessons to learn!'

In his Berlin review, and again in an article of 1959 on Marianne Moore, Auden categorised artists as Alices or Mabels:

ALICES	MABELS
Thucydides	Tacitus
Horace	Juvenal
Montaigne	Pascal
Marvell	Donne
Lovelace	Rochester
Leibnitz	Schopenhauer
Jane Austen	Richardson
Turgenev	Dickens
Verdi	Wagner
Henry James	Dostoevsky
de Tocqueville	de Maistre
Tolstoy	Joyce
Colette	Gide
E. M. Forster	Heidegger

According to Auden, 'Alices never make a fuss. Like all human beings they suffer, but they are stoics who do not weep or lose their temper or undress in public. Though they are generally people with stout moral standards, they are neither preachers nor reformers. They can be sharp, usually in an ironical manner, and tender, but the passionate outburst is not for them. As a general rule, also, while perfectly well aware of evil and ugliness in the world, they prefer to dwell on what is good and beautiful. Alices are always in danger of over-fastidiousness, as Mabels are of vulgarity.' Tolstoy was a typical Alice. 'What shocks him most about human nature is not its love of violence, its capacity for hatred, but its willful stupidity, its preference for illusions to truth.' De Maistre exemplified the Mabels, 'a type that is becoming, unfortunately, commoner – the intellectual with weak nerves and a timid heart, who is so appalled at discovering that life is not sweetly and softly pretty that he takes a grotesquely tough, grotesquely "realist" attitude'. The Mabels want 'man to be perfectible; if that cannot be, then man must be utterly depraved ... and the public executioner is the savior of society'.

Part of the impetus for Auden's Alice and Mabel game was his counter-revolutionary wish to resist the medicalisation of ethical issues. As he had suggested in *The Orators*, practical jokes were the surest way to resist indoctrination and censorship. He knew from his father's example as school medical officer for Birmingham that the welfare of children was best served by practical, unflamboyant, materialistic measures and that the subjugation of human freedom of choice to notions of the naked baby's right to health chiefly served the ends of adult regimes. If Auden was one of Isaiah Berlin's hedgehogs, then the centre of his system in the 1950s was his belief that 'the first step toward the realization of a universal good society is a belief in the fall of man' not as a symbol of the birth of morality but as a symbol of the human desire for autonomy. He was seeking a Christian–Freudian synthesis that would preserve his integrity, that is to preserve his mind's purposive wholeness and resist disintegrative influences. The naked anonymous baby was the secularised image, formed for a reductive age, of the Holy Child. He honoured Freud as the arch-priest of a new religion whose ideas might save people who could not be reached by another religion. Both the Bible and Freudian literature offered 'a world where novelties exist with ancient monuments, a world of guilt and responsibility, a world, heaven help us, that has to be described with analogical *metaphors*'. Auden wanted these metaphors to represent not diffused and fragmentary feelings and values, but a system of intellect and emotions that would, as Charles Williams had said of Kierkegaard, coinhere. But they also satisfied other needs in Auden. Christianity and Freudianism were ways of coping with or reimagining pain; they mirrored one another in such metaphors as the yearning for the Eden or the womb, or in their reliance on unseen, intangible forces like original sin or the recalcitrant libido. More personally, in Auden's case, they both explained, or minimised, the role of the accidental. With his insistence on strict routine, and anxious rage at even the most mundane diversions from his schedule, Auden needed systems which attributed most apparent accidents to internal, long-suppressed, subconscious wishes or to the workings of providence: which insisted that the accidental was deliberate.

'There was nothing more admirable in him than his complete sanity,' said Hannah Arendt, who became a friend in 1958. 'All kinds of madness were in his eyes lack of discipline – "naughty, naughty," as he used to say.' He equated sin with neurosis, and believed that neurotics had chosen their fate. 'Why are people neurotic?' he once asked Griffin. 'Because they refuse to accept suffering.' He blamed the Church for encouraging a conception of the Day of Judgment as 'like a law court where the sinners are despatched to punishment against their will, whereas the necessity for a Christian to believe in Hell as a possibility depends upon believing that

God will never compel anyone to do anything,' Auden told Gorer in 1955. 'The obvious aesthetic image for a damned soul is not a prisoner being tortured by sadists but a neurotic who defiantly clings to his neurosis though it makes him suffer.' He wished:

> that all those people who think of analysis as a device for getting a brand-new personality in place of their own would read Freud's warning: 'A man should not strive to eliminate his complexes but to get in accord with them: they are legitimately what directs his conduct in the world.' Freud cannot be blamed for what journalists and literary folk have done with his ideas, but there are too many persons today who believe they have Freud's sanction for measuring their value and state of psychological health by the quantitative amount of sexual gratification they are getting, just as there are others who imagine that an unhappy childhood relieves them of all obligation to behave well.

Seven years later he declared, 'if there are any souls in Hell, it is not because they have been sent there, but because Hell is where they insist upon being'. Auden approached pain as a stoic. 'As long as your suffering makes you defiant or despairing, as long as you identify your suffering with yourself as an existing individual, and are defiantly or despairingly the exception, you are not a Christian,' he declared in 1952. Yet he despised 'spiritual snobbery', and warned in 1960, 'unless introspection is accompanied, as it always was in Kafka, by an equal passion for the good life, it also too easily degenerates into a spineless narcissistic fascination with one's own sin and weakness'. He quoted Cesare Pavese with approval – 'One ceases to be a child when one realizes that telling one's truth does not make it any better' – and then added the gloss, 'not even telling it to oneself'. Human pain was only interesting when it exemplified the human condition: otherwise it chiefly induced self-pity. 'A suffering, a weakness, which cannot be expressed as an aphorism, should not be mentioned,' he felt by the 1950s. Psychoanalysis or even introspection were a variant of Roman Catholicism. 'The same rules apply to self examination as apply to confession to a priest: *be brief, be blunt, be gone*. Be brief, be blunt, forget.' He had a very English horror of public scenes, confessions, emotional stridency. As he wrote in 1953, 'love, or truth in any serious sense,/Like orthodoxy, is a reticence'. He practised this virtue among most friends.

'Reticence may be the *déformation professionelle* of the poet,' as Arendt mused in her recollection of Auden.

Overall his attitude was courageously ambivalent. Though he disliked the omnipotence and insularity of psychoanalytically informed critics ('the trouble about the Freudian approach to literature is that it is always heads-I-win-tails-you-lose'), he admired the altruism of psychoanalysis and the courage of analysands. In 1953 he wrote, 'I have no idea how many people have been "cured" by psychoanalysis . . . but one of the proofs of Freud's greatness is that he as good as said he didn't care.' His mistrust was for the more mediocre rump of therapists. 'You go to one of them attracted by his claim to free you, to unchain you from your fears and obsessions but after talking to him for a while you discover that he himself is not free: he is ruled by an interest in money,' he told Griffin. 'Some of them are power-maniacs. Almost half of them are quacks. They think they have all the answers. I would much rather have the police in charge than psychiatrists. The police can always be bribed.'

Under the medical-model system of rules in the 1950s, men who did not marry or father naked, anonymous babies were treated by gangs of less imaginative beings as heretics. Though the English academic F. R. Leavis is now a negligible figure, his attitude to Auden exemplifies the difficulties of a great poet with critical schools, and highlights a particular animosity with which Auden had to contend in the 1950s. 'Dr Leavis believed that literature was a moral discipline, a substitute for religion,' as Al Alvarez has written. 'Behind the key terms and catch-phrases solemnly parroted by Leavis's disciples' – of which maturity was the most used – lurked a bossy secularised piety resembling the child-centred progressive ideals that had irritated Auden on his visit to Dartington in 1932. They reflected the psychoanalytical derogation of homosexuality as an arrested emotional development and the corresponding over-valuation of the ethical power of family life. The Leavisites were like literary Kleinians, welcoming the symbol of the naked anonymous baby for the sake of whose health there must be indoctrination, censorship and the suppression of social or sexual deviance. 'We lusted after responsibility, and in the fifties responsibility meant marriage – the wife, the kids, the little home, the dog,' Alvarez recalls. 'Marriage (even a quarrelsome, unhappy marriage like that of Lawrence and Frieda) was the ultimate vindication of literary seriousness.' Their equivalents in New York were also, as Norman Podhoretz depicted,

'caught in that niggardly and lugubrious style of life so characteristic of the
first postwar decade and which Philip Roth was to evoke so cruelly in
Letting Go – the life of the married graduate student dragging his slow
length along the endless road to a Ph.D. with an increasingly resentful
wife', the pair of them anxious lest 'they would remain buried forever in
that tunnel of five-by-seven index cards; or perhaps they would crash
through it only to find themselves with no other honorable place to go'.

Young Leavisites enforced their leader's morality like the vigilantes of a
provincial Watch Committee. Robin Mayhead, who reviewed Auden's
poetic collection *Nones* for Leavis's periodical *Scrutiny* in 1952, began by
referring to Auden's 'failure of growth' and 'absence of . . . maturity' –
coded references to homosexuality as represented in psychoanalysis –
resulting in his 'irresponsible feeling for language'. Auden's 'striking and
amusing' verbal virtuosity was, Mayhead sniffed, 'hardly what one
expected from a responsible man growing older'; in case one had missed
the hint, a few lines later he dismissed Auden's fondness for neologisms
and slang as 'a schoolboy habit that one had hoped he would grow out of'.
In these reiterations one hears the railing self-righteous voice of Leavis.
Mayhead could not acknowledge that *Nones* was among the strongest of
Auden's collections, containing such major poems as 'In Praise of
Limestone', 'The Fall of Rome', 'Under Which Lyre', 'Memorial for the
City' and 'A Walk After Dark' as well as significant smaller pieces like 'In
Schrafft's', an arresting description of sublime contentment which, as
Elizabeth Bishop noticed, reworked the idea of Hardy's 'Her Apotheosis'.
Instead Mayhead singled out as 'salacious' Auden's poem of Firbankian
Eden, 'Pleasure Island'. Auden's 'disgust, if genuine disgust it be, can
hardly be called healthy or mature. It is little more than the disgust of the
sensitive, adolescent schoolboy' – the words ducked here are sissy or nancy
– 'outraged by his gross contemporaries.' Mayhead also judged 'A
Household' to be 'embarrassing' because he imagined homosexual sado-
masochism to be found in the lines about 'thrashings' between 'chums'. It
was this sort of tosh that provoked Auden to advise in 1953,

> Be subtle, various, ornamental, clever,
> And do not listen to those critics ever
> Whose crude provincial gullets crave in books
> Plain cooking made still plainer by plain cooks,
> As though the Muse preferred her half-wit sons;

Good poets have a weakness for bad puns.

Even honourable criticism of Auden was entangled in academic vendettas. During 1951 D. J. Enright wrote an article on Auden and Rilke accusing the former of 'playing into the hands of the new reaction' by treating 'imagination as dereliction of duty and perhaps even treason'. Enright's essay was published in *Essays in Criticism* of 1952, and though he doubts 'that I would have offered that piece to Leavis, knowing his views on Auden', the editor of *Essays in Criticism*, F. W. Bateson, believed otherwise. 'The private history of Enright's article is that it was originally written for *Scrutiny*,' he wrote in 1952. 'Hence the heavy anti-Auden line. But Leavis wouldn't print it, not because he didn't think much of the article, but because its appearance in *Scrutiny* would be tantamount to an admission that Auden exists as a poet (even as a bad poet) – which would be heresy!' This sense of Auden as a heretic occurred in a specific political context in Britain.

On 24 and 25 May 1951, while he was staying in London with the Spenders on his way from New York to Forio, Auden was twice telephoned by Guy Burgess, a diplomat who shared his dislike of English liberalism and whom he had known slightly for years (perhaps through Brian Howard or Tom Driberg). Auden was out on both occasions. Burgess then telegraphed to his mother that he was embarking on a Mediterranean holiday, and left Southampton on the cross-Channel steamer *Falaise* together with Donald Maclean, a fellow diplomat and former Gresham's pupil. Both men had been spying for the Stalinists and were now defecting to the Soviet Union. So Audenesque was this story of secret agents, false trails and border-crossings that Maclean's biographer in trying to describe their midnight passage on the *Falaise* quoted the lines from 'A Voyage' in *Journey to a War* ending, 'The journey is false; the false journey really an illness.' In the alarm that followed their flight it was suspected that Burgess might be making for Ischia, which Auden reached shortly afterwards. 'Stephen, dear,' Auden wrote on 14 June. 'The combination of that phone call and some lady who thought she saw la B in the train on his way to Ischia, has turned this place into a mad-house. The house watched night and day by plain-clothes men.' He was badgered by journalists, who invented ludicrous quotations. To Spender he confessed, 'the whole business makes me feel sick to my stomach. I still believe Guy to be a victim, but the horrible thing about our age is that one cannot be certain.'

Burgess, who spent the rest of his life in Moscow, regularly corresponded with Auden's old Christ Church tutor, Roy Harrod, to whom he often mentioned Auden. These letters vanished after Harrod's death, but Auden apparently had the same emblematic importance to Burgess as for thousands of other men of their generation. Auden became convinced, so he later told Harrod, that Burgess had intended to visit him, 'and was only diverted from this intention when he reached Prague', and despised the British government's insistence 'on a totally preposterous story about the love that dares not tell its name'. This affair provoked fears that national security was threatened by 'crypto-homosexuals', and the Home Secretary and other officials instituted a campaign of arrests, often resting on perjury and intimidation, which amounted to a sexual witch-hunt and ruined many lives in the 1950s. They fixed on several prominent men of whom to make a cruel example, whose cases Auden followed with fascinated horror and with the recognition that under the prevailing régime he too was 'capable of getting into trouble'. His own plans were disturbed by this continuing commotion. In 1953 he applied for a Fulbright fellowship at the University of Rome for 1954–5. 'Thanks to Italian indiscretion, I hear that, at the beginning of the summer, the local Mareschal of the Carabanieri received a telegram from New York, asking for a report on my conduct in Forio: he gave me a clean bill, I gather.' Nevertheless the Fulbright money was withheld, and when, in September 1953, Maclean's wife disappeared to join her husband in Moscow, the *carabinieri* investigated him again. 'I am rather mad about the business,' he told his brother John.

The Leavisites, with their self-conscious family frugality, provided the highbrow counterpart to the police bullying; both seemed concerned to ensure that homosexuality could never be thought compatible with personal happiness. Auden noted in 1953 that the American reviewers of Angus Wilson's 'awfully good' novel *Hemlock and After* 'were horrified, not at the subject, but at his portrayal of queers as no more unhappy than anyone else'. Such critics would have been contemptuous of Auden's version of family. Writing from New York City to Kallman in Ischia in February 1950, he declared, 'As to our place of reunion (1) I look to be met at what I think of as Home Sweet Home by whom I think of as my family

(2) I don't want the joy of seeing you again shadowed by that Big-City-Gleam in your eye.' He did not want his family life spoiled by interlopers and wrote in March: 'You've <u>got</u> to do something about Bu' (a boyfriend of Kallman's who was living in the Forio house). 'I'm not camping when I say it will *completely* ruin my time if he's there ... for some reason which I don't understand but which is, I'm afraid, more than a little connected with me, you seem to like him. I must say, knowing how I feel about having him around – it's an agony of embarrassment – I do think you might have discouraged him from returning. You've had his company for the whole winter – isn't that enough? <u>Please</u>, <u>Please</u>, <u>please</u>, do something. It means a very great deal to me.' Kallman's life on Ischia was a touching mixture of security and vulnerability. He became a keen vegetable gardener at Forio, where he grew Ischia's first brussels-sprout, but he was also the prey of loneliness and anxiety.

'Geoffrey honey,' Kallman wrote to Gorer at the end of summer in 1950, 'I'm feeling rather sad that it all seems to be drawing to an end, – and Wystan's cheery practicality ("Now, my dear, you must inform me immediately you get your passage, – so I know whether I should sub-let my apartment or not") ... oppresses me a bit.' He cheered himself with phantasies of dressing in disguise as Ingrid Bergman or Lincoln Kirstein, but concluded, 'Write again soon – the lonely season comes in ten days and I wither without some contact with real life.' Robert Craft visited Auden and Kallman at Forio in August 1951 and has left a vivid account of the two men's life together:

> The boat to Ischia, a packet steamer, absurdly class-segregated, is crowded and excruciatingly smelly.... At Forio I transfer to a scavenger-like trawler and am rowed ashore. Wystan meets me at the pier, barefoot and with the 'bottoms of his trousers rolled,' and he carries my bag through the toylike town to his house on the Via Santa Lucia. At street level this is an empty stable and carriage room, but the upstairs rooms are ample, bright, and immaculate, except for the burnt offerings in unemptied ashtrays, which may very well represent a protest against the sterility of American cleanliness. Americans are not responsible, in any case, but a handsome Neapolitan Ganymede with a manner like his not quite believable name, Giocondo.... We walk to a beach in the afternoon, Wystan at high speed (he is now wearing Plimsolls) in spite of the heat, and,

himself excepted, universal indolence.... On the return to Forio we
meet Chester Kallman, just back from a visit to another part of the
island. Wystan is always happier in tandem with Chester, and the
best of his former good spirits now seem like doldrums in
comparison. He dotes on the younger poet, in fact, listening
admiringly to his talk, calling attention to jeweled bits of it, and
supplying helpful interpretations for rougher gems, though as a rule
if Chester appears even to be on the verge of speaking, Wystan will
remain quiet. When the younger poet goes to the kitchen for a
moment, Wystan says of him that 'He is a very good poet and a far
cleverer person that I am.' Whatever the truth of these assessments,
Chester most certainly *is* a very good cook. By some oversight,
however, the spinach has not been washed tonight, and after what
sounds like a painfully gritty bite, Wystan reports a considerable
presence of sand; then lest we think him pernickety, he quickly adds
that he doesn't in the least mind, and even manages to suggest that he
has become quite fond of it.

In the summer of 1952 Auden suggested marriage to an elegant and
generous young American woman, Thekla Pelletti, whom he had met the
previous year on Ischia. She declined the proposal, wisely given his
remark that if they had a son, 'we must call him Chester'. (In any case his
marriage to Erika Mann had never been dissolved.) His proposal showed
his wish for emotional permanence, and was a reaction from the despair
which sometimes engulfed both him and Kallman during their Ischia
holidays. In proposing marriage to a woman Auden was resisting what he
was drawn to. In 'The Age of Anxiety' Malin had denounced 'the noble
despair of poets' as 'posturing':

> We would rather be ruined than changed,
> We would rather die in our dread
> Than climb the cross of the moment
> And let our illusions die.

He wrote against this fake aestheticism precisely because he felt tempted
by deliberate and even factitious suffering to maintain his creative tension.
His proposal to Thekla Pelletti, coupled with his stand against the
medicalisation of ethics and the related idolatry of an idealised middle-
class family life, was a similar phenomenon of temptation and reaction.
Auden sometimes thought that marriage betokened maturity, although he

must have realised that the reasons why people marry can be sad or ignoble. He identified the role of husband with cherished authority, regretted that 'the Edwardian paterfamilias who knew what was right is almost extinct', but was consoled to realise that though 'the bearded thunder god has turned into a clean-shaven pal, there is still the iron-toothed witch' of motherhood to keep children from complacence. 'When I seek an image / For our Authentic City,' he wrote in 1953,

> I see old men in hall-ways
> Tapping their barometers
> Or a lawn over which
> The first thing after breakfast,
> A paterfamilias
> Hurries to inspect his rain-gauge.

It was as a symbol to go with his imaginary rain-gauge that Auden wanted a wife. He was always attracted to the idea of other people's family life, and was a particular *ami du maison* of a young American couple, Anne and Irving Weiss, who rented a house at Forio until 1954 and whom he later saw often in New York. Auden once defined an American as 'a person who is as reluctant to give orders as he is to obey them', which he believed led to the inadequacy of American husbands. 'Marriage involves children and children have to be given orders. Every woman knows this, so that if the American male refuses to claim authority she has no option but to become the American Mom' – a role that he did not suppose was enjoyable. He nevertheless admired the Weiss marriage, and was godfather to their son born in 1957. In turn Irving Weiss was touched and impressed by Auden's relationship with Kallman. 'When one of them approved or did not approve of something in the literary taste of the other, the objection would come out or the approval, but the range of reference was so intimate and yet so apt and so far reaching, that it was not surprising that they had remained together for so long,' he told Dorothy Farnan in 1983. 'Because they were both intellectually powerful, each in his own right, they could talk to each other and have a lasting relationship ... one felt between them an instant electrical connection, particularly when they were talking about literature or music.'

Arthur Koestler, who had rented a house on Ischia at this time, found Auden 'very warm and cosy', though Bernard Berenson mistrusted 'the dubious society presided over by Auden on Ischia'. Auden's old mentor from Gresham's days Michael Davidson, who visited the island in 1953, wrote:

> No bank manager keeps stricter hours than he; woe betide the man who calls on him before 6.30 p.m. His days run to a timetable. Eight to 12:30 writing: new poems and criticism ... After lunch, revision; from three to four, a swim or walk; then reading. Sharp at 5.00, a couple of negronis, a powerful Italian cocktail, before dinner. At 8.30 precisely he appears on the little paved piazza to drink wine outside Maria's bar, to talk with severe brilliance, or – if the company bores him – to sit and glower, smoking the cheapest Italian cigarettes through a holder ... Around ten o'clock, he gets up suddenly, snapping off his discourse. 'I like to go to bed early,' he says severely; and stalks off home.

During the 1950s Auden was involved in increasing numbers of public functions. In March 1951 he went to India 'to speak at one of Sidney Hook's Anti-Communist Liberal Congresses', Ansen reported. 'He liked it not at all, what with non-alcoholic vegetarian dinners and other amenities.' He continued to attend international conferences, despite recognising their futility; in 1952 he attended a meeting in Paris organised by the recently formed Congress for Cultural Freedom (clandestinely funded by the CIA). Katherine Anne Porter made a disastrous speech on behalf of the American delegates after which Auden muttered to Allen Tate 'that she was an absolute crook'. His account of this meeting to the Sterns was hilarious:

> The Amerloque writers contingent consisted of Katherine Anne (who kept having heart attacks), Glenway Wescott (who seemed to know some very grand people), Allen Tate, Robert Lowell, me and Faulkner. We had an anxious time with the last for he went into a bout on arrival, shut up in his hotel throwing furniture out of the windows and bottles at the ladies and saying the most *dreadful* things about coons. However we managed to get him sober and onto the platform on the last day to say that the Americans had behaved badly but that he hoped they would behave better in the future and sit down. Malraux looked and spoke rather like Hitler but the public loved it. I was the first speaker at that meeting and as I rose a shower of pamphlets descended from the gallery. Naturally, I thought it was

the Commies starting up, but it turned out to be les lettristes accusing Malraux of being a sous-Gide and Faulkner of being a sous-Joyce.

In the next twenty years Auden attended many such bean-feasts. 'The sessions were, of course, appallingly boring,' he wrote of a writers' conference at Budapest, 'but the personal contacts were worth it.'

Auden in 1952 undertook his first major lecture tour in the United States. He was increasingly in demand for public performances, although he refused to give readings in southern states to segregated audiences. Since his first successes at Oxford he had been, as Harold Acton noticed, 'generous in reading his latest poem aloud, diffident about his celebrity'. Indeed his poetry is best appreciated if recited aloud. His words turned the public occasion of a reading into a counterpart of the musical evenings at Elizabeth Mayer's house, where briefly in the listeners' minds there was 'a civitas of sound'. Nevertheless these trips dissipated time and energy, and were not always worthwhile. There are too many indications that most of his audiences regarded him chiefly as a personality. Thus in February 1960 he gave a reading under the auspices of the *Harvard Advocate*. 'He was evidently a little tight but articulated perfectly distinctly and now puts on a much better performance than he used to,' one of his audience noted. He read from the galleys of his forthcoming book, *Homage to Clio*, 'and did not seem to have picked out beforehand the poems that he wanted to read. The proofs would slip out of his grasp and fall on the floor as he fumbled with them, and then he would have to plunge down after them ... like one of those comic paperhanger acts.' Ian Hamilton has described Auden's reading to the Oxford University Poetry Society a few months later in terms of 'that master's irritability, his gluttonous drink intake, his astonishing complexion'. Hamilton judged that 'these grand figures put themselves to this inconvenience – no fee, no audience to speak of, and a dinner that few of them ever seemed to touch' as part of 'the limitless vanity of poets: they'll put up with anything, provided that they can get to read the works'. Hamilton and his patronising friends were 'determined to be unimpressed'. They thought poets like Auden 'had dragged themselves to Oxford in order to be thought well of by the likes of us. They were afraid of becoming back numbers. They wanted to keep in with the young.' This interpretation was deeply unjust to Auden.

In 1951 Auden joined Jacques Barzun in the management of a highbrow book club founded by Lionel Trilling called The Readers' Subscription. This distinguished trio made a regular selection of books which could be bought at a reduced price by subscribers. The Readers' Subscription also published a circular entitled *Griffin* in which their selections were described in elegant critical essays. Auden, who first wrote for this magazine (on the subject of Colette) in December 1951, remained a prolific contributor until 1959: his *Griffin* pieces comprise a narrative of his ideas and interests in the 1950s. Thus he wrote in April 1952,

> To all of us, I believe, in the middle of the twentieth century, the Roman Empire is like a mirror in which we see reflected the brutal, vulgar, powerful yet despairing image of our own technological civilisation, an imperium which now covers the entire globe, for all nations, capitalist, socialist and communist, are united in their worship of mass, technique and temporal power. What fascinates and terrifies us about the Roman Empire is not that it finally went smash, but that, away from the start, it managed to last for five centuries without creativity, warmth or hope.

In 1959 The Readers' Subscription was superseded by the Mid-Century Society, in which Auden and Barzun were again associated with Trilling and his students. Auden often contributed to the society's magazine *Mid-Century* until its demise in 1962. Both book clubs were a feature of what Jarrell called 'the age of criticism', lasting in the United States from about 1950 until the crisis of dissent over the Vietnam war, when professors in the humanities were accorded rich and pompous accolades as the new Solomons. Trilling, even more than Tate, Blackmur, Rahv or Kazin, came to exemplify the public prestige of the humanities academics. Kenneth Tynan described a television programme in 1960 in which Barzun, Trilling and Auden:

> discussed 'The Crisis in Our Culture' with such fussy incoherence that they seemed to be not so much debating the crisis as embodying it. Mr Barzun sat bolt upright and smirked, while Mr Trilling leaned so far forward in cerebration that he appeared, in close shots, about to butt the camera. Mr Auden, looking like a rumpled, bulkier version of Somerset Maugham, slumped in his chair and squinted gaily at everyone, flicking ash at random, grinning mysteriously....

They spoke with the corporate drone of a house organ (Mr Barzun's 'House of Intellect,' no doubt), beside which Mr Auden sounded like a mouth organ – i.e., a very human instrument, capable of expressing great skittishness and great melancholy, but difficult to integrate into an orchestra. Together they formed a triptych of official American culture, and their appeal, especially to intelligent viewers under forty, must have been almost nil.

Auden enjoyed his association with Trilling and Barzun, but in many public ways signalled his higher admiration for the intellectual mode represented by Edmund Wilson.

As early as 1940 he had praised *To the Finland Station* as a 'scholarly and beautifully written book' steeped with 'moral passion'. Twenty years later, recommending *Apologies to the Iroquois* in *Mid-Century*, he celebrated Wilson as 'a specimen of that always rare and now almost extinct creature, the Intellectual Dandy': which is to say the antithesis of Leavis, someone neither a conformist nor a rebel, but indifferent to public opinion and therefore without any school of followers. 'One of the ways in which an Intellectual Dandy can be recognized is by the unpredictability of his work; no knowledge of his previous books offers any clue as to what he will write next.' But in addition to valuing Wilson's solitariness, he admired him as a stylist. 'The test of good prose is that the reader does not notice it any more than a man looking through a window at the landscape outside notices the glass ... The most famous of all dandies, Beau Brummell, made inconspicuous dress the height of elegance; by the same standard, Mr Wilson is ... one of the most elegant prose writers alive.' Auden, it will be clear, identified with Wilson. His admiration was reciprocated. Wilson thought Auden a 'genius', who 'has produced in poetic form, a comprehensive description of the whole English-speaking, industrial-ugly, democratic-levelling-oppressive, urban and suburban world'. He and Lowell had greater stature than any other contemporary poets. 'They have higher and more serious ambitions and they also have big enough talents to achieve poetic careers on the old nineteenth-century scale.' Wilson also found a generous explanation for Auden's enthusiasm in the 1950s for the quest novels of J. R. R. Tolkien: 'he no doubt so over rates *The Lord of the Rings* because he reads into it something that he means to write himself'. Wilson was unimpressed, though, by Kallman, who 'now resembles a tame goblin', he wrote in 1955. 'He carries on self-effacingly –

perfectly passive, a sallow-faced wife who is not supposed to be charming
... He never says anything to me, never comes to see us with Wystan –
from a distance he seems grisly, disgusting.' For perhaps related reasons
Wilson thought 'Auden's attempt to do a libretto for the Stravinsky opera'
together with Marianne Moore's translation of La Fontaine were 'the two
major literary mistakes of our time'.

Auden in 1951 rented an apartment to share with Kallman on the fifth
floor of a fur warehouse at 235 Seventh Avenue in New York City. It was
the first New York home that they had shared. Auden was delighted with
it, and told Wilson happily that it had a spare room in which Spender or
Isherwood could stay. 'The place was completely without heat when we
entered (it was sometime in late fall or winter), and Wystan started up
some queer kind of little stove, but we sat in our raincoats and our breath
went up in a vapor,' Wilson wrote of his first visit. 'A long curtainless
window gave a view on the shabbiness of Sixth [sic] Avenue with its cheap
stores and small neon signs. The guest room was a thing like a doghouse
built completely *inside* the loft.' There was some compressed-air
machinery belonging to a sculptor lying about; also a case of hock on the
floor, from which Auden produced a bottle while showing Wilson his
beloved treatise on Victorian plumbing. 'Wystan has condemned himself
to this,' Wilson wrote, 'for all the rest of his life – as he has to
homosexuality – and, in a puritanical way, seems to feel he is acquiring
merit by living – with a touch of fantasy – în the most unattractive way
possible.' (A few years later Auden however exclaimed to Wilson, 'I hate
living in squalor – I detest it! – but I can't do the work I want to do and live
any other way.')

Robert Craft has described Christmas dinner at the Seventh Avenue
loft in 1952. 'He kisses us as we enter, the prerogative being a sprig of
mistletoe dangling over the barricade of book-filled crates by the door
(which does not shut tightly and exposes the residence to footpads).
Shuffling about in *pantoufles* (bunion-accommodating babouches,
actually) he distributes a pile of fetchingly wrapped and ribboned
Christmas presents.' The apartment was strewn haphazardly 'with empty
bottles, used martini glasses, book, papers, phonograph records'. The air
was stale and boozy, the furniture cheap and dusty. 'The plates and
silverware are greasy, and, such is the dishwasher's myopia, not entirely
free of hardened remnants of previous meals. The dinner – smoked clams,

steak, potatos with dill – is excellent, and Wystan tucks in like Oliver Twist, which helps to account for his marsupial-like paunch; his plate soon looks as if it had been attacked by locusts. Five bottles of Pommard, from a case deposited on the floor at the end of the table, are drained.' The meal ended in cheerful disarray for Vera Stravinsky had been to the lavatory, and finding 'a mirror in which it would be impossible even to *recognise* oneself, a towel that would oblige the user to start over again, and a basin of dirty fluid on the floor, she unthinkingly empties the basin and fills it with fresh water. Not until dessert time do we discover, with mixed emotions, that she has flushed away Chester's chocolate pudding.' As Stravinsky said of Auden to Wilson, 'He is the dirtiest man I have ever liked.'

Yet Auden had become prudish. 'Paul Bowles has excreted a volume of sado-masochistic phantasies,' he reported after the publication in 1950 of *The Delicate Prey and other stories* by his fellow lodger in Middagh Street, and he walked out of a production of *Pal Joey* in disgust at its bawdiness in 1953. On another occasion that year he was himself walked out on. Robert Medley and Rupert Doone had invited him to dine with Spender and Francis Bacon in Kensington. As Medley wrote, 'in the middle of the main course Francis turned in sudden fury on Wystan: "Never before have I had to submit to such a disgusting display of hypocritical *Christian* morality!" Declaring that he could no longer sit at the same table with such a *monster* who considered himself an *artist* he leapt to his feet and before you could say "knife," was out of the front door and into the street.' Not everyone found him as unimpressive and disgusting as Bacon. 'One has but to hear him talk to realise not only the magnitude of his mind and the astounding memory ... but also the tremendous amount of almost surgical thought that has gone into the making of his opinions,' Michael Davidson reported after visiting Ischia in 1953. 'He is didactic because, one feels, he *knows* he is right; he has thought the thing out with the thoroughness of a cement mixer. But if his manner is hortative, he can, like Socrates, also be wildly funny.'

Auden had to vacate his Seventh Avenue apartment after the building was sold in 1952. Early in the following year he rented an apartment at 77 St Marks Place, on a continuation of Eighth Street between First and Second Avenue. This remained his New York home until he left the United States in 1972. It was an old-fashioned railroad apartment with a front parlour facing south on to St Marks Place used as Auden's work room and an adjacent (and spartan) bedroom. This was Auden's area of the flat. The book-lined alcove which served as a study and dining area was neutral. Beyond the alcove stood a music room with a record-player, speakers and impressive record collection which was the domain where Kallman entertained his friends. The sun room leading off this music room was converted by Auden into two alcove bedrooms for Kallman and another young tenant. The kitchen and bathroom were primitive, and shocked their more hygienic friends. The apartment's previous tenant had been an abortionist: 'occasionally nervous people come knocking at the door, asking for the doctor', he told Hedwig Petzold in 1954. The neighbourhood had many Italians, Poles and Ukrainians, which meant that there were good food stores.

Larry Rivers, who lived one flight down from them, has described their house-warming. 'Chester invited a tall, muscular sailor who showed up in uniform, a boy from Iowa, who after three cups of Chester and Wystan's concoction of English tea, white wine, and hundred-proof vodka slipped into a pair of black silk stockings and sheer lace panties and demurely worked a kosher salami into his asshole, singing "Anchors Aweigh".' Auden whispered to Kallman to 'get that hidee-ola out immediately'. He was being a protective host whose 'rage was provoked by the frivolous misuse of the kosher salami brought by Mr and Mrs Noah Greenberg of the Pro Musica Antiqua ensemble'. (With Noah Greenberg he and Kallman compiled a collection of lute songs and madrigals published as *An Elizabethan Songbook* by Doubleday in 1955.) When Auden and Kallman were invited to the apartment of Rivers's friend John Myers, Kallman brought some 'thugs from the Holiday Inn on St Marks Place' who 'began robbing everyone at the party; one stuck his knife in a gay guy's ass and asked him how he liked it'; robbers henceforth dogged their lives. Marianne Moore wrote to Elizabeth Mayer in 1959, 'I was sad to know that Wystan and Chester have been robbed again.'

Auden's tenant told Dorothy Farnan in 1982 of the 'great intellectual affinity' between Auden and Kallman, though their habits were barely reconcilable. 'With Wystan, everything was very structured. Everything had to be done according to a time schedule. There was, for example, always a cocktail hour at five o'clock and dinner had to be served exactly at six.' Auden often complained that Kallman would work all night and sleep until noon. Though Auden was a copious talker, 'Chester's main complaint about Wystan was that he did not engage in small talk in company but rather lectured or relied upon set-pieces ... Wystan's letters to me are campy and funny, but that's not the way he was in conversation.' Their occasional rows quickly subsided. 'Chester did all the screaming; Wystan never made scenes.' There is nothing unusual in two people who have ceased to be lovers remaining intimate friends, and there were deep and rich reserves of love and understanding between the two men. Nor is it unique for ex-lovers to share an apartment and enjoy one another's lives. The rare feature of Auden's relationship with Kallman in the 1950s is its intensity: as he wrote in 1957, 'If equal affection cannot be, / Let the more loving one be me.'

The poems written by Auden in the early 1950s were collected together in *The Shield of Achilles* published by Random House in February 1955 and by Faber in November. The title poem (written in 1952) is 'an impressive, carefully planned, entirely comfortless poem', as Randall Jarrell conceded; Laurence Lerner noted that its poignancy is all the keener 'because we cannot be sure if it is wholly a disaster we are learning about'. Auden himself warned that 'to read snippets of great poems is always bad', and this is certainly true of 'The Shield of Achilles', but two verses should be quoted:

> Barbed wire enclosed an arbitrary spot
>> Where bored officials lounged (one cracked a joke)
> And sentries sweated for the day was hot:
>> A crowd of ordinary decent folk
>> Watched from without and neither moved nor spoke
> As three pale figures were led forth and bound
> To three posts driven upright in the ground.
>
> The mass and majesty of this world, all
>> That carries weight and always weighs the same
> Lay in the hands of others; they were small
>> And could not hope for help and no help came:
>> What their foes liked to do was done, their shame
> Was all the worst could wish; they lost their pride
> And died as men before their bodies died.

This image of hopelessness is as terrifying as Auden thought John Marcher's paralysis of will in Henry James's 'The Beast in the Jungle'.

The poem also treats other great Auden themes. Achilles' mother Thetis is, in Auden's poem, another of the over-protective but in effect destructive mothers in the Auden canon whose idealisation of their children is wilful stupidity. Hephaestos, the crippled armourer who labours to produce the shield of Achilles, stands for all prolific creators: the shield is a work of art reflecting the world around it, it is made with painful labour; yet Hephaestos is powerless to change anything, and 'hobbles away' from what 'the god had wrought'.

The Shield of Achilles included occasional verses, love lyrics and a sequence in praise of nature collectively entitled 'Bucolics'. But even more momentous than the title poem were the seven poems together known as 'Horae Canonicae'. This was the culmination of his 'religious phase; hurt, tentative, masked', as Hayden Carruth noted; in sorrowful, vigorous language he wrote this sequence, 'poems too ashamed to be devotional, too bitter to be ceremonious, though they had a shot at both; poems close, peculiarly close, to the puckered spirituality of the age'. They trace the canonical hours of Good Friday, although Auden did not describe Christ's crucifixion because he thought that poetry's religious witness must be 'indirect and negative', that Christian beliefs could not be represented in aesthetic images. 'Poems, like many of Donne's and Hopkins', which express a poet's personal feelings of religious devotion or penitence, make one uneasy,' he wrote in *The Dyer's Hand*. 'Is there not something a little odd, to say the least, about making an admirable public object out of one's feelings of guilt and penitence before God?'

Auden's sequence opens with 'Prime', a poem set at 6 a.m. describing the holy, precious moment of a man awakening. 'Terce' is 9 a.m. when people, including the hangman and the judge, set to work; the crucifixion of Jesus in its biblical account lasted from 9 a.m. until noon, and they say, 'it is only our victim who is without a wish'. Twelve noon is represented in the poem 'Sext': Auden praises vocation, secular power, human progress, without which, 'at this noon, there would be no authority/to command this death'. The fourth of the sequence, entitled 'Nones' and set at 3 p.m., describes the stunned indifference after the horror of the crucifixion with the blood of sacrifice already dry on the grass. In a crucial passage, Auden notes that henceforth, despite all the games, there will always be remembrance of human violence:

We shall always now be aware

> Of the deed into which they lead, under
> The mock chase and the mock capture,
> The racing and tussling and splashing,
> The panting and the laughter,
> Be listening for the cry and stillness
> To follow after: wherever
> The sun shines, brooks run, books are written,
> There will also be this death.

Auden thought 'the only way in which one can possibly visualise Christ and the Devil is the same, by looking in the mirror'. A sudden instant of mirrored recognition produces the climax of the next poem of the canonical hour, 'Vespers', set at 6 p.m. This is the most autobiographical of the sequence: a long, elegant, teasing contrast between two opposing mentalities, the Arcadian and the Utopian, in which the Arcadian narrator makes himself sound altogether more attractive, as Alices are to Mabels. The Mabel-like Utopian (he resembles de Maistre) looks away from a 'chubby' child because his system of indoctrination is based on the pretext of protecting vulnerable children, the symbolic naked babies with which this chapter opened. But the Arcadian is as smug and self-deceiving as Prospero in 'The Sea and the Mirror'. The Arcadian avoids suffering: 'Passing a slum child with rickets, I look the other way.' Auden disapproved of looking away. He had seen great symbolism a few years earlier in a *New Yorker* cartoon depicting 'a little man struggling madly with a huge octopus issuing from a man-hole' and surrounded by 'an utterly passive crowd'. Two men are walking by – one carries an umbrella resembling Prospero's magic wand – shielded from what is happening by the backs of the crowd. The man with the wand says to his companion, 'It doesn't take much to attract a crowd in New York.' Auden's gloss on this joke was of huge significance to his poetry of the late 1940s and early 1950s. 'The individual struggling with fate is hemmed in by the crowd, some of whom say to themselves: Thank God, it isn't me. Others think: Nothing exciting ever happens to me! And the two men on the periphery assume that it doesn't take much to make people look; therefore they'll do the opposite; they'll solve the problem by not looking. How did the German people react to Hitler? Some thought: He is suffering for us. See how he suffers! Others thought: He is full of power. I envy him! – Whereas America and England turned and refused to look.' The Arcadian narrator of 'Vespers' turns from the rachitic child like the New Yorker with Prospero's wand, yet by his 'fortuitous' meeting with the Utopian the Arcadian's self-enchantment is pricked; for a moment, at least, he loses the distorting detachment of the artist decried by Caliban. He recalls Christ's substitution on the Cross and has an enforced remembrance of the victim

> on whose immolation (call him Abel, Remus, whom you will, it is
> one Sin Offering) arcadias, utopias, our dear old bag of a democracy,
> are alike founded:
> For without a cement of blood (it must be human, it must be
> innocent) no secular wall will safely stand.

These scarifying lines, so pessimistic in human terms, capture the essence of Auden's post-war thought.

The next poem in the sequence, 'Compline', is set at 9 p.m., when 'should come / The instant of recollection / When the whole thing makes sense'. The poem is the first in the sequence to contain a prayer, taken from the Requiem Mass, and the poet stumbles into prayer with a confession of the difficulties:

> It is not easy
> To believe in unknowable justice
> Or pray in the name of a love
> Whose name one's forgotten: *libera*
> *Me, libera* C (dear C)
> And all poor s-o-b's who never
> Do anything properly.

The final poem of the sequence is 'Lauds', a morning prayer, in which the poet wishes 'God bless'. It reads like the verbal accompaniment of a joyous dance, recalling the little golden dancing characters in perpetual motion who represent the joy of resurrection and eternal life in Charles Williams's novel *The Greater Trumps*.

In the early spring of 1953 Auden spent two months at Smith College in Massachusetts, where he gave lectures but had no teaching duties. There he met Wendell Stacey Johnson, a young member of the English faculty whom he found 'charming, bright and lascivious'. They had an affair which gave Auden great sexual pleasure: the letters that he sent Johnson after going to Ischia in May are suffused with gratitude. 'Even your leathery old mother finds your brew of decency and scampishness more powerful than any martini,' he wrote in June. He dedicated his poem 'Plains' of July 1953 to Johnson, recommended him to Spender as a contributor to *Encounter* and in September gave him the ultimate accolade: 'you and Chester are the *only* people in the world that I can talk to about such things' as poetic metre. Briefly, at least, Johnson was counted as one of Auden's 'few dear names'. Nevertheless the radiant love song (reminiscent of de la Mare) 'The Willow-wren and the Stare' with which Auden celebrated this affair is gently doubtful of the lover's sincerity in anything except the 'holy selfishness' of desire ('the most convincing love poems', he wrote in 1959, were 'the fa-la-la's of a good-natured sensuality which made no pretence at serious love.... the least convincing were those in which the poet claimed to be in earnest, yet had no complaint to make'). On 4 August he sent Johnson characteristic advice on depression. 'The cure – work and counting up the people who love one. Its curious, at least this is my experience, than [sic] when one is blue it is easier to believe that one is loved than that one loves. – one goes over one's affections and they all start to seem false – which aint really so, or rather one learns to love by believing that one can.' The two men apparently lost touch during 1954.

In August 1955 Auden was approached by Enid Starkie to stand as a candidate for the Oxford Professorship of Poetry. The holders of this chair, which had been endowed in 1708, are elected every five years by those Masters of Arts who come to Oxford to vote in person. Since the election of Day Lewis in 1951 dons like Starkie who wished the post to be held by poets had been opposed by a group with more urbane literary and social tastes. Their nominee was 'a tolerant, slightly cynical man of the world', as Auden described Sir Harold Nicolson, 'whose forte has always been the comic and slightly malicious'. A Shakespeare scholar, G. Wilson Knight, also entered the lists. Senior male members of the university opposed Auden as an American citizen with a bad war record; but he had the support of women dons, many scientists and all the interested undergraduates (who did not have a vote) and was elected in February 1956. British officials initially put up paltry difficulties to Auden as an American citizen taking a job in Britain, but these obstacles were surmounted, and after anxiously working for a month at his inaugural lecture, Auden reached Oxford in late May of 1956. He was given rooms at his old college, Christ Church. 'Auden has a hard time in the Common Room at Christ Church, where several of the dons twit him about being an American,' Spender noted on a visit in June. 'He is half fascinated, but also half bored by the endless cliquey donnish conversation.' Some of his colleagues were provincial pedants, and Auden perhaps tactlessly showed his impatience: 'A don at the House asked me if Eisenhower was a Democrat or a Republican. So I gave him a little lecture on the American electoral system.'

Auden's inaugural lecture was delivered on 11 June 1956 under the title 'Making, Knowing and Judging', was partly reproduced in the *Sunday Times* and eventually republished in his major critical volume, *The Dyer's Hand*, in 1963. The philosopher Stuart Hampshire, who attended the lecture, thought Auden 'inspired' but that some passages were 'false', and he was disheartened by the quotations from Charles Williams. In the most challenging passages of the lecture Auden depicted poetry-writing as a ritual act in celebration of a sacred object: every poem should be rooted in 'a passion of awe'. He ended magnificently by reciting Hardy's poem 'Afterwards' with its poignant close,

> And will any say when my bell of quittance is heard in the gloom,
>> And a crossing breeze cuts a pause in its outrollings,
> Till they rise again, as they were a new bell's boom,
>> 'He hears it not now, but used to notice such things'?

Some diffident undergraduates were intimidated by this performance. 'Here were "blinding theologies of flowers and fruits", a monogrammed set of myths and memories carried over from a bulging childhood,' Alan Bennett recalled. 'Obsessions, landscapes, favourite books, even (one's heart sank) the Icelandic sagas.' Bennett decided that his literary ambitions were hopeless if authorship required Auden's credentials; younger American writers, like Ned Rorem and Kallman's friend James Merrill, felt similarly overwhelmed when they met the formidable Auden. Yet not all undergraduates were discouraged. His Michaelmas-term lecture of 1960 'Genius and Apostle' concluded ringingly, in words that were full of excitement for Anne Ridler, 'Analogy is not identity. Art is not enough.' During all his visits to Oxford between 1956 and 1960 Auden tried to make himself approachable to young poets. 'At three o'clock every afternoon, he set off from his rooms, red slippers flapping, and sometimes a demure twist of shirt tail fluttering under his coat, for a teashop in St Giles, where he said the only good coffee in Oxford was obtainable.' He made it known that he was available here for conversation with undergraduates who wished to show him their verses. 'Every afternoon, in consequence, the place was packed by Somerville poetesses clutching folders full of sonnets about unrequited love.... They stared at Auden from afar, but seldom dared to approach him. When they did, he was unfailingly courteous.' His chief advice to all young poets was, 'Learn everything there is to know about metre.' Among the poets who sought him in 1958 was a young American visitor, Gregory Corso, who distressed him by trying to kiss the hem of his trousers. When Corso turned cute and poetical by asking, 'Are birds spies?', Auden sensibly replied, 'No, I don't think so. Who would they report to?'

Dom Moraes first went to consult Auden in college clutching a sheaf of his poems. 'I came into the room as into church,' he recalled. 'It was a strangely bare room, and the curtains were drawn on the sunshine, so it was sepulchral as well.' Auden's criticism 'was the best I had ever had. He did not seem to believe, as most critics do, that a poem should or shouldn't be written in a certain way: he took it as it was, as a shaped object, and told one where it was misshapen.' He was full of good sense and sound advice. When Moraes developed a prolonged writing block, Auden treated him 'like a veteran doctor prescribing for a hypochondriac' and suggested, with a kind, weary stare, 'Perhaps you ought to be in love.' Moraes protested, 'But I am.' 'Then it's the wrong person,' said Auden shortly.

Auden did not want to make himself at home. 'British intellectual society is less boring, more intelligent and infinitely more charming than its American counterpart, which makes its collective influence much more dangerous to the intellectual – to resist seems rather piggy,' Auden wrote after three years' experience of Oxford common rooms. It was easier in the United States 'to be alone, to be left alone (in England, all one's intellectual relatives live within calling distance, and they keep dropping in)'. There was perhaps an element of deliberate pigginess in Auden's behaviour at Christ Church: he was trying to resist some of the charmers. But he was also estranged from British ways by over fifteen years in the United States, and he was neither forgiven nor forgiving of the differences. 'When I went back to Oxford,' he told Robin Maugham and Michael Davidson in 1957, 'I just found I didn't belong. I said to them: "It's all fine, but where's the gravy?" In America I won't open my mouth for less than three hundred dollars. In England I found people expected me to speak for five pounds.' His old friends were disappointed in him. Richard Crossman (to whom he had addressed one of his poetic letters from Iceland) met him at dinner with Spender shortly after the inaugural lecture. 'Stephen listened in agony, since the more Wystan talked – and he talked very volubly – the more he revealed that he is now a comfortable, unreflective pundit, with extremely conventional, washy views.' Crossman was a Labour politician of anti-American hue who with characteristic English edginess 'couldn't help saying to him that he's the only ex-Englishman I know who has become a thoroughly balanced American'.

Spender at about the same time noted, 'he becomes completely absorbed in his own preoccupations, and hardly gets outside them.... When he is anxious like this, conversation consists largely in his waiting for an opening for him to hold forth on some topic. On the other hand, when he is on a congenial subject, or when he heeds some other point of view of his own, he becomes his old self.' A month later Spender and Auden dined as guests of an undergraduate club called the Mermaid whose members were typified by 'a tiresomely effeminate young undergraduate who wore a cloak lined with red satin and carried a cane' talking 'in a camp way about his fiancée'. Auden complained when the food was late, and of the officious behaviour of the British authorities over his work-permit. Spender recorded Auden's tabletalk. 'He talked in his usual categorical way, which is sometimes agreeable, sometimes illuminating, sometimes brilliant, sometimes funny, sometimes irritating.' Auden announced that 'morally speaking, Dylan Thomas had committed suicide', and 'then made a curious assertion that he had been able to tell exactly which of his preparatory school pupils would be killed in the war. He even went so far as to say that in the cases of two sets of twins, he knew which twin of each set was doomed to die.'

Auden's last three teeth were extracted in January 1956, and after this depressing start he seems to have been deeply unhappy for much of the year. His unhappiness served him in writing his 1956 study of paranoia, 'There Will Be No Peace', which owes something to the enmity that he aroused in England during and after his election to the Oxford chair. 'One of the most purely personal poems I have ever written,' he told Monroe Spears on 11 May 1963. 'It was an attempt to describe a very unpleasant dark-night-of-the-soul sort of experience which for several months in 1956 attacked me.' Thom Gunn judged this 'the worst of Auden's poems I have seen in book form', but his weaker poems are often those with the most distinct biographical content, just as his greatest poems have had the personal element intensely refined. Two verses of 'There Will Be No Peace' have that sense of implacable suffering, beyond any assuagement or alleviation, that characterises Auden at his strongest in the 1950s. He is bewildered by the animosity he encounters in England, and decides that he must not submit to the pain:

> What have you done to them?
> Nothing? Nothing is not an answer:
> You will come to believe – how can you help it? –
>   That you did, that you did do something;
> You will find yourself wishing you could make them laugh:
>   You will long for their friendship.
>
> There will be no peace.
> Fight back then, with such courage as you have
> And every unchivalrous dodge that you know of,
>   Clear in your conscience on this:
> Their cause, if they had one, is nothing to them now;
>   They hate for hate's sake.

Given Auden's experience of Oxford in 1956 his decision to settle there in 1972 seems all the more desperate or misjudged.

His feelings for Ischia waned from this time. In the winter of 1955–6 he had a financial misunderstanding with his houseboy there, Giocondo. The latter left Auden's employment abruptly and, working as a bartender, regaled his customers with gossip and complaints about Auden's household. This made for local unpleasantness, and in other ways the atmosphere at Forio was becoming less congenial. 'Forio has been invaded by Limey lushes,' Auden told Robin Maugham and Michael Davidson (a remark that surprisingly they did not take personally). John Osborne, who visited Ischia at this time with Tony Richardson, has left a similar account: 'Our fellow diners were usually groups of Englishmen in blazers and striped socks, all oppressively self-conscious, shouting at each other to keep up morale.' One evening there was a newcomer at a café table. 'He was flabby, debauched and was being fêted by a group of New York faggots and the local passing trade,' Osborne wrote. 'Tony stared at him with a kind of repelled excitement. It was Chester Kallman.' Richardson abandoned Osborne at a street corner and went in pursuit. Another visitor to Ischia was the young Allen Ginsberg, who in August 1957 found Auden in a bar with 'a tableful of dull chatty literary old fairies'. Ginsberg got drunk, and argued with Auden about Whitman. 'I doubt if Auden respects his own feelings any more,' he noted next day. 'His long sexual history has been relatively unfortunate and made him very orthodox and conservative and merciless in an offhand way. He sounds like an intelligent *Time* magazine talking, approaching such questions as capital punishment and literary censorship as if they were complicated bureaucratic problems, as if they have no right to private feelings but only a series of pseudo-factual logical considerations – a sort of fetish of objectivity – which strikes me as no objectivity at all, but a sort of abject distrust of people and their loves.' Another example of this false objectivity occurred at a dinner party of Auden, Spender, David Jones, Francis Bacon, Osbert Sitwell and others. Sitwell suffered from advanced Parkinson's disease and left early, whereupon Auden remarked that his best hope for Sitwell was a swift death. 'Like a lot of things Auden wishes for others, it seems a little too sensibly final,' Spender reflected. 'There is no margin for the possibility that Osbert may want to go on living, even under worsening circumstances.'

In June 1957 (a month after his father's peaceful death aged eighty-four) Auden was awarded the Antonio Feltrinelli Foundation prize worth over $33,000. Shortly afterwards he and Kallman decided to leave Ischia. The decade that they had spent there resembled the ten years from 1938 that Elizabeth Bishop had spent at Key West: both places had superb natural beauty, with fine though primitive buildings, and a cohesive community, but Auden and Bishop alike saw these features despoiled and the cultural integrity dispersed. In both cases, too, the poets formed an advance party of the despoilers: cultural interlopers whose arrival had foreshadowed the coming bewilderment and dissipation. 'The development of cheap mass travel since the war', Auden wrote, was opening Europe to 'the Low-Brows', people who should be visiting the Dominions, which were full of 'people like themselves, speaking English, eating English food, wearing English clothes and playing English games'. But he was implicated in the ruin of Ischia's traditions, as perhaps he sensed, for his adieus to Italy, 'Good-bye to the Mezzogiorno', written in September 1958, has an evasive and even trivial tone.

Following his decision to abandon Ischia, Auden asked the daughter of his old Austrian landlady, Hedwig Petzold, to find him a summer house within a reasonable distance of the Vienna Opera House (although he was not musically awed by 'the Karajan city where Wagner is played in complete darkness'). Shortly afterwards he saw an advertisement for a house at Kirchstetten, a village some thirty minutes by car west of Vienna. After an inspection with Kallman he bought his first and only house in October 1957 for the equivalent of £3000 sterling or US $12,000. His new home was a small, nondescript eighteenth-century farmhouse built of yellow clay close to an autobahn from which the drone of traffic was always audible. 'We both *love* it here and like the Austrians though I do think them a little Reichsinnig,' Auden wrote to Hedwig Petzold from Kirchstetten in October 1958. 'The Germans are much less sympathetic but they do feel *some* guilt at what they did – the Austrians none at all.' Auden had always been prone to use German words to indicate moral judgments (as when, in 1955, he was indicating weaknesses more profound than the English phrase 'third-rate' when he described Kingsley Amis as '*dritten Klasse*'). His first outlay on the Kirchstetten farmhouse was celebrated in a poem originally entitled 'On Installing an American Kitchen in Lower Austria', though later retitled 'Grub First, Then Ethics'. Otherwise the interior was nearly as spartan as Auden's bedroom at St Marks Place. The kitchen was Kallman's domain, and kept in an appalling clutter; Auden had an upstairs work room, reached by an external staircase, with a dormer window in a pantiled roof; his desk was set on a platform by the window, but there were no bookcases, and the room was therefore piled with books. The living room was dominated by the record collection and accompanying equipment. The guest bedroom contained two plain iron beds and a large crucifix. The ledges in the little entrance were piled with books and papers.

'When I lived in England, my reasons for going abroad were to get into the sun, to be able to drink what I liked when I liked and in general have the kinds of fun I could not have at home,' Auden had written a few years earlier. 'Now when I go to Europe from the States, the great relief is escaping from a non-humanised, non-mythologised nature and getting back to a landscape where every acre is hallowed. This is nothing to do with Culture with a capital c.... Architecture aside, there are very few artistic experiences which any American who lives within range of a big city cannot enjoy as well or better at home, but for a civilised landscape he still must go elsewhere, since his own is still the wild country of the open road where no one expects to stay, physically or spiritually, in one place for long.' Though to many of Auden's visitors the landscape around Kirchstetten seemed unremarkable, for Auden its plainness and the signs of good husbandry suggested a welcome containment: it was a relief for him that 'a house backed by orderly woods, / Facing a tractored sugar-beet country' would not attract people for whom 'drama was a craving'. It was a place where he expected to stay for long.

'Routine, in an intelligent man, is a sign,' he wrote in 1958, 'of ambition.' His routine at Kirchstetten was severe. He began work at six-thirty or seven, although around eleven, if there were visitors, he would often take them to a local *gasthaus* for a beer and a sandwich. He would return home for two glasses of dry vermouth and a tustle with the crossword puzzle before lunch cooked by Kallman. Auden would work in the afternoon, or walk, or go motoring. At six-thirty sharp he mixed lethally strong vodka-martinis. There would be lashings of wine during dinner, and afterwards; Auden went to bed equally sharply at 9.30, smoking in bed, drinking more wine and reading under a thick pile of blankets. He had become so set in routine that he wrote in 1962, 'My fantastic expectation that fate will do as I wish goes so far that my immediate reaction to an unexpected event, even a pleasant surprise, is anger.' This compulsive routine was a device to fend off the dramas that he went to Kirchstetten to avoid. 'A modern stoic,' he observed in the printed version of one of his Oxford lectures, 'knows that the surest way to discipline passion is to discipline time: decide what you want or ought to do during the day, then always do it at exactly the same moment every day, and passion will give you no trouble.' His insistence on punctuality disciplined the passions of others and required their attention. 'We do not want others to conform with our wishes because they must – life would be very lonely if they did – but because they choose to; we want DEVOTED slaves.'

It was under the influence of his happiness in Austria that Auden began to write 'a cycle about what worldliness really means'. The tone of gratitude for his Kirchstetten house is profound:

what I dared not hope or fight for
is, in my fifties, mine, a toft-and-croft
where I needn't, ever, be at home *to*
those I am not at home *with*.

Other rooms of the house are celebrated in poems dedicated to significant friends: Anne and Irving Weiss, the New Yorkers whose family life he much admired (and sometimes envied), received poems on the attic and basement cellar (both written in July 1963) which have a luxuriant pleasure and superb verbal confidence. The poem in praise of the guest bedroom was for John and Thekla Clark (his Ischia friend Thekla Pelletti and her husband), and a third couple Louis Kronenberger (with whom he collaborated on an anthology of aphorisms) and his wife Emmie received another joyous poem, 'The Cave of Nakedness', celebrating his sleeping room. Significantly the only room that Auden did not celebrate was the bedroom where Kallman slept with other men; instead the twelfth and final poem of the cycle, written for Kallman, rejoices in the shared area of their 'Common Life'. This poetic cycle was eventually published in the collection *About the House* (by Random House in 1965 and by Faber the following year) dedicated to Edmund and Elena Wilson. This cycle was, like all Auden's serious work at this time, 'a hymn to Natural Law and a gesture of astonishment at the greatest of all mysteries, the order of the universe'.

It was after settling at Kirchstetten that Auden became increasingly drawn to Goethe. His prose meditations on love written in 1959 were entitled 'Dichtung und Wahrweit' ('Poetry and Truth') after Goethe, and he embarked with Elizabeth Mayer on a translation of Goethe's Italian travel book eventually published in 1962. In the Introduction to this Auden praised Goethe for 'his amazing instinct, which he was to show all through his life, for taking the leap in the right direction'. This was how Auden liked to think of himself too. 'I have come to the conclusion that Goethe was a very lonely man,' he told his Austrian friend Baroness von Musulin in the early 1960s, again really speaking of himself. Though he described himself once as 'a minor Atlantic Goethe', he passionately celebrated national differences and cultural diversity. Thus he favoured Britain going into the Common Market, but distrusted the amorphous cultural effects of internationalisation, taking comfort from the Babel of language. 'So long as the Germans speak German and I speak English, a genuine dialogue between us is possible; we shall not simply be addressing our mirror images.'

Auden's maxims and reflections in 'Dichtung und Wahrweit' are about the feelings aroused by desire and defeat rather than directed at specific individuals. The impersonality is a deliberate characteristic of the piece. Yet the emotions it analyses were slightly represented by his relations with two young men whom he befriended in the late 1950s. One was Orlan Fox, an undergraduate at Columbia University, whom he met at a party in the spring of 1959. For several years they were lovers, and some friends hoped that Fox would replace Kallman in Auden's life. Latterly in the 1960s they ate together on every Friday evening that Auden was in New York. 'The relationship between the two of us was extremely complex,' Fox wrote after Auden's death. Initially it was 'a father–son relationship'. Auden instructed Fox on his reading, expected him to open the wine at dinner parties and serve the table as he carved. As they came to know one another better, and the sexual power receded, 'we became real pals', said Fox, 'and brother–brother'. But they also played together at boyish conspiracies and (for Fox was rather camp) schoolgirl jokes. Most of all Auden acted the role of an old mother He would scold Fox, 'Don't slouch in your seat; gentlemen sit upright' (a remark which, in conversation with John Heath-Stubbs, Auden attributed to his own mother). These roles were reversed when Fox came out of the kitchen with the food on Friday evenings. 'There would be Wystan anticipating the care and nourishment of mother. He always sat on a volume of the OED, as if he were a child too short for table.'

The other lover was a young Viennese called Hugerl, whom Auden met in a bar shortly after settling at Kirchstetten. Working-class youths who would turn a trick like Hugerl were not the sexual partners whom Auden preferred – Kallman, Wendell Johnson or Fox would have been best – but he was grateful for the pleasure and companionship. 'Hugo comes out every Sunday with his wife who is duly parked by the swimming pool or, if it is wet, ordered by hubby to take a nap,' Auden reported to Fox from Kirchstetten in 1960. 'We are past the cash-payment stage. (They are a very happy wedded couple, I must say.) The situation would make a jolly short story, but I suppose it would shock…. Last week we celebrated their wedding anniversary.' In April 1961 Auden wrote happily to Fox, 'Our sweet practical Hugie … has a driving licence now and is car crazy but, surprisingly, cautious.' Hugerl was allowed to drive Auden's Volkswagen, which in 1962 acquired a bullet-hole in the bonnet while serving as a getaway car after a burglary. This proved to be only one in a series of crimes perpetrated by Hugerl, including a break-in at the Kirchstetten house (though Auden and Kallman noted that Hugerl had not stolen their best silver). To Auden's distress Hugerl was sentenced to fifteen months' imprisonment in October 1962. 'Evidently the *Kurier* has somebody in the police in their pay, for the next morning appeared a filthy piece – all too well informed,' he wrote in distress to David Luke. 'Every possible innuendo was made.' As homosexual acts were criminal in Austria, as in Britain, Auden was relieved, as he wrote to Orlan Fox, that 'your mother is a free woman', but he was sorry for Hugerl, and feared his imprisonment would spoil their relationship. 'Even when he gets out I fear I must be just a sister to H, otherwise he will suspect my motives for "forgiving" him. God, what a bloody bore the whole thing is!'

In fact their friendship resumed on a stronger basis after Hugerl's release. Auden celebrated this relationship in a poem called 'Glad', written in March 1965 and circulated in his lifetime to a few trusted friends like Driberg. Though not technically a remarkable poem, nor even a love poem, it is tender, candid and perhaps Auden's most relaxed, unfeigning, grown-up poem about sexual pleasure. It expresses true gratitude 'For how much and how often / You have made me glad.' His gratitude was not only for their 'Mutual pleasure', for 'males are so constructed / We cannot deceive'; but also for Hugerl's arrest and incarceration. They had 'both learned a lesson', and their relation was finally freed from the roles of '*Strich* and *Freir*' (rent boy and trick). He was glad too of the tolerance of Hugerl's wife Christa: 'I can't imagine / A kinder set-up.' Husband and wife stayed with Auden at St Marks Place in January and February 1967: he felt that he owed them a look at his American home.

Homage to Clio was published by Random House in April 1960 and by Faber in July. It contains a few fine moments, especially 'Friday's Child', a poem dedicated to the memory of Dietrich Bonhoeffer, the theologian martyred by the Nazis in 1945. This poem is not immediately appealing or accessible to non-Christians, but offers a masterly summary of the twentieth-century theological predicament – it is 'Dover Beach' after the concentration camps – and of the dilemma of free will. It treats deadly serious subjects lightly because the contemporary mind had become so 'utterly banal', prosaic and materialistic. Auden warns that, with an increasingly secularised outlook, people are losing their patrimony of a common symbolic language, and hence the shared comprehension that unites human beings into humanity.

> Since the analogies are rot
> Our senses based belief upon,
> We have no means of learning what
> Is really going on.

The critical reception of the book was mainly negative. In the *Yale Review* Thom Gunn wrote in September 1960, '*Homage to Clio* is probably his worst book since *The Dance of Death*' – a judgment that seems reasonable for its poems are seldom exciting or memorable. In Britain the book's reception was equally unimpressed, although this was partly based on preconceptions and obtuse readings. Philip Larkin in the *Spectator* thought that Auden had done 'irreparable' damage to his poetry by emigrating in 1939: 'at one stroke he lost his key subject and emotion – Europe and the fear of war – and abandoned his audience together with their common dialect'. This is a judgment that says more about English insularity than Auden's limitations: it is to assume that Larkin's confined subject-matter, his steady focus on Englishness and the neo-Georgian stasis of his poetry are characteristics to be emulated. Larkin – who could not understand either the passionate courage of 'New Year Letter', which he called 'a rambling intellectual stew', or the aesthetic critique of 'The Sea and the Mirror', which he judged 'an unsuccessful piece of literary inbreeding' – thought that Auden should not have been more ambitious in his subjects than the political crisis of the 1930s. Dom Moraes was more perceptive than Larkin and more sympathetic than Gunn. He thought there were no 'outstanding' poems in the book, written by Auden under 'a suave, benevolent mask ... of a well-travelled member of the Senior Common Room at Christ Church'. For Moraes its highpoint was the prose meditations 'Dichtung und Wahrweit'. 'These are the most brilliant things in the book,' Moraes believed, 'and more revelatory than anything in the poems of the breadth, the depth and the knowledge of the mind of one of the most intelligent men and one of the finest poets alive.' Moraes was a reviewer of integrity, and his affectionate doubts about *Homage to Clio* would have given Auden good reason to stop short, and think; still more so, the fact that the libretto for Hans Werner Henze's 'Elegy for

Young Lovers' written by him with Kallman in 1959–60 was not an unvarnished success in productions at Schwetzingen and Glyndebourne in 1961. The early 1960s were a period of critical rebuffs, not altogether undeservedly.

Although the critical reception of *Homage to Clio* was disappointing, Auden had more success with his prose works. During 1960 he prepared with Louis Kronenberger a *Book of Aphorisms* which was published by Viking in the USA in November 1962 and by Faber in October 1964. Quoting is the sincerest form of gratitude; just as books formed Auden's world, so his lifelong collecting of aphorisms provided his ethical compasses around his personal planet. He was a supreme ironist, to whom the aphorism was an attractive mode of thought, always self-reliant, often aristocratic or pessimistic. He had begun recording aphorisms in the 1920s, and had presented Caroline Newton with the manuscript of an earlier collection around 1941. Auden and Kronenberger's glee in compilation is evident in the final product, 'a rich collection, a book to last a lifetime', as John Gross hailed it, treating the aphorism as 'an art-form, or a kind of game, rather than a medium of instruction'.

The Dyer's Hand, Auden's first great collection of critical essays (including some of his Oxford lectures), was published by Random House in November 1962 and by Faber in April 1963. The book was generously reviewed except, perhaps, by opponents of Christianity, for it has a strong, sometimes repetitive Christian agenda. 'A man converted to Christianity 20 years ago must be very strong and good not to have become corrupted into any of that religion's usual forms of nastiness,' William Empson wrote. 'The range and grasp of his mind is always evident in the present book; but it strikes me that his mind is increasingly hampered, and that the resulting thoughts are often wrong.... he twitters like a curate in W. S. Gilbert, emitting a steady rivulet of the opaque distinctions suited to a spiritual director. It must be rather baffling for the Americans, especially as it is so unlike his personal character.' American critics, as usual, were not as easily baffled as the English liked to hope. Jason Epstein in the *Partisan Review* recognised *The Dyer's Hand* as 'a kind of literary autobiography', and it is indeed a forerunner of his autobiographical anthology, *A Certain World*, published eight years later. Epstein thought *The Dyer's Hand* 'extraordinary' in its examination of how literature creates the effect of reality, 'a demanding and painful book in much the way that poems themselves used to be'. But it was the personal element, and the distinctively Audenesque isolation, that Epstein stressed. 'Much of what Auden says in *The Dyer's Hand* falls outside those realms of convenient discourse in which author and reader casually presuppose a ready made universe in common. The only world which Auden wants to presuppose is that of his own imagination and intelligence, concentrated in his recollections and feelings: a world which can truly be made to exist only insofar as he can find the language to create it and which, in order for it to exist at all, he has to create again and again.' Epstein concluded with a perception that is more subtle and suggestive, as well as more generous and accurate, than the Leavisites' crude fulminations about immaturity. 'His playfulness goes deep and at times one is forced to wonder to what extent Auden's concern with the world of pure play may not reveal a regressive temptation which he finds it hard to overcome,' or betrays a 'preference for ... the world of childhood over that in which he currently finds himself'.

In 1962 Auden began work translating the aphoristic spiritual journal of Dag Hammarskjöld, the Secretary General of the United Nations, who had been killed in 1961. Auden had met Hammarskjöld through Lincoln Kirstein and in 1960 had translated with him St John Perse's acceptance speech for the Nobel Prize for Literature; Auden was known to have been Hammarskjöld's candidate for the prize. He admired the Swedish statesman, and sympathised with his ideas, but he detected a trace of 'messianic delusion' in the journal which he did not shrink from mentioning in his introduction to the translation. Before the typescript (prepared jointly with Leif Sjoberg) had gone to press Auden was warned by a high Swedish official that his criticisms would prejudice the members of the Swedish Academy, who were responsible for awarding the Nobel Prize; but he would not modify his phrases. 'Well, there goes the Nobel Prize,' he said glumly at dinner with Lincoln Kirstein after his decision to ignore the Swedish official's hints. The Hammarskjöld book was published in 1964 under the English title *Markings*, and the Nobel Prize was offered to Sartre, who declined it. Auden was not discomfited at the time, though in the last years of his life he grieved obsessively about the money that he had lost.

'For better or worse, we have to live in a cultureless world, a world in which it is very difficult to believe in the reality of other people,' Auden wrote in 1960. As a child he had suffered this same difficulty and sought his reality in machines. His difficulty in respecting other people's reality led to increasing thoughts of censorship. He would have liked to testify that *Lady Chatterley's Lover* was pornographic when the English paperback edition was prosecuted for obscenity in 1960, for example, and was 'rather prissy about Cavafy's erotic poems', though he was teasing when he said Gerard Manley Hopkins was a poet who should be kept on the top shelf. Still his isolation became an increasing problem. 'He gives the impression of being somehow sated; fairly contented but self-sufficient and not wanting to see anyone,' Spender wrote during Auden's visit to London in June 1962. 'I don't think there is anyone from whom he gets anything new, unless perhaps a theologian.' His relationship with Spender was affectionate but competitive, and their comments on one another were often ambivalent; he was not unreachably self-absorbed with everyone.

Auden's social awkwardness may have been aggravated by the strains he had put on his physique. He had several habits which would not have seemed extreme or shocking to men of his generation, but which in the late 1990s would be regarded by many younger people as addictions to tobacco, amphetamines and alcohol. In 1960 he tried to renounce tobacco – 'It is *still* hell, but I pray,' he told Orlan Fox – though without success; by the late 1960s he was smoking at least 15,000 cigarettes a year according to James Stern's calculation. At Kirchstetten, at least, he and Kallman were 'eating their way into their graves', according to Stella Musulin. 'If they could possibly help it, of course, neither Wystan nor Chester ever walked a yard.' But most important of all was Auden's dependence on Benzedrine, which he had first used on his visit to the United States with Isherwood in 1938 and which he had consumed daily from 1939. The drug had lost its over-the-counter respectability by the 1950s: a manifesto issued by the American Medical Association in 1957 described amphetamines 'as by far the most dangerous drug existing today', potentially provoking 'violent, rapacious and criminal behaviour', which exaggeration was evidence of its newly illicit status. Kallman attributed Auden's premature ageing to his reliance on Benzedrine: 'Chester felt that he had used up his body at an accelerated rate.'

Auden took himself off it after starting to spend his summers at Kirchstetten, where it was unobtainable, though it is possible that he continued using it in New York for a few years longer. The withdrawal must have been stressful. Life without amphetamines was certainly slower, and perhaps felt emptier; the effects of detoxification (one can only speculate) may have contributed to the flatness of tone so often remarked in his poems of 1957–63. He had used amphetamines as a production engineer might use a chemical in a manufacturing process – "'I'm a working machine," he would say, smiling as if surprised and humbled by this fact' – and without it his functions faltered and misfired. He felt sapped of energy; and his sense of delight was weaker. Socially, for such a shy man, as Orlan Fox emphasised that he was, the strain of conversation without his Bennies could have been agonising. Without them he depended instead, like Kallman, far too heavily on alcohol. Ann Fleming in 1962 went to dine at Alan Pryce-Jones's New York apartment. 'I was only ten minutes late, but everyone was blind drunk,' she wrote. "'Everyone" was Auden, Isherwood and Tennessee Williams, each attended by a youthful curly-haired catamite.' Auden's level of drinking increased after he had discarded amphetamines, and is distressing to chronicle; the position deteriorated after a decisive change in his living arrangements in the early 1960s. At lunch in 1962 with St John Perse he said that his favourite French aphorism was from Proust: 'In matters of love it is easier to overcome a deep feeling than to renounce a habit.' Though the renunciation of amphetamines was a hellish experience, he was soon to be forced far more unpleasantly to renounce a habit of love. For in 1963 he reached the age of renunciation.

Auden in Italy in 1953. That year he
wrote, 'Love, or truth in any serious sense,
Like orthodoxy, is a reticence'.

The English Auden crosses the Atlantic on the *Queen Mary*.

The American Auden. In New York, said Harold Acton, 'he captured live images in mid-air, entranced by the racy slang, the garrulous cab drivers, the jets of steam in the streets.'

Auden in the 1950s. 'One ceases to be a child when one realizes that telling one's truth does not make it any better. Not even telling it to oneself.'

Auden broadcasting in the 1960s:
a public figure who believed that
'alienation from the collective is always a duty'.

Spender and John Ashbery with Auden at the Poetry
International. Auden had written a foreword to Ashbery's
Some Trees in the Yale series of Younger Poets.

Auden at an honorary degree investiture at Swarthmore
College in 1964. Lyndon Johnson, then President of the
United States, and U Thant, Secretary General of the
United Nations, also received honorary degrees.

Hannah Arendt said, 'Wystan is hideously
entangled and yet he longs for the simpler
certainties . . . he tries to reconcile the two
with a kind of spiritual masochism, but of
course it doesn't work'.

Auden near his apartment on St Mark's
Place in New York City. His Great Good
Place had turned into a futuristic badlands.

Sir Anthony Blunt with Auden at an
honorary degree ceremony in 1971.
'Oxford was fun,' Auden wrote after this
occasion, but he was breaking up.

Auden photographed by Nancy Crampton
shortly before his departure from New
York in 1972. A friend wrote at the time,
'He is going away (and not simply to
Oxford)'.

CHAPTER 10

'And I, submissive,
felt unwanted and went out'

In the last decade of his life, Auden became lonelier, more unhappy and vulnerable, seemed indeed to enter a physical decline. The constancy of his routine with Kallman was upset; his characteristic landscape became neither the great good places of the 1940s, nor the comfortless plain of 'The Shield of Achilles', but a futuristic badlands: 'all has gone phut in the future we paint', he wrote in 1967,

> where, vast and vacant, venomous areas
> surround the small, sporadic patches
> of fen and forest that give food and shelter,
> such home as they have, to a human remnant,
> stunted in stature, strangely deformed.

His last years had many depressing moments, though their reputation of unrelenting misery is too extreme. For his readers the ways in which he used this misery are more important than anecdotes about an ageing man struggling with increasing clumsiness to handle the machinery of life. In the six years before 1963 Auden's poetry was the least exciting of any period of his life; but his dying fall proved glorious, with many rich, luxuriant poems brimming with courage, consolation, gratitude and hope; steady, patient wisdom and sharp political comment interspersed with sparkles of campiness and rumbles of grumpiness. Gratitude provided the abiding note. He still rejoiced at his fortune in being alive and was startled at the ingratitude of others. In the mid-1960s he wrote,

> Scanning his fellow
> Subway passengers, he asks:
> 'Can I really be

> the only one in this car
> who is glad to be alive?'

For all that seemed to go wrong, he was always 'conscious of his good luck' at not being one of those described by Caliban in 'The Sea and the Mirror' falling to pieces in a grave.

But all his perceptions were complicated by a perpetual tension. As he asked around 1964,

> Flattered by Pleasure, accused by Pain,
> Which of the two
> Should he believe?

He had since boyhood shown a high-spirited love of pleasure and had loathed puritanism: 'as a rule', he had written in 1939, 'it was the pleasure-haters who became unjust'. Yet he eulogised pleasure precisely because he was tempted to seek aesthetic stimulation in mortification and found justice, even excitement in pain. The public prosecutor in 'The Public v. the Late Mr William Butler Yeats' (1939) or the implacable persecutors in 'There Will Be No Peace' (1956) are accusatory figures and therefore quintessential to one side of Auden, who in the 1960s still saw 'Each life an amateur sleuth, / Asking *Who did it?*' Though in the last years of life he tried to praise pleasure – particularly the discreet, scholarly, self-sufficient pleasures of 'The Horatians' (1968) – the accusation of pain took over. At the end of his life it was becoming difficult for him to believe in anything else.

Kallman remained crucial both to his experiences and to what he made of his experiences. Auden had longed for a settled domicile with Kallman, but only a few years after he had achieved his idyll in the valley at Kirchstetten – 'humanely modest in scale / and mild of contour', as he praised it in 1965 – the dream was disrupted. In the early 1960s Kallman decided to leave Kirchstetten each July for a month's visit to Greece. He had several reasons for his decision. The sexual opportunities in Athens and the islands were exciting. He needed to assert his independence from Auden's stifling attention, which Auden struggled imperfectly to restrain. As Auden wrote in the introduction to his anthology, *A Choice of de la Mare's Verse*, published by Faber in May 1963, 'To be well-bred means to have respect for the solitude of others, whether they be mere acquaintances or, and this is much more difficult, persons we love.' Kallman's desire for space away from Auden was accentuated by his own failure as a poet: his second collection, *Absent and Present*, published by the Wesleyan University Press in 1963, received little critical attention. (It is not incompetent and was praised in *Partisan Review* for 'ironic self-awareness' and 'deep knowingness', though, confessed its reviewer, a poem about death 'irresistibly raises the image in my mind of shrouds by Dior'.) The flop of *Absent and Present* was hurtful and disheartening for such a competitive man as Kallman, and he may have realised that Auden's clumsy championing of his work to editors and critics was sometimes ludicrous. In Kirchstetten the fact that, according to Stella Musulin, 'Chester's intelligence and wit' were 'liable ... to be under-estimated' by her fellow Austrians would have added to Kallman's sensitivity. Musulin's compatriot Emma Kann, who became a regular visitor to the Kirchstetten house, reported 'a slight tension between Kallman and me' until she 'told Auden that I would like to know Kallman in his own right'. They then established a routine whereby Auden cleared the lunchtable and went into the kitchen leaving Kann to give her entire attention to Kallman, whom she found 'a rather good conversationalist'. Without such careful exercises in etiquette, life for Kallman in Austria could be painful. 'Chester and Wystan most certainly adored and understood each other,' as Spender wrote after Kallman's death, 'yet it was impossible for them to live, except intermittently, together.'

Kallman usually brought a Greek youth back to Austria after his July holidays. These visitors caused predictable griefs. 'C went to meet Kosta for a week-end in München which seems to have been spent in fucking and crying and fucking and crying,' Auden wrote in June 1963. 'K has got that bloody Kraut cunt pregnant and will probably have to marry her. Chester, poor lamb, is utterly miserable, which doesn't make it so easy for me to be cheerful either.' Some of the toughs were nicer than Kosta. Konstantin, the Greek friend whom Kallman took to Kirchstetten in 1973, was described by Baroness von Musulin on the day that Auden's funeral arrangements were being settled as 'a warmhearted creature exuding tongue-tied sympathy with all around him'. But Kosta and Konstantin were less important to the lives of Auden and Kallman than another young Greek imported to Kirchstetten, Yannis Boras, who had been born in Arcadia in 1942. In 1963 Kallman fell more steadily in love with Boras than with any other younger sexual partner of his life.

Auden's dependence on Kallman – not merely as an object for his poetic imagination, but as someone he had loved in his eccentric way for a quarter-century – was ferocious and even oppressive. 'Whenever Wystan and I have met since 1939, or corresponded, it has been obvious that your happiness and affection were … his first considerations, *the things he aimed his life at*, and to which he inmostly dedicated every poem he wrote, as he wrote it,' Nevill Coghill once told Kallman. 'Whenever I met him he has spoken first and foremost of you, as if you were perpetually with him.' It was therefore demoralising for Auden when in 1963 Kallman decided that he would not return in the winter from Kirchstetten to New York, but in future would spend the months from October to April in Athens. 'It cannot have been easy living on a long-term basis with Auden in New York while attempting, however fitfully, to develop his own personality and talents,' Baroness von Musulin judged. When Elizabeth Hardwick and Robert Lowell had visited St Marks Place a little time before, Lowell had been impressed by Auden's 'beefy, slow, eccentric normality' while Kallman sat in another room without speaking but played a record of an Auden–Kallman libretto, perhaps as an assertive reminder of his achievements. Kallman for all his charm and intelligence had destroyed his looks by drinking heavily: Musulin thought he looked like a carp, and Allan Levy called him 'frog-faced'. He seemed desperate in his clinging to Greeks like Boras, and gave the impression of tormented and resentful failure. Visitors to Kirchstetten were drawn into his distress. In his poem about the Kirchstetten living room, 'For Friends Only', dedicated to Thekla Clark and her husband, Auden promised, 'Should you have troubles … / And confession helps, we will hear it, / Examine and give our counsel.' Ironically, after Auden had gone to bed at his regular early hour, it was friends like the Clarks who had to hear Kallman's confession and give their counsel, for Kallman would sit up drinking until the early hours, talking miserably of his wasted life and describing its latest indignities.

It must have been agonising to love Kallman as Auden did, and to watch his deterioration. 'A neurotic, an alcoholic, let us say, is not happy; on the contrary, he suffers terribly, yet no one can relieve his suffering without his consent and this he so often withholds,' Auden wrote in 1962, with Kallman surely in mind. 'He insists on suffering because his ego cannot bear the pain of facing reality and the diminution of self importance which a cure would involve.' Kallman cannot be faulted for wanting to spend more time with someone who gave him so many satisfactions as Boras, 'that dear good wild bad funny and now at last tragic boy', as James Merrill described him after his death. Kallman in 1963 took a furnished flat with Boras in Athens, where their life together was rather dominated by ouzo. Boras returned to Kirchstetten in the summers, where Auden would issue orders to him 'in the abrupt tones of a colonial English of yore speaking to the "boy"'. When at lunch one day Musulin asked where Boras was, Auden replied 'with a smirk of satisfaction: "I sent him up to the roof to mend tiles"'.

The effects of Kallman's preference for winter in Athens with Boras rather than New York with Auden were momentous. It seemed like a dire mutilation of their lives. In 1936 Auden had concluded one of his great love poems with an agonised question:

> Oh but what worm of guilt
> Or what malignant doubt
> Am I the victim of,
> That you then unabashed,
> Did what I never wished,
> Confessed another love;
> And I, submissive, felt
> Unwanted and went out?

It was a question to ask again, with sharper agony, in 1963. Auden felt unwanted, thought Kallman hurtful and shameless in his betrayal, and struggled to be submissive. His bitterness is evident in some of his prose writings of 1963, notably his Introduction to the Signet Classic edition of *Shakespeare's Sonnets*, where he wrote that the sonnets told 'the story of an agonized struggle by Shakespeare to preserve the glory of a vision he had been granted in a relationship ... with a person who seemed intent by his actions upon covering the vision with dirt'. Auden then quoted La Rochefoucauld – 'True love is like seeing ghosts: we all talk about it, but few of us have ever seen one' – and his friend, Hannah Arendt: 'Poets are the only people to whom love is not a crucial but an indispensable experience, which entitles them to mistake it for a universal one.' He told David Luke in 1963, 'When the vision fades ... the contrast between the glory of the vision and the sober world (I do *not* say reality) is too great to forgive.' The impact of Kallman's perceived desertion in 1963 is evident in the deterioration of Auden's morale. As their friend Vassily Yanovsky reflected, 'When Chester remained in Europe for good, Wystan quickly began to dry up.'

For years Auden's birthday each February had been celebrated with a party at St Marks Place at which his friends and Kallman's riotously congregated. With Kallman away in Athens, Auden lost heart to continue. The apartment became steadily less congenial to Auden and others. 'With Chester taking care of their domestic chores, the place seemed nice,' Yanovsky thought, 'but later it became really sad, hopeless.' By about 1966 Auden was superficially reconciled to Kallman's Athenian winters, although their annual separation was continuously depressing and he found living alone was an increasing strain. He struggled to accommodate himself to the change – 'A successful marriage represents the triumph of will over the immediate needs of the moment,' he wrote in 1969. 'Marriage has continually to be worked at' but the effort became too painful. For years he viewed life with ironic distance, but after 1963 irony became more elusive.

The other great feature of 1963 was the collaboration by Auden and Kallman in writing the libretto for Hans Werner Henze's opera, *The Bassarids*. The idea for the opera was Auden's. He wanted to develop the great and mysterious ideas embodied in Greek myths into a grand opera about the psychological origins of evil; the ambitiousness of his conception was wonderfully vindicated. By contrast his next most important libretto, for *The Rake's Progress*, seems less challenging, mainly because the opera was Stravinsky's idea inspired by Hogarth's unspectacular pictorial depiction of a commonplace morality tale. Auden and Kallman adapted the altogether uncommonplace story of Euripides' play, *The Bacchae*, the revenge tragedy which had been published in a critical text by Auden's friend E. R Dodds. Auden's father in a 1926 study of insanity as depicted in ancient Greek literature had praised Euripides 'as an acute psychological observer', shrewder than Sophocles on 'the psychology of sex-problems', who 'had he lived to the present day ... would have been an ardent disciple of Freud'. Auden and Kallman elaborated this psychology while constructing a more contemporary connection between divinity and humanity. In Auden's version the god Dionysus (son of Zeus by the dead Theban princess Semele) travels to Thebes, where his human grandfather Cadmus has abdicated his throne in favour of another grandson Pentheus, a repressed ascetic who is a version of a Mabel or the Utopian in 'Vespers'. Pentheus denies the divinity of his cousin Dionysus, orders his incarceration and the extirpation of the cult of Dionysus's mother Semele. Dionysus takes a terrible revenge by striking Pentheus' mother Agave and other Theban women with madness. They become Bacchantes, who join in the orgies of Dionysus. Pentheus has been a proud and unbending rationalist, but now breaks down and, wearing his mother's dress as a disguise, he goes to spy on the orgiastic rituals. After his trespass is spotted, a terrifying man-hunt ensues in the dark. His frenzied mother mistakes him for a lion and tears him to pieces. This plot with its theme of maternal destruction resembles the charade *Paid on Both Sides* written by Auden as early as 1928 or the doom of Ransom in *The Ascent of F6*. Interestingly Agave's behaviour after the death of Pentheus had been specified by Dr Auden as 'a rare appreciation of the re-integration of a split personality', and was analysed in detail in his article in the *Journal of Mental Science*; this scene in *The Bassarids* is Auden's finest achievement as a librettist. He and Kallman used ideas from both Christianity and Freudianism. Agave's mutilation of Pentheus' body is a metaphor for her castrating power as a mother. The fate of the Theban monarch and his people symbolises the terrible revenge taken by the sensual Dionysian aspect of human character if its existence is denied or its desires repressed. The conflict between Pentheus and Dionysus is between tense, repressive masculine intellect and passive, instinctual sensuality. The Bassarids themselves are familiar Audenesque figures of indifference:

> We heard nothing, we saw nothing.
> We took no part in her lawless frenzy,
> We had no share in his bloody death.

An effective touch by the librettists was to vest their characters in costumes of the historical eras that best represented their mentality. Pentheus is initially seen wearing monastic sackcloth; Tiresias, who has the religious flexibility of the vicar of Bray, appears as an Anglican archdeacon; Dionysus begins as a version of Dorian Gray and makes his apotheosis in the style of Beau Brummel in foppish red-silk and a stove-pipe hat; the Maenads resemble Left Bank waifs with 'hair à la Brigitte Bardot'; the Bacchants are beat poets in sandals, dirty dungarees and beards à la Ginsberg. *The Bassarids* is a story of passionate instincts destroying reason: the justice of its gods is arbitrary, vengeful and ruinous. It is the most powerful of the Auden–Kallman libretti, deriving its power from the searching ethical issues raised by Auden and the inspiration this gave him as a librettist. After the première at the Salzburg Festival in August 1966, the libretto was hailed in *The Times* as 'a beautifully constructed piece of writing, beautifully written, too, though often in more literary a manner than is ideal for setting to music'. Auden considered that Henze's composition made the opera a musical masterpiece.

Auden's approach to opera (fashioned under Kallman's influence) was unEnglish. In the 1940s and 1950s he had been sustained by the fine singers in American and Italian opera houses at a time when leading musicologists fashioning British operatic tastes were contemptuous of Italian composers, orchestras and singers. Robert Gittings wrote of Edward Sackville-West, the compiler of *The Record Guide* (1951) whom Auden had known as a young man, and his associates: 'The smug insularity of British taste in all its morbidity and self-satisfaction is only the cultural counterpart of the famous joke about the fog in the English Channel, which earned the newspaper headline: CONTINENT CUT-OFF BY FOG.' One London music critic, Desmond Shawe-Taylor, known to Auden and Kallman by the 'queen name' of Florence May, was notably unsympathetic to *The Bassarids*. 'As for Florence May,' Auden wrote to the music critic of the *Observer*, Peter Heyworth, after the reviews of the Salzburg première, 'she is jealous of our having made friends with you. I am convinced, I'm sorry to say – because it is a reflection on her as a critic – that, if Chester and I had been able to have drinks with her, during which she and Chester could have indulged in an orgy of opera-singer love, her review would have been different. The note of pique is too obvious.'

Kallman's abandonment of New York winters led Auden to resume his travels. He revisited Iceland in April 1964, and later that year agreed an arrangement whereby he avoided the misery of another winter in St Marks Place without Kallman. In the aftermath of John F. Kennedy's 'Ich bin ein Berliner' speech, the Ford Foundation was trying to establish a strong, non-communist cultural presence in the former German capital. As a result in September 1964 Auden went to live in Berlin for six months. He had mixed feelings about his return to Berlin. 'For the first time in my life,' he wrote to William Meredith, 'I feel like a rich man. The city has given me a bourgeois doll's house to live in – no guest room but *two* toilets and a TV.' But to his brother John he admitted that he found Berlin 'provincial' and felt 'a little lonely'. Shortly after his arrival he began keeping a journal. It was a resumption of his practice in Berlin thirty-five years earlier and, like its predecessor, formed a commentary on his current physical, psychological and spiritual interests. There are considerable divergences between the two journals. He showed a deep Christian bias in 1965, as when he mused 'perhaps Hell is a state of impotent hatred – to wish all other beings nothing but evil and at the same time to be incapable of doing them the slightest harm'. In other ways the later notebook is less rigorously argued, and his attempts to resume the Theophrastian verse-characters of the 1929 diary peter out dispiritedly. In places the 1965 journal indicates great weariness.

It was in Berlin that Auden met the musicologist Peter Heyworth, with whom he found a rich affinity. Heyworth joined the elect – Sheila and John Auden, and the Spenders – who acted as Auden's hosts on his London visits. He was perhaps the most forbearing of all, for he was an uncompromisingly fastidious man with an admiration for teutonic order who must have suffered greatly from Auden's filthy disorder. Auden, who liked Heyworth's German lover, took his advice on musical and business matters. Heyworth for example was shocked to find that Auden kept his savings lying in a non-interest-bearing bank account, and urged him to invest it more sensibly. 'Your old mother has at last taken your advice,' Auden wrote in December 1965. 'Three days ago she put thirty thousand dollars into an Investment Fund.' Heyworth also made sensitive and perceptive comments on the Salzburg production of *The Bassarids*. In 1969 Auden dedicated his new poetic collection, *City Without Walls*, to Heyworth with the couplet, 'At Twenty we find friends for ourselves, but it takes Heaven / To find us one when we are Fifty-Seven.'

In Berlin Auden had some tangles with the police. He was arrested for drunk driving, though the case was dismissed on 3 February. He picked up a 'steady' called Manfred whose wife appeared in a flurry at Auden's house early one morning in March. 'He was caught in a raid on a certain bar and discovered to have stolen something or other two years ago,' Auden reported to Fox. 'Your mother has saved him from jail at the expense of 700 DM.' It was of his involvement with men like Manfred that a few years later he wrote to a young New York friend, Robert Lederer,

'*Never* resort to sex in order to solve problems. It only complicates them. When one is "lonely" or "arserandy" one should either be chaste, or go with whores to whom one at least has something to give – i.e. money. The only proper time to have sex is when one is feeling happy and confident, for only then is one capable of giving as well as receiving.'

He recorded other sexual reflections around this time. In May 1965 Lord Arran initiated a British parliamentary debate on the decriminalisation of homosexuality which eventually led to the removal of the most oppressive features of the law in 1967. A great deal of nonsense was talked in the debates, both by bigots and by proponents of reform, who had to couch their arguments in unreal language. Auden felt tempted to intervene. 'As a homosexual nearing sixty years of age, I wish that the speakers on both sides knew more what they were talking about,' he wrote in a draft statement after the Arran debate. 'To begin with, they seem unaware that for over ninety-nine percent of us, it makes not the slightest difference, so far as our personal liberty is concerned, whether such a law be on the statute books or not.' He judged that 'the few who do get into trouble are either those with a taste for young boys – and I am surprised by how seldom they do – or those who cruise in public'. The pragmatic strategy of Arran and his supporters was to stress the separateness and freakish otherness of homosexuality. Auden disagreed. 'Most of the speakers seem under the illusion that only homosexuals, that is to say persons whose entire emotions are directed towards their own sex, commit homosexual acts. For anatomical, physiological & psychological reasons, male sexuality as such is playful, frivolous and impersonal. From experience I would say that there are few husbands under forty-five who, if the opportunity should exist, will not indulge in a homosexual diversion. At a queer Turkish baths, you will always see a number of wedding rings.'

One of his objections to the debate was its patronising insistence on the inherent misery of homosexuality. 'We are not nearly as unhappy as many people seem to think. Even those of us who believe that homosexual acts are sinful, cannot honestly say we feel guilty or remorseful, as one feels when one has been envious or angry or slothful.' Though these reflections were sensible, his poem 'Economics', written in Berlin in 1965 but published posthumously, in which he compared the rent boys of 'the Hungry Thirties', who sold their bodies for food, with those of 'the Affluent Sixties', who need to cover hire-purchase payments, was harsh and arguably foolish. He was becoming more relaxed about public descriptions of his own homosexuality: one sign of his disinhibition was his decision in 1965 to publish his poem 'Uncle Henry', written over thirty years earlier, about a lisping paederastic baronet travelling from Scotland to the Mediterranean in search of boys.

The most important episode during his stay in Berlin was the final illness of T. S. Eliot. 'Eliot's death has been sheer hell for me,' he wrote to his brother John on 11 January 1965. 'I feel like a professional ghoul.' He was interviewed by many journalists, and recorded an interview for BBC Radio Newsreel in which he spoke of Eliot in phrases resembling his earlier tribute to Charles Williams: 'To me the proof of a man's goodness is the effect he has upon others. So long as one was in Eliot's presence, one felt it was impossible to do or say anything base.' He harked upon this episode, which perhaps increased his own thoughts of mortality and his anxieties about the misuse of his work after his death. The press circus surrounding Eliot's death was an ugly presentiment of his own. He would have been deeply distressed, but not surprised, that on the morning that his death was announced in 1973 the BBC broadcast at breakfast-time a ghoulish radio interview with Isherwood, to whom the news had just been broken, sobbing about the loss of his oldest friend. Auden was later upset by the publication in 1971 of the drafts of *The Waste Land* because he felt a foreboding that his own drafts and revisions would inevitably be published in textual editions. 'Valerie Eliot didn't like having to publish the drafts, but, once they were discovered, she knew they would have to come out eventually – so she did it herself to ensure that it was done as well as possible,' he said in 1972. He was outraged by the presumption of the readers of the drafts and hated the inversion of values that might happen to his own poems posthumously. 'This sort of thing encourages amateurs to think, "Oh, look – I could have done as well." I think it shameful that people will spend more for a draft than for a completed poem.'

Though Kallman's decision in 1963 to leave New York City was the chief external event of Auden's last decade, it is in Berlin early in 1965 – coincidentally or otherwise after Eliot's death – that one sees a sudden deterioration. Auden had often recycled the same jokes or phrases in his letters, but it was in 1965 that his correspondence became more insistently and narrowly repetitive. Increasingly his letters to friends were written on the backs of carbon copies of his latest poems, which by the end of the decade were in certain moods the only messages he wished to give anyone. (Sometimes the poems were not carbons, but were typed specially for each recipient; this task was a way for him to improve details of the poems, which he found easier to do if treating them as messages to intimate friends.) Heavy ingestion of alcohol is likely to reach the brain faster in the case of a long-term amphetamine user, and can inflict more cerebral damage; Auden's premature fogeyness and grisly experience of ageing perhaps reflect this. His ageing became a complicated inner criterion of his ethical integrity and a penitential process in which he tried to atone for not being good enough for Kallman, or for his art, or for his God. 'I am now getting an old fogey,' he wrote in 1965 when he was only fifty-six. 'The sort of Old Age one gets is a test of whether one has lived one's life properly,' he told David Luke that same year. If he believed this, the increasing grimness of his life must at some moments have seemed retributive. He began to shut himself off: one symbol of the cordon he set around himself was his adoption, for no medical reason, of the habit of wearing very dark glasses even in winter or at night.

In 1965 too he began shrivelling as a prose-writer. For thirty-five years he had been a steady, sometimes brilliant commentator and critic. 'Much hard, ingenious, correct toil has gone into inconspicuous things: introductions, anthologies, translations,' Lowell wrote in 1967. 'When one looks at them closely, one is astonished at how well they have been done.' But in fact after his essays 'The Protestant Mystics' and 'Shakespeare's Sonnets' were published in 1964, nothing of great power or intellectual passion was written again, though his review (written in Berlin in 1965) of the memoirs of Evelyn Waugh and Leonard Woolf is semi-autobiographical and full of intriguing reflections. 'Auden's talk about himself,' Cleanth Brooks had said in 1957, 'is as good as it is because he knows so much about aesthetics and because he steadily maintains an interest in general problems.' But after 1965 his interest in general problems receded, and as a result his anthology of *Nineteenth Century Minor Poets* (published in 1966–7) or his 1967 T. S. Eliot lectures at the University of Kent, later published as *Secondary Worlds*, are slackly shaped. The reviews that he wrote in the 1970s are sterile. As he grew wearier, he reserved his energies for poetry and let the prose become more mechanical; without this choice, he could not have written his great poems of the late 1960s with all their technical and imaginative power.

'What Auden fears is an idolatry of taking literature too seriously,' two critics wrote in the *Sewanee Review* in 1964. Later that year there was a repellent public episode which must have heightened his fear. As early as 1944 Auden had dropped from 'September 1, 1939' the stanza which included his most famous line, 'We must love one another or die.' He explained that the line was a lie, for we must die anyway whether or not we love, which some of his critics thought was frivolous. 'Perhaps they prefer literature to tell lies: that way it frees itself from responsibility to the world of ethics, where lies have real and painful consequences,' his executor Edward Mendelson reflected later. Now during the US presidential election of 1964, when the incumbent Lyndon Johnson was publicly denouncing his opponent as a warmonger while privately planning to obliterate Vietnam by bombing, Johnson's campaign ran a television advertisement which caused such controversy that a still photograph from it was used on the front cover of *Time* magazine. The advertisement featured 'a little girl counting the petals of a flower, then interrupted her with a stern male voice counting down from ten to zero – when the little girl was abruptly replaced on the screen by a nuclear explosion. This left viewers rather shaken. Before they recovered, they heard Johnson's voice intoning, "These are the stakes: to make a world in which all of God's children can live, or go into the dark. We must love each other or we must die".' The dark, and possibly the children, as well as Johnson's misquotation, echo Auden's poem.

This was a shockingly offensive incident to which Auden never referred directly, though the degradation of his ideas clearly rankled. 'One cannot let one's name be associated with shits,' Auden wrote shortly afterwards to Stella Musulin. It was no wonder that after this Auden felt repelled by 'September 1, 1939', 'the most dishonest poem I have ever written', he told Naomi Mitchison: 'I pray to God that I shall never be memorable like that again.' The chief upshot of his rhetoric being enlisted in a Texan rascal's election campaign was a year later, in August and September 1965, when Auden prepared a new edition of his *Collected Shorter Poems* for publication. He deleted 'September 1, 1939' from the book and was severe with all his work from the 1930s, particularly those poems or phrases with potential political uses. He excised poems from the canon and revised the wording of those poems that survived. 'I am going through everything, revising, cutting, etc., a depressing boring job,' he wrote to Fox in August.

'I have no interest in my past.' In fact he was repudiating his past; understandably, for no one likes to be reminded of how unhappy, clumsy, opportunistic or foolish they were. 'I get more of the crotchety, ritualistic bachelor every day,' he reported again to Fox in September. 'God! how careless I used to be. I feel as if I am only just beginning to understand my craft. The revisions will be a gift to any anal-minded PhD student.' His tinkering often seems fussy, self-chastising and otiose; in this biography the texts as originally printed in book form are preferred, but if the stimulus for his revisions was Lyndon Johnson's manipulative propaganda, one can only sympathise with his motive. (He remained implacable in his hostility to Johnson. After being awarded the National Medal for Literature in 1967, he 'was at first worried by the reward, because I didn't want to receive it in the White House; on the other hand, I did not want to make a Cal Lowell gesture by a public refusal'.)

For all his repudiations, he did not discard his political concerns. 'Events could stir him deeply – with anguish, with apprehension and occasionally with pleasure,' the poet Emma Kann recollected of her visits to Kirchstetten. 'One of his strongest points was that he could feel so intensely about many questions and events in the fields of religion, politics, literature.... his reactions did not always point in the same direction but he was aware of his contradictions and saw in them one of the sources of his art.' He never ceased to be a political poet, even when his enemies thought he had become smug and dull, but from the 1940s he wanted to write about political power without allowing the possibility of contamination by modern political rhetoric. In the years after preparing his *Collected Shorter Poems*, he wrote a series of poems about power. He began in May 1966 with his unjustly neglected 'Partition', which is eloquent about the exercise of power without giving any inspiration to presidential slogan-makers and is one of his great historical poems. Back in July 1947 Sir Cyril Radcliffe, a barrister with no knowledge of India who had held a wartime post with the Orwellian title of Director General of Information, had been sent out by the British government to delineate the borders between the Hindu and Muslim populations of the Indian Empire, thus creating the separate states of India and Pakistan. He was given a few weeks to undertake this task. After the British granted self-rule to the Indian sub-continent, and enforced Radcliffe's scheme of partition in August 1947, there were mass migrations across the new frontiers and at least a million civilians were massacred. War and famine ensued. John Auden was working in India at the time, and discussed the management of partition both during Auden's visit to India in 1951 and on later occasions in the mid-1960s when they met in New York. 'You can't write a poem about Auschwitz; it's absolutely impossible,' Auden told an interviewer about the time that 'Partition' was written. 'The facts are too awful, too appalling.' But in 'Partition' he found an oblique way to write about power and the sacrifice of life by focusing on an individual who represented human, secular failure. Perhaps significantly Radcliffe in 1951 had given a notably intellectual series of Reith lectures broadcast by the BBC, entitled *The Problem of Power*, and their publication as a book in 1958 had provoked an unusually astringent public discussion on the ethics of power. The lawyer's necessary belief that life is a series of hard cases that one must put behind one was for Auden like a parable about the problem of power: indeed it resembled his own determination to have no interest in his past.

'Partition' is an elegant, spare, comfortless poem. The lawyer arrives in India and sets to work; his maps are obsolete, the census returns are incorrect and he has no time to inspect the contested frontiers. He is isolated from the people whose destiny he decides, for assassins are hunting him and the police guard him in a lonely house.

> But in seven weeks it was done, the frontiers decided,
> A continent for better or worse divided.

Never before or since has there been such an example of the administrators' faith in reason and detached analysis; an empire disembodied by a dry, intellectual lawyer working to a tight brief. Radcliffe was a scrupulous man, yet his appointment was a triumph of human fatalism and his report was a triumph of the arbitrary.

> The next day he sailed for England, where he quickly forgot
> The case, as a good lawyer must. Return he would not,
> Afraid, as he told his Club, that he might get shot.

The lawyer in 'Partition' like the tycoon in Auden's self-portrait 'A Household' lives in a lonely country mansion, and there are other resemblances between the Radcliffe figure and Auden: one is immersed in finicky legal details, the other in obscure metrical rules; it takes seven weeks for the lawyer to redraw the frontiers of a sub-continent, which is about the time Auden in 1965 had spent changing the landmarks in the private geography of his *Collected Shorter Poems*.

The likelihood that 'Partition' is a parable about Auden as well as about power is strengthened by the evidence of another rich, elegant, disenchanting poem: 'Rois Fainéants', written in 1968, ostensibly concerns the political impotence and public martyrdom of the Merovingian dynasty which ruled France from 511 to 751. It is another parable of power written with irony, and set in a distant epoch, but the episodes which it describes are seen by Auden as part of a universally significant pattern extending far in time and painful in its implications. By 1968 Auden had become an international celebrity on the poetry-reading circuit, and the fake kings of the poem's title are emblematic of the way that poets are treated under public power-systems that subdue dissent and enforce group unity. 'On High Feast-Days they were given a public airing,' Auden opens: the kings paraded, fêted and praised in a style and situation that really degraded. But after 'their special outing was ended, / Off they were packed again to their secluded manors' – cordoned off like Radcliffe in his lonely mansion – and were encouraged in self-destructive courses: 'supplied with plenty / Of beef and beer and girls from which, as was intended, they died young.' It is not only middle-aged poets who are victims of success: though 'Rois Fainéants' is set in ancient times, it is also immersed in the culture of the 1960s, as Auden heard it being lived on St Marks Place. The adulated, wild, doomed young men with 'their shoulder-length blond hair' represent not only chinless kings manipulated by palace officials but rockstars martyred by their recording companies, for it felt to Auden that the natural law of celebrity is a law of self-destruction.

There were other uncompromising political poems. In 'Epistle to a Godson' (1969) Auden signalled that although he had renounced his sloganising of the 1930s, he still felt horror at what he had called at the Icelandic whaling-station 'the cold controlled ferocity of the human species':

> tomorrow has us
> gallowed shitless: if what is to happen
> occurs according to what Thucydides
> defined as 'human', we've had it, are in for
> a disaster that no four-letter
> words will tarry.

The crucial verb in his description of humanity in 1969 is 'gallowed', which was not chosen casually. It is derived from 'to gally', meaning to frighten, used only by whale fishermen, who say that bull whales must be approached cautiously for they are easily gallied or gallowed. In 1969 he had not relinquished his vision from the Icelandic whaling-station in 1936, but he was writing about the human disaster in words that could not be easily abused.

BBC Television made a documentary film about Auden during the summer of 1965 which was broadcast in England on 28 November. It was 'quite well done', he told his brother Bernard. 'The editor seems to have been nicely discreet.... There was one moment when I lost my temper and said "For God's sake, dont ask such bloody silly questions".' The programme was well received by television critics, and full of familiar Auden axioms: 'A poet enchants for the purpose of disenchanting people with their illusions about themselves and the world.' He chided poetic pretensions in his familiar post-Caliban way: 'Art is small beer. The really serious things in life are earning one's living so as not to be a parasite, and loving one's neighbour.'

Auden had been lonely and restless in Berlin, and was somewhat unsettled and discontent at Kirchstetten during the summer of 1965; but it was in the winter of 1965–6 that his feelings for New York City became more hostile. He enjoyed the notorious power failure in November: 'a very extraordinary experience, especially as there was a full moon', he told his brother John. 'Aside from those who got trapped in subways and elevators, everyone enjoyed themselves.' Yet the deterioration of life in the city seemed to mirror the decline in his own life. 'We have a Subway and Bus strike,' he wrote on 2 January 1966. 'My kitchen roof leaks. Cockroaches abound. O New York!' From this time onwards 'as the years passed, Auden became more and more English', Musulin observed. 'The process annoyed Chester, who would expostulate at any sign of it.' Symptoms of his English nostalgia included his intense admiration for Ronald Blythe's *Akenfield* and a visit in July 1967 to his boyhood home. 'It was a traumatic experience for the city is so changed that I could hardly recognise anything,' he told his old Birmingham friend E. R. Dodds afterwards. 'I got into 42 Lordswood Road, now a midwives home, and wished I hadn't.' After Kallman left New York, Auden gradually became less receptive to American friendships. (The New York-based neurologist Oliver Sacks to whom he became close around 1969 was English-born.) He relied heavily on his supper each Friday evening with Orlan Fox, but there were no new American men of great emotional importance. 'Most Americans are bores,' he wrote to Peter Heyworth in 1967, 'but, when they are not, I find them remarkable.' Instead he forged new friendships with Englishmen like Heyworth and strengthened his contacts with older acquaintances. One of these was his publisher at Faber, Charles Monteith. In 1965 he agreed to support Monteith's sponsorship of Robert Lowell for the Oxford poetry professorship with characteristically sensible caution. 'His supporters should be aware, if they aren't already, that Cal has times when he has to go into the bin. The warning signals are three a) He announces that he is the *only* living poet b) a romantic and usually platonic attraction to a young girl and c) he gives a huge party.' Faber paid Auden the unusually high royalty of 15 per cent partly for the prestige of publishing him, but perhaps also because he was 'the perfect author' from a publisher's point of view: 'deadlines were met, proofs were returned on time, letters were answered by return post'.

In 1965–6 Auden wrote a number of short, elliptical verses cumulatively entitled 'Profile' which form his closest self-portrait apart from 'A Household'. He recognised himself as dogmatic:

> In his cups neither savage nor maudlin,
> but all too prone
> to hold forth.

People's perceptions of this phenomenon varied. 'His strongly affirmed opinions – as startling as they were strong' were 'usually conveyed with a glint of conscious naughtiness', according to Coghill. David Jones, who met Auden late in their lives at the Spenders', commented, 'both times Auden talked interestingly but without let-up. When someone else was talking Auden was preparing remarks.' Perhaps he misbehaved particularly in front of Spender, for he was by no means always a conversational bully. John Bridgen, a young curate interested in becoming a psychoanalyst, who spent two hours talking to him in October 1971, found him breathless and weary, 'but I did get an impression of a man who was lovably good as well as great. He had been patient with me, answered my questions carefully and listened intently to all I told him, spicing the conversation with jokes.' As late as 1972, when he is usually depicted as a ruined bore, a young American called Michael Newman found 'his conversation was droll, intelligent and courtly, a sort of humanistic global gossip, disinterested in the machinations of ambition'. Auden could seem (to himself and others) like a spoiled brat testing how much he could get away with:

> The way he dresses
> reveals an angry baby,
> howling to be dressed.

But the anger is that of a prematurely ageing man accused by pain.

The most distressing account of him is perhaps that of Hannah Arendt. They were never intimate friends, but she saw much of him after 1958. In the following year he reviewed Arendt's *The Human Condition* for Spender's magazine *Encounter*. 'Every now and then,' he announced, 'I come across a book that gives me the impression of having been especially written for me.... it seems to answer precisely those questions which I have been putting to myself.' He wrote to her and telephoned about the book, and tried to initiate a friendship by inviting her to his birthday party in February 1960. He afterwards often visited the apartment where she lived with Heinrich Blücher, 'talking and staying so long that a dinner invitation was usually extended'. She visited his place only once, 'for a dinner party to which T. S. Eliot and an odd assortment of Auden's young friends had come'; but she 'mothered him – once taking him off to Saks and forcing him to buy a second suit'. She admired him deeply, thought him capable of many forms of perfection, but came to regard his life as, in many ways, abysmal.

Auden deteriorated markedly between her first sight of him at a publisher's party in the late 1940s and the beginning of their friendship. 'I would not have recognised him more than ten years later, for now his face was marked with those famous deep wrinkles as if life itself had delineated a kind of face-scape to make manifest the "heart's invisible furies".' She was dismayed by his pain. 'Time and again, when to all appearances he could not cope any more, when his slum apartment was so cold that the water no longer functioned and he had to use the toilet in the liquor store at the corner, when his suit ... was covered with spots or worn so thin that his trousers would suddenly split from top to bottom, in brief, whenever disaster hit before your very eyes, he would begin to kind of intone an

utterly idiosyncratic, absurdly eccentric version of "count your bles-
sings".' For a time she thought the squalor was the eccentricity of genius.
'I finally saw the misery, somehow realized vaguely his compelling need to
hide it behind the "count-your-blessings" litany, and still found it difficult
to understand fully what made him so miserable, so unable to do anything
about the absurd circumstances that made everyday life so unbearable for
him.'

Frederic Prokosch has summarised a conversation that represents
Arendt's position, though it may not be accurate in every word: Prokosch
was both a fabulist and an admirer whom Auden had spurned. 'I love
Wystan,' Prokosch reports her as saying.

> Wystan is hideously entangled and yet he longs for the simple
> certainties. He feasts on all the varieties of unreciprocated love, or
> call it, if you wish, unreciprocatable love, and he ends by growing
> ever more dissolute and alcoholic as simultaneously he grows more
> didactic and avuncular. He tries to reconcile the two with a kind of
> spiritual masochism but of course it doesn't work…. He has
> contrived it so that only the unreciprocated love has a zest for him.
> The pain becomes an addiction just as heroin becomes an
> addiction…. He has sunk into this *nostalgie de la boue* and he isn't the
> only one, there are thousands of others in this devastating city.

The collection of Auden's recent poetry published under the title of
About the House by Random House in July 1965 and by Faber in January
1966 was more vigorous than *Homage to Clio*, but nevertheless had a
lukewarm reception. 'Rather disappointing to read altogether – a kind of
determined coyness about the indignities and comforts of old age (a little
early, I think),' judged Elizabeth Bishop, though she liked the poem to
MacNeice, 'Cave of Making', and some others. The richness of the
language and metrical structure in this new book was conceded by English
reviewers, though few of them were excited. 'Being civilised is still for Mr
Auden a matter of fixing a reproving, saddened, faintly scoffing eye upon
the apes, on history, on other people's funny ways – and at this level his
touch is as certain and as surprising as of old – but most of all it here
requires civility,' declared the reviewer in the *Times Literary Supplement*,
before concluding that it was a 'disappointing, trivial volume'.

Auden's sixtieth birthday in February 1967 was marked in several ways.

Geoffrey Grigson wrote a poem, 'To Wystan Auden'. Spender and Edmund Wilson wrote alternate lines in another poetic tribute. Lowell praised him in *Shenandoah*: 'Auden's work and career are like no one else's, and have helped us all. He has been very responsible and ambitious, constantly writing deeply on the big subjects, and yet keeping something wayward, eccentric, idiosyncratic, charming, and his own.' The public impression that Auden made at this time was similarly idiosyncratic. In October 1967 he gave the T. S. Eliot lectures at the University of Kent. 'At Canterbury his demeanour was unbending, his delivery unvaried; the script contained some dry jokes and little explosions of temper,' wrote Frank Kermode. 'He stood rock-like, paid his dues to Eliot and read his pieces.'

A few months earlier, in July, he attended the first Poetry International in London. This gathering, which appealed to his love of carnival, became an important feature of his last years. It was directed by Ted Hughes and Patrick Garland, with much of the organisation undertaken by an Australian, Charles Osborne, 'young, choleric, excitable and with a spectacular gift for insult which he indulged to the full', who developed a heartfelt admiration for Auden and wrote a biography of him published in the USA and Britain in 1979–80. The festival in 1967 attracted an impressive pride of poets in addition to Auden: Neruda, Ungaretti, Berryman, Graves, Olsen, Ginsberg, Sexton, Empson and Spender. 'The tone of the evening was to be reverential,' the *Guardian* reported. 'As soon as W. H. Auden began, the audience, of more than 1,000, was rapt. He explained that it might help us to know that the odd lines ended in dactyls, and then recited a little piece about his house in Austria, for his friend Louis MacNeice' – this was 'The Cave of Making', whose importance Elizabeth Bishop had spotted. After an outburst of applause, Malcolm Muggeridge walked over and, taking him by the shoulders, incited him to recite 'Fleet Visit', which is ostensibly about the American fleet in Naples but reaches its climax in praise not of the sailors but of the design of their killing machines. Auden and Neruda were the great successes of the evening, although the Englishman was unimpressed by his rival, as he teasingly told Orlan Fox. 'There were some poets, notably Neruda, who obviously never were at a British Public School, and wouldnt stop reading his not very good poetry. Anne Sexton read an acutely embarrassing poem about her attempted suicide and losing her baby.' Auden's displeasure with Sexton was manifest. 'While she was reading one of her dreadful confessional pieces, Anne Sexton was audibly heckled from the stage by Auden,' Osborne wrote. 'Wystan was rude to her because he found her poems boring ("Who the hell cares about Anne Sexton's grandmother?") and because she read them for about twice as long as we had asked her to.' Backstage afterwards, he reduced her to tears.

Auden was too harsh on Sexton, but agonised confessional poetry had always repelled him, and by the late 1960s it was clear that this repulsion was the source of great poetic and personal strength. 'W. H. Auden is the rarest kind of poet in a post-romantic age: interested not in himself but in the plural aspects and manifestations of the world which he turns into his art; interested in people and animals as in ideas and landscapes, rivers, buildings, metres, histories, coigns and quirk,' John Bayley wrote in 1969. 'All this is rare in an age in which even reportage can become a sort of self-caress (witness Norman Mailer's pieces on the Moonshot).' Shortly afterwards Auden told J. I. M. Stewart 'that he could recall absolutely nothing disagreeable that had ever happened to him. Although he had much trafficked with Freud in his time he rejected the notion that there was anything insalubrious of this suppressing of painful experience.... it was, he believed, one of nature's better ideas.' Despite his rudeness to Sexton, Auden became the 'mascot' of the Poetry International, and returned every year, even when he was not invited. He enjoyed the festivals and relished judging other poets. 'The only disaster,' he reported of the 1969 festival, 'Mr Robert Bly – who wore a shepherd's blanket, and recited Protest Poetry of an appalling badness.'

His successes at the Poetry Festival cheered him. After 'The Platonic Blow' was published without authorisation by *Fuck You* magazine, he admitted, 'in depressed moods I feel it is the *only* poem by me which the Hippies have read'. He admired the Flower People on St Marks Place for trying 'to revive the spirit of Carnival' but was 'afraid that when they renounce work entirely, the fun turns ugly'. He wailed to Coghill, '*why* O why will the young be so formless?' Cultural nihilism and personal annihilation scared him. He became more keenly and reiteratively obsessed with the decay of language and the formless use of words as his own body decayed, for by the age of sixty there was something palpably wrong with his body and his health. The corruption of language 'terrifies me', he said in 1972. 'I try by my personal example to fight it; and I say it's a poet's role to maintain the sacredness of language.' The integrity of language, he recognised like Orwell, was an indispensable part of political decency. When the troops of the Soviet ogre crushed Czechoslovakian independence in 1968, he wrote:

> one prize is beyond his reach,
> The Ogre cannot master Speech:
> About a subjugated plain,
> Among its desperate and slain,
> The Ogre stalks with hand on hips,
> While drivel gushes from his lips.

That same year, in 'Ode to Terminus', describing 'this world our colossal immodesty / has plundered and poisoned', he warned how easily the human mind, 'discarding rhythm, punctuation, metaphor, / sinks into a drivelling monologue, / too literal to see a joke or / distinguish a penis from a pencil'.

As to the mass dissent and madness of the United States under Johnson and Nixon, he wrote to the *New York Times* on 12 March 1968, 'If we withdraw from Vietnam, thereby admitting military defeat, we must expect very ugly troubles at home from embittered chauvinists, both military and civilian.' He seems to have envisaged a violent campaign such as French die-hards had amounted during the French withdrawal from Algeria a few years earlier. 'Withdrawal from Vietnam may, or almost certainly will, mean civil conflict at home, but at least we shall know what we are fighting about.' He wrote to Dodds on the following day, 'Vietnam is ghastly. If Rockefeller is nominated, I shall vote for him; if the choice is between Johnson and Nixon, I don't see how one can vote at all.' He suddenly felt that he had aged. 'This year, for the *first* time,' he wrote to Stern on 13 March 1968, 'I notice, with some shock, that most of the people on the street are my juniors.' His seniority was overpowering. Yet for all his love of routine he could not eliminate the accidental. First he fractured his shoulder when his car hit a telegraph pole in May 1968. 'What worries me most is that, since the accident, I have been constipated – I who was always the most regular of men.' Kallman had been complaining for some time of 'incessant fatigue', and in the summer of 1968 developed a numbness in his limbs known as peripheral neuritis, which was discreetly attributed to a tick-bite although the usual cause is alcohol.

A few months later he was dealt a knock-out blow. On 13 December 1968, near Vienna, while Boras was driving Auden's car back from Greece to Austria, he stopped at a red light and was rammed from behind by a truck whose driver was drunk and unlicensed. Boras, aged only twenty-six, was killed. Kallman was heartbroken, and his life took a steadily downward spiral. His long elegy to Boras, of which the following extract is typical, gives a sense of his pain:

> How, darling, this incontinent grief
> Must irk you, more
> Even than those outraged, mute
> Or pleading jealousies, though now
> This you are too pitiless to refute,
> Making me all you disapprove:
> Selfishly sodden, selfless, dirtier, a prodigal
> Discredit to our renewed belief in love.

Auden said of Kallman the following April, 'I don't know how he's going to get through the summer.' Kallman's private hell must have agonised Auden, who wrote to Coghill in 1968, 'If there are any souls in Hell, then, like alcoholics or terminal drug addicts, that is where they insist on being.' By 1971 Kallman had become neglectful of keeping in contact with Auden during their winter separation, even though Auden continued to remit him money. His friend Kosta was 'irritating, cold, distant', he complained to Fox in 1972, 'and too many of the other jolly companions suddenly turned demanding and/or THIEVISH. All too wearing.'

Auden had apparently been suffering since early manhood from Touraine-Solente-Gole syndrome in which the skin of the forehead, face, scalp, hands and feet becomes thick and furrowed and peripheral periostitis in the bones reduces the patient's capacity for activity. There was no therapy for the syndrome, which does not affect either life expectancy or mental status, but which accounted for Auden's striking appearance of grave, lined melancholy. For many years he had depended for both friendship and medical advice on a physician named David Protetch, whom he had first met at Ann Arbor. (It was Protetch who provided the LSD on the one occasion when Auden decided to test the effects of that hallucinogenic, and he in turn used Auden as a sexual confidant.) Protetch knew himself to be mortally ill – mistreatment of his diabetes resulted in cancer of the pituitary which killed him aged forty-six

– and his life took a somewhat desperate turn. In the late 1960s 'David was well on the way to *total* insanity, diabetic debilitation – and pretty deep into hard drugs besides,' another Protetch patient later wrote to Kallman. 'He was incapable of accurate diagnosis by that time – and I simply cannot go into the horror of my experiences with him in the last two years.' After Protetch's death in May 1969, Auden mourned him in 'The Art of Healing':

> For my small ailments,
> You, who were mortally sick,
>   prescribed with success:
>   my major vices,
> my mad addictions, you left
>   to my conscience.

The elegy to Protetch was the first of a sequence of poems in which Auden teased the theme of bodily decay. In the same month Auden wrote 'A New Year Greeting', dedicated to another medical friend whom he sometimes consulted after Protetch's death, Vassily Yanovsky. It is an oddly charming poem in which Auden, speaking as a warm, friendly host, addresses the yeasts, bacteria and viruses who visit his body. There is a snug comfort about Auden's existence but he ends by warning,

> sooner or later, will dawn
> A Day of Apocalypse, when my mantle suddenly turns
> too cold, too rancid, for you,
> appetising to predators
> of a fiercer sort, and I
> am stripped of excuse and nimbus,
> a Past, subject to Judgement.

He followed this in 1970 with a poem to his Kirchstetten physician, 'Lines to Dr Walter Birk on his retiring from general practice', celebrating the natural routine of the seasons ('When summer plumps again, our usual sparrows / will phip in the eaves of the patulous chestnuts') and the serenity of retirement: 'it is genuine in age to be / happily selfish'. Finally in 1971 he wrote 'Talking to Myself', dedicated to the New York physician Oliver Sacks and addressed to his own body: 'You can serve me as my emblem for the Cosmos.'

During 1969 he worked with Kallman on a libretto of *Love's Labour's*

Lost with music by Nicolas Nabokov. It was not performed until the year of Auden's death, and has not survived in the operatic repertoire (although for Auden specialists the libretto has much of interest). Auden also collaborated that year with Paul Taylor and Peter Salus in preparing a modern English text of *The Elder Edda*, a collection made in about AD 1200 of old Icelandic poems on cosmogony, mythology and epic heroes and dedicated by Auden to Tolkien. His great stroke among the reviewers was the publication by Faber in September 1969 of Auden's latest collection of his own poems, *City Without Walls* (Random House published in January 1970). The critical reception from his fellow poets was especially gratifying. 'This is a marvellous collection,' declared Roy Fuller, who judged that Auden's syllabic metres and alliterative verse were of the highest virtuosity and that he had proved himself 'a great comic poet'. The collection was a mixture of major works for the canon, like the title poem, 'Joseph Weinheber', 'Rois Fainéants', 'Partition' and 'Ode to Terminus'; occasional poems like that marking the Soviet invasion of Czechoslovakia 'August, 1968'; songs for a production of Brecht's *Mother Courage* at the National Theatre in London; short verses resembling abbreviations of Theophrastus' *Characters*; and commissioned texts. The Brechtian ballads have an air of simplicity concealing not only immense metrical sophistication, but an ethical seriousness and ambition that is easily overlooked. 'The tone, the trivialities, must be accepted, for out of all that comes the triumph of Auden's celebration of happiness in an age (and at an age) when everything militates against it,' Fuller concluded. 'There is nothing in the slightest degree false in his stream of praise of friendship, of bodily pleasures, of art and nature, and the praise is securely underwritten by his constant, wry consciousness of what in the way, say, of political involvement or aesthetic desperation is, like the picnic thunder, just outside his immediate business.' Peter Porter (who emerged in the 1960s as one of Auden's wisest readers) also enthused about *City Without Walls*. 'In the nonce words, the Sargasso sounds, the Jamesian syntax, the refusal to be simple-minded, there is an astonishing amount of nature, a nearly flawless knack at getting things right. Stravinsky says we should worship God with a little art if we have any. In the best poems of *City Without Walls*, the art concerned is prodigious.' Geoffrey Grigson wrote a poem in praise of the book:

We elderly wake in the night,

> Say by your rhythm,
> *I am glad to be living.*

Another success followed in 1970 with the publication of *A Certain World*. 'One of his most important books, and as one gets into it his presence is directly felt, as if he had come to stay for a weekend,' Cyril Connolly judged. 'I can hear his very voice and very sentences as I read *A Certain World*,' confirmed a later friend, Peter Walker. Auden described the book as 'a map' of his 'personal planet'. It is an extended autobiographical cypher: many of its entries providing explanations of Auden's life and ideas. His interest in landscape is well known; but he also laid clues to his interests in, for example, autism, castration and violence. Biographically it is one of his most significant works. The section on 'Enchantment' contains one aphorism from Hugo von Hofmannsthal, and nine maxims from Auden himself reflecting his beliefs after Kallman had settled in Athens: 'All true enchantments fade in time. Sooner or later we must walk alone in faith. When this happens, we are tempted, either to deny our vision, to say that it must have been an illusion and, in consequence, grow hardhearted and cynical, or to make futile attempts to recover our vision by force, i.e. by alcohol or drugs.' (Had he been younger, he suggested in 1971, he 'might well have mischiefed' himself injecting drugs.)

Around 1970 Auden contemplated publishing a collection of his essays and reviews but was deterred by the difficulty of remembering what he had written. In the event he delegated the task of selection to a young instructor at Yale, Edward Mendelson, who had a stack of xeroxes of Auden's uncollected prose writings. Together they settled on the pieces to be reprinted. One sign of Auden's qualities is recalled by Mendelson. 'He asked me why I didn't include his essay on Romeo and Juliet, and I simply shook my head no, as a slightly nervous way of saying I didn't think it equalled the rest. At this, he beamed at me, and I realized he was delighted that I didn't think everything he wrote was worthy to be engraved in gold.' At Kallman's prompting, Auden appointed Mendelson as his literary executor in the spring of 1972. This selection covering the period since 1943 was published by Random House and then Faber in 1973 under the title *Forewords and Afterwords*. The book gives an exciting sense of his interests and beliefs, rather in the manner of *A Certain World*, and has much of the argumentative strength of *The Dyer's Hand*. Though Auden often in these reviews commented on writers' emotional lives, it was not in the small-minded, excitable tones of a gossip columnist. As the *New York Review of Books* commented, 'Mr Auden is not primarily interested in the *bricolage* of a man's life but in ideas which become experience when they are interrogated: the interrogation must be conducted with zest but also with a sense of propriety.'

During 1969 Auden hinted that he would like to return to Christ Church on the same basis that E. M. Forster had been provided with a set of rooms at King's College, Cambridge since 1946. He became keener in the pursuit of this idea after Orlan Fox had gently rejected his suggestion that they should share an apartment in New York, and Hannah Arendt firmly declined his proposal of marriage in November 1970. She was aghast when, about three weeks after the death of her husband, Auden arrived at her apartment 'looking so much like a *clochard*' that the building's doorman accompanied him to her door. Erika Mann's death a year earlier in 1969 had freed Auden to marry. He 'said he had come to New York only because of me', Arendt wrote on 20 November, 'that I was of great importance to him, that he loved me very much'. She rejected his proposal. 'I am almost beside myself when I think of the whole matter,' she told Mary McCarthy. 'I hate, am afraid of pity ... and I think I never knew anyone who aroused my pity to this extent.' The intrusiveness of his declaration so soon after Arendt had been widowed and the plaintive desperation with which he spoke are equally shocking. Arendt, like Fox, was anguished when Auden died in 1973, and indeed had less public composure than after her husband's death. 'I am still thinking of Wystan ... and of the misery of his life, and that I refused to take care of him when he came and asked for shelter.'

Yet Arendt and Fox, who both loved Auden in different ways, realised that he would be impossible to live with: touchy, demanding, tyrannical, disruptive. Years earlier Dr Auden had boasted to a granddaughter that he had once caught one of his own farts in a bottle, and Auden as he grew older tended to dwell on similar topics. 'Wystan back from tour,' Vassily Yanovsky, whom Auden had known since the end of the war, noted in his diary in 1971. 'Unpleasant.... Spoke about peeing in the bathtub, farting – could imagine a couple communicating in this way, picking one's nose, eating snot ("delicious"). Something is falling apart in this huge clay body.' Auden seems to have considered his excretory interests as an alternative to talking to himself: 'Finding Echo repelient, / Narcissus ate his snot, / Pee'd in his bath.' This conversational mannerism was to prove disastrous when, having been rejected in his suits first to a man and then to a woman, he somewhat desperately wooed an institution, his old college, Christ Church. He was delighted to receive an honorary degree from Oxford in 1971, writing to Michael Newman, 'Oxford was fun as I liked Heath, the Prime Minister, very much.' In December Auden had an attack of vertigo, about which he consulted both Yanovsky and Sacks. He began worrying that he would have a coronary, and that his body would lie unfound for days; so it came as an intense relief when in January 1972, chiefly at David Luke's instigation, Christ Church offered him a tenancy of a cottage in its grounds known as the Brewhouse. It is to that college's credit that it took him in when no one else would. His preparations to leave New York City were immediate.

He had exhausted many old friendships. He was still receptive and generous with young people – a collection by the young black poet N. J. Loftis published in 1973 by Black Market Press was dedicated 'To my first friend, W. H. Auden' – but despaired among his contemporaries, particularly after he had begun drinking in the evening. It was as if his life had come to resemble Proust's final volume, *Le Temps Retrouvé*, in which the narrator and his surviving contemporaries, all horribly aged, gather for a last round of parties: 'a frightening book', he said, 'because all those people, not excepting the I, are in Hell, and don't know it'. It was a Proustian hell when, on 21 February 1972, shortly after the announcement of Auden's proposed return to Oxford, Random House held a party in the private rooms of a New York restaurant to celebrate his sixty-fifth birthday. 'Wystan not really drunk but dead (first dead, and then, to disguise it, drunk),' Yanovsky noted in his diary. 'We all, despite the champagne, feel as if at a funeral ... Nothing could overcome this deadly frost around him. He is going away (and not simply to Oxford).'

Around this time Auden heard from friends at the *New York Review of Books* about Robert Lowell's latest poetic collection, *The Dolphin*, which had not yet been published. (Kallman joked that Berryman, before jumping to his death from a bridge over the Mississippi in January that year, had left a suicide note saying only, 'Your move, Cal.') *The Dolphin* was a searing poetic account of the break-up of Lowell's marriage to Elizabeth Hardwick and the birth of his son Sheridan Lowell by Caroline

Blackwood. Lowell included in the book versified versions of Hardwick's letters to him during their marital crisis, using them without her consent and in a way that was humiliating. This seemed unforgivable to Auden, who hated the way, as he wrote in 1969, 'the ochlocratic media, / joint with under-the-dryer gossip, / process and vent without intermission / all today's ugly secrets'. In March he told a friend of Lowell that he would no longer speaken to Cal because of his indiscretion. When the friend retorted that 'he sounded like God the Father', Auden merely 'gave ... a tight smile'. Lowell was 'astounded' by Auden's insult. 'I think he's not a snubber and has never stopped talking to anyone, except Rudolph Bing, even then I think it was the Met he stopped talking to,' Lowell complained. But by March 1972 Auden was stopping talking, moving towards a frontier of silence. He made a last visit to the Kronenbergers in Boston, with whom he had stayed for years: hitherto always 'jolly sessions given to anecdotes, to jokes, to unmalicious gossip, to trading childhood experiences and amusements'; but this time 'Wystan lacked his usual animation and often showed no interest.'

His valediction to New York City ('not simply a Metropolis: it is also a city of Neighborhoods') was published on 18 March in the *New York Times*. 'Whoever invented the myth that America is a Melting Pot?' he demanded. 'It is nothing of the kind and, as a lover of diversity, I say thank God. The Poles, the Ukrainians, the Italians, the Jews, the Puerto Ricans, who are my neighbors, may not be the same as they would be in another country, but they keep their own characteristics. It is a neighborhood of small shops where they know one another personally, and how nice they have all been to this Wasp! Let me take this opportunity to thank in particular Abe and his co-workers in the liquor store, Abe the tobacconist, On Lok my laundryman, Joseph, Bernard and Maurice in the grocery store at Ninth and Second Avenue, Harold the druggist, John my mailman, Francy from whom I buy my newspaper and Charles from whom I buy seeds.' The packing up of his flat, and the dispersal of its belongings, was a tense, unhappy business; and his departure for Europe on 15 April was a sad, desperate leave-taking for his closest New York friends like Fox and Sacks.

Once in Europe there was a respite to his pain. 'Wystan, I'm happy to say, is relaxed and pleasant again,' Kallman wrote on 22 May to Fox, 'after the rather hair-raising tension he imposed on everyone near him in New

York, me especially.' Still he was in poor shape. During the summer he spent an evening with Larkin. 'I thought he seemed pretty broken up, & agreed with hardly anything he said, though he tried to be nice,' Larkin reported. In September he returned briefly to New York to complete his packing, and on 30 September left the United States for the last time. He was seen off at the airport by Orlan Fox and the Yanovskys: 'On our way back, the three of us felt as if we were returning from a funeral,' Vassily Yanovsky noted.

When he reached Oxford, the Brewhouse was not ready for occupation, and Charles Monteith of Faber, who was a fellow of All Soul's, arranged for Auden to stay at his college for a few weeks. He was euphoric at arriving in Oxford, but was denuded of his good spirits two days later when he was robbed in his rooms. The youth whom he accused of the crime – a labourer called Keith Tilley – was acquitted at Oxford Crown Court in January. As the *Sun* reported, 'Poet W. H. Auden went to court yesterday, unshaven and wearing carpet slippers, and told of the night he gave a man a £50 cheque after listening to a hard luck story. But two hours later, the man burgled his rooms and stole his wallet, £50 cash and an IOU, he claimed.' The incident depressed and shocked him; it was widely assumed in the university that Auden had been unlucky in his choice of rough trade, although he denied any sexual element in his contact with Tilley. 'He was quite blameless in the matter, except in being too Christian and too confiding,' as Rowse admitted, 'but it was a bad start ... and it was an ill omen.'

In October 1972 his new poetic *Epistle to a Godson* was published by Faber. 'What we have now is a public Auden who is gently conservative,' wrote Philip Toynbee, 'impeccably good humoured and kindly, yet sceptical, caustic, teasing and epigrammatic.' Toynbee thought Auden's taste for neologisms odd in an opponent of liturgical reform, and saw no public indulgence of private pain 'These are the poems of a man who has aged well: their most obvious quality is wisdom ... though his frequent teasing of the silly-young is never violent or vicious, it carries plenty of punch.'

The Brewhouse, in which Auden settled, was a little stone cottage which had not previously been inhabited. It had a complicated jutting roof and abutted on to a pretty little garden – both features that delighted Auden and increased his gratitude for his new home. But his immediate surroundings were neither large nor sumptuous. His front door was reached by metal stairs set among ugly sheds; the ground floor of the Brewhouse comprised vacant storerooms (in one of which Kallman stayed for a few nights). To reach his quarters, Auden had to mount a staircase at the top of which his bedroom was on the right and a small sitting room on the left, with the connecting corridor divided by hardboard partitions into a bathroom, lavatory and (what it would have pained Auden to hear called) a kitchenette. In bright weather these rooms were pretty, but in dark seasons they could be oppressively glum (although Auden since adolescence had liked to work with the curtains closed against the daylight of the outside world).

Oxford had changed immeasurably for the worse since the 1950s. When he had been Professor of Poetry he had enjoyed the convivial amenities of the Common Room, a semi-ceremonial after-dinner gathering of the Christ Church dons; but in the intervening years the sense of a clerisy had receded in Oxford and senior members of the college seldom tarried after the meal. Sometimes in 1972–3 he was the only person drinking port or brandy in the Common Room after dinner. 'Who on earth invented the silly convention that it is boring or impolite to talk shop?' he had demanded in *A Certain World*. 'Nothing is more interesting to listen to, especially if the shop is not one's own.' But it was generally considered bad form to talk shop in the Common Room, and his efforts in this direction were usually rebuffed: a young research lecturer called Roger Mallion, who was willing to talk science with him, gave him some rare moments of intellectual pleasure in these months. He made a new but not intimate friendship with the then Canon of Christ Church, Peter Walker, who found him 'a husk of a great man' but still with much to respect and admire: 'battered, rather tired, more sick, I suppose, than anyone knew'. Initially at Christ Church he tried to pitch his conversation to his companions, so that with Walker he played 'the theological gambit, whether Grace at dinner, or the Purgatory game of placing incompatibles next to each other for the duration – who would go with Simone Weil?' There was a great mutual sympathy between Auden and David Luke, and another Christ Church don with whom he retained a rapport was the novelist J. I. M. Stewart. But there was also unfriendliness partly provoked by his insistence on a routine that his New York friends had only narrowly tolerated. 'You can make something neurotic of his "ritualistic" obsession with time, but the amount it let him write in his lifetime remains, and he knew, no doubt, that time was not on his side,' Walker felt.

He was very soon depressed, and spent Christmas sozzled with vodka at the Sterns' Wiltshire house (Sonia Orwell was the other guest). It was a sad, awkward occasion for the Sterns, which Auden characteristically turned into a cause of celebration in his poem 'Thank You, Fog' of May 1973. He felt more than ever cut off from those he really loved. He was 'very worried' and hurt to receive no message from Kallman on his birthday in February. 'After having seen you, I wonder if this means that you are seriously ill.' Kallman did not reply, and Auden beseeched in March, 'Dearest Chester, *Please* let me know how you are.' Kallman briefly visited Christ Church, where to Roger Mallion he seemed 'diffident' in behaviour and conversation, and was treated 'nannyishly' by Auden.

Admiral Richard Byrd, describing Antarctic explorers camped together on the polar ice-cap, wrote: 'The time came when one has nothing to reveal to the other; when even his unformed thoughts can be anticipated, his pet ideas become a meaningless drool.... There is no escape anywhere. You are hemmed in on every side by your inadequacies and the crowding pressure of your associates.' Glaciers and icy fjords had all Auden's life been part of his poetic landscape; but now, in his last year of life, he found himself in an Antarctic camp of his own devising called the Christ Church Common Room. His meaningless drool was usually excretory or sexual. 'Look here, if Auden wants to drink himself to death, please could you ask him to do so in the Brewhouse and not in the Common Room,' one senior colleague implored David Luke. Representations were made to him that he was boring the Common Room with his scatalogical repetitions. Auden was mortified by these objections and particularly by the imputation that he did not know how to behave among gentlemen. He became 'markedly depressed', as Oliver Sacks judged, 'so much so that he wrote scarcely any letters'. David El-Kabir (a distinguished physician and discriminating musician whom Auden would previously have found fascinating) sat next to him at one Oxford dinner, and met him on other occasions. He found him 'closed up, utterly uncommunicative' and 'very disappointing'. When Yanovsky in 1972 telephoned with an anecdote of Turgenev at Oxford, Auden snapped, 'That's of no interest to me.' Yanovsky reflected, 'he was very much engrossed in something far away and could not be reached anymore'. Another example of snubbing occurred when Auden gave a reading at the University Theatre in Newcastle-upon-Tyne on 17 December. The organisers arranged that he should be taken on a tour of the cultural amenities, but he wanted to skulk in his hotel bedroom. One of the people brought in to entertain him was a very agreeable local author, Sid Chaplin, who had begun work as a coalminer at the age of fifteen. They were introduced, but when Chaplin ventured some polite remark, Auden demanded to know who he was. Chaplin repeated his name, and said apologetically that he wrote. 'Oh I see,' replied Auden witheringly, 'a *regional* author.' His victim did not open his mouth again. This was the unkindness of someone who was both miserable and ill. At the end he was losing what Coghill had admired all Auden's adult life, 'that formidable charity of heart'.

It was painful for his old friends to see a clear intelligence waver. 'I don't think the move to Oxford has had a good result; he seems to be lonely there apart from the free high table meals; and he is getting more and more irrational about money,' Auden's great friend Geoffrey Gorer wrote in an appeal to Kallman at this time. 'I don't know if you think there is anything any of us can do to stop him cutting himself off from his surviving friends or do you think there is a real and irreversible cerebral change? He is making us all anxious and unhappy.' It had been agreed that Auden would spend only the autumn and spring terms in Oxford, and he duly returned to Austria in May. For him it was a release from desperate failure. He had written no poems since August 1972, but had a creative renewal in May, when he wrote 'Thank You, Fog', which became the title poem of his posthumous last collection, and two other pieces, 'No, Plato, No' and 'A Thanksgiving'. A few final poems were managed later in the summer in Austria.

Yet he had little respite at Kirchstetten. 'I arrived to find Chester very sick – unable to lift his head, hands trembling, oedema on the legs, etc.,' he reported to Orlan Fox on 30 May. Kallman was hospitalised for a fortnight, and after his release limited himself briefly to one shot of vodka on Sunday and one cigarette an hour. 'To support him I've cut my own smoking down to one pack a day.' Equally distressingly Auden received a large, unreasonable and ignorantly framed tax demand from the Austrian Fiscus. In practice, had he lived, it would have been easily resisted; but he was very upset, dreading that his savings would be eroded, and Kallman believed that his fiscal anxieties hastened his death. He wrote a vigorous rebuttal to the tax-collectors, concluding, 'if this in my view unjustifiable nonsense does not cease, I shall leave Austria, never to return, which would be very sad for me and perhaps too for the shopkeepers at Kirchstetten. One thing, Gentlemen, I cannot conceal from you: if this should happen it might give rise to a scandal of worldwide dimensions.' The threat of being forced from his last sanctuary in Austria was terrible to him, especially as he had privately decided that he could not endure Oxford. He arranged to take a job in the City University in New York for a few weeks of the spring of 1974 and asked Orlan Fox to find him a suitable apartment. But he was weakening fast. 'A new village doctor, very nice, by origin a Syrian,' he reported to Fox. 'My mind still seems to function, thank God, as it should, but my body gets tired very easily. His diagnosis – a weak heart, whatever that means.' Shortly afterwards, at the close of summer, he wrote three lines that may constitute his last poem:

> He still loves life
> But O O O O how he wishes
> The Good Lord would take him.

At the end of September he and Kallman closed the Kirchstetten house to return to Oxford and Athens respectively. He gave a poetry reading on the evening of 28 September to the Austrian Society of Literature in Vienna and, after returning to his hotel, died in his sleep of heart failure. Kallman was sure that, like Constance Auden, he died before midnight, but the coroner officially stated that Auden died early on the morning of the 29th. It seems more than chance that he died on the very night that he left Kirchstetten, on the eve of the first anniversary of his move from New York, just hours before returning to Oxford, where in the preceding twelve months he had felt more miserable and rejected than at any time in his life. 'I have a sure sense of timing,' he had told Oliver Sacks. 'I always know the next thing to do.' Elizabeth Hardwick told Kallman, 'he was as prepared to accept death as anyone could be'. Dreading to return to Oxford, once again submissive, he felt unwanted and went out.

'God may reduce you on Judgment Day'

'Every day for the past year,' Kallman said after Auden's death, 'I have stood outside his door in the early morning, afraid to go in.' On the morning of 29 September, when he entered, he found Auden 'turning icy-blue on a hotel bed'. He was devastated by his discovery, and never recovered. The grief and loss and shock to Auden's friends, and to his readers, were overpowering. Isherwood was anguished in California. Ginsberg wept all afternoon when he heard. Many others were very deeply shaken. He remains the poet of this century about whom other poets continue to write most.

Some friends and acquaintances in New York and Oxford, who knew how miserable Auden had been, speculated whether he had killed himself either deliberately or accidentally with alcohol and pills. When David Luke raised the possibility with Kallman, the latter was not shocked or indignant, and thought it might explain something that oddly troubled him: he had found Auden dead on his left side, although it was his absolute rule to sleep on his right side. A limited autopsy was performed and indicated that he had died of heart failure. There is no evidence of a fatal overdose, intentional or otherwise; and perhaps the speculation arose because Auden in his last years often volunteered the remark that he had never contemplated suicide, with an insistence which made some of his friends doubtful.

The funeral at Kirchstetten on 4 October drew mourners from Britain and the United States. At Auden's wish a recording of Siegfried's funeral march from *Götterdämmerung* was played by Kallman. Then, following local custom, the funeral procession, accompanied by a band, paraded from the Kirchstetten house to the church, led by Kallman, with John Auden on his left and Michael Yates on his right. The day has remained vivid to many of those present. Afterwards David Luke and Edward

Mendelson arranged for a local lawyer to have the house sealed, for there had been depredations on the books and manuscripts.

Kallman's destruction was ensured by Auden's death. He was disorientated and inconsolable without his friend. He disposed of the Kirchstetten house on reckless terms to their former housekeeper and returned to Athens. 'I'm married to him,' Auden had said of Kallman shortly before his death. 'Of course he must have all my money.' Auden wished his entire estate to pass to John Auden's daughters, Rita Mudford and Anita Money, after Kallman's death, but was so infatuated with the gesture of naming Kallman as the sole beneficiary that he did not stipulate his contingent wishes in the will. Kallman himself was too depressed and disordered to amend his own will, which left everything to Auden. He survived only briefly, dying in Athens on 17 January 1975 aged fifty-four. His liver was enlarged and his heart was damaged by alcohol, but those who saw him in the last eighteen months judged that he died of grief. As his will was invalid, his estate (which was mainly Auden's property, derived from royalties) passed to his octogenarian father, Edward Kallman, and later to the latter's widow Dorothy Farnan.

Auden had often spoken or written of his death. 'If there is some kind of after-life, one can only be certain that it will be so utterly different from this one, as to be unimaginable,' he had written to Coghill in 1968. 'It's clear that "Life" as *we* know it ends with death, and one can only pray that one can make a good end. So long, too, as we walk the earth, we have the duty to remember our dead, and, if we possibly can, with more joy than grief.' Yet his last words should be on the death of the poet rather than of the man. Some critics had thought him too smug in his last decade, but there was no complacence in the terrifying postscript to his elegy to MacNeice written in 1964. He had always disliked the attitudinising of *fin de siècle* poets and the mediocrities who coyly aped Baudelaire's self-destruction: his postscript is a repudiation of their facile justifications for self-indulgence. MacNeice, like Auden, Lowell, Bishop and others poets of their generation, had inadvertently hastened his death with alcohol and cigarettes. Auden wrote with a tart irony that has been mistaken for self-satisfaction:

> Time has taught you
>   how much inspiration

> your vices brought you,
>   what imagination
> can owe temptation
>   yielded to,
> that many a fine
>   expressive line
> would not have existed,
>   had you resisted.

The poet's contrition is fake, his hopes that his books will be an exoneration 'from hell' merely a tempting, soothing phantasy: in fact what Auden, disparagingly, in 'Lakes' had called 'ever so comfy'. But poetry must disenchant and strip people of delusive comforts, as he had so often said. In his postscript to the MacNeice elegy the corrupt wishful-thinking poet is followed by a figure who is both incorruptible and everlasting. Auden produced for his conclusion a more comfortless, endangering possibility and finished with the pain of accusation:

> God may reduce you
> on Judgment Day
>   to tears of shame,
> reciting by heart
>   the poems you would
> have written, had
>   your life been good.

Even in death Auden was hard on himself.

Acknowledgments

I have always had a distaste for long, diffuse, emotional acknowledgments presenting their author as the centre of a uniquely loving, supportive network of scholars and admirers; but it is difficult not to be emotional in thanking Edward Mendelson, Katherine Bucknell and Nicholas Jenkins for their contributions to this book. Mendelson as Auden's executor, and Bucknell and Jenkins as co-editors of *Auden Studies* and of the *Auden Newsletter*, would have to be thanked *ex officio*; but their passion, intellect and generosity have been constant forces for me to try to emulate. Each of them has read this book in draft, and their intuitions, factual corrections and interpretative hints have been enormously enriching. My association with each of them has brought me great pleasure, and has filled me with the utmost admiration for them all. I must specially record my debt to Bucknell's thesis cited on page 351.

Without my mother's gift to me when I was a schoolboy of some new Auden volumes, and her material generosity since then, this book would not have been written. My wife's financial support, her merriness and her Anglo-Catholicism have been equally indispensable. The sermons of Father George Bright, of St John the Baptist, Holland Road, Kensington have influenced some key passages.

Charles Osborne and Humphrey Carpenter both published biographies of Auden within a decade of his death. I feel a particular debt to Humphrey Carpenter, whose account of Auden's life and work is so meticulous and even-handed that it was evidently redundant for me to write a similar book. Thanks to the existence of his detailed chronological study published in 1981, I was free to write a biography that is more thematic, or selectively emphatic. My book has been written throughout in a spirit of respect and gratitude for what his earlier work has clarified and facilitated.

I am specially grateful for permission to consult the pre-publication typescripts of Baroness von Musulin's fascinating memoir of Auden at Kirchstetten, and of Nicholas Jenkins's edited selection of Auden's important correspondence with James and Tania Stern. Both sets of documents, which are published by Oxford University Press in September 1995 in *Auden Studies*, volume 3 (entitled *'In Solitude, For Company'*: *W. H. Auden after 1940*, edited by Katherine Bucknell and Nicholas Jenkins), are far more exciting even than my brief extracts convey. The generosity of those concerned was very great.

For interviews, correspondence and information I am grateful to Janet Adam Smith, Rita Auden, Sheila Auden, Don Bachardy, Paul Bailey, Phil Baker, Lord Cobbold, David El-Kabir, D. J. Enright, Jane Hanly, Sir Rupert Hart Davis, David Kynaston, David Luke, Marina Majdalany, Roger Mallion, Anita Money, Alan Myers, Peter Nathan, Peter Parker, A. L. Rowse, Lord Shaughnessy, Sir Stephen Spender, Nikos Stangos, Martin Starkie and the Rt Rev. Peter Walker.

Letters and other unpublished manuscripts by Auden are copyright 1995 by the estate of W. H. Auden, and may not be reprinted without permission.

For permission to quote from *Collected Poems* and the *Complete Works* of W. H. Auden, and from *About the House, A Certain World, Another Time, City Without Walls, Dyers Hand, Epistle to a Godson, Forewords and Afterwords, For the Time Being, Homage to Clio, Journey to a War, Letters to Iceland, Look, Stranger, New Year Letter, The Age of Anxiety, The Orators*, and *Thank You, Fog*, I am grateful to Faber & Faber, Random House and the estate of W. H. Auden.

For permission to quote from unpublished material or for other assistance I am grateful to the Berg Collection at New York Public Library; the Humanities Research Center of the University of Texas at Austin (HRC); the Bodleian Library, Oxford; Boston Public Library; the British Library; the British Psycho-Analytical Library (Ernest Jones papers); Terence Cross (Margaret Rawlings Cross papers); Crusaid (Peter Heyworth papers); the London Library; the Dartington Trust Archives, Totnes (Dorothy Elmhirst papers); the University of Sussex Library (Geoffrey Gorer papers); University College, London (Max Plowright and Sir Richard Rees papers); and Dr Katherine Bucknell (Layard memoir).

Almost every page bears the influence of the ideas of Christopher Phipps, whose advice on my preliminary drafts proved him to be one of Auden's masters of nuance and scruple. The book's dedication to him is a weak expression of what my readers owe him.

Abbreviations used in source notes

The following abbreviations are used in these source notes to indicate Auden's principal works:

AA. *The Age of Anxiety*. Random House, 1947; Faber, 1948.
ACW. *A Certain World*. Viking Press, 1970; Faber, 1971.
Aphorisms. *The Viking Book of Aphorisms*. Viking Press, 1962 [Faber, 1965, as *The Faber Book of Aphorisms*].
AT. *Another Time*. Random House, 1940; Faber, 1940.
ATH. *About the House*. Random House, 1965; Faber, 1966.
CP76. *Complete Poems*. Faber, 1976.
CSP. *Collected Shorter Poems 1927–1957*. Faber, 1966.
CWW. *City Without Walls*. Faber, 1969; Random House, 1970.
DH. *The Dyer's Hand*. Random House, 1962; Faber, 1963.
EA. *The English Auden: Poems, Essays and Dramatic Writings 1927–1939*. Faber, 1977; Random House, 1978.
EF. *The Enchafèd Flood*. Random House, 1950; Faber, 1951.
ETAG. *Epistle to a Godson*. Faber, 1972; Random House, 1972.
FA. *Forewords and Afterwords*. Random House, 1973; Faber, 1973.
FTB. *For the Time Being*. Random House, 1944; Faber, 1945.
HTC. *Homage to Clio*. Random House, 1960; Faber, 1960.
J. *Juvenilia*. Princeton University Press, 1994; Faber, 1994.
JTW. *Journey to a War*. Faber, 1939; Random House, 1939.
L. *Libretti*. Princeton University Press, 1993; Faber, 1993.
LFI. *Letters from Iceland*. Faber, 1937; Random House, 1937.
LS. *Look, Stranger!* Faber, 1936 [Random House, 1937, as *On This Island*].
N. *Nones*. Random House, 1951; Faber, 1952.
NYL. *New Year Letter*. Faber, 1941 [Random House, 1941, as *The*

Double Man].

O. *The Orators*. Faber, 1932; Random House, 1967.

OBLV. *The Oxford Book of Light Verse*. Clarendon Press, 1938.

PB. *Paul Bunyan*. Faber, 1988.

PD. *The Prolific and the Devourer*. The Ecco Press, 1994.

PDW. *Plays, and Other Dramatic Writings*. Princeton University Press, 1988; Faber, 1988.

PT. *The Poet's Tongue*. G. Bell, 1935.

SW. *Secondary Worlds*. Faber, 1968; Random House, 1969.

TSOA. *The Shield of Achilles*. Random House, 1955; Faber, 1955.

TYF. *Thank You, Fog*. Faber, 1974; Random House, 1974.

The following abbreviations are used in the notes to indicate secondary sources:

Ansen. Alan Ansen, *The Table Talk of W. H. Auden*. Princeton, 1990; London, 1991.

AS1. Katherine Bucknell and Nicholas Jenkins eds, *Auden Studies 1: W. H. Auden, 'The Map of All My Youth': Early Works, Friends and Influences*. Oxford, 1990.

AS2. Katherine Bucknell and Nicholas Jenkins eds, *Auden Studies 2: W. H. Auden, 'The Language of Learning and the Language of Love': Uncollected Writings; New Interpretations*. Oxford, 1994.

AS3. Katherine Bucknell and Nicholas Jenkins eds, *Auden Studies 3: 'In Solitude, For Company': W. H. Auden, after 1940*. Oxford, 1995.

Bloomfield. B. C. Bloomfield and Edward Mendelson, *W. H. Auden: A Bibliography 1924–1969*. Charlottesville, 1972.

Bucknell. Katherine Bucknell, 'W. H. Auden: The Growth of a Poet's Mind (1922–1933)'. Columbia University PhD, submitted 1986.

Carpenter. Humphrey Carpenter, *W. H. Auden*. London, 1981.

CHK. Christopher Isherwood, *Christopher and His Kind*. London, 1977.

Coghill. Nevill Coghill, 'Thanks Before Going, for Wystan', in Peter Salus and Paul Taylor eds., *For W. H. Auden, February 21, 1972*. New York, 1972.

Davidson. Michael Davidson, *The World, the Flesh and Myself*. London, 1962.

Day Lewis. Cecil Day Lewis, *The Buried Day*. London, 1960.

Farnan. Dorothy Farnan, *Auden in Love*. New York, 1984.

Fuller. John Fuller, *A Reader's Guide to W. H. Auden*. London, 1970.

Griffin. Howard Griffin, *Conversations with Auden*. San Francisco, 1981.

Hynes. Samuel Hynes, *The Auden Generation*. London, 1976.

Jarrell. Randall Jarrell, *Kipling, Auden & Co*. New York, 1980.

Medley. Robert Medley, *Drawn from the Life*. London, 1983.

Mendelson. Edward Mendelson, *Early Auden*. London, 1981.

Miller. Charles Miller, *Auden, an American Friendship*. New York, 1983.

Osborne. Charles Osborne, *W. H. Auden*. London, 1980.

Paris Review. George Plimpton ed., *Writers at Work: the Paris Review Interviews, fourth series*. New York, 1976.

Smith. Stan Smith, *W. H. Auden*. Oxford, 1985.

Spears. Monroe Spears, *The Poetry of W. H. Auden*. New York, 1963.

Tribute. Stephen Spender ed., *W. H. Auden: A Tribute*. London, 1975.

WWW. Stephen Spender, *World Within World*. London, 1951.

Yanovsky. V. S. Yanovsky, 'W. H. Auden', *Antaeus*, 19 (autumn 1975).

ALS: autograph letter signed
TLS: typed letter signed

Sources

Prologue: 'What goal but the black stone?'

p. 1: Life, as. W. H. Auden, 'At the End of the Quest, Victory', *New York Times Book Review* (22 January 1956), section 7, 5.

p. 1: The journey. *FTB*, 48.

p. 1: From this. *FTB*, 55.

p. 2: Follow poet. *AT*, 109–10.

p. 2: Praise that. *Tribute*, 186.

p. 2: God knows. Carol Brightman, *Writing Dangerously* (London, 1993), 581.

p. 2: Poetry is. T. S. Eliot, *The Sacred Wood* (London, 1920), 53.

p. 3: Genius has. W. H. Auden, 'The Rewards of Patience', *Partisan Review*, 9 (July/August 1942), 336.

p. 3: If biographies. W. H. Auden, 'The Fabian Figaro', *Commonweal*, 37 (23 October 1942), 12.

p. 3: I don't. Alan Ansen journal, 5 March 1948, Berg.

p. 3: Auden retired. *Tribute*, 70.

p. 4: The poet. Paul Johnson, *A History of the Modern World from 1917 to the 1980s* (London, 1983), 337.

p. 4: The slaves. *EF*, 33; Wordsworth, 'Prelude', VII, 700–4.

p. 4: One goes. Henry James, 'The Private Life', in Leon Edel ed., *The Complete Tales of Henry James* Vol. 8 (London, 1963), 210, 225.

p. 4: Our dreaming. *N*, 50.

p. 5: Unless I. Auden to James Stern, ?25 April 1942, in Nicholas Jenkins, 'The Stern Letters', *AS3*, 72.

p. 5: To mature. *PD*, 8.

Chapter 1: 'A typical little highbrow and difficult child'

p. 6: Father's forbears. *LFI*, 203.

p. 6: Gun-shy myopic grandchild. *ETAG*, 58.

p. 6: Auden descendants. Arthur Fox-Davies, *Armorial Families*, 1 (London, 1929), 63–4; see also *Burke's Landed Gentry*, 1921 edition, 50–1.

p. 6: Much reverenced. *Tribute*, 44.

p. 7: Retired to. *Tribute*, 27.

p. 7: Evidently a sadist. *FA*, 498.

p. 7: Charles Bicknell. John Lloyd-Fraser, *John Constable 1776–1837* (London, 1976), 48–9.

p. 7: Lived under. Lady Augusta Fane, *Chit-Chat* (London, 1926), 16–17.

p. 8: Henry Mildred. Sir Sidney Lee, *King Edward VII* (London, 1925), 29; Sir Philip Magnus, *King Edward the Seventh* (London, 1964), 6–8; *The Times* (1

July 1884), 9.

p. 8: Augustus Frederick. James Brinsley-Richards, *Seven Years at Eton* (London, 1883), 52; Alfred Ainger, *Memories of Eton Sixty Years Ago* (London, 1917), 239.

p. 8: Business. David Kynaston, *The City of London*, 1 (London, 1994), 297.

p. 8: Newspaper obituary. *Birmingham Post* (23 August 1941).

p. 8: Constable connection. *Paris Interview*, 263.

p. 8: If you marry. *FA*, 496; *Paris Interview*, 264.

p. 9: Had a. Information from Jane Hanly, November 1994.

p. 9: Children's medicine. G. A. Auden, 'The Focus of Tuberculous Infection in Children', *St Bartholomew's Hospital Reports*, 35 (1899/1900), 79–90; G. A. Auden, 'Diphtheria in the Newlyborn', *Lancet* (19 April 1902), 1104; G. A. Auden, *A Notable Experiment in the Feeding of Children* (London, 1910).

p. 9: Dr Auden. *Lancet* (11 May 1957), 999.

p. 9: On the whole. *FA*, 499.

p. 9: The true. Cyril Connolly, *The Unquiet Grave* (London, 1945), 64.

p. 10: Ma should. *Observer Magazine*, 7 November 1971, 41, 43.

p. 10: He was. *FA*, 500–1.

p. 10: My Father goes. Auden, Berlin journal, 1929, Berg.

p. 10: John on. Berlin journal, 1929, Berg.

p. 10: Taller than. Medley, 44.

p. 10: This solemn. *CHK*, 200.

p. 10: Spoke of. John Heath-Stubbs, *Hindsights* (London, 1993), 68–9.

p. 11: As a small. W. H. Auden, 'In Defence of Gossip', *Listener* (22 December 1937), 1371.

p. 11: He developed. *Tribute*, 28.

p. 11: His was. Dr Malcolm Allan, *British Medical Journal* (18 May 1957), 1187.

p. 11: Numinous map. *CWW*, 123.

p. 12: Wasn't out. Information from Jane Hanly, November 1994.

p. 12: His family. Information from Jane Hanly, 17 March 1995.

p. 12: An extreme neurotic. Day Lewis, 152.

p. 13: Our anxieties. *Tribute*, 27.

p. 13: His fierce. *The Times* (24 January 1991).

p. 13: I am. Information from Jane Hanly, 17 March 1995; *Sunday Times* (28 October 1973).

p. 13: That, as. *Tribute*, 25.

p. 13: I, after all. *AT*, 27.

p. 13: A very bad. *LFI*, 115.

p. 14: The lifelong. *FA*, 503.

p. 14: A fatal. *ACW*, 5.

p. 14: In our. John Pudney, *Home and Away* (London, 1960), 45.

p. 14: Sturdy, podgy. Christopher Isherwood, *Lions and Shadows* (London, 1938), 181.

p. 14: A rather chubby. *Tribute*, 34.

p. 14: I grew. *PD*, 9. When not being sung around, the crèche was covered with a scarlet curtain bearing silver paper letters, 'GLORIA IN EXCELSIS DEO'.

p. 14: Most of. Auden, Berlin journal, 1929, Berg. There is a misreading of this quotation in *EA*, 299–300.

p. 15: Unsophisticated and provincial. W. H. Auden, 'A Literary Transference', *Southern Review*, 6 (1940), 81.

p. 15: He thanks God. *CWW*, 36.

p. 15: Mentally precocious. *EA*, 322.

p. 15: Your god. W. H. Auden, 'In Search of Dracula' (1934), *AS2*, 20.

p. 15: Always a thirsty. Gillian Brown (a cousin-germane of W. H. Auden). *Guardian* (21 May 1993).

p. 15: His learning. P. R. K., *Lancet* (18 May 1957), 1050.

p. 15: But little crime. *PDW*, 168.

p. 16: Proud, self-sufficient. George Auden to Elizabeth Mayer, 14 November 1946 and 27 August 1949, Berg. Wystan Auden by contrast was often a slack or negligent correspondent. Auden to Rupert Doone, 2 July 1932, *PDW*, 490; *LFI*, 203; Auden to Hedwig Petzold [January 1938], Berg; Grover Smith, *Letters of Aldous Huxley* (London, 1969), 458.

p. 16: Sophocles. G. A. Auden, 'Malaria in Ancient Greece', *Nature*, 82 (6 January 1910), 278; Sir William Osler and Sir Clifford Allbut, *Greek Medicine in Rome* (1910), 335.

p. 16: The long line. G. A. Auden, 'The Madness of Ajax, as Conceived by Sophocles, Clinically Considered', *Journal of Mental Science*, 72 (1926), 512.

p. 16: For of the soul. G. A. Auden, 'On Endogenous and Exogenous Factors in Character Formation', *Journal of Mental Science*, 72 (1926), 24. See also the letters of Dr Auden on Malthus in *The Times* (2 January 1935), 6, and on Juvenal, *The Times* (31 January 1935), 10.

p. 16: Cattle refuge. Alec MacDonald, *A Short History of Repton* (London, 1929), 15.

p. 16: I'm nordic. *TSOA*, 21; compare *JTW*, 228.

p. 16: They obviously. Ansen journal, 17 May 1947, Berg.

p. 17: My feelings. W. H. Auden, 'I Like It Cold', *House and Garden* (December 1947), 110.

p. 17: Were it. W. H. Auden, 'The Practiced Topophile', *Town and Country*, 101 (July 1947), 101.

p. 17: A Victorian. Auden, 'Practiced Topophile', 101.

p 17: Pyrites. *Tribute*, 25.

p. 17: It's a great. *LFI*, 145.

p. 18: He beheld. Hans Christian Andersen, *The Ice-Maiden*, translated by Mrs Bushby (London, 1863), 102.

p. 18: Favourite tale. *EA*, 191.

p. 18: The only English. *Tribute*, 90; *FA*, 269.

p. 18: Bicknells at Bordighera. William Raeper, *George MacDonald* (London, 1987), 348–9, 414.

p. 18: These hills. *AA*, 62.

p. 18: The chief defence. George MacDonald, *The Princess and the Goblin* (London, 1872), 64.

p. 19: The sole autocratic. Auden, 'Literary Transference', 78.

p. 19: A private sacred. *FA*, 502.

p. 19: Perhaps I. *AT*, 29.

p. 19: It is. Stella Musulin, 'Auden at Kirchstetten', 224.

p. 19: Machines are. *ACW*, 238.

p. 19: The line. *LFI*, 51.

p. 20: Strict beauty. *EA*, 38.

p. 20: Without a. *TSOA*, 38.

p. 20: Think of questions. *LFI*, 91.

p. 20: Faith in. *AA*, 55.

p. 20: Of two kinds. Auden, Berlin journal, 1929, Berg.

p. 20: What man. Auden, Berlin journal, 1964, Berg.

p. 20: Eating is. *ACW*, 134.

p. 20: We find. Eugen Bleuler in *American Journal of Insanity*, 69 (1912), 874.

p. 20: Idiots savant. Dr G. A. Auden, 'Arithmetical Prodigies', *Lancet* (2 December 1922), 1205–6.

p. 20: Sort of autobiography. *ACW*, vii.

p. 20: The world. *ACW*, 71–2.

p. 21: Intense joy. *J*, xxix.

p. 21: You know. George Auden to

Wystan Auden, 10 February 1940, Berg.

p. 21: My symbol. *NYL*, 55.

p. 22: How, but. *CWW*, 42.

p. 22: Father by son. *CP*76, 54.

p. 22: Hoary medical jokes. Interview with Peter Nathan and Martin Starkie, 27 April 1993.

p. 23: Perceptions of delinquency. G. A. Auden, 'Encephalitis Lethargical – Its Psychological Implications', *Journal of Mental Science*, 76 (1925), 647–58.

p. 23: Ancient Greek. G. A. Auden, 'The Madness of Ajax', 503–12; *Lancet* (4 September 1926), 521.

p. 23: Pre-pubescent. *TYF*, 39.

p. 23: A cliff. *NYL*, 55.

p. 23: My first remark. *LFI*, 205.

p. 23: Would leave. Claud Cockburn, *In Time of Trouble* (London, 1956), 46.

p. 24: I do not / But Reason. *J*, 16–17; Bucknell, 23–25.

p. 25: Thought / fairyland. *FTB*, 70.

p. 25: The use of magic. BBC Television interview, 28 November 1965.

p. 25: Charitable men. *Times Literary Supplement* (16 January 1976), 53.

p. 26: Showed us. *AT*, 118.

p. 26: The artist. W. H. Auden, 'The Wandering Jew', *New Republic*, 104 (10 February 1941), 185–6.

p. 26: He objected. *ACW*, 331.

p. 27: In England. Alan Ansen journal, 16 March 1949, Berg.

p. 27: Mildred. *PDW*, 204–5, 287–8.

p. 27: Poor Mrs Auden. Diary of Kathleen Isherwood, 26 February 1937, HRC.

p. 27: The son who. *PDW*, 412.

p. 27: What is. *FA*, 490.

p. 27: In poetry. W. H. Auden, 'Yeats as an Example', in John Crowe Ransom ed., *The Kenyon Critics* (New York, 1951), 108–9.

p. 27: Patriarch, whose. *Times Literary Supplement* (16 January 1976), 53.

p. 28: In poetry. Auden, 'Yeats as an Example', 108.

p. 28: Landscape. *O*, 9.

p. 28: Wystan taking. *FA*, 501; *Tribute*, 27.

p. 29: The Tristan–Isolde. Auden to Peter Salus, 31 May 1966, Berg.

p. 29: The second. *O*, 41.

p. 29: Religion was. W. H. Auden in *Oxford and the Groups* (Oxford, 1934), 90.

p. 29: Unusually devout. W. H. Auden, essay in James Pike, *Modern Canterbury Pilgrims* (London, 1956), 33.

p. 29: My mother's pet. Ansen journal, 5 November 1947, Berg.

p. 29: By the time. Auden, 'Practiced Topophile', 64.

p. 30: Dear chilblained. Auden, 'Practiced Topophile', 64.

p. 30: As a choirboy. *ACW*, 73.

p. 30: School entertainment. *St Edmund's School Chronicle*, 7.6 (November 1919), 91.

p. 30: Rossetti and Barham. *Tribute*, 36.

p. 30: Closed doors. Gabriel Carritt to K. Bucknell, November 1992.

p. 31: The mother. Auden, Berlin journal, 1929, Berg.

p. 31: Walking out. Interview with Peter Nathan and Martin Starkie, 27 April 1993.

p. 31: We imitate. *LFI*, 204.

p. 31: Of late. H. S. Webb, 'Annals in the Life of a Country Doctor Between 1852–1898', *St Bartholomew's Hospital Reports*, 34 (1899/1900), 239; Francis B. Smith, *The People's Health* 1830–1910 (London, 1979), 299.

p. 31: Comparison of. Auden, Berlin journal, 1929, Berg.

p. 32: The fact. Georg Groddeck, *The Book of It* (London, 1935), 163.

p. 32: To hear. Auden, Berlin journal, 1929, Berg.

p. 32: Offered a choice. Auden, Berlin journal, October 1964, Berg.

p. 32: Influence was. Walter Allen, *As I Walked Down New Grub Street* (London, 1981), 54.

p. 32: Not about thumb-sucking. *ACW*, 52. See also Leon Edel, 'Wystan Auden and the Scissors-Man', *Stuff of Sleep and Dreams* (London, 1982), 209.

p. 33: Very different. *ACW*, 53.

p. 33: The women in. *EA*, 130.

p. 33: In their Royal. *FTB*, 23.

p. 33: Let each. *LFI*, 206.

p. 33: So, under. *PDW*, 279.

Chapter 2: 'I knew that very moment what I wished to do'

p. 34: It is impossible. W. H. Auden, 'How Not to be a Genius', *New Republic* Vol. 97 (26 April 1939), 348, 350.

p. 34: My political. *EA*, 398.

p. 35: The last day. Kathleen Isherwood diary, 21 January 1916, HRC.

p. 35: He probably. *Tribute*, 27.

p. 35: Ordnance survey. *Time* (21 July 1947).

p. 35: Very military. Kathleen Isherwood diary, 2 June 1917, HRC.

p. 35: We drilled. *FA*, 505.

p. 35: Had no reality. *FA*, 504.

p. 36: God must. *Paris Interview*, 249.

p. 36: Seven against. W. H. Auden, Berlin journal, 1929, Berg.

p. 36: He was precociously. Isherwood, *Lions and Shadows*, 181–2.

p. 36: Antiseptic objects. *LFI*, 51.

p. 36: Wystan hasn't. *CHK*, 180.

p. 37: Defenestration. *Times Literary Supplement* (5 November 1971), 1390.

p. 37: A rather clumsy. Sir James Richards, *Memoirs of an Unjust Fella* (London, 1980), 35.

p. 37: The result was. *The Times* (10 January 1919), 11.

p. 38: Jesus Christ Cuts. *Tribute*, 38.

p. 38: Indecency, bad. Richard Cecil, *A Divided Life: A Biography of Donald Maclean* (London, 1988), 13–15.

p. 38: No more. *EA*, 325.

p. 38: Lost interest. *Modern Canterbury Pilgrims*, 33–4.

p. 39: Don't hoard. *The Times* (13 September 1956), 14.

p. 39: A scandal. *FA*, 52.

p. 39: All too. *FA*, 47.

p. 39: An immense. *EA*, 323.

p. 39: My first. *EA*, 323–4.

p. 40: I can. *LFI*, 111.

p. 40: Sources of. Laurence Le Quesne ed., *Frank McEachran: A Cauldron of Spells* (Somerset, 1992), xxxi; John Bridgen, 'Frank McEachran', *ASI*, 117–33; from Peter Davenport, August 1992.

p. 40: He told. Medley, 32–3.

p. 41: Even the. *AT*, 38.

p. 41: Crazes. *LFI*, 208.

p. 41: I have. Auden, 'Literary Transference', 78 9.

p. 42: More than. W. H. Auden, 'Jacob and the Angel', *New Republic*, 101 (27 December 1939), 292.

p. 42: Their straightforward. Auden, Berlin journal, 23 October 1964, Berg.

p. 42: Suspected / colder. Auden, 'Literary Transference', 81.

p. 42: Wordsworth. Bucknell, 3–9, 18, 26–33, passim.

p. 42: O look. *AT*, 56.

p. 43: Would-be poet. *DH*, 37–8.

p. 43: Nature's griefs. *J*, 11.

p. 43: A man could. *J*, 3.

p. 43: For more. Auden, 'Literary Transference', 80.

p. 44: There were several. Auden, 'Literary Transference', 81.

p. 44: His hawk's vision. Auden, 'Literary Transference', 83.

p. 44: Live as. Dr Malcolm Allan, *British Medical Journal* (18 May 1957), 1187.

p. 44: The debris of. G. A. Auden (quoting Oliver Wendell Holmes), 'The School Medical Service in Relation to Mental Defects', *Journal of Mental Science*, 67 (1921), 475.

p. 45: All at once. *J*, 95.

p. 45: The tarn. *J*, 62.

p. 45: Simply walked. John Pudney, *Home and Away* (London, 1960), 45.

p. 45: At Holt. Auden to Pudney, 28 July 1932, Berg.

p. 46: Love frustrated. Auden, 'Literary Transference', 79.

p. 46: Old drain-pipes. *J*, 55.

p. 46: Here now. *J*, 67; Bucknell, 45, passim.

p. 46: In my Eden. *TSOA*, 75.

p. 47: I was bewitched / sent every. Michael Davidson, *The World, the Flesh and Myself* (London, 1973), 127–8.

p. 47: Answered some. *LS*, 33.

p. 48: RUR. *The Times*, 25 April 1923, 12; Basil Dean, *Seven Ages* (London, 1970), 192–4.

p. 48: Consummated. *The Times* (7 May 1923), 10.

p. 48: They are. *ETG*, 36.

p. 48: I cannot. *LFI*, 123.

p. 48: Wystan predictably. Medley, 39.

p. 48: Dr Auden explained. Medley, 44.

p. 49: He knew. Davidson, 129.

p. 49: I wanted. *EA*, 399.

p. 49: Heaven and Hell. *EA*, 361–2.

Chapter 3: 'I mean to be a great poet'

p. 51: A time. *CWW*, 24.

p. 51: That, at. *WWW*, 53.

p. 52: Why must. Auden to John Auden, nd [?late 1963.]

p. 52: Willingly became. Day Lewis, 177.

p. 52: The exclusiveness. James Lees-Milne, *Another Self* (London, 1970), 92–3.

p. 52: Auden then. Louis MacNeice, *The Strings Are False* (London, 1965), 114.

p. 52: Literary and. Sir Roy Harrod, *The Prof* (London, 1959), 39–40.

p. 53: To an introvert. Auden to Harrod, postmarked Spa, 31 July 1928, BL Add 71181.

p. 53: His small. Isherwood, *Lions and Shadows*, 183.

p. 54: A novelist. W. H. Auden, 'A Novelist's Poems', *Poetry*, 49 (January 1937), 224.

p. 54: The chaos. W. H. Auden and C. Day Lewis, *Oxford Poetry 1927* (Oxford, 1927), v–vii.

p. 54: Puritanism became. T. S. Eliot, *The Sacred Wood* (London, 1920), 122.

p. 54: An upper. Isherwood, *Lions and Shadows*, 18–19.

p. 54: During the. *J*, 137.

p. 54: The Photograph. *J*, 124. I owe this point to Peter Parker.

p. 54: Uncle Henry. *CSP*, 48–9.

p. 54: Without these. *FTB*, 37.

p. 54: For years. Thom Gunn, *Shelf Life* (London, 1994), 178.

p. 55: Snooty. *CWW*, 25.

p. 55: I'm going. Coghill, 35.

p. 55: Was better. Lord David Cecil, 'Nevill Coghill', *Times Literary Supplement* (21 November 1980), 1334. See also Cecil's tribute in the Merton College magazine, *Postmaster*, 1981.

p. 55: Liveliest. Coghill, 37–8.

p. 55: He had. Coghill, 38.

p. 56: Really, how. *DH*, 39.

p. 56: Sardonic, restless. Day Lewis, 176.

p. 57: Given more. Auden, draft letter of 1968 to Day Lewis, in holograph notebook 1965–8, Berg.

p. 57: Wystan's favourite. Day Lewis, 177.

p. 57: You are. *WWW*, 52–5.

p. 57: That anxiety. *AA*, 13.

p. 58: When a. Spender, *Journals*, 356.

p. 58: Poetic competitiveness. Interview with Sheilah Auden, 24 November 1993.

p. 58: The common. Auden to John Auden, ?June 1927, Anita Money papers.

p. 58: Becoming a. Auden to William McElwee, Easter vacation 1928, BL Add. Ms. 59618.

p. 58: This was. J. I. M. Stewart, *Myself and Michael Innes* (London, 1987), 65.

p. 58: I certainly. Auden to Harrod, postmarked 31 July 1928, BL Add. Ms. 71181.

p. 58: Wystan's cleverness. ALS from A. L. Rowse, 1 January 1993.

p. 59: And would. Allen, *As I Walked Down New Grub Street*, 34.

p. 59: Remain frozen. *EA*, 326.

p. 59: Neither of Medley, 62.

p. 59: An institution. Tom Driberg, *Ruling Passions* (London, 1977), 2, 29, 43.

p. 59: Every family. W. H. Auden, 'The Double Focus', *Common Sense*, 9 (3 March 1940), 25.

p. 59: Read it. Driberg, *Ruling Passions*, 58; Marie-Jacqueline Lancaster ed., *Brian Howard: Portrait of a Failure* (London, 1968), 130.

p. 60: Given any. *EA*, 322–3.

p. 60: Idealize the labourer. *J*, 111.

p. 60: Really gratifies / brandishing my. Auden, Berlin journal, 1929, Berg.

p. 60: Too timid. *CWW*, 36.

p. 60: The European. Alan Ansen journal, 20 October 1947, Berg.

p. 60: Infinite sacred. *FA*, 101.

p. 61: Caricatures. *LFI*, 123.

p. 61: A word. Lord Radcliffe, *The Problem of Power* (London, 1952), 8.

p. 61: The analysis. W. H. Auden, review of Thouless, *Modern Poetic Drama* in *Listener* (9 May 1934), 808.

p. 61: Types. *Times Literary Supplement* (11 July 1935), 444.

p. 61: Cartoon-like. *Times Literary Supplement* (29 October 1938), 689.

p. 61: Though Auden. John Bayley, *The Romantic Survival* (London, 1957), 156.

p. 61: School life. *EA*, 399.

p. 61: Apart from. Auden to John Auden, nd [?June 1927].

p. 62: It was. *FA*, 514.

p. 62: Lamp-post. A. J. P. Taylor, *A Personal History* (London, 1983), 81–2.

p. 62: I don't. Auden to Nevill Coghill, 22 February 1972, Berg.

p. 62: I have. Nevill Coghill, 'Sweeney Agonistes', in Richard Marsh and Tambimuttu eds, *T. S. Eliot: A Symposium* (London, 1948), 82.

p. 62: His inspiration. Auden, 'T. S. Eliot', *Listener* (7 January 1965), 5.

p. 63: Had the. W. H. Auden, 'The Poet of the Encirclement', *New Republic*, 109, (24 October 1943), 579.

p. 63: Thomas Epilogises. *J*, 146–7.

p. 63: Dawn rose. *J*, 149–51.

p. 63: By great. T. S. Eliot, *Selected Essays 1917–1932* (London, 1932), 14–17.

p. 64: No man. Auden to John Auden, nd [Christ Church, 1926–7].

p. 64: Extraordinary gift. Auden, 'T. S. Eliot', 5.

p. 64: I don't. Auden to John Auden, nd [Oxford, probably December 1927]; in the following passages I am specially indebted to the ideas of Katherine Bucknell.

p. 64: Read Catallus. Auden to John
Auden, nd [from Hotel Espla-
nade, Zagreb, Croatia, late July
1927].

p. 64: Great masters. *NYL*, 20–1.

p. 65: A continual surrender. Eliot, *Selected
Essays 1917–32*, 17.

p. 65: The person. Auden to John Auden,
nd [?June 1927].

p. 65: Whimpers to. *J*, 130.

p. 65: Auden's life. *WWW*, 61.

p. 65: An adolescent. *J*, 137.

p. 65: The only. Auden to John Auden, 15
December 1926.

p. 65: As far. Auden to John Auden, nd
[?June 1927].

p. 67: That notable / Gauze. *J*, 227.

P. 67: Our youth. *Oxford Poetry 1927*,
Introduction, v.

p. 67: Pressure. *J*, 144.

p. 67: Young Desmond. *J*, 146–7.

p. 67: He feels. G. A Auden, 'Factors in
Character Formation', 11. Compare this with Auden to
McElwee, [?28 June 1927], BL
Add. Ms. 59618; the description
of the eclipse beginning at 5.29
a.m. on 29 June in the vicinity of
the Audens on the fells of the
West Riding in *The Times* (30
June 1927), 17. See also *ACW*,
144–6.

p. 67: Relation seemed. *J*, 161.

p. 67: Maturity. *Times Literary Supplement*
(16 January 1976), 53.

p. 68: There still. Carpenter, 49.

p. 68: Love / too curious. *J*, 214.

p. 68: Two pathics. *J*, 220–1.

p. 68: As a bugger. Auden to John Auden,
nd [1926–7]; *J*, xxxix.

p. 68: The constant. George Auden, 'Character Formation', 23.

p. 69: A hierarchy. *Times Literary Supplement* (8 December 1927), 925.

p. 69: I personally. Auden to John Auden,

nd [?June 1927].

p. 69: The so-called. George Auden,
'Character Formation', 23.

p. 69: Wished I. Richard Davenport-Hines
and Nicholas Jenkins, 'Poems and
Prose', *AS2*, 21.

p. 70: The lethal. *J*, 217.

p. 70: Heredity. George Auden, 'The Biological Factors in Mental Defect',
Psyche, 3 (1923), 248, 255.

p. 70: Wish to. Auden to John Auden, nd
[late July 1927]; *J*, xl.

p. 70: One of those. *J*, 212.

p. 70: Trained as. Day Lewis, 149–51. Her
first husband Raymond Pinson's
medical practice in Nottinghamshire was ruined by the break-up
of his marriage and he was
reduced to a medical job among
the planters and remittance men
of Singapore.

p. 70: Psychology was. *The Times* (16 June
1922), 7.

p. 70: Incarnation of. 'Another Gentleman
With a Duster', *Is Coué a Foe to
Christianity?* (New York, 1923),
83.

p. 71: Only a. *Psyche*, 3 (July 1922), 3.

p. 71: Equipped with. *The Times* (3 July
1926), 14, 15, 19.

p. 71: The man. W. H. R. Rivers, 'The
Aims of Ethnology', *Psyche*, 3
(1923), 136.

p. 71: We will. *Tribute*, 47.

p. 72: Self-sacrifice. Constance Auden to
Stanley Fisher, 20 April 1926,
Christ Church Library.

p. 72: I can. Auden to Harrod, postmarked
31 July 1928, BL Add. Ms.
71181.

p. 72: Agnostic, unconventional. Day
Lewis, 151.

p. 72: The penchant. Day Lewis, 152.

p. 72: I think. Auden to John Auden, nd
[from Zagreb, ?July 1927].

p. 72: Brilliant and domineering. John

Auden, undated note on back of photograph (information from Anita Money).

p. 72: She almost. John Auden to Edward Mendelson, 6 September 1982 (information from Anita Money).

p. 72: She can. Day Lewis, 152.

p. 72: The Auden meanness. Auden, Berlin journal, 1929, Berg.

p. 72: Bitterness and despair. John Auden, undated note (information from Anita Money).

p. 72: I shall. Auden to John Auden, 11 April 1932. See also Sean Day-Lewis, *C. Day-Lewis* (London, 1990), 86–7, 92.

p. 73: Had a. *J*, xl.

p. 73: Best in. Day Lewis, 152.

p. 73: I suddenly. Nicholas Jenkins, 'Letters to James and Tania Stern', *AS3*, 83.

p. 73: To throw. *J*, 246.

p. 74: The heroic. *LS*, 46.

p. 74: All buggers. Auden, Berlin journal, 1929, Berg.

p. 74: It's a. Interview with Sir Stephen Spender, 5 September 1994.

p. 74: Now tell. *Times Literary Supplement* (16 January 1976), 53.

p. 74: A good. Ansen, 87.

p. 75: Eliotian Intellectual. *J*, 139.

p. 75: Oedipal dialogues. Stan Smith, 'Persuasions to Rejoice', *AS2*, 155–63.

p. 75: Fascination. Auden, 'Yeats as an Example', 112.

p. 75: The dead hand. Auden, 'Yeats as an Example', 114.

p. 75: The occasional. Auden, 'Yeats as an Example', 113.

p. 75: How could. Auden, 'Yeats as an Example', 108–9.

p. 76: Should be. Deborah Baker, *In Extremis: The Life of Laura Riding* (London, 1993), 329.

p. 76: He has. Auden to Spender, 20 May 1964, Berg.

p. 76: Homosexual and parlour. Paul O'Prey, *In Broken Images: Selected Letters of Robert Graves 1914–1946* (London, 1982), 263.

p. 76: Cowardice. Robert Graves, *The Crowning Privilege* (London, 1955), 130–1.

p. 76: To read. W. H. Auden, 'A Poet of Honor', *Mid-Century*, 28 (July 1961), 9.

p. 77: Between you. Auden to Coghill, 6 Dec 1961, Berg.

p. 77: He nearly. Margaret Gardiner, *A Scatter of Memories* (London, 1988), 151.

p. 77: He had. *WWW*, 59.

p. 77: An infinitesimal. *Oxford Poetry 1927*, vii.

p. 77: With the. Auden, 'Yeats as an Example', 111.

p. 77: Had the courage. Francis Scarfe, *Auden and After* (London, 1942), 12.

p. 77: The army. T. S. Eliot, *Complete Poems and Plays* (London, 1969), 30.

p. 77: In an absolute. Robert Graves, *Poetic Unreason* (London, 1922), 42.

p. 77: Learn from. Graves, *Poetic Unreason*, 47.

p. 78: Rarely purely. Auden, 'Yeats as an Example', 107. The following passage closely follows ideas of Katherine Bucknell.

p. 78: A quotation. Auden to John Auden, nd [Zagreb, ?July 1927].

p. 78: Had one. Auden, Berlin journal, 1929, Berg.

p. 78: The possibility. I. A. Richards, *Science and Poetry* (London, 1926), 49.

p. 78: The neutralization. Richards, *Science and Poetry*, 52.

p. 79: Pseudo-statement. Richards, *Science and Poetry*, 62–4.

p. 79: It is never Richards, *Science and Poetry*, 31.

p. 79: Ars Poetica. Archibald MacLeish, *Poems 1924–1933* (New York, 1933), 123.

p. 79: Brain is. *Times Literary Supplement* (15 December 1927), 966.

p. 79: Works of. W. H. Auden to John Auden, nd [1927]. See also Katherine Bucknell, 'Writing', *AS1*, 21–2.

p. 80: Ideas strike. Louis MacNeice, *Selected Literary Criticism* (Oxford, 1987), 115.

p. 80: The language. Eliot, *Sacred Wood*, 136.

p. 80: Written ravishing. *WWW*, 50.

p. 80: Lands on. *PDW*, 279; James Fenton, 'Coghlan's Coffin Revisited', *Auden Newsletter*, 3 (April 1989), 5.

p. 80: The Adversary. *J*, 240.

p. 81: A manifesto. Mendelson, 15.

p. 81: We are shut. Bucknell, 'Writing', *AS1*, 40.

p. 81: Most of. Bucknell, 'Writing', *AS1*, 42.

p. 81: Is like a. Bucknell, 'Writing', *AS1*, 40–1.

p. 81: When communities. Bucknell, 'Writing', *AS1*, 45; William McDougall, *The Group Mind* (Cambridge, 1920), 12–13.

p. 81: Generally speaking. Bucknell, 'Writing', *AS1*, 44.

p. 81: That they. John Matthias, *Reading Old Friends* (New York, 1992), 91.

p. 82: In general. Auden to John Auden, nd [?1927].

p. 82: Memorable speech. *PT*, v.

p. 82: I cannot. *HTC*, 51.

p. 82: The gaps. John Bayley, *Selected Essays* (Cambridge, 1984), 79.

p. 83: Children swarmed. *AT*, 25.

p. 83: Became his admirers. *AT*, 107

p. 83: If the apprentice. Auden, 'Phantasy and Reality in Poetry' *AS3*, 191.

p. 83: Frustrate and vexed. *J*, 218.

p. 83: Country on. Auden, Berlin journal, 1929, Berg.

p. 83: You yourself. D. H. Lawrence, *Women in Love* (London, 1920; 1931 edn), 131, ch. 11.

p. 84: Powerful, underworld. Lawrence, *Women in Love*, 119, ch. 9.

p. 84: Control of. *J*, 239.

p. 84: Poems with. *WWW*, 51.

p. 85: Pure gold. *Times Literary Supplement* (8 December 1927), 925, 939.

p. 85: The management. *Times Literary Supplement* (8 December, 1927), 925, 939.

p. 85: Discipline of. Robert Thouless, *The Control of the Mind* (London, 1927), 64, 202.

p. 86: Cajoling, scolding. *AT*, 41.

p. 86: Their syllabus. *Times Literary Supplement* (16 January 1976), 53.

p. 86: He wrote. Jarrell, 230.

Chapter 4: 'I'm king of Berlin'

p. 87: The conventional. W. H. Auden, 'Short Novels of Colette', *Griffin*, 1 (December 1951), 1.

p. 87: I and. W. H. Auden, 'Our Italy', *Griffin*, 1 (April 1952), 1.

p. 87: Ceased to *LFI*, 209.

p. 87: I am incredibly. Auden to Spender, nd [1928], Berg.

p. 88: Never attempted. Edith Sitwell, 'Auto-Obituary: The Late Miss Sitwell', *Listener* (29 July 1936), 192.

p. 88: It is. John Hayward, *Criterion*, 12 (1932), 134.

p. 88: Someone . . . nearly unconscious motive. *O66*, 7–8.

p. 88: A device. W. H. Auden, 'The History of an Historian', *Griffin*, 4

(November 1955), 10.

p. 88: More sex-obsessed. Arthur Koestler, *Stranger on the Square* (London, 1984), 182.

p. 88: A man should. Auden, 'History of an Historian', 10.

p. 88: Is all. *EA*, 334.

p. 88: The real 'life-wish'. Auden Berlin journal, 1964, Berg. In this chapter all unacknowledged Auden quotations are from this source, which is to be published in a later volume of *Auden Studies*.

p. 88: The immense bat-shadow. *O*, 24.

p. 89: Yours you. *EA*, 48.

p. 89: By the symbolism. George Auden, 'An Unusual Form of Suicide', *Journal of Mental Science*, 73 (1927), 429.

p. 90: He was. *CHK*, 19–20.

p. 90: Our lives. Auden, 'History of an Historian', 10.

p. 90: Because he. Elaine Showalter, *The Female Malady* (New York, 1985), 183–4.

p. 91: Chief father-figure. Sir Rupert Hart-Davis ed., *Siegfried Sassoon Diaries 1920–1922* (London, 1981), 32, 163, 170.

p. 91: Those talks. Arnold Bennett, 'W. H. R. Rivers: Some Recollections', *New Statesman* (17 June 1922), 290. For another view of Rivers, see Max Plowman, *Bridge into the Future: Letters* (London, 1944), 65, 130.

p. 92: An undisturbed belief. Edith Wharton, *The Age of Innocence* (New York, 1920), book 1, ch. 11.

p. 92: I found. Layard memoir. All Layard quotations in this chapter are from this source, which has been generously provided to me by Katherine Bucknell.

p. 92: We have. Havelock Ellis, *Affirmations* (London, 1897), 115.

p. 93: John Layard / cow. Kathleen Isherwood diary, 6 November 1938, HRC.

p. 93: Helpless and ugly. *EA*, 37.

p. 93: Raised me. *PDW*, 478–9.

p. 94: Novel writing. *LFI*, 20.

p. 94: Quoted in. *EA*, 423.

p. 94: The would-be. W. H. Auden, 'Some Notes on D. H. Lawrence', *Nation* (26 April 1947), 482.

p. 95: Our highly prized. Groddeck, *The Book of the It*, 24.

p. 95: A capricious. Groddeck, *Book of the It*, 274.

p. 95: Repenting its. *LFI*, 136.

p. 95: Loved / to perdition. D. H. Lawrence, *Fantasia of the Unconscious* (London, 1922), 71, 131.

p. 95: Man lives. Groddeck, *Book of the It*, 26–7.

p. 95: As to. *J*, 217.

p. 95: A dangerous. *The Times* (18 March 1925), 11.

p. 95: The most. Jonathan Croall ed., *All the Best, Neill: Letters from Summerhill* (London, 1983), 94. For other accounts see F. T. Bazeley, *Homer Lane and the Little Commonwealth* (London, 1928) and W. David Wills, *Homer Lane* (London, 1964).

p. 97: I am. Auden to McElwee, 31 December 1928, BL, Add. Ms. 59618.

p. 97: My boy. Auden to Prudence McElwee, ?31 December 1927, BL Add. Ms. 59618.

p. 97: I do. Coghill, 39.

p. 97: Romantic emotional. David Luke, 'Gerhart Meyer and the Vision of Eros', *AS2*, 110.

p. 98: The end. Ansen, 24.

p. 98: The sailor. Auden, *EF*, 123.

p. 98: Absence of fear. *EA*, 37.

p. 99: My name. Auden to Jimmy and Tania Stern, 1 May [1955], in

Nicholas Jenkins, 'The Stern Letters', *AS3*, 102.

p. 99: So insecure. *EA*, 39.

p. 99: Perceives the. Luke, 'Gerhart Meyer', 108.

p.100: His clap. David Constantine, 'The German Auden', *AS1*, 15.

p.100: Only the. Charlotte Wolff, *Magnus Hirschfeld: A Portrait of a Pioneer in Sexology* (London, 1986), 116–17.

p.100: Childish condition. Carl Jung, *Collected Works*, 7 (London, 1966), 107.

p.100: Always a defective. Jung, *Collected Works*, 6 (London, 1981), 471.

p.100: A faulty development. Jung, *Collected Works*, 7, 106.

p.100: Bravo me. Carpenter, 104.

p.101: I was. Auden to McElwee, [nd, summer, 1929], BL Add. Ms. 59618.

p.101: The dragon's. *EA*, 40.

p.101: I am. Naomi Mitchison, *You May Well Ask* (London, 1979), 122.

p.102: Man-woman. Marcel Proust, *Cities of the Plain*, 1 (London, 1929), 1 (quoting Alfred de Vigny).

p.103: Frowning, conscious. *O*, 57.

p.103: An immature. *O*, 29

p.103: Touch-line admirers. *O*, 46.

p.103: The muscular. *O*, 34.

p.103: A long. *EA*, 42–3.

p.104: Guerilla warfare. William Plomer, *At Home* (London, 1958), 61.

p.104: Remarkable ear. Louis MacNeice, *Selected Literary Criticism* (Oxford, 1987), 2, 36.

p.104: It puts. William Empson, *Argufying* (London, 1987), 371.

p.104: I'm sending. F. R. Leavis to Ronald Bottrall, 5 January 1931, HRC.

p.104: A liar's quinzy. *CHK*, 13.

p.104: So tall. Isherwood, *Lions and Shadows*, 303.

p.105: Writing a. Auden to Naomi Mitchison, postmarked 9 April 1930,

Berg.

p.105: He was. BL Add. Ms 52430.

p.105: At first. Spender, 'Oxford to Communism', *New Verse* (November 1937), 10.

p.105: I don't. *O*, 46.

p.105: If we really. *EA*, 49.

p.105: The mere. W. H. Auden, *Criterion*, 12 (January 1933), 288–9.

p.106: We can. John Haffenden, *W. H. Auden: The Critical Heritage* (London, 1983), 102.

p.106: Great Works. Justin O'Brien ed., *The Journals of André Gide*, 3 (London, 1949), 106.

p.106: When I. John Berryman, 'Shirley & Auden', *Collected Poems 1937–1971* (London, 1989), 172.

p.106: Metropolitan high. Stan Smith, 'Remembering Bryden's Bill: Modernism from Eliot to Auden', *Critical Survey*, 6 (1994), 318.

p.106: Day is. *O*, 104; *EA*, 105.

p.107: Persons unknown. *O*, 20.

p.107: Poetry is. J. B. Yeats, *Letters to his Son W. B. Yeats and Others, 1869–1922* (London, 1944), 178.

p.107: Bad men. W. H. Auden, 'The double focus', *Common Sense*, 9 (March 1940), 25; see also Richard Bozorth, 'Whatever You Do Don't Go Into the Wood,' *AS2*, 113–36.

p.107: Speaking as. *O*, 55.

p.107: BEF in 1914. *O*, 72–3.

p.107: The last. *O*, 72.

p.107: In public. Kenneth Ingram, *The Modern Attitude to the Sex Problem* (London, 1930), 68.

p.107: A flying trickster. *O*, 46–8 and passim.

p.107: Unholy hunting. *O*, 52.

p.107: If the Lord. *O*, 45.

p.107: Day-dreams. *O*, 45.

p.107: Soft seat / pivot of power / revolving roarer. *O*, 51–2.

p.108: A rugger hearty. Auden to Prudence McElwee, ?31 December 1928, BL Add. Ms. 59618.

p.108: £5. Bevis Hillier, *Young Betjeman* (London, 1988), 177–8.

p.108: *****.*O*, 34. The word 'buggers' had been printed in a poem of November 1929: see W. H. Auden, *Poems* (London, 1930), 41. In 1931 the poet Geoffrey Potocki de Montalk sent five poems for private circulation to a printer, who showed the manuscript to the police, who launched a prosecution for obscenity. Prosecuting counsel mentioned in his opening address that Potocki owned a copy of Radclyffe Hall's *Well of Loneliness*. Sentencing Potocki to six months' imprisonment, the Recorder of London, Sir E. Wild, said, 'A man must not say he is a poet and be filthy. He has to obey the law the same as ordinary citizens, and the sooner the highbrow school learns that, the better for the morality of the country.' Charles Hobday, *Edgell Rickword* (Manchester, 1989), 141–3.

p.109: The glutton. *O*, 34.

p.109: Passed away / the little Mickey. *LFI*, 55.

p.109: About the. *ACW* 382.

p.109: Previously the. W. H. Auden, 'k's quest', in Angel Flores ed., *The Kafka Problem* (New York, 1946), 51.

p.109: Excessive lovers. *O*, 14.

p.109: He who. *ACW*, 347.

p.110: You have. Lawrence, *Fantasia*, 100.

p.110: You are. *O*, 18.

p.110: Undercarriage. *O*, 53.

p.110: Outside I. *O*, 37.

p.110: Thanks to. *O*, 38.

p.111: True ancestor. *O*, 45.

p.111: The lethal. *J*, 217.

p.111: Hinting at. *AT*, 35; *EA* 236.

p.111: I thought. *O*, 61.

p.111: Uncle Sam. *O*, 51.

p.111: Self-care. *O*, 42.

p.111: Psycho-analyst and Christian. *LFI*, 204.

p.112: From all. *O*, 24–5.

p.112: What Freud. Lawrence, *Fantasia*, 13.

p.113: One charms. *O*, 30–1.

p.113: Three enemy. *O*, 55–6.

p.114: At the pre-arranged. *O*, 77.

p.114: The smaller. *O*, 104.

p.114: Man … can. Auden, 'k's quest', 52.

p.114: We are all. Auden to John Pudney, 1932, Berg.

Chapter 5: 'To love; to be loved; to be a teacher; to be a pupil'

p.115: The concept. Connolly, *Unquiet Grave*, 112

p.115: Numinous object. W. H. Auden, 'A World Imaginary, but Real', *Encounter*, 3 (November 1954), 59.

p.115: Makes possible. Mendelson, 163.

p.115: Poetry can. *DH*, 60.

p.116: Facile optimism. Anthony Hecht, *The Hidden Law, The Poetry of W. H. Auden* (Cambridge, Mass., 1993) 44.

p.116: For the wicked/Can Hate. *LS*, 68.

p.116: Moneybug. *LS*, 52.

p.116: Businessman. Auden to Pudney, 28 July 1932, Berg.

p.116: I am not. Auden to Harrod, postmarked 31 July 1928, BL Add. Ms. 71181.

p.116: As the one. Auden to Spender, nd [? June 1933], Berg.

p.117: What I think. Auden to Michael Roberts, 22 April 1935, Berg.

p.117: While we. *LS*, 42–3.

p.117: Violent faces. *LS*, 67.

p.117: Lucky, this. *LS*, 13.

p.117: The four. BL Add. Ms. 52430.

p.117: The healers. *LS*, 14.

p.117: Witty, playful. *CHK*, 82.

p.118: A leather. Joe Ackerley, *My Father and Myself* (London, 1968), 142.

p.118: Huxley knowaldous. Auden to Mrs Dodds, postmarked 29 August 1939, Bodleian.

p.118: He looked. Guy Davenport, *Every Force Evokes a Form* (London, 1989), 169.

p.118: Malinowski, Rivers. *AT*, 68–9; Gerald Heard, *Social Substance of Religion* (London, 1931), 34, 40, 112.

p.118: O what is. *LS*, 20–1; Katharine Bucknell, 'Freud is OK', *AS3*, 193–4.

p.118: The Gospel. Heard, *Social Substance*, 204–5, also quoted by W. H. Auden, 'The Group Movement and the Middle Classes', in R. H. S. Crossman ed., *Oxford and the Groups* (Oxford, 1934), 98–9. Auden praised 'noble amateurs like Gerald Heard … who … have promoted social justice' in a poem of 1934: *Times Literary Supplement* (16 January 1976), 53.

p.119: The Middle Class. Auden, 'Groups and the Middle Classes,' 98.

p.119: I teach rugger. Auden to Spender, nd [c. June 1933], Berg.

p.119: Materially I. Auden to John Auden and Margaret Marshall, 20 November 1931.

p.120: A posh liberal. Auden to Coghill, nd (? January 1933), Berg.

p.120: Frightfully busy. Auden to Rupert Doone, postmarked 19 October 1932, Berg.

p.120: Although this. Lancaster ed., *Brian Howard*, 382.

p.120: Our school. Auden to Walter de la Mare, 17 June 1935, Bodleian.

p.120: His arrival. Michael Yates, *Badger* (autumn 1974), 34.

p.120: Full of doubts. Auden to Michael Roberts, 5 April 1935, Berg.

p.121: Highbrow. *EA*, 317.

p.121: This fellow. B. C. Bloomfield and Edward Mendelson, *W. H. Auden: A Bibliography* (Charlottesville, 1972), 3.

p.121: Almost as. Sir Richard Rees to Max Plowman, 21 January 1937, Plowman papers, University College, London.

p.121: Through a. Auden to Max Plowman, 2 October [sic; surely November] 1930, Plowman papers, UCL.

p.121: Hopeful young. Sir Richard Rees to Geoffrey Sainsbury, nd [1932], Rees papers, UCL.

p.121: A misery. Max Plowman, *Bridge into the Future* (London, 1944), 643.

p.121: Affectation, Day Lewis to Sir Richard Rees, 10 August [? 1931–2], Rees papers; compare Spender to Rees, 15 June [? 1931], Rees papers.

p.121: Early in. Janet Adam Smith, 'Auden and The Listener', *Listener* (18 October 1973), 532.

p.122: Spender party. Interview with Janet Adam Smith, 10 June 1994.

p.122: Silenced. Janet Adam Smith, 'Tom Possum and the Roberts Family', *Southern Review*, vol. 21, no. 4 (autumn 1985), 1057.

p.122: Much too. Peter Parker, *Ackerley* (London, 1989), 201.

p.122: Debt. *FA*, 450.

p.122: Chuck it. Auden to John Auden, 18 November 1930.

p.122: Anomymously written reviews. Interview with Janet Adam Smith, 10 June 1994.

p.122: This book. *Listener* (9 May 1934),

908.

p.123: Trashily written. Auden, *Scrutiny*, 2
(December 1933), 307–10.

p.123: Moral degenerates. *PDW*, 238.

p.123: Imperial Chemicals. *LFI*, 256.

p.123: Glorified circular. Michael Howard,
Jonathan Cape, Publisher (London, 1971), 53.

p.123: A shilling life. *LS*, 33. My reading
of this poem is influenced by Bayley, *Romantic Survival*, 80–1.

p.123: Cross-roads where. Marcel Proust,
Cities of the Plain, (London,
1971), 34–6.

p.124: Whenever an. *CHK*, 197.

p.124: Two friends. *NYL*, 165.

p.124: Psychological ramifications. Heard,
Social Substance, 11 and chart II.

p.125: Presenting the future. *News
Chronicle*, (11 June 1937), 6.

p.125: The problem. Auden to Pudney, 28
July 1932, Berg.

p.125: Even when. Auden in *Criterion*, 11
(January 1932), 319.

p.125: The school. Bonamy Dobree, 'New
Life in English Poetry', *Listener*
(14 June 1933), 958.

p.126: Where now. Rex Warner, 'Choruses
from "The Dam",' in Michael
Roberts ed., *New Country* (London, 1933), 251.

p.126: In the hopes. TLS from Sir Rupert
Hart-Davis, 19 March 1994; Sir
Rupert Hart-Davis. *The Power of
Chance* (London, 1991), 83.

p.126: Aspects of. Michael Roberts and
John Lehmann eds, *New Signatures* (London, 1932), 13.

p.126: Psychological revolutionaries. Connolly,

p.126: Frontier officials. *PDW*, 224.

p.126: The only useful. Peter Stansky and
William Abrahams, *Journey to the
Frontier* (London, 1966), 173–4.

p.127: A new type. Bayley, *Romantic Survival*, 169.

p.127: He put on. Edward Upward,
'Remembering the Earlier
Auden', *Adam*, nos 379–84
(1973/4), 19.

p.127: The clown. *FTB*, 7.

p.127: Why do you. Auden to Grigson, 11
October 1932, HRC (where it is
misdated 10 November 1932).

p.127: One of. *PT*, ix.

p.127: I am for. Sean Day Lewis, *C. Day
Lewis*, 72.

p.128: Quite a. Auden to Alan Sinkinson,
postmarked 31 December 1932,
Berg.

p.128: A private school. *PD*, 15.

p.128: Just like. Auden to Dodds, 3 May
1947, Bodleian.

p.128: A state. Auden. 'Life's Old Boy',
Scrutiny, 2 (March 1934), 408–9.

p.128: A useful citizen. *EA*, 313.

p.128: Topsy-turvy. W. H. Auden, *Criterion*, 12 (April 1933), 538.

p.128: The tenth week. Wystan Auden to
John Auden, 15 November 1930.

p.129: Occasional exquisite. Auden to
Spender, nd [June 1933?], Berg.

p.129: A teacher soon. *EA*, 401.

p.129: His classes. Yates, *Badger* (autumn
1974), 34.

p.129: He was fascinated. Gurney Thomas,
'Recollections of Auden at the
Downs School', *W. H. Auden
Society Newsletter*, 3 (April 1989),
1.

p.129: Love, satisfaction. *LS*, 30.

p.130: I shall. Auden to Dorothy Elmhirst,
3 April 1932, Dartington Trust
Archives, Totnes.

p.130: I've just. Auden to John Auden, 11
April 1932.

p.130: An excessive. W. H. Auden, *Criterion*, 12 (April 1933), 537.

p.130: The high thin. *LS*, 43.

p.130: Folk-dancer. *EA*, 312.

p.131: Air of injured. *LFI*, 203.

p.131: I find. Auden to Ernest Jones, 4

November 1953, Archives of the British Psycho-Analytical Society.

p.131: The whole self. *EA*, 302.

p.131: We are not. *FA*, 48.

p.132: One fine summer *FA*, 69–70.

p.133: Many writers. Auden, 'John Skelton', in Katharine Garvin, *The Great Tudors* (London, 1935), 67.

p.133: He knows. A. J. M. Smith in *Poetry*, 47. (1935), 46.

p.133: Out on the lawn. *LS*, 13–14.

p.133: The vision seriously. *CP76*, 245.

p.133: At last. *AT*, 39.

p.134: It is the life. *EA*, 319–20.

p.134: The subject. *WWW*, 51.

p.134: Argues that. Mendelson, 162–3.

p.135: It's such. *LFI*, 203.

p.135: Seems to. Edmund Wilson, *Shores of Light* (New York, 1952), 669.

p.135: Let the florid. *LS*, 18.

p.135: Really beautiful. Anthony Thwaite ed., *Selected Letters of Philip Larkin 1940–1985* (London, 1992), 28.

p.135: Easy for. *LS*, 50–1.

p.136: Oncers do. *ETAG*, 41.

p.136: Was perhaps. David Marr, *Patrick White* (London, 1991), 272.

p.136: Rooted horror. *CHK*, 157.

p.136: Rather a. Diary of Kathleen Isherwood, 16 December 1936, HRC.

p 136: What are buggers. P. N. Funbank, *E. M. Forster: A Life*, 2 (London, 1978), 213.

p.136: Wystan wanted. Paul Vaughan, *Something in Linoleum* (London, 1994), 143.

p.137: The pomposity. *Times Literary Supplement* (29 February 1936), 181.

p.137: Johnny, who. Cyril Connolly, *New Statesman* (29 February 1936), 313–14.

p.137: Unjustifiable presumption. Auden notebook, 1936, Berg.

p.137: Between two. Auden, notebook of 1964/5, Berg.

p.137: A realist. Auden to Spender, nd [after June 1935], Berg.

p.137: A friend. Auden, 'The Group Movement', 100.

p.137: Maturity – to recover. 'Squares and Oblongs', in Charles Abbott ed., *Poets at Work* (New York, 1948), 162.

p.137: A pair. Valentine Cunningham, *British Writers of the Thirties* (London, 1988), 374.

p.137. Mata Hari. *The Times* (25 April 1932), 12.

p.137: Can't you. Peter Alexander, *William Plomer* (Oxford, 1989), 186.

p.137: Coghill and Garrett. E. W. F. Tomlin, *T. S. Eliot* (London, 1988), 33.

p.138: School Song. *AS2*, 32–3.

p.138: Have you. Vaughan, *Linoleum*, 135.

p.138: The unhappy face. *PT* vi. See also W. H. Auden, 'The Average Man', *Listener* (7 November 1936), 741–2.

p.138: Over the. A. L. Rowse, 'Trowbridge' in *A Life - Collected Poems* (Edinburgh, 1981), 326–7.

p.138: You were. Vaughan, *Linoleum*, 106.

p.138: You all. Vaughan, *Linoleum*, 116.

p.138: With those. 'W. H. Auden on George Orwell,' *Spectator* (16 January 1971), 86.

p.139: One of. A. T. Davies and David Jones, *Letters to a Friend* (Swansea, 1980), 84.

p.139: So essentially. Auden, *Listener* (9 May 1934), 808.

p.139: Auden is. Ann Olivier Bell ed., *The Diary of Virginia Woolf*, 4 (London, 1982), 324.

p.140: Drama began. *PDW*, 497; Medley, 160.

p.140: Abstract drama. Mitchison, *You May Well Ask*, 120.

p.140: I went down. Medley, 152–3. See also Michael J. Sidnell, *Dances of*

Death: The Group Theatre of London in the Thirties* (London, 1984).

p.141: I can't. Susan Chitty ed., *Antonia White: Diaries 1926-1957* (London, 1991), 53.

p.141: Who do. *PDW*, 491–2.

p.141: This brash. *PDW*, xx.

p.141: In this episodic. *The Times* (2 October 1935), 12.

p.142: This is. Earl of Cromer, minute of 23 July 1935, BL, Lord Chamberlain's archives.

p.142: It is. G. S. Street, report of 23 July 1935, Lord Chamberlain's archives.

p.142: They have invented. *The Times* (31 January 1936), 12.

p.143: Many people. G. S. Street, report of 21 October 1935, Lord Chamberlain's archives.

p.143: An unnecessary. Earl of Cromer, minute of 22 October 1935, Lord Chamberlain's archives.

p.143: It would. Lord David Cecil, report of 24 October 1935, Lord Chamberlain's archives.

p.144: We were. Elizabeth Sussex, *The Rise and Fall of British Documentary: The story of the Film Movement Founded by John Grierson* (Berkeley and London, 1975), 79.

p.144: O Lurcher-loving. *PDW*, 421.

p.144: Because he. *J*, 125.

p.144: Happiness comes. *LFI*, 21.

p 144: He kept. Sussex, *British Documentary*, 71.

p.145: That it. Donald Mitchell ed., *Letters from a Life: Selected Letters and Diaries of Benjamin Britten, 1913-1976*, 1 (London, 1991), 379.

p.145: Underneath the. *LS*, 54.

p.145: I was. Kathleen Bell, 'Nancy Spender's Recollections of Wystan Auden', *W. H. Auden Society Newsletter*, 10/11 (September 1993), 3.

p.145: Towns take. *LFI*, 215.

p.145: Exasperatingly slow. *EA*, 355.

p.145: You only. Quoted obituary of Sir Lawrence Growing, *The Times* (7 February 1991), 12.

Chapter Six: 'The cold controlled ferocity of the human species'

p.146: Like a sentinel. *AT*, 42.

p.146: The clutch. *JTW*, 299.

p.146: In a low. *AT*, 112.

p.146: One must. W. H. Auden, 'The Wandering Jew', *New Republic*, 104 (10 February 1941), 185.

p.147: An effect. *LFI*, 141.

p.147: No one thinks. *LFI*,

p.147: Nothing is made / its routine. *AT*, 59–60.

p.148: I had. *LFI*, 30.

p.148: Paid to teach. Draft poem to Gabriel Carritt, BL Add. Ms. 52430.

p.148: Perfectly happy. *AT*, 41.

p.148: Until the. *LFI*, 105.

p.148: A scivvy. *LFI*, 104.

p.148: A new class. *LFI*, 105.

p.148: To strive to seek. Vaughan, *Linoleum*, 64.

p.148: You can't. Auden to Coghill, 11 January 1965, Berg.

p.148: Tennyson was. *FA*, 231.

p.149: Remember you. Interview with Janet Adam Smith, 13 June 1994.

p.149: Auden made. Michael Meyer, *Not Prince Hamlet* (London, 1989), 25.

p.149: Construing ... Auden. Lord Annan, *Our Age* (London, 1990), 183.

p.149: I should be. Robert Giroux ed., *Elizabeth Bishop: One Art* (London, 1994), 16.

p.149: For six. Frederic Prokosch, *Voices* (New York, 1983), 44.

p.150: Auden is not. *New Verse*, no. 15 (June 1935), 22.

p.150: Random House. Barry Ahearn ed., *The Correspondence of Ezra Pound: Pound/Zukofsky* (London, 1987), 161.

p.150: Contrary to. Thomas C. Kemp, *Birmingham Repertory Theatre* (Birmingham, 1943), 87. See also John Trewin, *The Birmingham Repertory Theatre 1913–1963* (Birmingham, 1963), 115–16.

P.150: An exciting. *Birmingham Post*, 28 March 1938, 12.

p.150: The cynical. *Birmingham Post*, 4 April 1938, 3.

p.150: The play. *Birmingham Post*, 6 April 1938, 5.

p.150: That famous. Ralph Fox, 'Worker's Notebook', *Daily Worker* (6 February 1936), 4.

p.151: Hugh Weston. Diary of Kathleen Isherwood, 24 January 1939, HRC.

p.151: To love fame. Paul Valéry, *Analects* (London, 1970), 21.

p.151: Auden understood. Interview with Sir Stephen Spender, 5 September 1994.

p 151: Would be. Auden to Mrs Dodds, postmarked 21 April 1940, Bodleian.

p.151: Thousands are. Lavater quoted in Auden's commonplace book given to Caroline Newton Berg.

p.151: Europe lies. *PDW*, 417.

p.152: Liberal Democrats. W. H. Auden, 'Democracy's Reply to the Challenge of Dictators', *New Era in Home and School*, 20 (January 1939), 6.

p.152: Our international rout. *N*, 27.

p.152: During our. *Tribune*, 66–7.

p.153: Except perhaps. Stephen Spender, *Letters to Christopher* (Santa Barbara, 1980), 76.

p.153: It seems. CHK, 226.

p.153: There was. *LFI*, 148.

p.153: Dreaming permits. *ACW*, 126.

p.154: I wish. *LFI*, 149–50.

p.154: Importance. Louise Bogan, *Poet's Alphabet (New York, 1970), 34.

p.154: Let me. *LFI*, 223–4.

p.155: Nice English. *Tribute*, 60.

p.155: The poet's eye. *LFI*, 221.

p.155: Thanks to. *HTC*, 24.

p.155: About suffering. *AT*, 47.

p.156: That is. *N*, 34.

p.156: The primary function. *EA*, 371.

p.156: It is to-day. *AT*, 62.

p.156: Thought of. W. H. Auden, 'Rilke in English', *New Republic* (6 September 1939), 135.

p.156: External disorder Epigraph to *LS*.

p.156: In every body. *JTW*, 294.

p.157: Its difficult. Auden to John Auden, 16 September 1932.

p.157: Empires stiff. *LS*, 44.

p 157: No I am. Auden to Rupert Doone, nd [autumn 1932], Berg.

p.157: The Russians. Auden to John Auden, 14 [?January 1932.]

p.157: The interest. W. H. Auden, 'Authority in America', *Griffin*, 4 (March 1955), 8–9.

p.158: Armaments manufacturers. Malcolm Muggeridge, *The Green Stick* (London, 1972), 69. See also Hugh Dalton, House of Commons debates, 192 (11 March 1926), col. 2736.

p.158: The Balkan conscience. *LFI*, 240.

p.158: Sermon by. *EA*, 138–41. See also *EA*, 123 for armaments firms.

p.158: That man's. *EA*, 314.

p.158: The task. *EA*, 347.

p.159: Thinking about. *LFI*, 142.

p.159: Who can ever. *LFI*, 143.

p.159: Madness, and the. *LFI*, 257.

p.159: All the hate. *LFI*, 258.

p.159: All rather subdued. Auden, 'Dracula', *AS2*, 21–2.

p.160: Violence successful. *JTW*, 281.

p.160: A cross. *PDW*, 598.

p.160: Scoundrels. Auden, 'The Wandering Jew', 185.

p.160: He was most. Robert Skidelsky, *John Maynard Keynes*, 2 (London, 1992), 628.

p.161: Ransom is. *The Times* (27 February 1937), 10.

p.161: My minor place. *PDW*, 336.

p.161: *F6* was. Carpenter, 195.

p.162: We must. Sir Richard Rees, *A Theory of My Time* (London, 1963), 107.

p.162: That movement. *PD*, 18.

p.162: Bloomsbury and Greenwich. Arthur Koestler, *The Invisible Writing* (London, 1954), 326–7.

p.162: Saga-novels. Stuart Gilbert and Alastair MacDonald trans., *André Malraux's Days of Hope* (London, 1938), 285.

p.162: There was. Day Lewis, 210.

p.162: All intellectuals. Auden to Dodds, postmarked 8 December 1936, Bodleian.

p.163: Seduced. Auden to Dodds, nd [mid-December 1936], Bodleian.

p.163: War's greatest. Hynes, 23.

p.163: Believe that. Auden to Dodds, nd [?8 December 1936], Bodleian.

p.163: Wystan … was. Marr, *Patrick White*, 173, 672–3.

p.163: He goes off. Mitchell, *Britten Letters*, 1, 461.

p.164: Despite all. *CHK*, 197.

p.164: It went. Diary of Kathleen Isherwood, 26 February 1937, HRC.

p.164: By the pilot. Koestler, *Invisible Writing*, 337.

p.164: Nobody I. W. H. Auden, 'Authority in America,' *Griffin*, 4 (March 1955), 9.

p.165: Makeshift consolations. *AT*, 106.

p.165: One cannot walk. *PD*, 17.

p.165: The machine. *EA*, 317.

p.165: The radio, suddenly. *AA*, 17.

p.165: Quant pointed. *AA*, 28.

p.166: I am your. *AT*, 105.

p.166: The sheer sense. Nicholas Jenkins, 'Auden and Spain', *AS1*, 93.

p.166: Fit to stand. Donald Moggridge ed., *The Collected Writings of John Maynard Keynes*, 28 (London, 1982), 61–5.

p.166: Maintained that. Diary of Kathleen Isherwood, 5 November 1937, HRC.

p.166: The acceptance. George Orwell, 'Political Reflections on the Crisis', *Adelphi* (December 1938), 110.

p.166: Often thoughts. *L*, 40.

p.166: Eric Blair. Rayner Heppenstall to Sir Richard Rees, 29 April 1936, Rees papers, UCL.

p.167: Mr Auden's brand. Sonia Orwell and Ian Angus eds, *The Collected Essays, Journalism and Letters of George Orwell*, 1 (London, 1969), 516.

p.167: Densely unjust. Spears, 157.

p.167: Time is short. *AT*, 106.

p.167: Equate goodness. *CSP*, 15.

p.167: Auden's most. Mendelson, 348.

p.168: Exigence. Spender, *The Thirties and After* (London, 1978), 31.

p.168: This rare. Auden, 'Men of Thought and Action', *Town Crier* (14 October 1938), 2.

p.168: Behind pity. W. H. Auden, 'The Heresy of Our Time', *Renascence*, 1 (spring 1949), 24.

p.169: I could. Auden, *Modern Canterbury Pilgrims*, 41.

p.169: And the nations. *AT*, 104.

p.169: In a publisher's. Auden, *Modern Canterbury Pilgrims*, 41.

p.169: Behind the. T. S. Eliot, 'The Significance of Charles Williams', *Listener*, 36 (19 December 1946), 894.

p.170: More playful. C. S. Lewis, *Essays*

Presented to Charles Williams (Oxford, 1947), ix–x.

p.171: Our greatest. W. H. Auden, 'Ironworks and University', *Town Crier* (21 October 1938), 2.

p.171: As we run. *JTW*, 11.

p.171: There is. *Times Literary Supplement* (29 October 1938), 689.

p.171: Lord how. Nigel Nicolson, *The Letters of Virginia Woolf*, 6 (London, 1980), 318.

p.171. Unquestionably it. Keynes, *Collected Writings*, vol. 28, 128.

p.172: Only that. Bogan, *Poet's Alphabet*, 34.

p.172: To show. Earl of Gowrie, 'Accomplishing Auden', *Agenda*, 32 (1994), 212.

p.172: 'Benjie' played. Diary of Kathleen Isherwood, 18 January 1938, HRC.

p.172. Started brawl. Sir James Richards, *Memoirs of an Unjust Fella* (London, 1980), 118–19; Christopher Hassall, *Edward Marsh* (London, 1959), 611.

p.172: Do not think. Diary of Kathleen Isherwood, 19 January 1938, HRC.

p.172: CAIRO: that. W. H. Auden and Christopher Isherwood, 'Escales', *Harper's Bazaar*, 72 (October 1938), 79.

p.173: Am I to. *JTW*, 19.

p.173: Wystan endured. *CHK*, 222.

p.173: The oxtail soup. *CHK*, 223.

p.173: Looking for. Auden to Dodds, 20 April 1938, Bodleian.

p.173: A Lewis Carroll. *JTW*, 33.

p.173: I have spent. *JTW*, 206.

p.174: Lunch was argumentative. *JTW*, 162–3.

p.175: To be saved. Auden, 'The Wandering Jew', 185.

p.175: One sector. *JTW*, 292.

p.175: And, if we. *JTW*, 298–9.

p.175: The little natures. *JTW*, 272.

p.175: I am very. Auden to Mrs Dodds, nd [late 1938], Bodleian.

p.176: Since Yeats. Kirstein, 'Poets Under Fire', 151–2.

p.176: Reported to. 'The American Scene', *Times Literary Supplement* (24 August 1951), xxxiv.

p.176: He had already. Martin Stannard, *Evelyn Waugh; No Abiding City* (London, 1992), 299.

p.176: Lectures on China. Diary of Kathleen Isherwood, 6 November, 28 November and 2 December 1938, HRC.

p.177: I get very. Auden to Mrs Dodds, nd [May 1939], Bodleian.

p.177. Wystan Auden. Diary of Kathleen Isherwood, 12 October 1938, HRC.

p 177. Midland service. W. H. Auden, 'What the Chinese War Is Like', *Listener* (2 February 1939), 247–8.

p.177: Publicity is. Denis Healey, *The Time of My Life* (London, 1989), 130.

p.177: These public men. *NYL*, 114.

p.177: We're VERY. *L*, 31.

p.177: Few of. *PD*, 18.

p.178: The Great Game. Geoffrey Grigson, 'A Letter from England', *Poetry*, 49 (1936), 102.

p.179: England is terribly. Robin Maugham, *Escape from the Shadows* (London, 1972), 203.

p.179: In order. Auden to Geoffrey Gorer, 26 July 1971, University of Sussex Library.

p.179: Clever hopes. *AT*, 112.

p.179: Strange young. Diary of Kathleen Isherwood, 25 January 1939, HRC.

p.179: Resentful. Diary of Kathleen Isherwood, 26 January 1939, HRC.

p.179: Rather inclined. Diary of Kathleen Isherwood, 24 January 1939, HRC.

p.180: At the first. Evelyn Waugh, 'Two Unquiet Lives', *Tablet* (5 May 1951), 356.

p.180: Obviously a brave. Kirstein, 'Poets Under Fire', 152.

p.180: A Viper. See extract from *New Statesman* of 17 February 1940 copied into notes of 1940 diary of Kathleen Isherwood, HRC. See also *Spectator* (21 June 1940).

p.180: No more. Sir Kingsley Amis, *Memoirs* (London, 1991), 151. See also Anthony Powell, *Journals 1982-1986* (London, 1995), 213.

p.180: An artist. Louis MacNeice, 'American Letter', *Horizon*, 1 (July 1940), 464.

p.180: He could. Davenport, *Every Force Evolves a Form*, 169.

Chapter 7: 'Mr Right has come into my life'

p.182: Auden is. Robert Phelps and Jerry Rosco eds, *Continual Lessons: The Journals of Glenway Wescott 1937-1955* (New York, 1990), 49.

p.182: He's pretty. Jeffrey Miller ed., *In Touch: The Letters of Paul Bowles* (New York, 1994), 171.

p.182: Just a. Ruth Limmer ed., *What the Woman Lived: Selected Letters of Louise Bogan* (New York, 1973), 185.

p.182: He looked. Prokosch, *Voices*, 110-11.

p.183: Immense Park. Jessica Mitford, *Hons and Rebels* (London, 1960), 181.

p.183: The most. *DH*, 335-6.

p.183: His manner. *Tribute*, 98.

p.184: A slight erotical. Carpenter, 296.

p.184: Writer's functions. Klaus Mann, *The Turning Point* (London, 1984), 341-2.

p.184: Tried to. Auden to James Stern, 23 July 1942. Jenkins, 'Stern Letters', *AS3*, 77-8.

p.184: Ladies who. Auden to Angelyn and Albert Stevens, 30 July 1942, University of Michigan Library, Ann Arbor.

p.184: A great. Auden to Kallman, 27 December 1949, Berg.

p.184: Never one. *EF*, 60.

p.184: Exceptional individual. *DH*, 155. See also *LFI*, 101; *ACW*, 183-4; Jarrell, 226.

p.184: A connection. *EA*, 390.

p.185: We can. *FTB*, 124.

p.185: The prosecutor *TSOA*, 66.

p.185: Pleasure is. *DH*, 5.

p.185: Auden never. *Tribute*, 99.

p.185: Poets here. John Butler Yeats, *Letters to his Son W. B. Yeats and Others, 1869-1922* (London, 1944), 130.

p.185: European crisis. *New York Times* (5 April 1939), 10.

p.186: Came after. Auden to Mrs Dodds, postmarked 11 July 1939, Bodleian.

p.186: New York is. Auden to John Auden, nd [April 1939.]

p.186: Seconal. Auden to Mrs Dodds, postmarked 29 May 1939, Bodleian.

p.186: Beautiful / the same rapt. *TSOA*, 65.

p.186: Inefficiency / pathetic. Auden, 'Heretics', *New Republic* (1 November 1939), 373.

p.186: Alcohol coffee. Auden, 'Squares and Oblongs', in *Poets at Work*, 173.

p.186: Pep-up. Anon, 'Use and Abuse of Drugs by Athletes', *Lancet*, 1 (1958), 252; see also *Journal of the American Medical Association*, 164 (13 July 1957), 1244.

p.187: Elation, confidence. Andrew Tyler, *Street Drugs* (London, 1986), 39.

p.187: A single. P. H. Connell, *Amphetamine Psychosis* (London, 1958), 58.

p.187: Did you. Harold Norse, *Memoirs of a Bastard Angel* (London, 1990), 61.

p.187: Both sexes. Norse, *Memoirs*, 52.

p.187: Miss Mess. Norse, *Memoirs*, 62.

p.187: Was the star. Norse, *Memoirs*, 63.

p.187: Awful. Auden to Mrs Dodds, postmarked 29 May 1939, Bodleian.

p.187: A man. Howard Griffin, 'A Dialogue with W. H. Auden,' *Partisan Review*, 20 (1953), 76.

p.188: It's the wrong. Norse, *Memoirs*, 64.

p.188: When it comes. *AT*, 91; Norse, *Memoirs*, 64.

p.188: Mad with. Auden to Britten, nd [May 1939], Berg.

p.188: Just a line. Auden to John Auden, nd [April 1939].

p.189: Perhaps it. Auden to James Stern, 25 April 1942. Jenkins, 'Stern Letters', *AS3*, 74.

p.189: I'm the. Ansen journal, 23 November 1947, Berg.

p.189: The power. *LS*, 52.

p.189: Chester was. Nicholas Jenkins, 'A Conversation with Lincoln Kirstein', *Auden Newsletter*, no. 7 (October 1991), 6–7.

p.190: What the. *Antaeus*, 23 (autumn 1976), 195.

p.190: After about. Kallman to Auden, 11 May 1939, Berg.

p 190: The king. *NYL*, 170.

p 190: Charming anecdotes. Limmer ed., *What the Woman Lived*, 221.

p.190: Fastidious as. *CP76*, 243.

p.191: The experience. Charles Williams, *He Came Down from Heaven* (London, 1938), 92–4.

p.191: An accident. *NYL*, 14; Auden, 'A Preface to Kierkegaard', *New Republic* (15 May 1944), 684.

p.191: An indirect. David Luke, 'Gerhart Meyer and the Vision of Eros', *AS2*, 109.

p.191: Anytime, how. *NYL*, 47.

p.192: Like love. *AT*, 19.

p.192: That thrilling. Charles Williams, *The Descent of the Dove* (London, 1939), 136.

p.192: The young. Griffin, 103.

p.192: You know. George Auden to Elizabeth Mayer, 1 February 1953, Berg.

p.192: Now I have. *AT*, 29.

p.192: A Mission. *L*, 6.

p.192: The person. Miller, 34.

p.192: In the. Griffin, 98–9.

p.193: Wystan: Are you. Alan Ansen journal, 30 January 1947, Berg.

p.193: The passengers. Norse, *Memoirs*, 70–1.

p.194: Interview. *New York Times*, 12 March 1939, 24.

p.194: Vastly resonant. Richard Eberhart, *Collected Poems* (London, 1976), 238–9.

p.194: The staff. Auden to Mrs Dodds, nd [May 1939], Bodleian.

p.194: O but I. Davenport-Hines, 'School Writings', *AS2*, 42.

p.194: Wystan calls. Norse, *Memoirs*, 75; Auden to John Auden, nd [May 1939].

p.195: Wystan's state. Norse, *Memoirs*, 75.

p.195: Paradise is / The memory *PD*, 37–8.

p.195: An omnipotent *PD*, 81.

p.195: Industrialism is. *PD*, 40–1.

p.195: The teaching. *PD*, 41.

p.196: Only our. *PD*, 47.

p.196: The original. Auden to Edward Kallman, 5 July 1939, HRC.

p 196: The country. Auden to Mrs Dodds, postmarked 11 July 1939, Bodleian.

p.196: Dressed for. Margaret Lefranc, 'W. H. Auden in the Southwest', *El Palacio*, 98 (winter 1992/3), 50–1.

p.196: Auden was. Lefranc, 'W. H. Auden', 49.

p.197: We had. Lefranc, 'W. H. Auden', 50.

p.197: In earlier. Lefranc, 'W. H. Auden', 50.

p.197: Perceptibly tense. Lefranc, 'W. H. Auden', 52.

p.198: Arizona and Nevada. Auden to Mrs Dodds, 7 August 1939, Bodleian.

p.198: Human life. Auden, 'Rilke in English', *New Republic*, 100 (6 September 1939), 135.

p.198: There is. Auden to Mrs Dodds 28 August 1939, Bodleian.

p.198: We all kept. Mitchison, *You May Well Ask*, 231.

p.198: The dive. Norse, *Memoirs*, 78–9.

p.198: I sit. *AT*, 112.

p.199: We must love. Joseph Brodsky, *Less Than One* (New York, 1981), 353.

p.199: A self-portrait. Brodsky, *Less Than One*, 355.

p.200: Elizabeth was. Charles Miller, *Auden: An American Friendship* (New York, 1983), 57.

p.200: There are. Auden to Elizabeth Mayer, February 1943; Carpenter, 316.

p.200: I revisage. *ETG*, 51.

p.200: Kill them. Alan Levy, 'On Audensstrasse – In the Autumn of the Age of Anxiety', *New York Times Magazine* (8 August 1971), 42.

p.200: The English intellectuals. *Tribute*, 102.

p.200: Jung hardly. W. H. Auden, 'Romantic or Free?', *Smith Alumnae Quarterly*, 31 (August 1940), 357.

p.200: The arid prudence. *NYL*, 96.

p.201: Auden gave. John Constable ed., *Selected Letters of I. A. Richards, CH* (Oxford, 1990), 105.

p.201: We are. Auden, 'Jacob and the Angel', *New Republic*, 101 (27 December 1939), 292.

p.201: After a. Griffin, 106.

p.202: Christianity is. W. H. Auden, 'The Means of Grace', *New Republic* 104 (2 June 1941), 765.

p.202: Lack of faith. *PD*, 45.

p.202: I can. W. H. Auden, 'In Poor Shape', *Sewanee Review*, 52 (1944), 596.

p.202: The whole. Auden, 'A Preface to Kierkegaard', *New Republic*, 110 (15 May 1944), 684.

p.202: The fatal. Auden, 'Preface to Kierkegaard', 686.

p.202: Without blinding. Auden, 'Preface to Kierkegaard', 683–4.

p.203: One must. *Antaeus*, 23 (autumn 1976), 195.

p.203: It is defeat. *FTB*, 28.

p.203: Many times. *FA*, 33.

p.203: But they. *Tribute*, 106.

p.203: A true gestalt. *NYL*, 19.

p.203: Much the best. Edmund Wilson, *Letters on Literature and Politics 1912–1972* (New York, 1977), 369.

p.204: Was denouncing. Mary Jarrell ed., *Randall Jarrell's Letters* (London, 1985), 47.

p.204: Hesitates on. Spears, 134.

p.204: O unicorn. *NYL*, 73.

p.204: In its. P. K. Walker, 'Auden Thoughts', *Theology*, 80 (November 1977), 433.

p.204: Dear friend. *NYL*, 74.

p.204: Some notes. Randall Jarrell, *Kipling, Auden & Co* (New York, 1980), 57.

p.204: Former manner. Bogan, *Poet's Alphabet*, 38.

p.205: The more poets. G. W. Stonier, 'Auden Meditates', *New Statesman* (5 July 1941), 16.

p.205: Pompous. Auden, 'Open Letter to Knut Hamsun', *Common Sense*, 9 (August 1940), 22–3.

p.205: In the. Maurice Cranston, 'Poet's Retreat', *John O'London's Weekly* (6 February 1948), 50.

p.205: Lidice. Auden, 'Squares and Oblongs', 174.

p.206: Anaemic, muscularly. *O*, 17.

p.206: Sensed an. John Lehmann, *I Am My Brother* (London, 1960), 31.

p.206: Nude figures. Cyril Connolly, 'Spymania', *New Statesman* (15 June 1940), 748.

p.206: Seeking refuge. House of Commons debates, 361 (13 June 1940), col. 1361.

p.206: Suede shoes. Julian Critchley, *Westminster Blues* (London, 1985), 30.

p.206: Minor personal. Auden to John Auden, nd [postmarked 21 June 1940].

p.207: The Left. MacNeice, *Strings Are False*, 35.

p.207: Normality. *LFI*, 207.

p.207: A long. Anon, 'Reports on England', *New Statesman*, 21 June 1941, 638.

p.207: Dirtiest witticism. Geoffrey Grigson, *The Crest on the Silver* (London, 1950), 216.

p.207: George's account. Kallman to Auden, 24 May 1939, Berg.

p.207: Richard Wright. Jeffrey Miller ed., *In Touch: The Letters of Paul Bowles* (New York, 1994), 363–4. See also Paul Bowles, *Without Stopping* (London, 1972), 233–4; Millicent Dillon, *A Little Original Sin: The Life and Work of Jane Bowles* (New York, 1981), 94–5; Paul Muldoon, *Meeting the British* (London, 1987), 36–60.

p.208: He kept. *Tribute*, 100–11.

p.208: He could. Lefranc, 'W. H. Auden', 52.

p.208: Striking and. *Tribute*, 98–9.

p.208: One of. Auden, 'A Great Democrat', *Nation*, 147 (25 March 1939), 352.

p.208: Preachy / shattering. Norse, *Memoirs*, 86.

p.208: Playing the. Donald Mitchell, *Britten and Auden in the Thirties* (London, 1981), 162.

p.208: The most. Delmore Schwartz, 'Auden and Stevens', *Partisan Review*, 14 (1947), 529; see also James Atlas, *Delmore Schwartz* (New York, 1977), 217–20.

p.208: Why do. Sir Stephen Spender, 'You were funny like us; your gift survived it all', *Spectator* (24 September 1994), 41.

p.209: Drive a. Norse, *Memoirs*, 65.

p.209: Instead of. Joel Roache, *Richard Eberhart* (New York, 1971), 104.

p.209: Auden's look. Jenkins, 'Conversation with Kirstein', 2.

p.209: Crooked immoralist. Auden, 'Double Focus', 26.

p.209: An entirely verbal. Stephen Spender, 'Auden's Achievement', *Spectator* (29 February 1952), 267.

p.209: Always made. Jarrell, 229.

p.210: The one infallible. Auden, 'Double Focus', 25–6.

p.210: Freud is. Empson, *Argufying*, 372.

p.210: Half angel. *NYL*, 50.

p.210: Love must be. *NYL*, 128.

p.210: Do not. Auden, Introduction to Henry James, *The American Scene* (New York, 1946), xxi.

p.210: In their loves. *AT*, 72.

p.211: Love does. *Faber Book of Aphorisms*, 186 (quoting from Chapter 8 of Saint-Exupéry, *Winds, Stars and Sand*).

p.211: Life after death. *FTB*, 116.

p.211: These dissent. *AT*, 21.

p.211: Like a child. *LFI*, 93.

p.211: A land. *CP76*, 247–9.

p.212: To me. Auden, Berlin journal, 1964, Berg.

p.212: Regarded sex. Auden, 'Ambiguous Answers', *New Republic* 104 (23 June 1941), 861.

p 212. Those who. Auden, Berlin journal, 1964, Berg.

p.212. When I do. Kallman to Norse, 11 July [?1940], Berg.

p.212. Real men. Kallman to Auden, 10 November 1941, Berg.

p.212: Court jester. Interview with Sir Stephen Spender, 5 September 1994.

p.212. Sexual fidelity Ansen journal, nd [February 1948], Berg.

p.212. I was. Farnan, 55.

p 213: Many people. Auden, review of Theodore Roethke's *Open House*,

Saturday Review of Literature, 5 April 1941, 30–1.

p.213: Full of. Richard Gillman and Michael Novak eds, *Poets, Poetics and Politics: The Letters of Rolfe Humphries 1910–1969* (Kansas, 1992), 175.

p.213: Chester ... to. Auden to Caroline Newton, postmarked 5 June 1941, Berg.

p.213: Hints. Auden, 'Eros and Agape', *Nation* (28 June 1941), 756–7.

p.213: Chester retired. Farnan, 56.

p.213: A violent. Farnan, 55–6.

p.213: Evil. Interview with Sir Stephen Spender, 5 September 1994.

p.214: Because an. Griffin, 33.

p.214: Providentially. Auden, *Modern Canterbury Pilgrims*, 41.

p.214: To make. Ansen, 91.

p.214: It was Chester's. Farnan, 61.

p.214: For a. *Tribute*, 109.

p.214: We're not. Carpenter, 313.

p.215: She had. George Auden to Kaye Richardson, 13 October 1941.

p.215: The good. Auden, 'Last Words', *Harper's Bazaar* (October 1941), 83.

p.215: Bert Savoy. Auden, 'Last Words', 119.

p.215: I'm afraid. Alan Ansen journal, 20 October 1947, Berg.

p.215: Of course. Information from Sir Stephen Spender.

p.215: O my dear. 'Miss God on Mr Stevens', Berg.

p.215: I'm fairly. Auden to Caroline Newton, postmarked 7 October 1941, Berg.

p.216: But there. Kallman to Auden, 3 November 1941, Berg.

p.216: Divine soldier. Kallman to Auden, 7 December 1941, Berg.

p.216: Christopher having. Kallman to Auden, 7 December 1941, Berg.

p.216: At the Manns. Miller, 65.

p.216: Just a. Auden to Mina Curtiss, 14 January 1942, Berg.

p.216: He makes. Auden to Caroline Newton, 10 January 1942, Berg.

p.216: Suffering is. Auden, 'Fabian Figaro', 12.

p.217: An artist. Auden, 'Fabian Figaro', 13.

p.217: If one. Miller, 3–4.

p.217: Because one. Auden to James Stern, 23 July 1942. Jenkins, 'Stern Letters', *AS3*, 79.

p.217: Charlie, it's. Miller, 32.

p.217: My chief. Auden to Sterns, c. 7 November 1941 *AS3*, 67–8.

p.217: I never. Auden to James Stern, ?25 April 1942. *AS3*, 73–4.

p.217: A whole cloud. Limmer ed., *What the Woman Lived*, 213.

p.218: The best. Elizabeth Frank, *Louise Bogan* (New York, 1985), 296; Limmer ed., *What the Woman Lived*, 221.

p.218: The first. W. H. Auden, 'The Rewards of Patience', *Partisan Review*, 9 (July/August 1942), 336.

p.219: I saw. Helen Sonthoff to Chester Kallman, 30 September 1973, HRC.

p.219: The plot. *PB*, 131.

p.219: Flaccid. *PB*, 134–5.

p.219: The relation. Auden, 'Rewards of Patience', 336.

p.220: In 1912. Auden to James Stern, 30 July 1942. Jenkins, 'Stern Letters', *AS3*, 81.

p.220: I was. Auden to George Auden, 13 October 1942.

p.220: To choose. *FTB*, 81.

p.220: Though written. *FTB*, 91.

p.220: Psychiatrist who. Auden to Caroline Newton, 2 September 1942, Berg.

p.221: Poor little. *O*, 68.

p.221: If I'd. Alan Ansen journal, 12 April 1947, Berg.

p.221: *Very* tired. Auden to James Stern, 1 November 1942, *AS3*, 85–6.

P.221: For an. Alan Ansen journal, Halloween 1947, Berg.

p.221: The more. Auden to James Stern, 5 July 1944. Jenkins, 'Stern Letters', *AS3*,

p.222: Art is not Magic. Auden, 'The Poet of the Encirclement', *New Republic*, 109 (25 October 1943), 579.

p.222: The sounded note. *FTB*, 58.

p.222: The railroad. *FTB*, 36.

p.222: Gallows and battlefields. *FTB*, 45.

p.222: Only fictional. W. H. Auden, 'Red Lizards and White Stallions', *Saturday Review of Literature*, (13 April 1946), 23.

p.222: As I. *FTB*, 18.

p.222: On account. Farnan, 66.

p.222: Paul Valéry, 'Note and Digression on da Vinci' (1919). See *Complete Works*, 8 (London, 1972), 105.

p.223: To think. *FTB*, 26–8.

p.223: Only your. *FTB*, 23.

p.223: Believe your. *FTB*, 25.

p.223: Henry James's prefaces. *Tribute*, 113.

p.223: We should. *FTB*, 38.

p.224: Whatsoever thy. Ecclesiastes, 9: 10.

p.224: How soon. *FTB*, 24–5.

p.225: There are times. Auden, 'Keats in His Letters', in William Phillips and Philip Rahv, *The Partisan Review Anthology* (London, 1982), 431.

p.225: Out of. Griffin, interview 1.

p.225: The point. Julian Symons, 'The Double Man', in B. Rajan and Andrew Pearse eds, *Focus Two* (London, 1946), 132.

p.225: Cones. *FTB*, 51.

p.225: The massacres. *FTB*, 58.

p.225: Final prudery. Auden, 'Means of Grace', 765.

p.226: The world problem. Auden to Dodds, 20 January 1945, Bodleian.

p.226: The most. Louis Untermeyer, *Yale Review*, 34 (December 1944), 345–6.

p.226: Very high. Symons, 'Double Man', 137.

p.226: The two. Bogan, *Poet's Alphabet*, 38.

p.226: To do my. Quoted Auden, 'The Things Which Are Caesar's', *Theology*, 53 (1950), 411.

p.227: Once King. *FTB*, 25.

Chapter 8: 'Disgraces to keep hidden from the world'

p.228: At the age. *CSP*, 15.

p.228: Life crisis. W. H. Auden, Introduction to J. W. von Goethe, *Italian Journey* 1786–1788 (London, 1962), xvii–xviii.

p.228: It is not. *EF*, 126.

p.228: Because they. *DH*, 305.

p.228: It is. Erik H. Erikson, *Young Man Luther* (London, 1959), 254, reviewed in W. H. Auden, 'Greatness Finding Itself', *Mid-Century*, 13 (June 1960), 9–18.

p.229: Every ordinary. Auden, 'Young Boswell', *New Yorker* (25 November 1950), 136.

p.229: Poetry is. *L*, 610–11.

p.229: The Capital. *AT*, 35; *EA*, 235–16.

p.229: The mental. *LFI*, 201.

p.229: The caves. *AT*, 39.

p.229: That state. *AA*, 55.

p.229: At all. *N*, 21.

p.230: As a. Auden, 'The Things Which Are Caesar's', 417.

p.230: If Wystan's. Kallman to William Rogers, 27 April [1945], Berg.

p.230: My dear. *Times Literary Supplement* (28 March 1975), 827.

p.230: Lucian Freud. Stephen Spender, *Journals* (London, 1985), 158.

p.230: Ha ha. Martin Seymour-Smith, *Robert Graves* (London, 1982), 372.

p.230: In fundamental. Edmund Wilson,

Letters on Literature and Politics 1912–1972 (New York, 1977), 429; see also Lehmann, *I Am My Brother*, 290.

p.230: In youth. W. H. Auden, *Tennyson: An Introduction and Selection* (London, 1946), x.

p.231: Poor, congenitally. Sir Desmond MacCarthy, *Memories* (London, 1953), 154.

p.231: I became. Auden to Dodds, 3 May 1947, Bodleian.

p.231: Views of. George Auden to Elizabeth Mayer, 10 March 1946, Berg.

p.231: Where there. Auden to Elizabeth Mayer, 9 May 1945, Berg.

p.231: We asked them. Carpenter, 335.

p.231: We are very / I keep wishing. Auden to Elizabeth Mayer, 9 May 1945, Berg.

p.232: The Kinsey. Ansen journal, 31 December 1947, Berg. Unlike Isherwood, 'no one is more notably opposed to the [Kinsey] research than Auden', Wescott noted in 1951. Phelps and Rosco eds, *Continual Lessons*, 307. On prostitutes surviving revolutions, see also *PD*, 16. For Lionel Trilling's views, see Lionel Trilling, *The Liberal Imagination* (London, 1951) 223–42.

p.232: I feel. Ansen journal, 20 October 1947, Berg.

p.232: Sexual experience. Griffin, typescript of seventh dialogue, Berg; compare Griffin, 103.

p.232: Loneliness waited. *ATH*, 75.

p.232: Odious. Carpenter, 338.

p.233: It's such. *LFI*, 203.

p.233: Too expensive. Auden to Rhoda Jaffe, postmarked 27 August 1946, Berg.

p.233: New but drab. Norse, *Memoirs*, 148–9.

p.233: With its. Griffin, typescript of first

dialogue (14 November 1949) with Auden, Berg.

p.234: He captured. Harold Acton, *More Memoirs of an Aesthete* (London, 1970), 253.

p.234: The most. Yanovsky, 107–8.

p.234: The city. Griffin, 108.

p.234: Barely looking. Norse, *Memoirs*, 149–50.

p.234: It is in. *FTB*, 48.

p.235: An immense. *The Complete Tales of Henry James*, vol. 11 (1964), 13, 17.

p.235: A sort of. *Complete Tales of Henry James*, vol. 11, 31, 37–8.

p.235: Writing a religious. Auden, Introduction to Henry James, *The American Scene* (New York, 1946), xxii–xxiii, reproduced in *DH*, 322–3.

p.236: The day. Auden, 'Squares and Oblongs', 176.

p.236: My Great Good. Auden to Grigson, 17 January 1950, Berg.

p.236: Venice was. Auden, Foreward to Frederick Rolfe, *The Desire and the Pursuit of the Whole* (London, 1953), ix.

p.236: My Negro. Ansen journal, 19 February 1948, Berg.

p.236: BE MORE. Auden to Ansen, 31 December 1948 Berg.

p.236: Étude de. Dedication of *EF*.

p.236: Rents were. Anatole Broyard, *Kafka Was the Rage* (New York, 1993), 7–8.

p.236: I often. Broyard, *Kafka*, 9.

p.237: She clung. Broyard, *Kafka*, 10.

p.237: She worries. W. H. Auden, 'Then and Now: 1935–1950', *Mademoiselle*, 30 (February 1950), 162.

p.237: Books steadied. Broyard, *Kafka*, 30.

p.237: I thought over. Griffin, typescript of second dialogue with Auden, Berg.

p.238: We were not. *DH*, 334.

p.238: I am compulsive. Griffin, typescript of fifth dialogue with Auden, Berg.

p.238: Noise of. *AA*, 26.

p.238: An unprejudiced. *AA*, 11.

p.239: Human beings. *AA*, 103.

p.239: Who will trust. *AA*, 83–4.

p.239: Constant regets. Auden, 'Practiced Topophile', 101.

p.240: Stupid world. *AA*, 45.

p.240: Factories bred. *AA*, 24.

p.240: This guilt. *AA*, 28.

p.240: In our anguish. *AA*, 125–6.

p.241: Appearance of. Alan Ross, 'Third Avenue Eclogue', *Times Literary Supplement* (23 October 1948), 596, reprinted in John Gross ed., *The Modern Movement*, (London, 1992), 137–8.

p.241: The purpose. Patric Dickinson, *Horizon*, 19 (1949), 377.

p.241: Spent twenty. *DH*, 52.

p.241: Thought *The Age*. Wilson, *Letters*, 431.

p.241: Fascinating and hair-raising. Spears, 239, 250.

p.241: That it. Ansen journal, 6 December 1947, Berg.

p.242: Times like. *N*, 32.

p.242: *The Age*. Jarrell, 145.

p.242: The basic. Robert FitzGerald, 'Eclogue, 1947', *Time* (21 July 1947), 98–100.

p.242: The ideal audience. Auden, 'Squares and Oblongs', 176.

p.242: Frost / Cavafy. *DH*, 342.

p 242: Carlos Williams. Norse, *Memoirs*, 208–9, William Carlos Williams, *Autobiography* (New York, 1951), 310–11; John C. Thirlwall ed., *Selected Letters of William Carlos Williams* (New York, 1957), 245, 313.

p.242: We drank. Ralph Mills ed., *Selected Letters of Theodore Roethke* (London, 1970), 115.

p.242: I want. Limmer ed., *What the Woman Lived*, 243.

p.243: Awfully nice. Mary Jarrell ed., *Randall Jarrell's Letters*, 287.

p.243: St John Perse. Arthur Knodel ed., *St John Perse Letters* (Princeton, 1979), 617.

p.243: Mr Auden. Marianne Moore to Elizabeth Mayer, 8 July 1945, Berg; Auden to Dodds, 21 August 1949, Bodleian; *DH*, 305.

p.243: Love undying. Marianne Moore, 'Voracities and Verities Sometimes Are Interacting', *Collected Poems* (London, 1951), 147.

p.243: Homosexual chauvinist. Wilson, *Letters*, 430.

p.243: *The Bostonians*. Auden to Rhoda Jaffe, postmarked 25 June 1947, Berg; Alan Ansen journal, 21 November 1947, Berg.

p.243: I'd rather. Ansen journal, 9 March 1948, Berg.

p.243: Auden appears. Robert Phillips ed., *Delmore Schwartz and James Laughlin: Selected Letters* (New York, 1993), 333.

p.243: That horrible. Ansen journal, 30 April 1947, Berg.

p.243: I think. Farnan, 119.

p.244: Current rumor. Auden to Rhoda Jaffe, postmarked 14 April 1946, Berg.

p.244: He slept. Farnan, 113.

p.244: But after all. Information from Edward Mendelson, 12 January 1995.

p.244: Rhoda turned. Ansen journal, 17 December 1947, Berg.

p.244: Psychology in general. Farnan, 119–20.

p.244: I hide. *AA*, 116.

p.244: All her friends. Farnan, 120.

p.245: The girl whose / I would rather.

Auden, 'Squares and Oblongs', 175.

p.245: Proper concern. Sean Day-Lewis, *C. Day-Lewis* 239.

p.245: Miss God. Auden to Jaffe, postmarked 17 June 1947, Berg.

p.245: So my. *N*, 16.

p.245: I've come. Ansen journal, 17 and 21 February 1948, Berg.

p.245: One shouldn't. Ansen, 87.

p.246: Deciding that. Auden to Kallman, 13 December 1948, Berg. The poem was printed in *Fuck You/a magazine of the arts*, no. 5 (March 1965); also printed as 'The Gobble Poem' in *Suck: the first European sex paper* [Amsterdam], 1 (October 1969), 8.

p.246: All American Ansen journal [nd, late February 1948], Berg.

p.246: As far as. Auden, 'Some Notes on D. H. Lawrence', *Nation* (26 April 1947), 483.

p.247: Wystan has. Edmund Wilson, *The Fifties* (New York, 1986), 297.

p.247: I don't. Kallman to Geoffrey Gorer, 26 April 1950, University of Sussex Library.

p.247: Firbank's extraordinary. Auden, 'Firbank Revisited', *New York Times* (20 November 1949), section 7, 5.

p.248: Chester came. Auden to Jaffe, postmarked 10 June 1947, Berg.

p.248: He's through. Auden to Jaffe, 17 June 1947, Berg.

p.248: A little vague. Auden to Jaffe, 25 June 1947, Berg.

p.248: She is. Auden to Jaffe, 2 July 1947, Berg.

p.248: Work has. Auden to Jaffe, 14 July 1947, Berg.

p.249: People are born. Griffin, 24.

p.249: The paths. Maurice Cranston, 'Poet's Retreat', *John O'London's Weekly* (6 February 1948), 49–50.

p.249: A poem is. *DH*, 70–1.

p.250: What there. *N*, 24–6.

p.251: Looking at. Yanovsky, 108.

p.251: You either. Ansen journal, 17 February 1948, Berg.

p.251: That since. Norse, *Memoirs*, 152–3.

p.251: Old men. Chester Kallman, 'Old Men Are Funny', *Commonweal* (8 February 1946), 431.

p.251: Wonderful old gent. Chester Kallman, 'Portraits and Parables', *Commonweal* 4 January 1946.

p.252: Its lowest ebb. Norse, *Memoirs*, 153.

p.253: Opera … is. *DH*, 470.

p.253: An old friend. Igor Stravinsky, *Selected Correspondence*, 1 (London, 1982), 304.

p.253: Sexual hoax. Robert Craft, 'Words for Music Perhaps', *New York Review of Books* (3 November 1994), 53.

p.253: A corporate personality. *DH*, 483.

p.253: The finished. *L*, xxi.

p.253: Really lovely. Auden to Sterns, *AS3*.

p.253: Wystan, finding. Robert Craft, *Stravinsky: Chronicle of a Friendship* (London, 1972):

p.254: Auden is. Craft, *Stravinsky*, 43.

p.254: Wildly enthusiastic. Auden to James and Tania Stern, 28 February 1953. *AS3*, 99.

p.254: The verses. *L*, 611; *DH*, 473.

p.254: Self-deception. *DH*, 471.

p.255: To hear people. Auden, 'Squares and Oblongs', 169.

p.255: Deftly, admiral. *N*, 17.

p.256: Of personal. Bayley, *Romantic Survival*, 38–9.

p.256: One thing only. Auden, 'Henry James and Artist in America', 39.

p.256: How does. Michael Shelden, *Friends of Promise* (London, 1989), 192.

p.256: Day Lewis was. Christopher Hewett ed., *The Living Curve* (London, 1984), 115.

p.257: My first image. Auden, 'Our Italy', *Griffin*, 1 (April 1952), 1.

p.257: A society. Auden, 'Squares and Oblongs', 178.

p.257: A verbal. *DH*, 338.

p.257: Because it. *N*, 11.

p.257: Imagines a. Laurence Lipking, 'Faults', *AS3*.

p.257: One of the. Stephen Spender, title?, *Poetry* (September 1951), ?

p.258: Its such. Auden to Jaffe, 30 May 1948, Berg.

p.258: We live. Lancaster ed., *Brian Howard*, 492.

p.258: Ischia – For Brian. *N*, 21–3.

p.258: Wystan's influence. Lancaster ed., *Brian Howard*, 494.

p.258: The sex situation. Auden to Jaffe, 6 July 1948, Berg.

p.258: The women here. Auden to Jaffe, 17 May 1949, Berg.

p.259: Never far. Anne Valery, *The Edge of a Smile* (London, 1977), 203.

p.259: Italy may. Auden, 'Our Italy', 2–3.

p.259: All my. Auden to Kallman, 1 November 1948, Berg.

p.259: If I'm. Auden to Kallman, 21 February 1949, Berg.

p.259: I'm a little. Auden to Kallman, 24 February 1949, Berg.

p.259: Serious prophets. Auden, 'A Playboy of the Western World: St Oscar, the Homintern Martyr', *Partisan Review*, 17 (April 1950), 390–4, reprinted in William Phillips and Philip Rahv eds, *The New Partisan Reader 1945–1953* (New York, 1953), 603–7.

p.260: The whole. Auden to Jaffe, 16 August 1949, Berg. See also W. H. Auden, 'The Question of the Pound Award', *Partisan Review*, 16 (May 1949), 512–13; Humphrey Carpenter, *A Serious Character* (London, 1988), 788–92; R. H. Winnick ed., *Letters of Archibald MacLeish, 1907 to 1982* (Boston, 1983), 344–5; Laurance Thompson and

R. H. Winnick, *Robert Frost: The Later Years* (New York, 1976), 174–6; Gail McDonald, *Learning to Be Modern* (Oxford, 1993), 198–9; Randolph Hughes ed., *Lesbia Brandon, by Algernon Charles Swinburne* (London, 1952), xxxi–xxxv.

p.260: I work. Auden to Jaffe, postcard 7 May 1949, Berg.

p.261: To my great. Auden to Jaffe, 17 May 1949, Berg.

p.261: There is. Auden to John Hayward, 14 August [1950], Berg.

p.261: Sexuality. Albert Camus, *Selected Essays and Notebooks* (London, 1979), 265.

p.261: The crematorium. *N*, 34.

p.261: The humour. *N*, 36.

p.261: Without me. *N*, 38.

p.262: He would die. *N*, 53.

p.262: Like most. Auden, 'Port and Nuts with the Eliots', *New Yorker*, 25 (23 April 1949), 85 (or 92 in some editions).

p.262: The Yiddish. Stella Musulin, 'Auden in Kirchstetten', *AS3*, 213.

p.262: Don't tell. Auden to Monroe Spears, 11 May 1963, Berg.

p.263: When to. *N*, 52–3.

Chapter 9: 'I was glad I could be unhappy'

p.265: Since the Auden, 'History of a Historian', 9.

p.265: I was glad. *HTC*, 16.

p.265: A plain. *TSOA*, 35.

p.265: A stoic. Brodsky *Less Than One*, 355.

p.265: Nothing is. *TSOA*, 29.

p.266: The lasting. W. H. Auden, 'Jean Cocteau', *Flair*, 1 (February 1950), 102.

p.266: One of our. W. H. Auden, 'A Jolly Magpie', *New Yorker* (15 February 1958), 129.

p.266: I hate. Auden to Spender, 28 February 1953, Berg.

p.266: His inability. W. H. Auden, 'Through the Collarbone of a Hare', *New Yorker* (2 May 1953), 114.

p.266: Comedy. W. H. Auden, 'Crying Spoils the Appearance', *New Yorker*, 7 September 1957, 146.

p.266: A committed. TLS from Nikos Stangos, 22 March 1995.

p.266: Just reeling. *TSOA*, 24.

p.266: No longer. Jarrell, 228.

p.266: Alienation from. *ETAG*, 49.

p.267: Far from. *Tribute*, 185.

p.267: The disgusting. Prokosch, *Voices*, 295.

p.267: The real passion. W. H. Auden, 'Fog in the Mediterranean', *Christian Scholar*, 27 (December 1954), 531.

p.267: In 1914. W. H. Auden, Introduction to *Poets of the English Language*, 5 (London, 1952), xxiv–xxv. Compare with W. H. Auden, 'A Guidebook for All Good Counter-Revolutionaries', *Nation* (8 April 1950), 328; Marianne Moore, *Predilections* (London, 1956), 84.

p.268: Isn't it true. *LFI*, 91.

p.268: Christ's body. I Corinthians 13; Musulin, 'Auden at Kirchstetten', *AS3*, 223

p.268: Every beautiful. W. H. Auden, 'Nature, History and Poetry', *Thought*, 25 (September 1950), 422.

p.268: To express. W. H. Auden, 'A Song of Life's Power to Renew', *New York Times* (27 July 1958), section 7, 1.

p.268: The sense of Nature. Auden, 'Fog in the Mediterranean', 533.

p.268: Wystan tries. Kallman to Gorer, 26 April [1950], University of Sussex Library.

p.269: Pseudo-sciensy rubbish. Auden to Gorer, 23 May [?1950], University of Sussex Library.

p.269: Relate everything. W. H. Auden, 'Holding the Mirror Up to History', *New Yorker* (25 September 1954), 116.

p.269: Sometimes I. Spender, *Journals*, 118–19.

p.269: She began. Auden, 'Holding the Mirror', 118–19; W. H. Auden, 'Miss Marianne Moore, Bless Her!', *Mid Century*, no. 5 (fall 1959), 6.

p.271: The first step. Griffin, 25.

p.271: A world where. Auden, 'Sigmund Freud', *New Republic*, 127 (6 October 1952), 17.

p.271: There was. *Tribute*, 184.

p.271: Why are people? Griffin, 28.

p.271: Like a. Auden to Gorer, 9 July 1955, University of Sussex Library.

p.272: That all. Auden, 'History of a Historian', *Griffin* (November 1955), 10.

p.272: If there are. Auden, 'Anger', *Sunday Times*, 21 January 1962, 26.

p.272: As long as. Auden, *Kierkegaard* (London, 1955), 3.

p.272: Spiritual snobbery. Auden, 'K', *Mid-Century*, 17 (fall 1960), 10–11.

p.272: One ceases. *DH*, 99. This is Auden's translation of the entry in Pavese's journal for 31 October 1937. The translator of the English edition of these journals, *This Business of Living* (London, 1961), renders this as 'one stops being a child when one realises that telling one's trouble does not make it better' (p. 42).

p.272: A suffering / The same rules. *DH*, 99.

p.272: Love, or truth. *TSOA*, 46.

p.273: Reticence may. *Tribute*, 181.

p.273: The trouble. Auden to Wendell Johnson, 9 November 1953, Berg.

p.273: I have no. W. H. Auden, 'The Greatness of Freud', *Listener* (8 October 1953), 594.

p.273: You go. Griffin, 28.

p.273: Some of them. Griffin, 29.

p.273: Dr Leavis. A. Alvarez, 'Marvell and Motorcycles', *New Yorker* (1 August 1994), 78.

p.274: Caught in. Norman Podhoretz, *Making It* (London, 1968), 172.

p.274: Failure of. Robin Mayhead, 'The Latest Auden', *Scrutiny*, 18 (June 1952), 315–19; Giroux ed., *Elizabeth Bishop, One Art* 442.

p.274: Be subtle. *TSOA*, 44; see also W. H. Auden, 'A Consciousness of Reality', *New Yorker* (6 March 1954), 112.

p.275: Playing into. D. J. Enright, *The Apothecary's Shop* (London, 1957), 196.

p 275: That I. TLS from D. J. Enright, 3 February 1995.

p.275: The private history. F. W. Bateson to Margaret Rawlings Cross, 5 June 1952.

p.275: The journey. *JTW*, 17; Robert Cecil, *A Divided Life* (London, 1988), 143.

p.275: Stephen, dear. Auden to Spender, 14 June 1951, Berg.

p.276: And was only. Roy Harrod to Goronwy Rees, 1 March 1972, Berg.

p.276: On a totally. Auden to Spender, 20 June 1951, Berg.

p.276: Capable of. Auden to Wendell Johnson, 9 November 1953, Berg; Auden to Gorer, 9 July [1955], University of Sussex Library; Richard Davenport-Hines, *Sex, Death and Punishment* (London, 1990), 299–309.

p.276: Thanks to. Auden to John Auden, 10 October [1953].

p.276: Awfully good. Auden to Tania and James Stern, 28 February 1953 *A53*, 100.

p.276: As to our. Auden to Kallman, 17 February 1950, Berg.

p.277: You've got to. Auden to Kallman, 7 March 1950, Berg.

p.277: Geoffrey honey. Kallman to Gorer, 3 September 1950, University of Sussex Library.

p.277: The boat. Craft, *Stravinsky*, 25–7.

p.278: We must. Carpenter, 374.

p.278: We would rather. *AA*, 123.

p.279: The Edwardian paterfamilias. Auden, 'Sigmund Freud', *New Republic* 127 (6 October 1952), 16.

p.279: When I seek. *TSOA*, 15–16.

p.279: A person who. Auden, 'Authority in America', 6, 10–11.

p.279: When one. Farnan, 173–4.

p.279: Very warm. Iain Hamilton, *Koestler* (London, 1982), 246.

p.279: The dubious. Giles Constable ed., *The Letters Between Bernard Berenson and Charles Henry Coster* (Florence, 1993), 243.

p.280: No bank. Michael Davidson, 'The Poet Works To a Timetable,' newspaper cutting, untraced [but published after 9 November 1953].

p.280: To speak. Alan Ansen to Mary Valentine, 23 April 1951, Berg.

p.280: That she was. Joan Givner, *Katherine Anne Porter* (New York, 1982), 383.

p.280: The Amerloque. Auden to Tania and James Stern, 6 June 1952. Nicholas Jenkins, *AS3*, 96.

p.281: The sessions. Auden to Orlan Fox, 19 October 1964, Berg.

p.281: Generous in. Acton, *More Memoirs of an Aesthete*, 253.

p.281: A civitas. *NYL*, 18.

p.281: He was evidently. Edmund Wilson, *The Sixties* (New York, 1993), 18.

p.281: That master's. Ian Hamilton, 'Spender's Lives', *New Yorker* (28 February 1994), 72.

p.282: To all. Auden, 'Our Italy', 3.

p.282: Humanities. Mark Krupnick, *Lionel Trilling and the Fate of Cultural Criticism* (Evanston, 1986), 102–3.

p.282: Discussed the. Kenneth Tynan, *Curtains* (London, 1961), 376; Wilson, *Sixties*, 16.

p.283: Scholarly and beautifully. W. H. Auden, 'Who Shall Plan the Planners?', *Common Sense*, 9 (November 1940), 22.

p.283: A specimen. W. H. Auden, 'Apologies to the Iroquois', *Mid-Century*, 9 (February 1960), 2, 10–11.

p.283: They have/he no doubt. Edmund Wilson, *The Bit Between My Teeth* (New York, 1966), 547–8.

p.283: Now resembles. Wilson, *Fifties*, 297.

p.284: Auden's attempt. Wilson, *Letters*, 518.

p.284: The place/I hate. Wilson, *Fifties*, 292–3.

p.284: He kisses/He is Craft, *Stravinsky*, 39–40.

p.285: Paul Bowles. Auden to Gorer, 5 January [1951], University of Sussex Library.

p.285: In the middle. Medley, 211.

p.285: One has. Davidson, 'The Poet Works to a Time-Table'.

p.286: Occasionally nervous. Auden to Hedwig Petzold, 17 February 1954, Berg.

p.286: Chester invited. Larry Rivers, *What Did I Do?* (New York, 1992), 110.

p.286: Thugs from. Rivers, *What Did I Do?*, 205.

p.286: I was sad. Marianne Moore to Elizabeth Mayer, 7 December 1959, Berg.

p.286: Great intellectual. Farnan, 203–4.

p.287: If equal. *HTC*, 38.

p.287: An impressive. Jarrell, 227.

p.287: Because we. L. D. Lerner, untitled review in *London Magazine*, 3 (March 1956), 74.

p.287: To read snippets. Auden, 'Aeneid for Our Time', *Nation* (10 March 1951), 231.

p.287: Barbed wire. *TSOA*, 36.

p.288: Hobbles away. *TSOA*, 37.

p.288: Religious phase. Hayden Carruth, 'An Austria Remaining', *Poetry*, 108 (1966), 119.

p.288: Indirect and negative. *SW*, 136; Auden to Gorer, 9 July 1955, University of Sussex Library.

p.288: Poems, like. *DH*, 458.

p.288: It is only. *TSOA*, 63. In my account of this sequence I am indebted to P. K. Walker, 'Horae Canonicae: Auden's Vision of a Rood – A Study in Coherence', in David Jasper ed., *Images of Belief* (London, 1984), 52–79.

p.288: At this noon. *TSOA*, 68.

p.288: We shall always. *TSOA*, 71–2.

p.289: Passing a slum. *TSOA*, 77.

p.289: A little man. Griffin, 10.

p.290: On whose immolation. *TSOA*, 77.

p.290: Should come. *TSOA*, 78–9.

p.290: God bless. *TSOA*, 80.

p.290: Charming, bright. Auden to Howard Griffin, 22 April 1953, Berg.

p.291: Even your. Auden to Wendell Stacey Johnson, 10 June 1953, Berg.

p.291: You and Chester. Auden to Johnson, 1 September 1953, Berg.

p.291: *Encounter* contributor. Auden to Spender, 5 October 1953, Berg.

p.291: Few dear names. *TSOA*, 17.

p.291: Holy selfishness. *N*, 42.

p.291: The most. *HTC*, 49.

p.291: The cure. Auden to Johnson, 4 August 1953, Berg.

p.291: A tolerant. W. H. Auden, 'Talent, Genius and Unhappiness', *New Yorker* (30 November 1957), 221.

Become of Wystan?', *Spectator* (15 July 1960), 104.

p.302: Outstanding. Dom Moraes, 'Mr Auden's Many Masks', *Time and Tide* (9 July 1960), 803.

p.303: A rich. John Gross, 'The Aphorists', *New Statesman* (23 October 1964), 614.

p.303: A man. William Empson, 'The Just Man Made Innocent', *New Statesman* (19 April 1963), 592.

p.303: A kind. Jason Epstein, 'Auden's Essays', *Partisan Review*, 30 (summer 1963), 281–5.

p.304: Messianic delusion. Limmer ed., *What the Woman Lived*, 359.

p.304: Well, there. Information from Edward Mendelson, 26 February 1995.

p.304: For better. W. H. Auden, 'The Problem of Nowness', *Mid-Century*, 19 (November 1960), 19.

p.305: Chatterley. Spender, *Journals*, 291; compare Wilson, *Sixties*, 173.

p.305: Rather prissy. D. J. Enright, *Conspirators and Poets* (London, 1966), 162; Rae Dalven, *The Complete Poems of Cavafy* (London, 1961), vii–xv.

p.305: He gives. Spender, *Journals*, 242–3; compare Samuel Delany, *The Motion of Light in Water* (London, 1990), 144–9.

p.305: It is *still*. Auden to Orlan Fox, 5 September 1960, Berg.

p.305: 15,000 cigarettes. *Tribute*, 124.

p.305: Eating their. Musulin, 'Auden', 219.

p.305: As by. Anon, 'Use and Abuse of Drugs by Athletes', *Lancet*, 1 (1958), 252; 'Report of Reference Committee on Hygiene, Public Health, and Industrial Health', *Journal of American Medical Association* (13 July 1957), 1244.

p.305: Chester felt, Musulin, 'Auden', 214; Carpenter, 425, suggests that

Auden came off amphetamines later than the late 1950s.

p.306: I'm a working. Yanovsky, 108.

p.306: I was. Amory ed., *Letters of Ann Fleming*, 298; Alan Pryce-Jones, *The Bonus of Laughter* (London, 1987), 210.

p.306: In matters of love. Craft, *Stravinsky*, 152.

Chapter 10: 'And I, submissive, felt unwanted and went out'

p.307: All has. *CWW*, 13.

p.307: Scanning his. *CWW*, 38.

p.308: Flattered by. *ATH*, 72.

p.308: As a rule. *AT*, 42.

p.308: Each life. *ATH*, 74.

p.308: Humanely modest. *CWW*, 20.

p.308: To be well-bred. Auden, *A Choice of de la Mare's Verse*; Susan Chitty, *Antonia White: Diaries 1958–1979* (London, 1992), 86.

p.309: Ironic self-awareness. Marius Bewley, 'New Poems', *Partisan Review*, 30 (spring 1963), 146–7.

p.309: Chester's intelligence. Musulin, 217.

p.309: A slight. Emma Kann, 'Recollections of Auden in Austria', *W. H. Auden Society Newsletter*, 10/11 (September 1993), 12.

p.309: Chester and Wystan. Spender, *Journals*, 290.

p.309: C went. Auden to Peter Heyworth, 2 June 1963, Crusaid bequest.

p.309: A warm-hearted. Musulin, 222.

p.310: Whenever Wystan. Coghill to Kallman, 30 September 1973, HRC.

p.310: It cannot. Musulin, 217.

p.310: Beefy, slow. Paul Mariani, *Lost Puritan* (New York, 1994), 270.

p.310: Frog-faced. Levy, 'Audenstrasse', 43.

p.310: Should you. *ATH*, 37.

p.310: A neurotic. Auden, 'Anger', 26.

p.311: That dear good. James Merrill to

Kallman, 18 December 1968, HRC.

p.311: In the. Musulin, 212.

p.311: Oh but. *LS*, 61.

p.311: The story. *FA*, 103.

p.311: True love / Poets are. *FA*, 106.

p.312: When the. David Luke, 'Gerhart Meyer,' *AS2*, 110.

p.312: When Chester. Yanovsky, 108.

p.312: With Chester. Yanovsky, 114.

p.312: A successful. Auden to Robert Lederer, 29 May [1969], Berg.

p.312: As an. George Auden, 'The Madness of Ajax', 511.

p.313: A rare. George Auden, 'Madness of Ajax', 511–12.

p.313: We heard. *L*, 308.

p.313: Hair á la. 303.

p.314: A beautifully. Anon., 'Henze's Symphonic Opera,' *The Times* (12 August 1966), 6.

p.314: The smug. Robert Gittings, 'Significant Situations: Auden and the Idea of Opera', in Alan Bold ed., *W. H. Auden: The Far Interior* (London, 1985), 161.

p.314: Queen name. Auden to Peter Heyworth, nd [?April 1966].

p.314: As for. Auden to Peter Heyworth, nd [?August 1966].

p.314: For the first. Auden to William Meredith, 31 January 1965, Berg.

p.315: Provincial. Auden to John Auden, 11 January 1965.

p.315: Perhaps Hell. Auden, Berlin journal, 1965, Berg.

p.315: Your old mother. Auden to Peter Heyworth, 15 December 1965, Crusaid bequest.

p.315: At Twenty. *CWW*, 7.

p.315: He was caught. Auden to Orlan Fox, 9 March 1965, Berg.

p.316: *Never* resort. Auden to Robert Lederer, 29 May [1969], Berg.

p.316: As a homosexual. Auden, Berlin journal, 1965, Berg.

p.316: The Hungry. *TYF*, 31.

p.317: Eliot's death. Auden to John Auden, 11 January 1965.

p.317: To me. Auden, 'T. S. Eliot, O. M.', *Listener* (7 January 1965), 5.

p.317: Valerie Eliot. Michael Newman, 'W. H. Auden', *Paris Review*, 57 (spring 1974), 46.

p.318: Heavy ingestion. M. H. Seevers, 'Amphetamine and Alcohol', *Journal of American Medical Association*, 184 8 June 1963, 843.

p.318: I am now. Auden to William Meredith, 31 January 1965, Berg.

p.318: The sort. Auden to David Luke, 4 October 1965, Berg.

p.318: Much hard. Robert Lowell, *Collected Prose* (New York, 1987), 74.

p.318: Auden's talk. Cleanth Brooks, 'The State of Criticism', *Sewanee Review*, 65 (1957), 487.

p.319: What Auden. Roger Hecht and Charles Hallett, 'Porridge After Meat', *Sewanee Review*, 72 (1964), 539.

p.319: Perhaps they. Edward Mendelson, 'Editing Auden', *New Statesman* (17 September 1976), 376.

p.319: A little girl. Mendelson, 'Editing Auden', 376.

p.319: One cannot. Auden to Stella Musulin, 23 December 1964 *AS3*, 210.

p.319: The most dishonest. Auden to Naomi Mitchison, 1 April 1967, Berg.

p.320: I am going. Auden to Orlan Fox, 23 August 1965, Berg.

p.320: I get. Auden to Fox, 23 September 1965, Berg.

p.320: Was at. Auden to Peter Salus, 10 May 1967, Berg.

p.320: Events could. Kann, 'Recollections of Auden', 12.

p.321: You can't. Stanley Kunitz, 'Auden on Poetry', *Atlantic Monthly*, 218 (August 1966), 96.

p.321: But in seven. *CWW*, 89.

p.322: On High. *CWW*, 88.

p.322: Tomorrow has. *ETAG*, 10.

p.323: Quite well. Auden to Bernard Auden, 15 December 1965, Bodleian.

p.323: A poet enchants. Sean Day-Lewis, 'No Pomp or Pretence in W. H. Auden', *Daily Telegraph* (29 November 1965), 14.

p.323: A very extraordinary. Auden to John Auden, 8 December [1965].

p.323: We have. Auden to Dodds, 2 January 1966, Bodleian.

p.323: As the years. Musulin, 215.

p.323: It was. Auden to Dodds, 23 August 1967, Bodleian.

p.324: Most Americans. Auden to Peter Heyworth, 1 February 1967.

p.324: His supporters. Ian Hamilton, *Robert Lowell* (London, 1983), 345.

p.324: The perfect. Charles Monteith, 'W. H. Auden', *New Statesman* (5 October 1973), 479.

p.324: In his cups. *CWW*, 36.

p.324: His strongly. Coghill to Kallman, 30 September 1973, HRC.

p.324: Both times. William Blissett, *The Long Conversation* (Oxford, 1981), 139

p.324: But I. John Bridgen, 'Auden on Christianity', *W. H. Auden Society Newsletter*, 3 (April 1989), 3.

p.325: His conversation. Newman, 'Auden', 33–4.

p.325: The way. *CWW*, 36.

p.325: Every now. W. H. Auden, 'Thinking What We Are Doing', *Encounter* 12 (June 1959), 72.

p.325: Talking and staying. Elizabeth Young-Bruehl, *Hannah Arendt* (New Haven, 1982), 436.

p.325: I would not. *Tribute*, 182–3.

p.326: I love Wystan. Prokosch, *Voices*, 294–5.

p.326: Rather disappointing. Giroux ed., *Elizabeth Bishop, One Art*, 436.

p.326: Being civilised. Anon., 'Well Bred', *Times Literary Supplement* (17 March 1966), 224.

p.327: Auden's work. Lowell, *Collected Prose*, 74.

p.327: At Canterbury. Frank Kermode, 'Secondary Worlds' review, *Guardian* (29 November 1968), 5.

p.327: Young, choleric. Lord Goodman, *Tell Them I'm on My Way* (London, 1993), 325.

p.327: The tone. Terry Coleman, 'Poetry International at the Queen Elizabeth Hall', *Guardian* (13 July 1967), 5.

p.327: There were. Auden to Fox, 4 August 1967, Berg.

p.328: While she. Charles Osborne, *Giving It Away* (London, 1986), 197, 296.

p.328: W. H. Auden. Bayley, *Selected Essays*, 67.

p.328: That he. Stewart, *Myself and Michael Innes*, 55.

p.328: Mascot. Osborne, *Giving It Away*, 198.

p.328: The only disaster. Auden to Orlan Fox, 12 August 1969, Berg.

p.328: In depressed. Auden to Monroe Spears, 18 November 1967, Berg.

p.328: To revive. Newman, 'Auden', 47.

p.328: *Why* O. Auden to Coghill, 30 June [1967 or 1968], Berg.

p.328: Terrifies me. Newman, 'Auden', 41.

p.328: One prize. *CWW*, 90.

p.329: This world / discarding rhythm. *CWW*, 98–9.

p.329: If we withdraw. Auden, 'Domestic Turmoil', *New York Times* (12 March 1968), 42.

p.329: Vietnam is. Auden to Dodds, 13 March 1968, Bodleian.

p.329: This year. Auden to Stern, 13 March 1968, *AS3*, 105.

p.329: Incessant fatigue. Auden to Peter Heyworth, 15 March 1966, Crusaid bequest.

p.329: Tick-bite. Auden to Peter Salus, 17 July 1968, Berg.

p.330: How darling. Kallman, 'Address to Yannis Boras, b. Livadaki, Arcadia 3–3–1942, d. Vienna 13–12–1968', HRC.

p.330: I don't. Musulin, 212.

p.330: If there. Auden to Coghill, 22 August 1968, Berg

p.330: Irritating, cold. Kallman to Fox, 22 May 1972, Berg.

p.331: David was. Charles Heilemann to Kallman, 15 March 1974, HRC.

p.331: For my small. *ETAG*, 14.

p.331: Sooner or later. *ETAG*, 19.

p.331: When summer. *ETAG*, 16–17.

p.332: You can. *ETAG*, 72.

p.332: This is. Roy Fuller, 'At the Picnic', *New Statesman* (26 September 1969), 421.

p.332: In the. Peter Porter, 'Faber and Faber Limited', *London Magazine*, 9 (October 1969), *81*.

p.333: We elderly. Geoffrey Grigson, *Collected Poems 1963–1980* (London, 1982), 81.

p.333: One of. Cyril Connolly, *The Evening Colonnade* (London, 1973), 367.

p.333: I can. Peter Walker, 'Auden Thoughts', *Theology*, 80 (November 1977), 430.

p.333: All true. *ACW*, 150.

p.333: Might well. *ETAG*, 71.

p.333: He asked. Information from Edward Mendelson, 6 February 1995.

p.334: Mr Auden is. Denis Donoghue, 'Good Grief', *New York Review of Books* (19 July 1973), 18.

p.334: Looking so. Young-Bruehl, *Arendt*, 455.

p.334: Bottled fart. Information from Jane Hanly, March 1995.

p.334: Wystan back. Yanovsky, 131.

p.335: Finding Echo. *ATH*, 75.

p.335: Oxford was. Auden to Michael Newman, 13 July 1971, Berg.

p.335: A frightening. Griffin, 84.

p.335: Wystan not. Yanovsky, 131; information from Edward Mendelson, 27 February 1995.

p.336: Your move. Hamilton, *Robert Lowell*, 438.

p.336: The ochlocratic. *ETAG*, 10.

p.336: He sounded/not a snubber. Mariani, *Lost Puritan*, 410.

p.336: Jolly sessions. *Tribute*, 160.

p.336: Whoever invented. Auden, 'I'll be seeing you again, I hope', *New York Times* (18 March 1972), 31.

p.337: Wystan, I'm. Kallman to Fox, 22 May 1972, Berg.

p.337: I thought. Thwaite ed., *Selected Letters of Philip Larkin*, 460.

p.337: On our way. Yanovsky, 133.

p.337: Poet W. H. Anon., 'Poet says: I was robbed', *Sun* (5 January 1973), 7.

p.337: He was quite. A. L. Rowse, *The Poet Auden* (London, 1987), 128.

p.337: What we have. Philip Toynbee, 'Mellow Fruitfulness', *Observer* (8 October 1972), 38.

p.338: Oxford City. Auden to Michael Newman, 7 December 1972, Berg.

p.338: Who on earth. *ACW*, 43.

p.338: Talked science. Memorandum from Dr Roger Mallion, 6 March 1995.

p.338: A husk. Interview with Rt Rev. Peter Walker, 23 February 1995.

p.338: Battered, rather. Walker, 'Auden Thoughts', 429.

p.338: The theological gambit. Walker, 'Auden Thoughts', 430.

p.339: You can make. Walker, 'Auden Thoughts', 429.

p.339: Very worried. Auden to Kallman, 24 February [1973], HRC.

p.339: Dearest Chester. Auden to Kallman, 3 March [1973], HRC.

p.339: Diffident/nannyish. Interview with Dr Roger Mallion, 7 March 1995.

p.339: The time. Richard Byrd, *Alone* (London, 1938), 16–17.

p.339: Look here. Information from David Luke, 9 February 1995.

p.339: Markedly depressed. *Tribute*, 195.

p.340: Closed up. Information from David El-Kabir, 17 January 1995.

p.340: That's of. Yanovsky, 132.

p.340: Oh I see. Information from Paul Bailey, 30 October 1994; TLS from Alan Myers, 7 June 1994.

p.340: That formidable. Coghill to Kallman, 30 September 1973, HRC.

p.340: I don't. Gorer to Kallman, nd [1973], HRC.

p.340: I arrived. Auden to Fox, 30 May 1973, Berg.

p.341: If this. Musulin, 'Auden', 232.

p.341: A new. Auden to Fox, 31 August 1973, Berg.

p.341: He still loves. *TYF*, 7.

p.341: I have. *Tribute*, 194.

p.341: He was. Elizabeth Hardwick to Kallman, postmarked 10 December 1974, HRC.

Epilogue: 'God may reduce you on Judgment Day'

p.341: Every day. Musulin, 'Auden', 219.

p.343: Turning icy-blue. *Tribute*, 227.

p.343: I'm married. Interview with David Luke, 9 February 1995.

p.344: If there. Auden to Coghill, 22 August 1968, Berg.

p.344: Time has. *ATH*, 22–3.

p.345: Ever so. *TSOA*, 24.

Index

Note: Abbreviations used in the index are WHA for Wystan Hugh Auden; CK for Chester Kallman; NY for New York; WWI and WWII for World War I and World War II.